CW00742647

W0007000

THE
ETYMOLOGICON

THE
ETYMOLOGICON

A Circular
Stroll Through the
Hidden Connections
of the English
Language

MARK FORSYTH

ICON

Published in the UK in 2011 by
Icon Books Ltd, Omnibus Business Centre,
39–41 North Road, London N7 9DP
email: info@iconbooks.co.uk
www.iconbooks.co.uk

Sold in the UK, Europe, South Africa and Asia
by Faber & Faber Ltd, Bloomsbury House,
74–77 Great Russell Street,
London WC1B 3DA or their agents

Distributed in the UK, Europe, South Africa and Asia
by TBS Ltd, TBS Distribution Centre, Colchester Road,
Frating Green, Colchester CO7 7DW

Published in Australia in 2011 by Allen & Unwin Pty Ltd,
PO Box 8500, 83 Alexander Street,
Crows Nest, NSW 2065

Distributed in Canada by Penguin Books Canada,
90 Eglinton Avenue East, Suite 700,
Toronto, Ontario M4P 2YE

ISBN: 978-184831-307-1 (hardback)
ISBN: 978-184831-453-5 (paperback)

Typeset in Minion by Marie Doherty
Printed and bound in the UK by Clays Ltd, St Ives plc

Contents

About the author

Mark Forsyth is a writer, journalist, proofreader, ghostwriter and pedant. He was given a copy of the *Oxford English Dictionary* as a christening present and has never looked back.

In 2009 he started the Inky Fool blog, in order to share his heaps of useless information with a verbose world.

For John Goldsmith,
With thanks.

The author would like to thank everybody involved with
the production of this book, but especially Jane Seeber and
Andrea Coleman for their advice, suggestions, corrections,
clarifications and other gentle upbraidings.

*… they who are so exact for the letter shall be dealt with by the **Lexicon**, and the **Etymologicon** too if they please …*

JOHN MILTON

This book is the papery child of the Inky Fool blog, which was started in 2009. Though most of the material is new some of it has been adapted from its computerised parent. The blog is available at http://blog.inkyfool.com/ which is a part of the grander whole www.inkyfool.com.

Preface

(or that which is said – *fatus* – before)

Occasionally people make the mistake of asking me where a word comes from. They never make this mistake twice. I am naturally a stern and silent fellow; even forbidding. But there's something about etymology and where words come from that overcomes my inbuilt taciturnity. A chap once asked me where the word *biscuit* came from. He was eating one at the time and had been struck by curiosity.

I explained to him that a biscuit is cooked twice, or in French *bi-cuit*, and he thanked me for that. So I added that the *bi* in biscuit is the same *bi* that you get in *bicycle* and *bisexual*, to which he nodded. And then, just because it occurred to me, I told him that the word bisexual wasn't invented until the 1890s and that it was coined by a psychiatrist called Richard von Krafft-Ebing and did he know that Ebing also invented the word *masochism*?

He told me firmly that he didn't.

Did he know about Mr Masoch, after whom masochism was named? He was a novelist and …

The fellow told me that he didn't know about Mr Masoch, that he didn't want to know about Mr Masoch, and that his one ambition in life was to eat his biscuit in peace.

But it was too late. The metaphorical floodgates had opened and the horse had bolted. You see there are a lot of other words named after novelists, like Kafkaesque and Retifism …

It was at this point that he made a dash for the door, but I was too quick for him. My blood was up and there was always something more to say. There always is, you know. There's always an extra connection, another link that joins two words that most of mankind quite blithely believe to be separate, which is why that fellow didn't escape until a couple of hours later when he managed to climb out of the window while I was drawing a diagram to explain what the name Philip has to do with a hippopotamus.

It was after an incident such as this that my friends and family decided something must be done. They gathered for a confabulation and, having established that secure psychiatric care was beyond their means, they turned in despair to the publishing industry, which has a long history of picking up where social work leaves off.

So, a publisher was found somewhere near the Caledonian Road and a plan was hatched. I would start with a single word and then connect it to another word and then to another word and so on and so forth until I was exhausted and could do no more.

A book would therefore have a twofold benefit. First it would rid me of my demons and perhaps save some innocent conversationalist from my clutches. Second, unlike me, a book could be left snugly on the bedside table or beside the lavatory: opened at will and *closed* at will.

So a book it was, which set me thinking …

The Etymologicon

A Turn-up for the Books

This is a book. The glorious insanities of the English language mean that you can do all sorts of odd and demeaning things to a book. You can cook it. You can bring a criminal to it, or, if the criminal refuses to be brought, you can throw it at him. You may even take a leaf out of it, the price of lavatory paper being what it is. But there is one thing that you can never do to a book like this. Try as and how you might, you cannot turn up for it. Because *a turn-up for the books* has nothing, directly, to do with the ink-glue-and-paper affair that this is (that is, unless you're terribly modern and using a Kindle or somesuch). It's *a turn-up for the bookmakers*.

Any child who sees the bookmaker's facing the bookshop across the High Street will draw the seemingly logical conclusion. And a bookmaker was, once, simply somebody who stuck books together. Indeed, the term *bookmaker* used to be used to describe the kind of writer who just pumps out one shelf-filler after another with no regard for the exhaustion of the reading public. Thomas More observed in 1533 that 'of newe booke makers there are now moe then ynough'. Luckily for the book trade, More was beheaded a couple of years later.

The modern sense of the bookmaker as a man who takes bets originated on the racecourses of Victorian Britain. The bookmaker would accept bets from anyone who wanted to lay them, and note them all down in a big betting book. Meanwhile, a turn-up was just a happy chance. A dictionary of slang from 1873 thoughtfully gives us this definition:

> **Turn up**   an unexpected slice of luck. Among sporting men bookmakers are said to have a turn up when an unbacked horse wins.

So, which horses are unbacked? Those with the best (i.e. longest) odds. Almost nobody backs a horse at 1,000/1.

This may seem a rather counterintuitive answer. Odds of a thousand to one are enough to tempt even a saint to stake his halo, but that's because saints don't know anything about gambling and horseflesh. Thousand to one shots never, ever come in. Every experienced gambler knows that a race is very often won by the favourite, which will of course have short odds. Indeed, punters want to back a horse that's so far ahead of the field he merely needs to be shooed over the line. Such a horse is a *shoo-in*.

So you pick the favourite, and you back it. Nobody but a fool backs a horse that's unlikely to win. So when such an unfancied nag romps over the finish line, it's a turn-up for the books, because the bookies won't have to pay out.

Not that the bookmakers need much luck. They always win. There will always be many more bankrupt gamblers than bookies. You're much better off in a zero-sum game, where the players pool their money and the winner takes all. Pooling your money began in France, and has nothing whatsoever to do with swimming pools, and a lot to do with chickens and genetics.

A Game of Chicken

Gambling in medieval France was a simple business. All you needed were some friends, a pot, and a chicken. In fact, you didn't need friends – you could do this with your enemies – but the pot and the chicken were essential.

First, each person puts an equal amount of money in the pot. Nobody should on any account make a joke about a *poultry sum*. Shoo the chicken away to a reasonable distance. What's a reasonable distance? About a stone's throw.

Next, pick up a stone.

Now, you all take turns hurling stones at that poor bird, which will squawk and flap and run about. The first person to hit the chicken wins all the money in the pot. You then agree never to mention any of this to an animal rights campaigner.

That's how the French played a game of chicken. The French, though, being French, called it a game of *poule*, which is French for chicken. And the chap who had won all the money had therefore won the *jeu de poule*.

The term got transferred to other things. At card games, the pot of money in the middle of the table came to be known as the *poule*. English gamblers picked the term up and brought it back with them in the seventeenth century. They changed the spelling to *pool*, but they still had a pool of money in the middle of the table.

It should be noted that this pool of money has absolutely nothing to do with a body of water. Swimming pools, rock pools and Liverpools are utterly different things.

Back to gambling. When billiards became a popular sport, people started to gamble on it, and this variation was known as *pool*, hence shooting pool. Then, finally, that poor French chicken broke free from the world of gambling and soared majestically out into the clear air beyond.

On the basis that gamblers *pooled* their money, people started to pool their resources and even pool their cars in a *car pool*. Then they pooled their typists in a *typing pool*. Le chicken was free! And then he grew bigger than any of us, because, since the phrase was invented in 1941, we have all become part of the *gene pool*, which, etymologically, means that we are all little bits of chicken.

Hydrogentlemanly

The gene of *gene pool* comes all the way from the ancient Greek word *genos*, which means birth. It's the root that you find in *generation, regeneration* and *degeneration*; and along with its Latin cousin *genus* it's scattered generously throughout the English language, often in places where you wouldn't expect it.

Take *generous*: the word originally meant *well-born*, and because it was obvious that well-bred people were magnanimous and peasants were stingy, it came to mean munificent. Indeed, the well-bred *gen*tleman established such a reputation for himself that the word *gentle*, meaning *soft*, was named after him. In fact, some gentlemen became so refined that the *gin* in *gingerly* is probably just another *gen* lurking in our language. *Gingerly* certainly has nothing to do with ginger.

Genos is hidden away in the very air that you breathe. The chemists of the late eighteenth century had an awful lot of trouble with the gases that make up the air. Oxygen, carbon dioxide, nitrogen and the rest all look exactly alike; they are transparent, they are effectively weightless. The only real difference anybody could find between them was their effects: what we now call oxygen makes things burn, while nitrogen puts them out.

Scientists spent a lot of time separating the different kinds of air and then had to decide what to call them all. Oxygen was called *flammable air* for a while, but it didn't catch on. It just didn't have the right scientific ring to it. We all know that scientific words need an obscure classical origin to make them sound impressive to those who wouldn't know an idiopathic craniofacial erythema[1] if it hit them in the face.

Eventually, a Frenchman named Lavoisier decided that the sort of air that produced water when it was burnt should be called the *water-producer*. Being a scientist, he of course dressed this up in Greek, and the Greek for water producer is *hydro-gen*. The bit of air that made things acidic he decided to call the *acid-maker* or *oxy-gen*, and the one that produced *nitre* then got called *nitro-gen*.

(Argon, the other major gas in air, wasn't known about at the time, because it's an inert gas and doesn't produce anything at all. That's why it's called argon. *Argon* is Greek for *lazy*.)

Most of the productive and reproductive things in the world have *gen* hidden somewhere in their names. All words are not homo*gen*ous and sometimes they are en*gen*dered in odd ways. For example, a group of things that reproduce is a *gen*us and if you're talking about a whole *gen*us then you're speaking in *gen*eral and if you're in *gen*eral command of the troops you're a *gen*eral and a *general* can order his troops to commit *gen*ocide, which, etymologically, would be suicide.

---

[1] That's a blush to you and me.

Of course, a general won't commit genocide himself; he'll probably assign the job to his privates, and *privates* is a euphemism for *gonads*, which comes from exactly the same root, for reasons that should be too obvious to need explaining.

The Old and New Testicle

Gonads are *testicles* and testicles shouldn't really have anything to do with the Old and New *Testaments*, but they do.

The Testaments of the Bible *testify* to God's truth. This is because the Latin for *witness* was *testis*. From that one root, *testis*, English has inherited pro*test* (bear witness for), de*test* (bear witness against), con*test* (bear witness competitively), and *test*icle. What are testicles doing there? They are *testi*fying to a man's virility. Do you want to prove that you're a real man? Well, your *testi*cles will *testi*fy in your favour.

That's the usual explanation, anyway. There's another, more interesting theory that in bygone days witnesses used to swear to things with their hands on their balls, or even on other people's balls. In the Book of Genesis, Abraham makes his servant swear not to marry a Canaanite girl. The King James Version has this translation:

> I pray thee, thy hand under my thigh: And I will make thee swear by the LORD, the God of heaven, and the God of the earth

Now, that *may* be the correct translation, but the Hebrew doesn't say thigh, it says *yarek*, which means, approximately, *soft bits.* Nobody knows how oaths were sworn in the ancient world, but many scholars believe that people didn't put their hands on their hearts or their thighs, but on the testicles of the man to whom they were swearing, which would make the connection between *testis* and *testes* rather more direct.

Testicles. Bollocks. Balls. Nuts. Cullions. Cojones. Goolies. Tallywags. Twiddle-diddles. Bawbles, trinkets, spermaria. There are a hundred words for the danglers and they get everywhere. It's enough to make a respectable fellow blush. Do you enjoy the taste of avocado? So did I, until the terrible day when I realised that I was eating Aztec balls. You see, the Aztecs noticed the avocado's shape and decided that it resembled nothing so much as a big, green bollock. So they called it an *ahuakatl*, their word for testicle. When the Spanish arrived they misheard this slightly and called it *aguacate*, and the English changed this slightly to *avocado*. To remember that I used to like avocados with a touch of walnut oil only adds to my shame.

Even if you flee to an ivory tower and sit there wearing an orchid and a scowl, it still means that you have a testicle in your buttonhole, because that's what an orchid's root resembles, and *orchis* was the Greek for testicle. Indeed, the green-winged orchid used to rejoice in the name *Fool's Ballocks*. The technical term for somebody who has *a lot of balls* is a *polyorchid*.

And it's very possible that this *orb* on which we all live comes from the same root as *orchid*, in which case we are whirling around the Sun on a giant testis, six billion trillion tons of gonad or *cod*, which is where *cod-philosophy*, *codswallop* and *codpiece* come from.

There are two codpieces at the top right of your computer keyboard, and how they got there is a rather odd story.

Parenthetical Codpieces

Your computer keyboard contains two pictures of codpieces, and it's all the fault of the ancient Gauls, the original inhabitants of France. Gauls spoke Gaulish until Julius Caesar came and cut them all into three parts. One of the Gaulish words that the Gauls used to speak was *braca* meaning trousers. The Romans didn't have a word for trousers because they all wore togas, and that's why the Gaulish term survived.

From *braca* came the early French *brague* meaning trousers, and when they wanted a word for a codpiece they decided to call it a *braguette* or *little trousers*. This is not to be confused with *baguette*, meaning stick. In fact a Frenchman might brag that his baguette was too big for his braguette, but then Frenchmen will claim anything. They're *braggarts* (literally *one who shows off his codpiece*).

Braguettes were much more important in the olden days, especially in armour. On the medieval battlefield, with arrows flying hither and thither, a knight knew where he wanted the most protection. Henry VIII's codpiece, for example, was a gargantuan combination of efficiency and obscenity. It was big enough and shiny enough to frighten any enemy into disorganised retreat. It bulged out from the royal groin and stretched up to a metal plate that protected the royal belly.

And that is significant. What do you call the bit of stone that bulges out from a pillar to support a balcony or a roof? Until the sixteenth century nobody had been certain what to call them; but one day somebody must have been gazing at a cathedral wall and, in a moment of sudden clarity, realised that the architectural supports looked like nothing so much as Henry VIII's groin.

And so such architectural structures came to be known as *braggets*, and that brings us to Pocahontas.

Pocahontas was a princess of the Powhatan tribe, which lived in Virginia. Of course, the Powhatan tribe didn't *know* they lived in Virginia. They thought they lived in Tenakomakah, and so the English thoughtfully came with guns to explain their mistake. But the Powhatan tribe were obstinate and went so far as to take one of the Englishmen prisoner. They were planning to kill him until Pocahontas intervened with her father and Captain John Smith was freed. The story goes that she had fallen madly in love with him and that they had a passionate affair, but as Pocahontas was only ten years old at the time, we should probably move swiftly on.

Of course, it may not have happened exactly that way. The story has been improved beyond repair. But there definitely *was* a Pocahontas and there definitely *was* a Captain John Smith, and they seem to have been rather fond of each other. Then he had an accident with one of his guns and had to return to England. The cruel colonists told Pocahontas that John Smith was dead, and she pined away in tears thinking that he was lost for ever. In fact, he wasn't dead, he was writing a dictionary.

The Sea-Man's Grammar and Dictionary: Explaining all the Difficult Terms of Navigation hit the bookstands in 1627. It had all sorts of nautical jargon for the aspiring sailor to learn. But, for our story, the important thing is that Captain Smith spelt *braggets* as *brackets*, and the spelling stuck.

The original architectural device was called a bragget/ bracket, because it looked like a codpiece. But what about a double bracket, which connects two horizontals to a vertical? An architectural double bracket looks like this: [

Look around you: there's probably one on the nearest bookshelf. And just as a physical bracket got its name because it resembled a codpiece, so the punctuation bracket got its name because it resembled the structural component.

In 1711 a man called William Whiston published a book called *Primitive Christianity Revived*. The book often quotes from Greek sources and when it does, it gives both Whiston's translation *and* the original in what he was the first man to call [brackets].

And that's why, if you look at the top right-hand corner of your computer keyboard, you will see two little codpieces [] lingering obscenely beside the letter P for *pants*.

Suffering for my Underwear

Once upon a time there was a chap who probably didn't exist and who probably wasn't called Pantaleon. Legend has it that he was personal physician to Emperor Maximianus. When the emperor discovered that his doctor was a Christian he got terribly upset and decreed that the doctor should die.

The execution went badly. They tried to burn him alive, but the fire went out. They threw him into molten lead but it turned out to be cold. They lashed a stone to him and chucked him into the sea, but the stone floated. They threw him to wild beasts, which were tamed. They tried to hang him and the rope broke. They tried to chop his head off but the sword bent and he forgave the executioner.

This last kindness was what earned the doctor the name *Pantaleon*, which means *All-Compassionate*.

In the end they got Pantaleon's head off and he died, thus becoming one of the *megalomartyrs* (the great martyrs) of Greece. By the tenth century Saint Pantaleon had become the patron saint of Venice. *Pantalon* therefore became a popular Venetian name and the Venetians themselves were often called the *Pantaloni*.

Then, in the sixteenth century, came the *Commedia Dell'Arte*: short comic plays performed by travelling troupes and always involving the same stock characters like Harlequin and Scaramouch.

In these plays Pantalone was the stereotypical Venetian. He was a merchant and a miser and a lustful old man, and he wore one-piece breeches, like Venetians did. These long breeches therefore became known as *pantaloons*. Pantaloons were shortened to *pants* and the English (though not the Americans) called their underwear *underpants*. *Underpants* were again shortened to *pants*, which is what I am now wearing.

Pants are all-compassionate. Pants are saints. This means that my underwear is named after an early Christian martyr.

Pans

So *pants* and *panties* come from Saint Pantaleon and your undies are all-compassionate and your small-clothes are martyred.

St Pantaleon was therefore a linguistic relation of St Pancras (who *held everything*) and Pandora, who was *given everything* in a box that she really shouldn't have opened.

Pan is one of those elements that gets everywhere. It's pan-present. For example, when a film camera *pans* across from one face to another, that *pan* comes from the same Greek word that you'll find in your underpants. Cinematic *panning* is short for the *Panoramic Camera*, which was patented back in 1868 and so called because a *panorama* is where you see everything.

A *panacea* cures absolutely everything, which is useful if you're in the middle of a *pandemic*, which is one up from an *epidemic*. An epidemic is only *among the people*, whereas a pandemic means *all the peoples of the world* are infected.

Pan also gives you all sorts of terribly useful words that for some reason loiter in dark and musty corners of the dictionary. *Pantophobia*, for example, is the granddaddy of all phobias as it means *a morbid fear of absolutely everything*. Pantophobia is the inevitable outcome of *pandiabolism* – the belief that the Devil runs the world – and, in its milder forms, is a *panpathy*, or *one of those feelings that everybody has now and then*.

However, not all *pans* mean *all*. It's one of the great problems of etymology that there are no hard and fast rules: nothing is panapplicable. The pans and pots in your kitchen have nothing whatsoever to do with panoramas and pan-Africanism. Panic is not a fear of everything; it is, in fact, the terror that the Greek god Pan, who rules the forests, is able to induce in anybody who takes a walk in the woods after dark. And the Greek god Pan is not panipotent. Nobody knows where his name comes from – all we're sure of is that he played the pan-pipes.

Back in 27 BC the Roman general Marcus Agrippa built a big temple on the edge of Rome and, in a fit of indecision, decided to dedicate it to all the gods at once. Six hundred years later the building was still standing and the Pope decided to turn it into a Christian church dedicated to St Mary and the Martyrs. Fourteen hundred years after that it's still standing and still has its original roof. Technically it's now called the Church of Saint Mary, but the tourists still call it the *Pantheon*, or *All the Gods*.

The exact opposite of the Pantheon is *Pandemonium*, the place of all the demons. These days pandemonium is just a word we use to mean that everything is a bit chaotic, but originally it was a particular palace in Hell. It was one of the hundreds of English words that were invented by John Milton.

Miltonic Meanders

A boring commentary in ten books of meandering verse on the first chapter of Genesis …

… is how Voltaire described *Paradise Lost*, the great epic poem by John Milton. Voltaire was wrong, of course. *Paradise Lost* is mainly about Adam and Eve, and that pomavorous couple don't actually appear until the *second* chapter of the book of Genesis.

Paradise Lost is about the fall of Satan from Heaven and the fall of humanity from the Garden of Eden into the Land of Nod, and is generally speaking a downhill poem. However, it's still the greatest epic in English, an achievement that's largely due to its being almost the only epic in English that anybody has ever bothered writing, and certainly the only one that anyone has ever bothered reading. It's also the origin of *Pandemonium*.

In Milton's poem, when Satan is thrown out of Heaven and into Hell, the first thing he decides to do is to get a roof over his head. So he summons all the other fallen angels and gets them to build a huge and hideous palace. And just as the Pantheon is the temple of All the Gods, so Satan decides to name his new *pied-à-terre All the Demons* or *Pandemonium*, and that's how the word was invented.

Of course, since then pandemonium has come to mean anywhere that's a bit noisy, but it all goes back to Milton's idea, and his fondness for inventing language.

Milton adored inventing words. When he couldn't find the right term he just made one up: *impassive, obtrusive, jubilant, loquacious, unconvincing, Satanic, persona, fragrance, beleaguered, sensuous, undesirable, disregard, damp, criticise, irresponsible, lovelorn, exhilarating, sectarian, unaccountable, incidental* and *cooking*. All Milton's. When it came to inventive wording, Milton actually invented the word *wording*.

Awe-struck? He invented that one too, along with *stunning* and *terrific*.

And, because he was a Puritan, he invented words for all the fun things of which he disapproved. Without dear old Milton we would have no *debauchery*, no *depravity*, no *extravagance*, in fact nothing *enjoyable* at all.

Poor preachers! People always take their condemnations as suggestions. One man's abomination is another's good idea. This is the law of unintended consequences, and yes, Milton invented the word *unintended*. He probably didn't intend or imagine that one of his obscurer words would end up as the title for this book. *Etymologicon*, meaning a book containing etymologies, first crops up in his essay on *Nullities in Marriage*.

Whether you're *all ears* or obliviously *tripping the light fantastic*, you're still quoting Milton. '[T]rip it as ye go, / On the light fantastic toe' is from his poem *L'Allegro*, 'In a light fantastic round' and 'all ear' are from his play *Comus*. When a tennis player has an advantage, that's Milton's too, or at least he invented *advantage* in its sporting sense. When *all Hell breaks loose*, that's *Paradise Lost*, because when Satan escapes from Hell a curious angel asks him:

> Wherefore with thee
> Came not all Hell broke loose?

We rely on Milton. For example, he invented space travel, or at least made it linguistically possible. The word *space* had been around for centuries, but it was Milton who first applied it to the vast voids between the stars. Satan comforts his fallen angels by telling them that though they have been banned from Heaven,

> Space may produce new worlds

And that's why we don't have *outer distance* or *void stations* or *expanse ships*. Because of Milton we have *2001: A Space Odyssey* and David Bowie's song 'Space Oddity'. Indeed, if there were any justice in pop music John Milton would be raking in the royalties from Jeff Beck's 'Hi Ho Silver Lining', because Milton invented *silver linings*:[2]

> Was I deceived or did a sable cloud
> Turn forth her silver lining on the night?

This chapter is becoming rather *quotationist*, which is one of Milton's words that didn't catch on. So let us proceed to pastures new ('At last he rose and twitched his mantle blue,/ Tomorrow to fresh woods and pastures new'). Let us forget about the silver linings and concentrate on the clouds.

Bloody Typical Semantic Shifts

Do you know the difference between the clouds and the sky? If you do, you're lucky, because if you live in England, the two are pretty much synonymous. The clouds aren't lined with silver. The weather is just miserable. It always has been and it always will be.

Our word *sky* comes from the Viking word for *cloud*, but in England there's simply no difference between the two concepts, and so the word changed its meaning because of the awful weather.

If there's one thing that etymology proves conclusively, it's that the world is a wretched place. We may dream of better things, but the word *dream* comes from the Anglo-Saxon for *happiness*. There's a moral in that.

---

[2] He'd also be making a little less from Nick Cave's 'Red Right Hand'.

It has always rained, happiness has always been a dream, and people have always been lazy. I should know, I'm lazy myself. Ask me to do something like the washing up or a tax return and I'll reply that I'll do it *in five minutes.*

Five minutes usually means *never.*

If the task that I have been assigned is absolutely essential for my survival then I might say that I'll do it *in a minute.* That usually means *within an hour*, but I'm not guaranteeing anything.

Do not condemn me. Remember that a *moment* is the smallest conceivable amount of time. Now, turn on the radio or the television and wait. Soon enough an announcer will come on and say that 'In a moment we'll be showing' this, that or the other, 'but first the news and weather'.

There's an old pop song by The Smiths called 'How Soon is Now?' The writers of the song must have been even lazier than I am, because the answer is available in any etymological dictionary. *Soon* was the Anglo-Saxon word for *now.*

It's just that after a thousand years of people saying 'I'll do that soon', *soon* has ended up meaning what it does today.

These days, *now* has to have a *right* stuck on the front or it doesn't mean a thing. The same happened to the word *anon* (not the shortening for *anonymous*, but the synonym for *soon*). It derives from the Old English phrase *on an*, which meant *on one* or *instantly*. But humans don't do things instantly, we just promise to. And the word *instantly* will, of course, go the way of its siblings.

And people are nasty, condemnatory creatures. The way people overstate the faults of others is, frankly, demonic. There's a lovely bit in *King Lear* where the Duke of Gloucester is having his eyes gouged out by Regan and responds by calling her a 'naughty lady'.

Naughty used to be a much more serious word than it is now, but it has been overused and lost its power. So many stern parents have called their children naughty that the power has slowly drained from the word. If you were naughty it used to mean that you were a *no-human*. It comes from exactly the same root as *nought* or *nothing*. Now it just means that you're mischievous.

Every weakness of human nature comes out in the history of etymology. Probably the most damning word is *probably*. Two thousand years ago the Romans had the word *probabilis*. If something was *probabilis* then it could be *proved by experiment*, because the two words come from the same root: *probare*.

But *probabilis* got overused. People are always more certain of things than they really should be, and that applied to the Romans just as much as to us. Roman lawyers would claim that their case was *probabilis*, when it wasn't. Roman astrologers would say that their predictions were *probabilis* when they weren't. And absolutely any sane Roman would tell you that it was *probabilis* that the Sun went round the Earth. So by the time poor *probably* first turned up in English in 1387 it was already a poor, exhausted word whose best days were behind it, and only meant *likely*.

Now, if *probable* comes from the same root as *prove*, can you guess why the proof of the pudding is in the eating?

The Proof of the Pudding

As we've seen, both *probable* and *prove* come from a single Latin root: *probare*. But while *probable* has, through overuse, come to mean only *likely*, *prove* has prospered and its meaning has grown stronger than it ever used to be. However, you can still see its humble origins in a few phrases that don't seem to make sense any more.

Why would an exception *prove the rule*? And why do you have a *proofreader*? What happens on a *proving ground* that is so very definitive? And what kind of rigorous philosopher would require *proof of a pudding*?

The answer to all of these can be found in that old Latin root: *probare*. Despite what was said in the last section, *probare* didn't exactly mean *prove* in our modern English sense, but it meant something very close. What the Romans did to their theories was to *test* them. Sometimes a theory would be tried and tested and found to work; other times a theory would be tried and tested and found wanting.

That's the same thing that happens to a book when it's sent to the proofreader. What the proofreader gets is a proof copy, which he pores over trying to fnid misspellings and unnecessary apostrophe's.

That's also why an exception really does prove a rule. The exception is what puts a rule to the test. That test may destroy it, or the rule may be tested and survive, but either way the theory has been *proved*.

Similarly, when a new weapon is taken to the proving ground, it's not just to make sure that it exists. The proving ground is a place where a weapon can be tested to make sure that it's as deadly as had been hoped.

All of which should explain why the *test* of a good dessert and the *proof of a pudding* is in the eating. It's the old sense of *prove*.

Mind you, you probably wouldn't have wanted to *prove* old puddings. A pudding was, originally, the entrails of an animal stuffed with its own meat and grease, boiled and stuck in a cupboard for later. One of the earliest recorded uses of the word is in a medieval recipe from 1450 for Porpoise Pudding:

> **Puddyng of Porpoise**. Take the Blode of hym, & the grece of hym self, & Oatmeal, & Salt, & Pepir, & Gyngere, & melle [mix] these togetherys wel, & then put this in the Gut of the Porpoise, & then lat it seethe [boil] esyli, & not hard, a good while; & then take hym up, & broyle hym a lytil, & then serve forth.

The proof of porpoise pudding would definitely be in the eating. A pudding was effectively just a very strange (and possibly poisonous) kind of sausage.

Now, before the next link in the chain, can you take a guess as to why glamorous people put sausage poison in their faces?

Sausage Poison in Your Face

The Latin word for sausage was *botulus*, from which English gets two words. One of them is the lovely *botuliform*, which means *sausage-shaped* and is a more useful word than you might think. The other word is *botulism*.

Sausages may taste lovely, but it's usually best not to ask what's actually in them. Curiosity may have killed the cat, but it was a sausage-maker who disposed of the body. In nineteenth-century America, the belief that sausages were usually made out of dog meat was so widespread that they started to be called *hotdogs*, a word that survives to this day. Sausages are stuffed with pork and peril. They don't usually kill you, but they can.

There was an early nineteenth-century German called Justinus Kerner, who when not writing rather dreary Swabian poetry worked as a doctor. His poetry is now quite justifiably forgotten, but his medical work lives on. Kerner identified a new disease that killed some of his patients. It was a horrible malady that slowly paralysed every part of the body until the victim's heart stopped and he died. Kerner realised that all his dead patients had been eating cheap meat in sausages, so he decided to call the ailment *botulism*, or *sausage disease*. He also correctly deduced that bad sausages must contain a poison of some sort, which he called *botulinum toxin*.

In 1895 there was a funeral in Belgium. Ham was served to the guests at the wake and three of them dropped down dead. This must have delighted the undertakers, but it also meant that the remaining meat could be rushed to the University of Ghent. The Professor of Bacteria studied the homicidal ham under a microscope and finally identified the culprit, little bacteria that were, appropriately, shaped like sausages and are now called *Clostridium botulinum*.

This was an advance because it meant that Kerner's botulinum toxin could be manufactured. Now, you might be wondering why anybody would want to manufacture botulinum toxin. It is, after all, a poison. In fact, one microgram of it will cause near-instantaneous death by paralysis. But paralysis can sometimes be a good thing. If, for example, you're afflicted by facial spasms, then a doctor can inject a tinsy-winsy little dose of botulinum toxin into the affected area. A little, temporary paralysis kicks in, and the spasms are cured. Wonderful.

That, at least, was the original reason for manufacturing botulinum toxin; but very quickly people discovered that if you paralysed somebody's face it made them look a little bit younger. It also made them look very odd and incapable of expressing emotion, but who cares about that if you can remove a few years' worth of ageing?

Suddenly sausage poison was chic! The rich and famous couldn't get enough of sausage poison. It could extend a Hollywood actress's career by years. Old ladies could look middle-aged again! Injections of Kerner's sausage poison were like plastic surgery but less painful and less permanent. Sausage poison became the toast of Hollywood.

Of course, it's not called sausage poison any more. That wouldn't be very glamorous. It's not even called botulinum toxin, because everybody knows that toxins are bad for you. Now that botulinum toxin has become chic, it's changed its name to *Botox*.

So, if Botox is sausage poison and *toxicology* is the study of poison and *intoxication* is poisoning, what does *toxophilite* mean?

Bows and Arrows and Cats

A *toxophilite* is somebody who loves archery. The reason for this is that *toxin* comes from *toxon*, the Greek word for *bow*, and *toxic* comes from *toxikos*, the Greek word for *pertaining to archery*. This is because in ancient warfare it was common practice to dip your arrowheads in poison. The two ideas were so connected in the Greek mind that *toxon* became *toxin*.

Archery used to be ubiquitous. That's why there are so many people called Archer, Fletcher (arrow-maker) and Bowyer (bow-maker) in the phone book. In 1363 Edward III passed a law that required all men over the age of fourteen and under the age of 60 to practise the sport once a week. Obviously, it wasn't so much a sport back then as a means of killing people. Edward III's law has never actually been repealed.

So, terms from archery are hidden all over the English language, for example *upshot*. The *upshot* is the shot that decides who has won an archery contest. King Henry VIII's accounts for 1531 include his sporting losses and:

> To the three Cotons, for three sets which the King lost to them in Greenwich Park £20, and for one upshot won of the King.

Tudor archery was not necessarily a pleasant business. There are two theories on the origin of the phrase *enough room to swing a cat*. The first is that the *cat* is a cat-o'-nine-tails and that it's hard to whip somebody properly in a small room. The other theory is to do with marksmanship.

Hitting a stationary target was just too easy for the Tudors. So the best archers used to test themselves by putting a cat in a bag and hanging the bag from the branch of a tree. The ferocious feline would wriggle about and the sack would swing, and this exercise in animal cruelty provided the discerning archer with a challenge and English with a phrase.

Incidentally, this has nothing to do with *letting the cat out of the bag*. That's to do with pigs, obviously. In medieval markets piglets were sold in sacks, so that the farmer could carry them home more easily. This was *a pig in a poke*. A standard con at the time involved switching a valuable piglet for a valueless cat or dog. You were then being *sold a pup*, or, if you discovered the trick, you would *let the cat out of the bag*. Unlikely as that all sounds, there are equivalent phrases in almost every European language.

But to return to archery, all this sagittopotent[3] and toxophilite tosh brings us around to the odd phrase *point blank*.

The *blank* here is not your usual English *blank*, though it's closely related. The *blank* in *point blank* is the French *blanc*, which of course means *white*. The term *bullseye* is reasonably new. It was invented only in the nineteenth century. Before that, the white spot bang in the middle of an archery target was called the *white* or *blank*.

The funny thing about archery is that you don't usually aim at the target. Gravity decrees that if you aim straight at the blank your arrow will hit somewhere below. So you point the arrow somewhere above the blank, and hope that this cancels

---

[3] Good at archery, like Sagittarius, but we'll come to the Zodiac (or *little zoo*) later.

out the effects of Newton's troublesome invention. That's why *aim high* is another archer's term; it doesn't mean that you'll end up high, or it's not meant to. You aim high and hit on the level.

However, there's one situation in which this rule does not apply: if you are very, very, very, very close to the target. In that case you can aim straight at the *blank point* or white spot in the middle. If you're that close to the target, you're at *point blank* range.

Black and White

Etymologists have a terrible time distinguishing black from white. You'd think that the two concepts could be kept apart, but that wasn't how the medieval English thought about things. They were a confusing bunch of people and must have had a terrible time ordering coffee. The *Oxford English Dictionary* itself feebly admits that: 'In Middle English it is often doubtful whether *blac*, *blak*, *blacke*, means "black, dark," or "pale, colourless, wan, livid"'.

Chess would have been a confusing game; but on the plus side, racism must have been impractical.

Utterly illogical though all this may sound, there are two good explanations. Unfortunately, nobody is quite sure which one is true. So I shall give you both.

Once upon a time, there was an old Germanic word for *burnt*, which was *black*, or as close to *black* as makes no difference. The confusion arose because the old Germanics couldn't decide between black and white as to which colour *burning* was.

Some old Germans said that when things were *burning* they were bright and shiny, and other old Germans said that when things were *burnt* they turned black.

The result was a hopeless monochrome confusion, until everybody got bored and rode off to sack Rome. The English were left holding *black*, which could mean either *pale* or *dark*, but slowly settled on one usage. The French also imported this useless *black* word. They then put an N in it and later sold it on to the English as *blank*, leaving us with *black* and *blank* as opposites.

The other theory (which is rather less likely, but still good fun) is that there was an old German word *black* which meant *bare*, *void* and *empty*. What do you have if you don't have any colours?

Well, it's hard to say really. If you close your eyes you see nothing, which is *black*, but a *blank* piece of paper is, usually, *white*. Under this theory, *blankness* is the original sense and the two colours – *black* and *white* – are simply different interpretations of what *blank* means.

And, just to prove the point even more irritatingly, *bleach* comes from the same root and can mean *to make pale*, or any substance used for making things black. Moreover, *bleak* is probably just a variant of *bleach* and once meant white.

Such linguistic nonsenses are a lot more common than you might reasonably have hoped. *Down* means *up*. Well, okay, it means *hill*, but hills are upward sorts of things, aren't they? In England there's a range of hills called the Sussex Downs. This means that you can climb up a down.

Down, as in *fall down*, was originally *off-down*, meaning *off-the-hill*. So if an Old Englishman fell off the top of a hill he would fall *off-down*. Then lazy Old Englishmen started to drop the word *off*. Rather than saying that they were going *off-down*, they just started going *down*. So we ended up with the perplexing result that the *downs* are *up* above you, and that going *downhill* is really going *downdown*.

But we must get back to *blanks* and lotteries.

Once upon a time, a lottery worked like this. You bought a ticket and wrote your name on it. Then you put it into the name jar. Once all the tickets had been sold, another jar was filled up with an equal number of tickets, on some of which were written the name of a prize.

The chap running the lottery would pull out two tickets, one from the name jar and one from the prize jar. Thus, way back in 1653, the court of King James I was described as:

> A kind of Lotterie, where men that venture much may draw a
> Blank, and such as have little may get the Prize.

Blank lottery tickets were thus the financial opposite of *blank cheques* (if you're British) and *blank checks* (if you're American), although as we shall see, the American spelling is older.

Hat Cheque Point Charlie

Almost every word in the English language derives from *shah*.

Once upon a time, Persia was ruled by shahs. Some shahs were happy shahs. Other shahs were crippled or dead. In Persian that meant that they were *shah mat*. *Shah* went into Arabic as, well, *shah* (ain't etymology fascinating?). That went into Vulgar Latin as *scaccus*. That went into vulgar French (all French is vulgar) as *eschec* with the plural *esches*, and that went into English as *chess*, because a game of chess is a *game of king*, the king being the most important piece on the board. And what happened to *shah mat*? When the king is crippled, a chess player still says *checkmate*.

Chess is played on a chessboard. Chessboards are kind of useful because you can arrange stuff on them. For example, when Henry II wanted to do his accounts he did them on:

a quadrangular surface about ten feet in length, five in breadth, placed before those who sit around it in the manner of a table, and all around it it has an edge about the height of one's four fingers, lest any thing placed upon it should fall off. There is placed over the top of the escheker, moreover, a cloth bought at the Easter term, not an ordinary one but a black one marked with stripes, the stripes being distant from each other the space of a foot or the breadth of a hand. In the spaces moreover are counters placed according to their values.

Dialogus de Scaccario, c. 1180

It looked just like a chessboard and, as Henry II spoke French, it was called the *Escheker* – that's why the finances of the British government are still controlled by the *Chancellor of the Exchequer*. (The S changed to X through confusion and foolishness.)

But chess and Persian kings don't stop there. We are nowhere near the endgame. Let us continue unchecked.

You see, when your opponent puts you in *check*, your options become very limited. You have to get out of *check* in one move or it's *checkmate* and the game is over. From this you get the idea of somebody or something being *held in check*. *Checking* somebody *stops* them doing what they want, and that's why you can still body-*check* people, and why government is held *in check* by *checks and balances*.

Check or *cheque* began to mean somebody who stopped things going wrong. For example, the *Clerk of the Cheque*, whom Pepys mentions in his seventeenth-century diaries, was the chap who kept a separate set of accounts for the royal ship-yard. He *checked* fraud and served a good lunch.

> I walked and enquired how all matters and businesses go, and
> by and by to the Clerk of the Cheque's house, and there eat
> some of his good Jamaica brawne.

And from that you get the sense of a *check* as something that stops dishonesty. At a *hat-check*, for example, you get a *check* to prove that you're not stealing somebody else's hat. Bank *checks* (or *cheques*) were originally introduced as a replacement for promissory notes and got their name because they *checked* fraud.

Bank checks started out being spelled with a –*ck* on both sides of the Atlantic. But British people, perhaps under the influence of the Chancellor of the Exchequer, decided to start calling them cheques. This has a peculiar etymological result. A *blank cheque* is a *cheque* with no *check* on it. Given that blank cheques are found from as early as 1812, it's a miracle that the first *bouncing cheque* isn't recorded in the dictionary until 1927.

And from there you get *check off* (1839) and *check up* (1889). And then the Wright Brothers invented the aeroplane and people would fly around and navigate by distinctive landmarks called *checkpoints*. And then the Second World War broke out and pilots were trained and given an examination or *checkout*. Then shops got *checkouts* and *roadblocks* became *checkpoints* and people went to doctors for *checkups* and guests *checked out* of hotels and *checked in* at *check-ins* wearing a *checked* shirt and all, dear reader, *all* because of crippled shahs from ancient Persia.

All of this has nothing to do with the Czech Republic, which is ruled not by a shah but a president. However, Ivan Lendl's wife could reasonably be said to have a *Czech mate*.

Sex and Bread

Freud said that everything was secretly sexual. But etymologists know that sex is secretly food.

For example, *mating* with somebody was originally just sharing your food, or *meat*, with them (*meat* meant food of any kind and not just flesh). Likewise, your *companion* is somebody with whom you share your *bread* (from the Latin *panis*).

The Old English word for bread was *hlaf*, from which we get *loaf*; and the Old English division of labour was that women made bread and men guarded it. The woman was therefore the *hlaf-dige* and the man was the *hlaf-ward*.

Hlafward and Hlafdige
Hlaford and Hlafdi
Lavord and Lavedi
Lord and Lady

And Indian bread is in the nude, but to explain that I'm going to have to explain how half the languages in the world began, or at least the best theory on the subject.

Once upon a terribly long time ago, four thousand years before the birth of Jesus of Nazareth, there were some fellows living between the Black Sea and the Caspian. Whenever one of them died the others would bury him, or her, in a pit. They were therefore called the Kurgan Pit Burial culture. They also had some distinctive pottery and all the other tedious accoutrements of Neolithic man.

Well, *we* call them the Kurgans. We don't know what they called themselves. This was in the time before the invention of writing, or even of the internet, so we don't know what language they spoke, but we can take a very educated guess, and that educated guess is called *Proto-Indo-European*, or PIE for short.

The Kurgans probably invented the chariot, and probably used it to invade their neighbours. However, they did these invasions in a deplorably disorganised manner. Rather than all banding together and attacking in one direction, they split up and attacked hither and thither. Some of them ended up in northern India and some of them ended up in Persia. Some went to the cold, rainy lands around the Baltic, and some of them went to Greece and became Greek. Still others got lost and ended up in Italy and it was, to put it gently, a big mess.

We can tell where they went by digging up their burial pits and their distinctive pottery and whatnot. But their pottery is not what makes them interesting. They also took with them their language – Proto-Indo-European – and spread it all over Europe and Asia.

One would have hoped that this would operate like a reverse Tower of Babel, but it did not. You see, all the different groups developed different accents and these accents became so strong that their languages became mutually incomprehensible. After a few hundred years the Kurgans in northern India wouldn't have been able to make out what their cousins in Italy were saying. If you want to see this process in action today, visit Glasgow.

So the ancient Indians called their dads *pitar*, and the Greeks called their dads *pater*, and the Romans called them *pater*. The Germans, though, started pronouncing the letter P in a very funny way that made it sound more like an F. So they called their male parent *fater*, and we call him *father*, because English is descended from Old German.

Similarly, the PIE word *seks* became German *sechs*, English *six*, Latin *sex*, Sanskrit *sas* and Greek *hex*; because the Greeks pronounced their Ss funny.

There are rules of pronunciation like the German P-F and the Greek S-H that mean we can trace all these fundamental words. That's how we can work back and take an educated guess about what Proto-Indo-European was. However, it isn't always so simple.

Just looking at changes in pronunciation works very well on the great unchanging concepts like fathers and numbers. However, many words change their meaning as they go along. Let's look at the Proto-Indo-European word *neogw*, which meant *unclothed*.

In the German languages (of which English is one) *neogw* became *naked*. In the Latin languages *neogw* became *nude*. But a funny thing happened in Persia to do with cookery.

You see, the ancient Persians cooked their meat by burying it in hot ashes. However, they baked their bread *uncovered* in an oven. They still used the PIE *neogw*, and therefore called their bread *nan*.

Nan was taken into Hindi as *naan*, and if you go into an Indian restaurant today you can still buy a lovely, puffy sort of bread called *naan*, and it's etymologically *naked*.

Some bread names are even stranger. *Ciabatta* is the Italian for *slipper*, *matzoh* means *sucked out*, and *Pumpernickel* means *Devil-fart*.

Now what has *Pumpernickel* got to do with *partridge*?

Concealed Farts

Aubrey's *Brief Lives* contains this sad story about the seventeenth Earl of Oxford:

> This Earle of Oxford, making of his low obeisance to Queen Elizabeth, happened to let a Fart, at which he was so abashed and ashamed that he went to Travell, 7 yeares. On his return the Queen welcomed him home and sayd, My Lord, I had forgot the Fart.

Farts are quickly delivered and slowly forgotten. The English language, though, has had much more than seven years to let the world forget its flatulence. The smell of the original meaning slowly peters out.

Take, for example, the phrase *peter out*. Nobody is quite sure where it comes from, but one of the best theories is that it comes from the French *peter*, which meant *fart*. *Peter* definitely gave us the word *petard*, meaning a little explosive, for reasons that should be obvious to anyone who has eaten beans.

However, when Hamlet says, "'Tis sport to have the engineer hoist with his own petard', he doesn't mean that the poor engineer is raised into the air by the jet-power of his own flatulence, but that he's blown upward by his own explosive. The fart had ceased to smell.

The same thing has happened with the phrase *fizzle out*, which once meant cutting the cheese and was delicately described in one nineteenth-century dictionary as 'an escape backwards'. The same dictionary describes a *fice* as:

> A small windy escape backwards, more obvious to the nose than ears; frequently by old ladies charged [blamed] on their lap-dogs.

And *fice* itself comes from the Old English *fist*, which likewise meant fart. In Elizabethan times a smelly dog was called a *fisting cur*, and by the eighteenth century any little dog was called a *feist*, and that's where we get the word *feisty* from. Little dogs are so prone to bark at anything that an uppity girl was called *feisty*, straight from the flatulent dogs of yore. This is a point well worth remembering when you're next reading a film review about a 'feisty heroine'.

The fart lingers.

Our word *partridge* comes from the Old French *pertis* which comes from the Latin *perdix* which comes from the Greek *perdix* which comes from the Greek verb *perdesthai* which means *fart*, because that's what a partridge sounds like when it flies. The low, loud beating of the wings sounds like the clapping of the buttocks when the inner gale is liberated.

A polite, even beautiful, word for foods that make your bottom quack is *carminative*. There used to be carminative medicines, for it was widely believed that farting was good for you, as in the rhyme:

Beans, beans, they're good for the heart
The more you eat, the more you fart;
The more you fart, the better you feel;
So let's have beans for every meal.

This belief in the curative powers of flatulence was, originally, based on the idea of humours. The body was thought to be filled with substances that could get horribly out of balance. A fart was like a comb or card being pulled through wool and removing the knots. The Latin for a wool card was *carmen*, which has nothing to do with the opera, but is exactly the same as *heckling*.

Wool

Heckling is, or once was, the process of removing the knots from wool. Sheep are notoriously lackadaisical about their appearance, so before their wool can be turned into a nice warm jumper it must be combed.

It's easy to see how combing wool and teasing out the knots could be used metaphorically for *combing* through an oration and *teasing* the orator, but the connection is probably far more direct and goes to the Scottish town of Dundee.

Dundee was a radical place in the eighteenth century. It was the local centre of the wool trade and was therefore overrun with hecklers. The hecklers were the most radical workers of all. They formed themselves into what today would be called a trade union and used collective bargaining to guarantee themselves good pay and perks. The perks were mostly in the form of alcohol, but that was to be expected.

They were a political lot, the hecklers. Every morning while most of them were busy heckling, one of their number would stand up and read aloud from the day's news. They thus formed strong opinions on all subjects and when politicians and dignitaries tried to address them, their speeches were combed over with the same thoroughness as the wool. Thus *heckling*.

Wool is everywhere in language. If you possess a mobile phone you are probably wooling your friends every day without even realising it. You are, after all, currently reading wool.

Or had you never noticed the connection between *text* and *textile*?

That you send woolly messages on your telephone and read wool and cite wool from the Bible is all down to a Roman orator named Quintilian. Quintilian was the greatest orator of his day, so great that the Emperor Domitian appointed him as tutor to his two grand-nephews who were also his heirs. Nobody knows what exactly Quintilian taught them, but Domitian soon sent them both into exile.

The two lines of Quintilian that interest us are in the *Institutio Oratorico*, a gargantuan twelve-volume work on absolutely everything to do with rhetoric. In it, Quintilian says that after you have chosen your words you must weave them together into a fabric – *in textu iungantur* – until you have a fine and delicate *text*[*ure*[*ile*]] or *textum tenue atque rasum*.

It's the sort of thing we say all the time. We *weave* stories together and *embroider* them and try never to lose the *thread* of the story. Quintilian's metaphor lasted. Late classical writers took up *text* to mean any short passage in a book and then we took it to mean anything that was written down and then somebody invented the SMS message. This sheep-skin writing is all rather appropriate, given that the size of books depends upon the size of sheep.

Paper was invented in China about two thousand years ago, but we in the West didn't take up the invention until the fourteenth century. Even then, paper was considered an oriental oddity. The first English paper mill was founded in 1588.

Before paper, readers had to make do with one of two alternatives. They could use the papyrus plant, which grew plentifully in Egypt. If you mashed up papyrus you could make something that resembled paper – indeed, it was similar enough that *papyr*us is where we get the word *paper*.

Unfortunately, there's very little papyrus in England. Instead, we used sheepskins, and now you can too. Here's the recipe.

1. Take one sheep.
2. Kill it and skin it (it's vital to do this in the right order).
3. Wash the bloody skin in water, then soak it in beer for a couple of days until the hair falls out.
4. Let it dry stretched out on a wooden rack called a *tenter*. To keep it taut and flat, attach it using *tenterhooks*.

5. After a couple of days you should have something that's approximately rectangular with four sad extrusions that used to be legs.
6. Cut off legs and discard.
7. Trim the remainder down until you have an exact rectangle.
8. Fold in half.
9. You should now have four pages (printed front and back) that are roughly the size of a modern atlas. This is called a folio. All you now need to make an atlas of more than four pages is more sheep.
10. Fold it in half again and you'll have eight pages at roughly the size of a modern encyclopedia. You'll need to slice the pages at the top to make the pages turnable. This is called a quarto.
11. Fold again.
12. Provided you started off with an average-sized medieval sheep, you should now be holding something pretty much the size of a hardback novel. This is called an octavo.
13. Fold again.
14. Mass-market paperback.

When Caxton built his printing press in the fifteenth century, he set it up to use sheepskin and not paper. When paper was finally introduced it was manufactured to fit the existing printing presses, and that's the reason that both the text you're reading and the book that contains it are dependent upon sheep.

Of course, you may be reading this on your e-book reader, but as those have been designed to mimic the size of normal books, you're still at the mercy of the sheep.

Wool gets everywhere in language. Muslim mystics are called *Sufis* because of the woollen, *suf*, garments that they wore. *Burlesque* dancers on the other hand are taking part in a non-sensical or trifling show named after the Latin *burra* meaning *a tuft of wool*. Burras were used as coverings for desks, and that gave us *bureaus* and then *bureaucracies*.

Then there are all different kinds of wool: cashmere came originally from Kashmir and Angora came from Ankara, the capital of Turkey.

Turkey is, of course, the country you eat for Christmas.

Turkey

Early explorers in the Americas saw flocks of turkeys singing in the magnolia forests, for the turkey is native to America. Indeed, it was domesticated and eaten by the Aztecs. Why it should therefore be named after a country in Asia Minor is a little odd, but explicable.

Many animals are misnamed. Guinea pigs, for example, aren't pigs and they aren't from Guinea. They are found in *Guyana* in South America, and it takes only a little mispronunciation to move them across the Atlantic. The pig bit is just weird.

The same is true of the helmeted guinea fowl, or *Numidia meleagris*, which was once native to Madagascar but not Guinea. The helmeted guinea fowl is an ugly bird. It has a big bony knob on the top of its head (hence the name), but it tastes *delicious*.

People started importing helmeted guinea fowl from Madagascar to Europe, and the people who did the importing were usually Turkish traders. They were known as Turkey merchants, and the birds that they brought were therefore called *turkeys*. But those aren't the turkeys that we eat at Christmas with bread sauce and relatives. That bird is *Meleagris gallopavo*, which is also delicious.

It was the Spanish conquistadors who found *Meleagris gallopavo* in the magnolia forests and brought it back to Europe. It became popular in Spain and then in North Africa. And though it's a different species from the helmeted guinea fowl, the two birds do look surprisingly alike.

People got confused. The birds looked the same, tasted similar and both were exotic new dishes brought from Somewhere Foreign. So it was assumed that they were the same thing, and the American bird got called turkey as well, in the mistaken belief that it was a bird that was mistakenly believed to come from Turkey.

In Turkey itself, of course, they didn't make this mistake. They knew the bird wasn't theirs. So the Turks made a completely different mistake and called it a *hindi*, because they thought the bird was probably Indian. The French thought the same and they still call turkey *dindon* or *d'Inde*, which also means *from India*. It's a most confusing bird but delicious.

In fact it was so delicious that, though it was introduced to England only in the 1520s or 30s, it had become the standard Christmas meal by the 1570s. None of which explains why people occasionally *talk turkey*. Indeed, they demand to talk turkey. This all goes back to an old joke, that isn't, I'm afraid, very funny.

The joke involves a turkey and a buzzard. Now, it may be possible to eat buzzard. I don't know. But the bird's absence from any menu that I've ever encountered makes me suspicious. I suspect the buzzard is a foul fowl, and that's certainly the point of the story.

Once upon a time, a white man and a Red Indian went out hunting together. They killed a tasty turkey and a buzzard. So the white man said to his companion: 'You take the buzzard and I'll take the turkey, or, if you prefer, I can take the turkey and you can take the buzzard.'

To which the Red Indian replied: 'You don't talk turkey at all.'

This joke was immensely popular in nineteenth-century America. It was even quoted in Congress, though history doesn't recall whether anybody laughed. But it was popular enough to spawn *two* phrases.

By 1919 *talking turkey* had been altered somewhat: people had started inserting the adjective *cold*. *Talking cold turkey* is like talking turkey only more so. You were getting beyond the brass tacks and down to the barest of bare essentials. Talking cold turkey was the bluntest, directest form of speech.

And a couple of years later, in 1921, people started to use the phrase *cold turkey* to describe the bluntest, most direct method of giving up drugs.

So going cold turkey has nothing whatsoever to do with the miserable leftovers so sorrowfully consumed in the week after Christmas. Cold turkey isn't a food at all, even though it sounds like one. It's a blunt way of talking, and a blunt way of giving up drugs.

However, when you *give someone the cold shoulder*, that is a food.

Insulting Foods

There are two sorts of guests: welcome and unwelcome. The host is not permitted to tell you which you are, though he may give you a clue.

If your host cooks you a nice hot dinner, you're probably welcome. If he gives you yesterday's leftovers – for example a *cold shoulder* of mutton – then he probably wishes you hadn't come around.

It could have been worse, though – he could have made you eat *humble pie*. Humble pie is made using the *umbles* or innards of a deer. Here's a recipe from Nathan Bailey's *Dictionarium Domesticum* of 1736:

> Boil the umbles of a deer until they are very tender, set them by till they are cold, and chop them as small as meat for minc'd pyes, and shred to them as much beef suet, six large apples and half a pound of currants, as much sugar; seasoning with salt, pepper, cloves and nutmegs, according to your palate; mix all well together, and when you put them into the paste, pour in half a pint of sack, the juice of one orange and two lemons, then close the pie, bake it, and serve it hot to table.

Of course, the umbles are the worst parts of the deer. After a hard day's stag-hunting a rich man will dine on venison. Only his servants beneath the stairs would have to make do with umble (and therefore humble) pie.

Folk Etymology

The addition of the H to *umble* is an example of what's known as folk etymology. Somebody who didn't know what an *umble* was saw the words *umble pie* and got confused. Then they saw that umble pie was a humble dish, assumed that somebody had just missed off the H, and decided to put it back. Thus umble pie becomes humble pie. That's folk etymology.

A *duckling* is a little duck and a *gosling* is a little goose and a *darling* is a little dear, and on the same principle a little fellow who stood at an important chap's side used to be known as a *sideling*.

Then the origin of the word *sideling* was forgotten and in the seventeenth century people decided that it must be the participle of a verb, just as *leaping* and *sleeping* are participles of *leap* and *sleep*. There was only one problem with this theory: there didn't seem to be a verb to fit the noun. So one was invented and from then on a *sideling* became somebody who *sidled*. These days there aren't nearly as many lords and servant boys and so *sideling* itself has vanished. People still *sidle around* and *sidle up* to each other, but they are able to do so only because of a mistake of folk etymology and the backformation of a new word.

Another common form of folk etymology happens when people alter the spelling of strange or unfamiliar words so that they appear to make more sense. For example, there's a drowsy little rodent that the French therefore used to call a *dormeuse*, which meant *she who sleeps*. In English we call the same creature a *dormouse*. That's despite the fact that it isn't a mouse and has no particular affinity for doors. The reason is that the English had *field mice* and *town mice* and so they were, of course, going to look at the word *dormeuse* and conclude that someone just didn't know how to spell.

The same principle applies to fairies, or rather to the disappearance of fairies. Once upon a time, belief in fairies was commonplace. They lived not at the bottom of the garden, but in the woods, where they would play all sorts of mysterious games. They would milk people's cattle in the night, or hide in flowers and under trees, and generally do the sorts of things that would get you or me arrested. They were known as the Folks. When it was cold the Folks liked to wear gloves, which is why there is, or used to be, a flower called a *folks' glove*.

But the fairies have all died (or maybe just got better at hiding) and people stopped referring to them as Folks many years ago, which is why the name *folks' glove* became rather peculiar. Then some clever fellow decided that they weren't *folks' gloves* after all, they must be *fox-gloves* because foxes have such dinky little feet, and the error set in. They are foxgloves now, and foxgloves they will remain, until somebody makes a better mistake.

By the same system, the old word *crevis* is now spelled and pronounced *crayfish*, even though it's not very fishlike. The Spanish *cucaracha* became a *cockroach*, and most wonderfully of all, the Indian *mangus* became a *mongoose*, although there's not a huge similarity between the furry, snake-devouring mammal and a goose.

An exception to these folk etymologies is the *butterfly*. Butterflies do have something to do with butter, although nobody is quite sure what. They like to flutter around milk pails and butter churns, which might explain it. Many butterflies are yellow, which would be a good reason for the name. But there's another, more troubling possibility: butterflies, like the rest of us, are subject to the call of the lavatory, and butterfly poo is yellow, just like butter.

Now, you may ask yourself, what sort of person goes around peering at butterfly poo and then naming an insect after it? The answer, it would appear, is that Dutch people do that. Or at least, an old Dutch word for butterfly was *boterschijte*.

Of course, you may dismiss that last theory as poppycock, but if you do, please remember that *poppycock* comes from the Dutch *pappe-cack*, meaning *soft shit*.

Before the next link, can you guess what butterflies have to do with psychiatry and pasta?

Butterflies of the World

For some reason the languages of the world put more effort into the names of butterflies than those of any other creature. From Norway to Malaysia the words are extraordinary.

Malay doesn't have plurals like ours. In English you simply add an S to the end of the word. But in Malay you form your plural by repeating the noun, so *tables* would become *table table*. It's a system with some sort of logic to it. When there's more than one word, that means there's more than one thing.

It works out fine for the speaker of Malay, so long as the original singular noun wasn't formed by reduplication itself, as is the case with their butterflies. The Malay for *butterfly* is *rama-rama*, so *butterflies* is *rama-rama rama-rama*. And it doesn't stop there. The Malays also repeat verbs to intensify them, so *I really like* would be rendered as *I like like*, or *suka suka*. We occasionally do this in English, when somebody says, 'I've got to, *got to* see that film'. All of which means that the Malay for *I love butterflies* is:

Saya suka suka rama-rama rama-rama

In Italian, butterflies are called *farfalle* and there's a kind of butterfly-shaped pasta named after them that you can buy in most supermarkets. Outside Italy, though, most people don't realise that it's *butterfly pasta*, and in America they ignore the Italian name entirely and call *farfalle bow-ties*, because a butterfly resembles a bow-tie, and in an emergency could probably serve as a substitute.

This is a point of dress not lost upon the Russians, who call a bow-tie a butterfly. And as a butterfly is, in Russian, a little lady, bow-ties, butterflies and girls are all called *babochkas* (like *babushkas*).

In the bleak Norwegian winter there are no butterflies at all, so when they emerge from their chrysalises in the bleak Norwegian summer they are called *summer-birds, or somerfogl*.

In French they rather boringly just took the Latin *papilio* and called their butterflies *papillons*. But then, in a fit of inventiveness, they realised that the grand tents in which kings sat at tournaments and jousts were shaped like the wings of a butterfly, so they called them *papillons*, and we call them *pavilions*, which means that there's a butterfly at one end of Lord's Cricket Ground.

Why all these intricate and exquisite names? Nobody bothers with the humble fly (which does exactly what it says on the tin) or the beetle (*biter*) or the bee (*quiverer*), or the lousily-named louse. Butterflies hog all the attention of the word-makers.

Perhaps this is because in many quite distinct and unconnected cultures the butterfly is imagined to be a human soul that has shaken off this mortal coil of woes and now flutters happily through a gaily-coloured afterlife.

This was the belief of the Maoris, and of the Aztecs in whose mythology Itzpapalotl was the goddess of the Obsidian Butterfly: a soul encased in stone who could be freed only by another tongue-twisting god called Tezcatlipoca.

There also seems to have been a ghost of this belief among the ancient Greeks. The Greek for butterfly was *psyche*, and Psyche was the goddess of the soul. There's a lovely allegorical poem about her called 'Cupid and Psyche', and she's also the origin of the *study of the soul*: *psychoanalysis*.

Psychoanalysis and the Release of the Butterfly

The great thing about creating something is that you get to give it a name. Who would endure the expense and incontinence of babies, were it not for the fun of saddling another human with a moniker that you chose yourself?

With this in mind one can imagine Sigmund Freud sitting in his study in Vienna and considering Psyche, the Greek goddess of the soul and mystical butterfly. That's what he was analysing (with the stress on the first two syllables), so he decided to call his new invention psychoanalysis. *Analysis* is Greek for *release*. So Freud's new art would be, literally, the *liberation of the butterfly*. How pretty! Freud was probably so pleased with himself that he became lazy, for most of the other psychological terms are Jungian.

Carl Jung was Freud's protégé. Then one day Carl had a dream that wasn't about sex. He hesitated before telling Freud something quite that embarrassing. Confessing to a psychoanalyst that you've had an innocent dream is rather like confessing to your grandmother that you've had a dirty one. Freud was outraged. What sort of fruitcake, he demanded, has a dream that isn't dirty? It was inconceivable. Freud decided that Jung had gone quite mad, that the dream really had been dirty, and that Jung was just being coy.

Jung insisted that his dream wasn't about sex and that, in fact, it was about his grandparents being hidden in a cellar. So he rejected Freud's pansexualism (not a sin of cookery, but the belief that everything comes down to nooky) and ran off to become a Jungian.

Having invented his own form of psychoanalysis, Jung now had naming rights. So it was Carl and not Sigmund who decided that a psychological problem should be called a *complex*. Then he thought up *introverts* and *extroverts*, and finally, realising that naming was a doddle, he invented *synchronicity* and *ambivalent*. And with that he sat down to rest on his laurels and consider his subterranean grandparents.

But the grand panjandrum and greatest inventor of psychological terms was neither Sigmund Freud nor Carl Jung. It was a man who was just as important but is far less known today: Richard von Krafft-Ebing.

Krafft-Ebing was born sixteen years before Dr Freud and 35 years before Jung. He was, essentially, the first doctor to start writing case histories of people whose sexual behaviour wasn't entirely respectable.

The book that resulted, *Psychopathia Sexualis* (1886), was so scandalous that large chunks of it had to be written in Latin, in order to keep it out of the hands of the prurient public. The idea was that if you were clever enough to understand Latin, you couldn't possibly be a pervert (something that nobody mentioned to Caligula).

Because Krafft-Ebing was a pioneer he had to invent terms left, right and centre. Humanity had a long history of condemning peccadilloes, but not of classifying them. So it was in the translation of *Psychopathia Sexualis* that English first got the words *homosexual, heterosexual, necrophilia, frotteur, anilingus, exhibitionism, sadism* and *masochism*.

Sadism had in fact been around for a while in French. The French writer Donatien Alphonse François Marquis de Sade was famous for producing horrid books about people being horrid to each other in bed. Really horrid. Catchy titles like *One Hundred and Twenty Days of Sodom* should give you some idea, but a clearer image of the nature of Sade's work comes from the fact that in the 1930s a historian by the name of Geoffrey Gorer, who was researching the marquis, went to the British Museum to read some of de Sade's works that were stored there. However, he was told by the British Museum that it was a rule that people were only allowed to read de Sade's books 'in the presence of the Archbishop of Canterbury and two other trustees'.

So it's easy to see how de Sade's notoriety meant that his favourite activity became known as *sadism* in French. But Richard von Krafft-Ebing also needed a name for sadism's opposite: masochism.

Leopold von Sacher-Masoch, who gave us the word *maso-chism*, is known to few, or less. This seems rather appropriate. While the Marquis de Sade strides around spanking Fame's bottom with a hardbacked copy of *The Hundred and Twenty Days of Sodom*, little Leo is forgotten in some ratty cellar, wearing a gimp-suit and whimpering over a copy of *Venus in Furs*.

Venus in Furs (1870) was Masoch's great work. It describes a chap called Severin who signs a contract with a lady (I use the term loosely) who is thereby:

> … entitled not only to punish her slave as she deems best, even for the slightest inadvertence or fault, but also is herewith given the right to torture him as the mood may seize her or merely for the sake of whiling away the time …

As you can imagine, *Venus in Furs* would make a splendid book-group read, or christening present. Yet even Masoch's masterwork is better known these days as a song by the Velvet Underground, whose lyrics have a fragile connection to the original novel, mainly in the use of the name Severin.

Venus in Furs was rather closely based upon Leo's own life. Masoch met a girl with the ridiculous name of Fanny Pistor. They signed just such a contract as the one above and set off to Florence together, with him pretending to be her servant. Exactly how much time Fanny Pistor whiled away and how is not recorded, and it's probably best not to try to imagine.

When, in 1883, Krafft-Ebing was casting around for a name for a newly classified perversion, he thought of Sacher-Masoch's novel. He wrote in *Psychopathia Sexualis* that:

I feel justified in calling this sexual anomaly 'Masochism,' because the author Sacher-Masoch frequently made this perversion, which up to his time was quite unknown to the scientific world as such, the substratum of his writings ... he was a gifted writer, and as such would have achieved real greatness had he been actuated by normally sexual feelings.

Poor Leo was still alive when Krafft-Ebing appropriated his name for a psychological disorder. He was, apparently, peeved by the terminology. Mind you, he probably rather enjoyed the humiliation.

The Villains of the Language

History is written by victors. The Elizabethan poet Sir John Harington once wrote:

> Treason doth never prosper: what's the reason?
> Why, if it prosper, none dare call it Treason.

But history is a lot fairer than language. Language takes your name and applies it to whatever it likes. Sometimes, however, it *is* fair, as with the word *quisling*.

Vidkun Quisling was a Norwegian maths prodigy and invented his own religion. He also embarrassed himself rather during the Second World War by trying to get Norway to surrender to the Nazis so that he could be the puppet Minister-President. He succeeded in his plan and ten weeks after his appointment *The Times* wrote:

Major Quisling has added a new word to the English language. To writers, the word Quisling is a gift from the gods. If they had been ordered to invent a new word for traitor … they could hardly have hit upon a more brilliant combination of letters. Aurally it contrives to suggest something at once slippery and tortuous. Visually it has the supreme merit of beginning with a Q, which (with one august exception) has long seemed to the British mind to be a crooked, uncertain and slightly disreputable letter, suggestive of the questionable, the querulous, the quavering of quaking quagmires and quivering quicksands, of quibbles and quarrels, of queasiness, quackery, qualms and quilp.

And it serves him right. However, language isn't always on the side of justice. Consider these three names: Guillotine, Derrick and Jack Robinson. Which of those do you think was the nasty one?

Two Executioners and a Doctor

Once upon a time, hanging was the punishment for almost any crime. Even the great Elizabethan poet Ben Jonson, for the trivial offence of murder, was sentenced to death. The sentence was commuted when Jonson proved that he could read and thus got Benefit of the Clergy. Instead of being executed, he had a T branded on his thumb and was sent home with a warning.

The T stood for Tyburn, which is where the hangings used to take place. We even know the name of the man who would have hanged Ben Jonson: he was called Thomas Derrick.

Thomas Derrick was a nasty man. There hadn't been enough applicants for the role of executioner and so the Earl of Essex pardoned a rapist on condition that he would take on the job. That rapist was Derrick.

Derrick was a bad man and a good executioner. The two are probably connected. In fact, Derrick was something of an innovator. Rather than just slinging the rope over the beam, he invented a complicated system of ropes and pulleys. He even, in 1601, executed the Earl of Essex, though being a noble Essex was allowed the dubious honour of having his head chopped off, rather than hanging.

There's a moral in that, but I haven't the foggiest notion what it is – and the ethics get more complicated when you consider that Derrick's name survives and Essex's doesn't. The rope system he invented started to be used for loading and unloading goods down at the docks and that's why modern cranes still have a *derrick*. It's named after a rapist and executioner. There's no justice in this world: look at Jack Robinson.

There are three main theories on why things happen *before you can say Jack Robinson*. The first is that Robinson used to be the French term for an umbrella (because of *Robinson Crusoe*, in which the hero has an umbrella and very little else), and that French servants were usually called *Jacques*. This meant that when rich Frenchmen visited England and were surprised by the inevitable shower of rain, they would shout, 'Jacques, robinson!' There is, though, no evidence for this theory at all.

The second theory is that there was an eccentric fellow in early nineteenth-century London who would walk out of parties without warning, often before you could even say his name, which was Jack Robinson. However, there's no contemporary evidence for this strange Jack Robinson's existence, so the second theory looks as dicey as the first.

The third and most plausible theory is that the phrase comes from Sir John Robinson, who definitely existed and was constable of the Tower of London from 1660 to 1679. He was therefore in charge of executions and was a stickler for efficiency rather than solemnity. The prisoner was marched out, put on the block and shortened without any opportunity for famous last words or blubbering. He didn't even have the time to appeal to the overseer of the execution. He was beheaded *before he could say Jack Robinson.*

So derricks and brief spans of time were both named after cruel and psychotic executioners. The guillotine, on the other hand, was named after a jolly nice chap.

Dr Joseph-Ignace Guillotin had nothing whatsoever to do with the invention of the guillotine. In fact, so far as anybody can tell, he was against the death penalty. Nobody is sure who designed the first modern guillotine, but we know that it was built by a German harpsichord-maker called Tobias Schmidt.

It was Guillotin's kindness that got the machine named after him. You see, in pre-revolution France poor people were hanged, whereas nobles had the right to be beheaded, which was considered less painful (although it's uncertain how they worked that out). So when the poor of France rose in revolution, one of their key demands was the right to be decapitated.

Dr Guillotin was on the committee for reforming executions. He decided that hanging was horrid and that axes were inefficient. However, a newfangled mechanism from Germany was, probably, the least painful and most humane method available. If there *had* to be executions, it was best that they were done with this new device. He recommended it.

In the debate that followed, on 1 December 1789, Dr Guillotin made one silly remark: 'Avec ma machine,' he said, 'je vous fais sauter la tête d'un coup-d'oeil, et vous ne souffrez point.' ('With my machine, I cut off your head in the twinkling of an eye, and you never feel it.')

The Parisians loved this line. They thought it was hilarious. In fact, they composed a comic song about it. And thus Dr Guillotin's name was attached to one of the most famous methods of execution. Thomas Derrick and Jack Robinson were both sadistic, heartless thugs, whose names live on in innocence, if not glory. Poor Dr Guillotin's family were so embarrassed that they had to change their surname. There's no justice.

And sometimes with these eponymous inventions it can be hard to work out which came first, the word or the man. This is the case with Thomas Crapper, who invented the crapper.

Thomas Crapper

There's a myth that the word *crap* was coined for the sake of Thomas Crapper, the inventor of the flushing lavatory. There's also a myth that the word *crap* was *not* coined for Thomas Crapper. It actually depends on where you come from, and if that sounds odd, it's because *crap* is a sticky subject. Luckily, I have, as it were, immersed myself in it.

The first mistake that must be wiped away is that Thomas Crapper (1836–1910) was the inventor of the lavatory. He wasn't. The first flushing lavatory was invented by the Elizabethan poet

Sir John Harington (who was quoted a couple of pages ago on the subject of treason).

Sir John installed his invention in his manor at Kelston, Somerset, where it's said that it was used by Queen Elizabeth herself. Harington was so pleased with the device that he wrote a book on the subject called *A New Discourse Upon a Stale Subject: The Metamorphosis of Ajax*. Ajax gets in there because in Elizabethan times the slang word for a privy was *a jakes*.

A whiff of the book's style and of the previous state of English crapping can be gained from the following extract:

> For when I found not onely in mine own poore confused cottage, but even in the goodliest and statliest pallaces of this realm, notwithstanding all our provisions of vaults, of sluces, of grates, of paines of poore folkes in sweeping and scour-ing, yet still this same whorson sawcie stinke, though he were commanded on paine of death not to come within the gates, yet would spite of our noses, even when we would gladliest have spared his company ... Now because the most unavoid-able of all these things that keep such a stinking stirre, or such a stinke when they be stirred, is urine and ordure, that which we all carie about us (a good speculation to make us remember what we are and whither we must) therefore as I sayd before, many have devised remedies for this in times past ... but yet (as the ape does his young ones) I thinke mine the properest of them all.

Americans like to talk about *going to the john*, and it has been suggested that this is in memory of John Harington. Unfortunately that's unlikely, as *john* in the lavatorial sense didn't appear until more than a hundred years after Harington's death. However, it *is* likely that *john* was an alteration of *jake*. Or perhaps we just like giving boys' names to the smelliest room in the house.

Harington's invention didn't catch on. Unless there are sewers and running water, a flushing lavatory is never really going to be viable for the mass market. It's like having an electric lamp without mains electricity, or skis without snow.

Sewers and running water arrived in Britain in the mid-nineteenth century, and what we generally think of as a lavatory was patented by Edward Jennings in 1852.

So who was Crapper? Thomas Crapper was born in Yorkshire in 1836. In 1853, a year *after* Jennings' patent, he came to London to start an apprenticeship as a plumber. He was jolly good at plumbing, and the 1850s were the golden age of the toilet trader. The new sewers meant that everyone could flush away their shame and smell. Business boomed.

Crapper set up his own company, Thomas Crapper & Co., and designed his own line of thrones. He invented the ballcock system for refilling, which stopped water being wasted, and added extra devices to stop anything unpleasant flowing back into the bowl after the flush. His were very superior lavatories, the pinnacle of plumbing.

Crapper lavatories were chosen for the residence of the Prince of Wales and for the plumbing of Westminster Abbey, where Crapper's name can be seen to this day on the manhole covers. The brand-name Crapper was everywhere, but *crap* had been around for a long time before.

All the dictionaries claim that *crap* first appeared in the 1840s, but in fact the word can be traced back to 1801 and a poem by a fellow called J. Churchill. Churchill's poem tells a story (which it claims is based on fact) about a subaltern in the army who feels the call of nature. He runs to the outhouse only to find that a major is already there, and as the major outranks him, he's forced to wait. The subaltern feels himself beginning to give way and his misery is compounded when a captain turns up and pulls rank:

Just adding (for some only mind number ONE)[4]
'I, I shall go in, when the major has done:'
The Sub, who was, now, a most terrible plight, in;
And, not quite aware of priority S---ING,
Squeez'd awhile; 'Well!' says he, 'then, the best friends MUST
    PART;'
Crap! Crap! 'twas a moist one! a right Brewer's ****!
And, finding it vain, to be stopping the lake;
'Zounds!' says he, 'then, here goes man! I've brew'd;
    so, I'll bake.'

That beautiful poem was written 35 years before Thomas Crapper was born, and half a century before he started plumbing. So *crap* is certainly not named after Crapper. Perhaps it was a case of nominative determinism. If you're unfortunate enough to be called Crapper, what are you going to do except work with it?

However, if Crapper didn't cause *crap*, he associated himself with it closely. All of his lavatories had Thomas Crapper & Co.

---

[4] This is also the first-ever reference to *number one* in a lavatorial context. Most authorities have it down as a twentieth-century term.

written on them in florid writing and these lavatories were installed all over Britain. But in America, nobody had ever heard of either Crapper the man, or *crap* the word.

There isn't an American reference to *crap* all through the nineteenth century. In fact, there's nothing before the First World War. Then, in 1917, America declared war on Germany and sent 2.8 million men across the Atlantic, where they would have been exposed to the ubiquitous Thomas Crapper & Co. on every second lavatory.

It's only after the First World War that *crap, crapper, crapping around* and *crapping about* appear in the United States. So it would seem that though the English word *crap* doesn't come from the man, the American one does. Crapper didn't invent it, but he spread the word.

Mythical Acronyms

Can you take another chapter on the same subject? Good, because we have something to clear up: *shit* and *fuck*, or more precisely, *SHIT* and *FUCK*.

You might have heard the story that both these words are acronyms. This is absolute twaddle.

The story goes that manure gives off methane. So far, so true. But then the story continues that when manure is transported on a ship, it needs to be stored right at the top of the boat to stop the methane building up to explosive levels in the cargo hold. So the words *Store High In Transit* used to be stamped on bags of manure before they were loaded onto a boat. *Store High*

In Transit then got shortened to its initials – *S.H.I.T.* – and that was the start of *shit*.

It's an ingenious explanation and whoever thought it up at least deserves credit for imagination. Unfortunately it's absolute manure. *Shit* can be traced back to the Old English verb *scitan* (which meant exactly what it does today), and further back to Proto-Germanic *skit* (the Germans still say *scheisse*), and all the way to the Proto-Indo-European word (c. 4000 BC) *skhei*, which meant to *separate* or *divide*, presumably on the basis that you *separated* yourself from your faeces. *Shed* (as in *shed your skin*) comes from the same root, and so does *schism*.

An odd little aspect of this etymology is that when Proto-Indo-European arrived in the Italian peninsula they used *skhei* to mean *separate* or *distinguish*. If you could tell two things apart then you *knew* them, and so the Latin word for *know* became *scire*. From that you got the Latin word *scientia*, which meant *knowledge*, and from that we got the word *science*. This means that *science* is, etymologically, *shit*. It also means that *knowing your shit*, etymologically, means that you're good at physics and chemistry.

Also, as *conscience* comes from the same root, the phrase *I don't give a shit* is thoroughly appropriate.

The other acronymic myth that we need to stamp out is that *fuck* is a legal term. The commonly believed myth runs that once upon a time, when sex could land you in jail, people could be taken to court and charged *For Unlawful Carnal Knowledge*. Nothing of the sort is true and there has never been such a term in English law.

The first recorded *fuckers* were actually monks. There was a monastery in the English city of Ely, and in an anonymous fifteenth-century poem somebody mentioned that the monks might have acquired some dirty habits. The poem is in a strange combination of Latin and English, but the lines with which we are concerned run thus:

Non sunt in celi
Qui fuccant wivys in Heli

Which seems to mean:

They are not in heaven
Who fuck wives in Ely

The modern spelling of *fuck* is first recorded in 1535, and this time it's bishops who are at it. According to a contemporary writer, bishops 'may fuck their fill and be unmarried'. In between those two there's a brief reference by the Master of Brasenose College, Oxford to a 'fuckin Abbot'. So it seems that the rules of celibacy weren't being taken too seriously in the medieval church.

Some scholars, though, trace the word *fuck* to even earlier roots. The etymologist Carl Buck claimed to have found a man from 1278 who rejoiced in the name *John Le Fucker*, but nobody since has been able to find the reference and some even suspect that Buck made it up as a joke. Also, even if John Le Fucker did ever exist, he was probably really *John Le Fulcher* or *John the Soldier*.

Acronyms are, I'm afraid, mainly myths. *Posh* does not mean *Port Out Starboard Home* and *wog* never stood for *Wily Oriental Gentleman*. There was a famous *cabal* formed of Clifford, Arlington, Buckingham, Ashley and Lauderdale, all conspiring against Charles II. But that was coincidence; the word had already been around for centuries.

But some acronyms do exist, just not where you might expect to find them. There's one hidden away in *The Sound of Music* that relates straight back to John the Baptist.

John the Baptist and *The Sound of Music*

About two thousand years ago a perfectly respectable lady called Elizabeth became pregnant and her husband lost his voice. He stayed silent as a silo until the child was born. The child was called John, and when John grew up he began telling people that they were naughty and chucking them in a river. Now, if you or I tried a stunt like that we'd be brought up by the police pretty sharpish. But John got away with it and, if you can believe it, was considered rather holy for all his attempted drownings. Chaps at the time called him John the Baptist.

Seven hundred years later somebody else lost his voice, or at least had a terribly sore throat. He was an Italian who went by the cumbersome moniker of Paul the Deacon, so he wrote a verse prayer to John the Baptist that ran thus:

Ut queant laxis
    resonare fibris
Mira gestorum
    famuli tuorum,
Solve polluti
    labii reatum,
Sancte Iohannes.

[O let your servants sing your wonders on,
With loosened voice and sinless lips, St John.]

Four hundred years after that, in the fourteenth century, some-body set this little poem to music. He (or maybe she) wrote a pretty, climbing melody, in which each line started a note higher than the last, until with the words *Sancte Iohannes* it dropped again to the bottom.

So the first note was on the syllable *Ut*, the second line began with the *re* in *resonare* on the note above, then *Mi* in *Mira*, *fa*, *So*, *la* …

The problem with *Ut*, though, is that it's a rather short syl-lable and difficult for a singer to hold. Try it. So *Ut* got changed to *Do* (perhaps for *Dominus*, but nobody's sure), and that gave *Do*, *re*, *Mi*, *fa*, *So*, *la* and, by extension, *Si* for **Sancte Iohannes**. Then somebody pointed out that there was already a *So* begin-ning with S and you couldn't rightly have two lines beginning with the same letter. So *Si* was changed to *Ti*.

Do re Mi fa So la Ti Do

Which is just a shortening of a hymn to John the Baptist. The shortening technique was invented by a fellow called Guido of Arezzo.

So *Do* is not a deer, a female deer, and *re* is not a drop of golden sun. The Von Trapp family were cruelly deceived.

Poor *Ut* was consigned to history, or nearly. It sort of sur-vives. The lowest note was also known as *gamma*, after the Greek letter. So the lowest note of the scale was once known as *gamma* or *ut*. Then a whole scale came to be known as *gamma-ut*.

And that's why when you go through the whole scale, you still run through the *gamut*. It all comes back to church music, rather like organised crime, which is, of course, crime played on a church organ.

Organic, Organised, Organs

Organic food is food grown in a church organ. Organised crime is crime committed by organists.

Well, etymologically speaking.

Once upon a time, the ancient Greeks had the word *organon*, which meant *something you work with*. An *organon* could be a tool, an implement, a musical instrument or a part of the body. For the moment, let's stick to the musical sense.

Originally, an *organ* was any musical instrument, and this was still the case when, in the ninth century, people decided that every church should have a *pipe organ* in it, for, as Dryden put it: 'What human voice can reach the sacred organ's praise?'

Slowly the *pipe* part of *pipe organ* got dropped and other instruments ceased to be *organs* (except the *mouth organ*, which, if you think about it, sounds a bit rude). And that's why an organ is now only the musical instrument you have in a church.

Now let's return to the Greeks, because *organ* continued to mean *a thing you work with* and hence *a part of the body*, as in the old joke: 'Why did Bach have twenty children? Because he had no stops on his organ.'

A bunch of organs put together make up an *organism*, and things that are produced by organisms are therefore *organic.* In the twentieth century, when artificial fertilisers were strewn upon our not-green-enough fields, we started to distinguish between this method and *organic farming* and thus *organic food.*

The human body is beautifully and efficiently arranged (at least my body is). Each organ has a particular function. I have a hand to hold a glass, a mouth to drink with, a belly to fill, a liver to deal with the poison and so on and so forth. Heart, head, lungs, liver, kidney and colon: each performs a particular task, and the result, dear reader, is the glory that is I.

If you arrange a group of people and give each one a particular job, you are, metaphorically, making them act together like the *organs* of a body. You are *organising* them.

Thus an *organisation*: something in which each person, like each *organ* of the body, has a particular task. That shift in meaning happened in the sixteenth century when everybody liked metaphors about the *body politic.* However, crime didn't get organised until 1929 in Chicago, when Al Capone was running the mob (or *mobile vulgus* to give it its proper name – *mob* is only a shortening).

Clipping

When a phrase like *mobile vulgatus* or *mobile peasants* gets shortened to *mob*, linguists call it clipping. And there are more clips around than you might think:

Taxi cab = **Taxi**meter **cab**riolet
Fan = **Fan**atic

Bus = Voiture omni**bus**
Wilco = **Will co**mply
Van = Cara**van**
Sleuth = **Sleuth**hound (a kind of sniffer dog)
Butch = **Butch**er
Cute = A**cute**
Sperm whale = **Sperm**aceti **whale**
Film buff = **Buff**alo

Buffalo

How did *buffalo* come to mean *enthusiast*? What's the connection between the beast and the music *buff*?

To answer that, you first need to know that buffalo aren't buffalo; and also that *buffalo* is one of the most curious words in the English language.

The ancient Greek word *boubalos* was applied to some sort of African antelope. Then *boubalos* was changed to *buffalo* and applied to various kinds of domesticated oxen. That's why you still have water buffalo (*Bubalus bubalis*). Any ox in Europe could once be called a buffalo.

Then the same thing happened to buffalos that had happened to turkeys. Explorers arrived in North America, saw some bison, and wrongly assumed that they were the same species as the European ox. Biologically they aren't related, and to this day scientists will become all tetchy if you call a bison a buffalo, but who cares? The name stuck.

Now, let's jump back across the Atlantic and take another look at those European oxen. They were called *buffalo*, but the name was often shortened to *buff*. European buffalo used to get killed and skinned and the leather that resulted was therefore known as *buff*, or *buffe leather*.

This leather was very useful for polishing, which is why we still *buff* things until they shine. When something has been properly buffed it looks good, and from that we get the idea that people who spend too much time at the gym running around like crazed gerbils are *buff*.

An odd thing about buff leather is that it's rather pale and, in fact, looks very like human skin. That's why naked people are referred to as being *in the buff*, because it looks as though they are dressed in buff leather.

Some people really did dress in buff leather, as it's a good strong material. For example, in the nineteenth century the uniform of the New York firefighters was made from buff and the firefighters themselves were often called *buffs*.

The firefighters of New York were heroes. Everybody loves a good conflagration, and whenever a New York building started burning the buffs would be called and crowds of New Yorkers would turn out to cheer them on. People would travel across the city just to see a good fire, and schoolboys would become aficionados of the buffs' techniques for putting them out. These devoted New York schoolboys became known as *buffs*. Thus the *New York Sun* said, in 1903, that:

> The *buffs* are men and boys whose love of fire, fire-fighting and firemen is a predominant characteristic.

And that's why to this day you have film *buffs* and music *buffs* and other such expert *buff*alos.

On the far side of New York state, beside the Niagara River, is a whole city called Buffalo, which is a bit odd as there aren't any bison there, and never have been. However, the Niagara River is very pretty, and the best guess about the origins of the city's name is that *Buffalo* is a corruption of the French *beau fleuve*, or *beautiful river*. But imagine if there *were* bison in the city of Buffalo. Pigeons in London are called London pigeons. Girls in California are called California girls. So any bison that you found in Buffalo would have to be called Buffalo buffalos.

Buffalos are big beasts and it's probably best not to get into an argument with one. That's why there's an American slang verb *to buffalo* meaning *to bully*. This means that if you bullied bison from that large city on the Niagara River, you would be *buffaloing Buffalo buffalos*.

But you can go further, and a linguist at the University of Buffalo did. He worked out that if bison from his native city, who were bullied by other bison from his native city, went and took their frustration out on still other bison from his native city, then:

Buffalo buffalo Buffalo buffalo buffalo buffalo Buffalo buffalo.

Confused? The grammar is easier if you compare it to this version:

Buffalo bison [whom] Buffalo bison bully [then] bully Buffalo bison.

It's the longest grammatically correct sentence in the English language that uses only one word. Word buffs love it.

Antanaclasis

Rhetorically, the sentence *Buffalo buffalo Buffalo buffalo buffalo buffalo Buffalo buffalo* is antanaclasic, which means that it keeps using the same word in different senses. People have been playing around with antanaclasis since language began. The Romans thought up the Latin sentence:

Malo malo malo malo.

Which means:

I would rather be in an apple tree than be a bad boy in trouble.

But neither the Romans nor the bison of Buffalo can come close to what you can achieve in Chinese if you really set your mind to it. Chinese is an incredibly tonally inflected language and you can change the meaning of a word by slightly changing the way you say it. When you add that advantage onto the principle behind *Buffalo buffalos* and *malo malo*, you can create something much longer. That's how a Chinese-American linguist came up with a poem that, in Westernised script, reads like this:

Shíshì shíshì Shī Shì, shì shí, shì shí shí shī.
Shì shíshí shì shì shì shī.
Shí shí, shì shí shī shì shì.
Shì shí, shì Shī Shì shì shì.
Shì shì shì shí shī, shì shí shì, shī shì shí shī shìshì.
Shì shí shì shí shī shī, shì shíshì.
Shíshì shī, Shì shí shì shì shíshì.
Shíshì shì, Shì shí shì shí shì shí shī.
Shí shí, shī shí shì shí shī, shí shí shí shī shī.
Shì shì shì shì.

Which means:

> In a stone den was a poet named Shi, who loved to eat lions,
>   and had decided to eat ten.
> He often went to the market to hunt for lions.
> At ten o'clock precisely, ten lions had just arrived at the market.
> At that moment, Shi had just arrived at the market as well.
> Seeing those lions, he shot them with his arrows.
> He brought the corpses of the ten lions to the stone den.
> The stone den was wet, so he had his servant clean it.
> After the stone den was cleaned, he tried to eat those ten lions.
> When he ate, he realised the corpses were really ten stone lions.
> Try to explain this matter.

That's one hell of a case of antanaclasis. However, like the buf-falo sentence, it makes no sense, even to the Chinese, unless it's explained.

China

Westerners find it terribly hard to pronounce Chinese words, and the Chinese find it hard to pronounce ours. In the nineteenth century when British merchants were over in China trying to trade opium, they found that the locals couldn't even say the word *business*, and instead pronounced it *pidgin*, which is why strange colonial dialects are still called *pidgin English*.

And we're so bad at pronouncing Chinese that when we want one of their phrases we don't adopt them as we would a French one, we just give in and translate. Do you have any idea how to pronounce *xi nao*? Luckily, you don't need to, as we translated it to *brainwashing* (it was originally a form of Buddhist meditation). We never lost face by trying to pronounce *tiu lien*, instead we took the phrase and translated it to *lose face*. As for Mao Tse Tung's *tsuh lao fu*, we call them *paper tigers*.

However, some Chinese words do get into the language, mostly because of the delicious food. These remain untranslated, which is generally a good thing. *Kumquats* and *dim sum* might sell more if English-speakers knew that they meant *golden orange* and *touch the heart*; however, *fish brine* would probably not sell as much as *ketchup*, *odds and ends* (basically leftovers) doesn't sound as exotic as *chop suey*, and nobody would eat *tofu* if they knew that it meant *rotten beans*.

However, as alien as the Chinese language may sound to Western ears, there are still some points where we can see that our languages connect, not because they are related (they aren't) but because humans form languages in the same way, for example by imitation of sound. That's why the Chinese word for *cat* is *miau*.

And here's a true oddity: the Chinese word for pay is *pei*.

Coincidences and Patterns

The Chinese for *pay* is *pei*, and the Farsi Iranian word for *bad* is *bad*. The Uzbek for *chop* is *chop*, and in the extinct Aboriginal language of Mbaram a *dog* was called a *dog*. The Mayan for *hole* is *hole* and the Korean for *many* is *mani*. When, in the mountains of the Hindu Kush, an Afghan wants to show you something, he will use the word *show*; and the ancient Aztecs used the Nahuatl word *huel* to mean *well*.

Any idiot can deduce from this that all the languages of the world are related. However, anyone of reasonable intelligence will realise that they are just a bunch of coincidences. There are a lot of words and a lot of languages, but there are a limited number of sounds. We're bound to coincide sometimes.

To prove that two languages are related you need to show a *pattern* of changes. It's not enough to say that the Latin word *collis* has a double L in it and so does *hill*. That wouldn't convince anyone of anything. But it's possible to show that hundreds of Latin words that begin with a hard C have German and English equivalents that begin with an H. Moreover, you discover that the rest of the consonants are pretty much unchanged. So the Latin *cornu* translates to Old German and English as *horn*. If you can show a pattern of changes, then you can be pretty damned sure that the languages are related. Let's give it a go.

So the English *horn of hounds* would be the *cornu canum* and the *horn of a hundred hounds* would be the *cornu centum canum* and the *hundred-headed hound with horns* would be *canis centum capitum cum cornibus*. And the …

Well, you get the idea.

The C to H shift that separates Latin from German is part of a group of shifts known as Grimm's Law, because they were set out by Jacob Grimm, who was one of the Brothers Grimm and who spent most of his time collecting fairy tales.

There are other parts to Grimm's Law; for example, Ps in Latin turn to Fs in German (and hence in many English words), which is how *paternal pisces* became *fatherly fishes*.

It's easy to see how this happens when you consider how it still goes on today. In the East End of London, people don't pronounce their Hs and haven't done for at least a hundred years. The *house of a hundred hounds in Hackney* would be pronounced the *'ouse of an 'undred 'ounds in 'Acne*. Nor do East Enders pronounce the G at the end of participles, so instead of *humming and hawing*, a Londoner would find himself *'ummin' and 'awin'*.

The important thing is that people do this *consistently*. Nobody listens to *'ip hop*, or even *hip 'op*. You either pronounce your Hs or you don't. Once one H has gone, they all disappear.

Of course, East London English is still English, for now. But if somebody built a big wall around the East End and didn't let anyone in or out for a few hundred years, the captives would probably make more and more changes until their language became utterly incomprehensible to the rest of the English-speaking world.

Can that still happen?

Nobody is quite sure how transport and communication will affect the splitting of languages. On the face of it, you'd expect accents to stop developing as everybody adjusted to the tyranny of television, but that doesn't *appear* to be the case. In the US, for example, there's a thing called the Northern Cities Vowel Shift, whereby people in Detroit and Buffalo have started pronouncing *block* as *black* and *cot* as *cat*. That, in turn, has pushed the A sound, so that *cat* is pronounced as *cee-at*: so folks in Detroit would call the famous children's book *The Cee-at in the Hee-at*.

And accent changes are unpredictable. In Jamaica they don't drop their Hs, they pick them up. A Jamaican with a strong accent will *hadd han haitch honto hany* word that begins with a vowel. In New Zealand E has become I, so they have *six*. And though in Britain a *medal* is made of *metal*, in America a *medal* is usually made of substance that's pronounced *medal*.

These laws are not absolutely consistent; but they're an awful lot better than you might expect. Also, words change their meaning and get shortened so you can't just take an English word, apply some transformations to it, and come out with perfect Italian. But all the European languages are closely enough related that for the basic words – like *father*, *eyes*, *heart* – there's probably a recognisable cousin.

This is particularly amazing when you consider how Europe has been overrun again and again by hordes of barbarians speaking barbarian languages like Frankish.

Frankly, My Dear Frankfurter

Once upon a terribly long time ago, there was a tribe called the Franks. They invaded Gaul and Gaul became *Franc*[k]*e*.

They oppressed the native Gauls horribly, forcing them to eat garlic and listen to Johnny Hallyday records. Only the Franks themselves were free. Thus they were en*franch*ised. They were able to speak freely, or *frankly*, and everybody else was disen*franch*ised and not able to approve things just by *frank*ing them.

How did the Franks get to France? Well, on the way they had to cross the River Main. This was easily done: they found a ford by which to ford it. The place became known as *Frank-ford on the Main*, or Frankfurt am Main.

Frankfurt is now best known as a financial centre, but also gave its name to a kind of low-rent sausage called a *frankfurter*. By the same token, a *hamburger* comes from Hamburg and involves no *ham* (or in the case of many modern hamburgers, no detectable meat at all). Also, a *berliner* is a kind of doughnut from Berlin, which made JFK's famous remark – 'Ich bin ein Berliner' – rather amusing to German audiences.

Back in ancient France the big export used to be incense, which therefore became known as *frankincense*, and at least one of the conquering Franks managed to cross the Atlantic still bearing his name of 'Son of the south freeborn landowner', which translates to *Benjamin Franklin*.

You may notice a pattern here. Naturally, the Franks named good things like *frankincense* and *speaking frankly* after themselves. It's an absolute truth of linguistics that bad things are foreign.

Beastly Foreigners

The history of English prejudice is engraved in the English language.

These days the Dutch are considered inoffensive, charming even; but it hasn't always been so. The Dutch used to be a major naval and trading power just across the North Sea from Britain, and so Holland and Britain were natural and nautical enemies. Even when the two countries weren't fighting outright battles, the English would subtly undermine their enemies by inventing rude phrases.

Dutch courage is the courage found at the bottom of a bottle, and a *Dutch feast* is a meal where the host gets drunk before his guests. *Dutch comfort* is no comfort at all. A *Dutch wife* is simply a large pillow (or in gay slang something far more ingenious). A *Dutch reckoning* is a fraudulent price that is raised if you argue about it. A *Dutch widow* is a prostitute. A *Dutch uncle* is unpleasant and stern, and only tight-fisted diners insist on *going Dutch*. That'll show them.

In 1934 the Dutch government finally noticed all these phrases. They decided that it was too late to change the English language and instead made it a rule that their ambassadors in English-speaking countries only use the term *The Netherlands*.

The Dutch probably invented their own equivalent phrases about the English, but nobody knows what they are, as the Dutch language is *double Dutch* to us. Anyway, the English were too busy thinking up nasty phrases about their other neighbours.

Welsh rarebit used to be called *Welsh rabbit*, on the basis that when a Welshman promised you something nice to eat like rabbit, you were probably only going to get cheese on toast. The English also used to believe that the Welsh were crazy for cheese. *Grose's Dictionary of the Vulgar Tongue* (1811) records that:

> The Welch are said to be so remarkably fond of cheese, that in cases of difficulty their midwives apply a piece of toasted cheese to the *janua vita* [gates of life] to attract and entice the young Taffy, who on smelling it makes most vigorous efforts to come forth.

By the same token, a *Welsh carpet* was a pattern painted, or stained, onto a brick floor; a *Welsh diamond* is a rock crystal; and a *Welsh comb* is your fingers.

When they had finished abusing the Welsh, the English phrase-makers turned their fury on the Irish, who made *Irish stew* out of leftovers. In fact, it was decided that the Irish were so nonsensical that nonsense itself was called *Irish*.

Yet the great enemy of England has always been France. We believed the French to be dishonest lechers, which is why a *French letter* is a condom and *French leave* is truancy, although here the French have got their own back by calling the same thing *filer à l'anglais*.

And when the English had got bored with just using the proper names of countries to insult them, they decided to think up nasty names for absolutely everybody.

Pejoratives

Here are some pejorative terms for the European nations and
their origins.

Frog Short for *frog-eater* (1798). Previously (1652) the pejorative for a Dutchman because Holland is so marshy.

Kraut From the German for *cabbage*. First recorded in 1841,
but popularised during the First World War.

Hun meant *destroyer of beauty* in 1806, long before it became
the pejorative for German. That's because the Huns, like the
Vandals, were a tribe who helped to bring down the Roman
empire (the actual order was Vandal, Goth, Hun pushing
each other from Germany through France to Spain and
North Africa). Matthew Arnold called art-haters *Philistines*
on the same basis of naming people you don't like after an
ancient tribe. It was Kaiser Wilhelm II who first applied *Hun*
to Germans in 1900 when he urged the army he was sending
to China to mimic the behaviour of their supposed Hunnish
forebears and 'Take no prisoners', a phrase that's usually
attributed to him, although someone had doubtless said
something like it before ('I'll be back' is similarly attributed
to the film *Terminator*). The word was taken up as a pejorative during the world wars as, though the Germans imagined
their ancestors to be raffish and rugged, the British thought
them beastly.

Wop (1912) American term, from Neapolitan dialect *guappo*, meaning *dandy* or *gigolo*.

Dago (1823) From *Diego* (obviously). Originally for either Spanish or Portuguese sailors.

Spic (1913) American term for anyone in the slightest bit Hispanic. Derives from 'No *speak* English'. Or maybe from *spaghetti* via *spiggoty* (1910).

However, language and history have been cruellest to the Slavs of Eastern Europe. Slavs such as the Bulgars spent many years battling against their neighbours. They weren't always successful. That there was a Byzantine emperor nicknamed Basil the Bulgar Slayer ought to give you some idea of what happened.

Basil the Bulgar Slayer once captured 15,000 Bulgars and blinded 99 per cent of them. Every hundredth Bulgar was left with one eye so that he could lead his 99 comrades home. Byzantine historians call this a clever tactic, but to our more modern minds it looks plain damned rude.

Basically, the Slavs had a hard time of it. When they weren't being slain by Basil in the south they were being subjugated by the Holy Roman Empire in the north and forced into lives of servitude. So many Slavs were defeated and oppressed that the word *Slav* itself became interchangeable with *forced labourer*, and that's where we got the word *slave*.

Now, before the next chapter, which common valediction surrenders you to a life of servitude: *adieu, toodle-pip*, or *ciao*?

Ciao Slave-driver

The word *slave* comes from *Slav*, and though it varies between Western languages the poor Slavs were everybody's original slave. The Dutch got *slaaf*, the Germans got *Sklav*, the Spanish got *esclavo* and the Italians got *schiavo*.

Medieval Italians were terribly serious fellows. They would wander around solemnly declaring to each other 'I am your slave'. However, being medieval Italians, what they actually said was *Sono vostro schiavo*.

Then they got lazy and shortened it to *schiavo*. In the north, where they were lazier still, this got changed to *ciao*.

Then, a few centuries later, the Italians got all energetic and tried to join in the Second World War. British and American troops were sent to tick them off.[5] These Allied troops picked up the word *ciao* and when they got back to their own countries they introduced it into English. It was considered a rather exotic new word. But be wary when you say *ciao*: however dashing and Mediterranean you may think you're being, you are, etymologically, declaring your own enslavement.

Ciao has an exact opposite, in the greeting *Hey, man*. In the United States, before the Civil War had finally established the idea that slavery isn't completely compatible with the Land of the Free, slave-owners used to call their slaves *boy*.

---

[5] This was a Good Thing, as the American troops were issued with rations of bacon and eggs. When an American GI was hungry he would pay a local chef to turn these basics into a pasta dish, and that's how spaghetti carbonara was invented. (At least, that's one theory, and there's certainly no record of carbonara before the Second World War.)

The Battle of Gettysburg freed the slaves and produced a memorable address, but it didn't, unfortunately, come with a socio-economic plan or a new language. Slave-owners weren't allowed to own slaves any more, but they continued to be rather nasty to their ex-slaves and kept calling them *boy* in a significant sort of way that annoyed the hell out of the manumitted.

All over America, infuriating white people would address black men with the words 'Hey, boy'. And it grated. It really grated.

That's why, in the 1940s, black Americans started taking the fight the other way and greeting each other with the words 'Hey, *man*'. The vocative was not inserted for the purposes of sexual identification, it was a reaction against all those years of being called *boy*.

It worked. White people were so confused by 'Hey, man' that the sixties happened and everybody, of whatever race, started calling each other *man*, until the original significance was lost. This is an example of Progress.

Now, before the next link, are *robots* Martian slave-owners, Bolivian peasants, or Czech serfs?

Robots

Once upon a time in the Austro-Hungarian empire, which ruled much of central Europe, there were lords and peasants. The lords owned all the land but peasants were granted portions of it to work for themselves. The peasant would then work his own little plot *and* the lord's. The bigger the peasant's plot, the longer he had to work the fields of the lord who had granted it to him.

This system, abolished by Emperor Josef II in 1848, was called *robot*.

The system was abolished, but the word, of course, survived. Seventy-two years later, in 1920, a Czech fellow called Karel Čapek was writing a play. It was a rather spooky, futuristic piece about a factory that produced willing servants out of biological matter. Mr Čapek decided to use the Latin root *labor* (that gives us *labour*) and call these manufactured servants *labori*.

And that would have been that, were it not for Karel's brother, Josef, who suggested calling them *robots* instead. Karel took the suggestion and made the changes. The play was performed under the title *RUR: Rossum's Universal Robots* and was such a success that the word arrived in English two years later.

Of course, *robot* had cropped up in English before, but only in references to European politics that seem rather odd to the modern reader. Take this complaint of 1854 by an Austrian aristocrat who believes that socialism has gone quite mad:

I can get no labor, as the robot is abolished; and my tenants have now land of their own, which once was mine, to cultivate.

The English-speaking equivalent of *robot* was *indentured labour*, whereby a fellow signed a contract that made him a slave for a limited period. There are no extant records of indentured dentists, which is a shame because they both involve teeth.

In fact, lots of things involve teeth. Tri*dent*s have three teeth; *al dente* food is cooked for the teeth; and dandelions are *lions'* *teeth*, or *dents de lions* in French. But I digress. For the moment, we must stick to *indentations*, which are, etymologically, *bite marks*.

Medieval contract law was a sorry affair, largely because very few people could read. This meant that contracts could be signed left, right and centre, but few could tell which one was which. Most of us already have enough trouble finding some important piece of paper that we know we put somewhere safe; imagine how much harder it is for the illiterate.

There are two solutions to this problem, but as one of them involved learning to read, there was really only one solution, and it involved scissors.

A contract would be written out by a priest, signed or sealed by both parties (probably with an X) and then cut in half. This would not, though, be a straight cut. Instead, the contract would be cut up in a thoroughly wonky zig-zag. Each party would then keep one half of the contract and, if they ever needed to prove whose it was, they would simply put the two pieces of paper together to show that the *indentations* matched. Thus indentured servants were indentured until the contract was terminated by a terminator.

Terminators and Prejudice

The *termination* is the end. That's because the Latin *terminus* meant *boundary* or *limit*, from which we get *bus terminals*, *terms and conditions*, *fixed-term parliaments* and indeed many *terms* for things (because a *term* has a *limited* meaning).

From that you get the idea of *terminating* somebody's employment. Legally speaking, you can do this in one of two ways: you can *terminate without prejudice*, meaning that you are open to the idea of re-employing the poor chap; or you can *terminate with prejudice*, meaning that you will never hire the scoundrel again. The latter is for employees who have done something awfully naughty and broken and betrayed your trust.

The CIA employs agents. If you break the CIA's trust and reveal their secrets to the Other Side, your employment will be terminated. Indeed, it will be terminated with prejudice. Indeed, the CIA often makes sure that nobody ever employs you again by the simple expedient of creeping up behind you and shooting you in the head. This they jokingly refer to as *termination with extreme prejudice*.

The CIA being awfully secret, it's hard to say exactly when the phrase *terminate with extreme prejudice* was invented. That it was revealed to the general public at all, was the fault of the US Army Special Forces: the Green Berets.

In 1969 a Vietnamese fellow called Thai Khac Chuyen was working as an agent or informer for the Green Berets (or possibly the CIA, or both). However, he was also working for the Viet Cong and when the Green Berets discovered this they became a little bit peeved.

They went (or didn't go, depending on whom you believe) to the CIA for advice on what to do about Chuyen. The CIA told the Green Berets to let bygones be bygones and to try to see it from the other chap's point of view, or at least that's what the CIA claim.

The Green Berets, on the other hand, say that the CIA told them that Chuyen (or his contract) should be *terminated with extreme prejudice*.

Exactly who said what is no longer of interest to Thai Khac Chuyen, as the upshot of the story is that he was shot. Eight Green Berets were arrested over the affair and, in the brouhaha and court martial that followed, the CIA joke about contract law was finally brought out into the open.

It was this incident that took the innocent word *terminate* away from contract law and bus depots and got it a part in the movies. First, there was a mention in *Apocalypse Now* (1979), where the hero is sent off to find Colonel Kurtz and *terminate* him *with extreme prejudice*. Soon, *terminate* was so sturdily established in the public mind as a big, tough, scary synonym for 'kill' that in 1984 James Cameron decided to call his big, tough, scary killer-robot *The Terminator*.

Terminators and Equators

If you look up *terminator* in a dictionary, you're unlikely to find any reference to death or cyborgs. The first definition will be an astronomical one, because the terminator is the line that divides the illuminated part of a planet from the darker half. So the straight line down the middle of a half-moon is a terminator.

Astronomy and astrology (which were once the same thing) used to be big business until somebody pointed out that huge and distant balls of hydrogen were unlikely to affect your love life. Horoscopes were sent to skulk at the back of the newspaper with the crosswords and personals. Yet the terminology of astrology survives all over the language. For example, if a fellow is of a friendly *disposition*, it's because his friendliness is the inevitable consequence of the positions of the planets at the moment of his birth, or rather the distances between the planets, hence *disposition*.

If Jupiter was in the ascendant when you were born, you are of a *jovial disposition*; and if you're not jovial but miserable and *saturn*ine that's a disaster, because a *disaster* is a *dis-astro*, or *misplaced planet*. *Disaster* is Latin for *ill-starred*.

The fault, as Shakespeare put it, is not in our stars; but the language is.

Culmination, *opposition*, *nadir*, *depression* and *aspect* are all words that we have purloined from the horoscopes and telescopes of antiquity. However, astrology is not the only reason that the heavens take precedence over the Earth. There's the simpler question of visibility. The North Pole, for example, is very far away, and inconveniently located for public transport, but you can *see* the pole star from your house (providing you're in the northern hemisphere). The celestial equator is an imaginary projection of the Earth's equator out into space, and the stars through which this celestial equator passes shine brightly every night no matter where you are, although to reach the real equator requires a journey. And that's why the word *equator* referred to part of the sky two centuries before it referred to part of the globe.

Equality in Ecuador

Because the Earth wobbles on its axis, the celestial *equa*tor is over the terrestrial *equa*tor only twice a year, at the *equi*noxes when night and day are of *equal* length. The Sun is a nomad and for the first half of the year it tramps slowly southwards until it gets to a latitude of 23 degrees, at which point it *turns* around and heads for 23 degrees north, where it *turns* again.

The Greek for *turn* was *tropos*, which is why a *turn of phrase* was for them a *rhetorical trope*. That's also the reason that the latitude of 23 degrees south is the *Tropic* of Capricorn and its northern equivalent is the *Tropic* of Cancer, and everywhere in between is *tropical*.

Bang in between the two tropics is the equator that runs like a 25,000-mile belt around the Earth.[6] The Spanish for *equator* is *ecuador*, so when they found a country through which the *ecuador* ran, they called it Ecuador.

The equator is called the equator because it divides the Earth into two equal sections, which therefore have *equality*. In most circumstances *inequ*ality is *iniqu*itous, but sometimes iniquity is necessary. Not everybody can be equal. Take, for example, sport. You have two teams that have equal status, but when they argue you need somebody of higher status to judge between them. This referee is *not on a par* with them. In Latin he was a *non-par* and in Old French he was *a noumpere*, but then something happened to the N and he became *an umpire*.

An undignified fate often awaits words that begin with an N. Cooks used to wear a *napron*. But *naprons* were more often stained than written down, and so the A was able to craftily steal the N away from *napron*, and now a cook wears *an apron*.

This fickle N is something to ponder next time you're bitten by *a nadder*, but I wouldn't ponder it for too long.

---

[6] In *A Midsummer Night's Dream*, Puck says that he will 'put a girdle round about the earth/In forty minutes'. This means that he must be able to travel at 37,000 miles an hour, or Mach 49.3.

Sometimes the inconstant N travels the other way. What was once *an ewt* is now *a newt*; and an extra name, *an eke-name*, is now *a nickname*.

The Latin *par* also gave us *parity*, *peer groups*, *peerless* and *peers of the realm*. It may seem rather odd that aristocrats, who are above everybody else, should be called *peers*. The reason is that Charlemagne had twelve noble knights who were all equal, and therefore *peers*. In fact, Charlemagne didn't have twelve knights, but there was a *legend* that he did, and that's quite good enough for spawning a word.

Par hides all over the place. If you do somebody down and make them feel less important than you, you dis*par*age them; and if you have a girl to live with you as an equal she is an *au pair*. But the most obvious place that the word *par* survives is on the golf course, as the score between a birdie and a bogey.

Bogeys

Why is a score of one over par called a *bogey*?

Any game of golf is played against two opponents. You are competing against the other golfer and you are competing against the ground score, the scratch value, the *par* – the number of strokes a professional golfer should take to complete the course. Of your two opponents, the ground is usually the harder to beat.

There was a terribly popular song in Victorian England called 'The Bogey Man'. It was about the nasty mythical fellow who creeps into the rooms of naughty children and causes all sorts of trouble to all sorts of people. This song was running through the head of Dr Thomas Brown as he played a round of golf in Great Yarmouth one day in 1890.

The idea of playing against the ground score in golf was quite new at the time. Originally, pars and eagles and birdies were unknown in golf. All you did was to add up your total number of shots, and whoever had the lowest was the winner.

This was the first time that Dr Brown had played against the ground and he didn't like it. He preferred to play against an opponent because, as he observed, the ground always seemed to beat him. It was an enemy that followed him around the course but never appeared in person, and in the end Dr Brown decided that his invisible opponent was the Bogey Man, just like in the song. His joke caught on in Great Yarmouth and then spread around the golfing world. The Bogey became a score.

Lone golfers were therefore playing against the Bogey and the word spread until it meant *par for the course*. It wasn't until the 1940s that the word shifted to mean *one over par*, and nobody is quite sure why.

Bugbears and Bedbugs

The previous story has an instructive little postscript. Within a few years, golfers had forgotten the origin of the word *bogey* and the par score for a course was blamed on a fictional golfer named Colonel Bogey. A book of golfing cartoons from 1897 contains the line: 'I, Colonel Bogey, whose score is so uniform, and who generally win …'

This meant that in 1914, when Kenneth Alford wanted a name for his brand-new marching tune, he called it 'Colonel

Bogey' and thus *bogey* returned to the world of song whence it had sprung.

So who or what was the bogeyman? Bogeymen come in all shapes and sizes. Some are shaped just like bears. They live in the woods and they eat small boys who don't do as they're told. These are *bogey-bears*. However, the bogey-bear has diminished over the years. He has faded from his ursine grandeur, both in threat and in the length of the term. Nowadays a bogey-bear is a mere *bugbear*, and far from devouring a child whole, he is an insignificant annoyance.

Likewise, a *bugaboo* is now scoffed at by everyone except James Bond. James Bond is very careful about *bugaboos* and usually checks for them under his bed. Well, etymologically he does.

In the eighteenth century a *bugaboo* (which is of course a variant bogeyman) became thieves' slang for a sheriff's officer, or policeman. Nineteenth-century burglars were therefore scared of bugaboos or *bugs* for short. But they kept burgling anyway, and burglaries continued all the way into the twentieth century. Indeed, they were so common that people started to set up burglar alarms, and in the 1920s burglars began to call burglar alarms *bugs* on the basis that they acted like an automated policeman. If a solicitous homeowner had fitted an alarm within his house, the joint was said to be *bugged*.

From there it was one small step for the word *bug* before it was applied to tiny listening devices that could be placed inside telephones or teapots. And that's why James Bond checks his room for *bugs*, and that's also why there could actually be an etymological *bogeyman* hidden beneath your bed.

Bogeys and *bugs* have always been pretty much interchangeable. Myles Coverdale's 1535 translation of the Psalms renders the fifth verse of the 91st Psalm thus:

Thou shalt not need to be afrayed for eny bugges by nights.

Most subsequent Bibles have used the word *terrors*; Coverdale's is therefore known as *The Bug's Bible*. Then, in the mid-seventeenth century, *bug* mysteriously started to mean *insect*. Perhaps this was because insects are terrifying, or perhaps because they used to get into your bed like a bogeyman. The first six-legged bug on record was a *bedbug* in 1622. Since then, though, the word has expanded to mean any sort of creepy-crawly, including insects that crawl inside machines and mess up the workings.

There's a story that one of Thomas Edison's inventions kept going wrong. Edison couldn't work out why his machine kept breaking down, but break down it did. He checked all the parts and they worked. He checked the design and it was flawless. Then he went back to check the machine one last time and discovered the cause of the problem. A small insect was crawling around over his delicate electronics and messing everything up. This, so the story goes, is the origin of *bug* in the sense of a technical failing.

This story may not be completely true, but it's certainly the case that Thomas Edison was the first person to use *bug* in the technological sense. In 1878 he wrote in a letter that:

It has been just so in all of my inventions. The first step is an intuition, and comes with a burst, then difficulties arise – this thing gives out and [it is] then that 'Bugs' – as such little faults and difficulties are called – show themselves and months of intense watching, study and labor are requisite before commercial success or failure is certainly reached.

And in 1889, the *Pall Mall Gazette* reported that:

Mr Edison, I was informed, had been up the two previous nights discovering 'a bug' in his phonograph – an expression for solving a difficulty, and implying that some imaginary insect has secreted itself inside and is causing all the trouble.

So the insect story *could* be true, or it could simply be that Edison was referring to *bogeyman* sprites that haunted his machines, working mischief in the mechanism.

Whatever the origin, the word *bug* caught on, and when your computer crashes due to a software *bug*, the fault lies with Thomas Edison and the bogeyman.

Von Munchausen's Computer

New things need new words, but they usually end up with old ones. Computers have been around since at least 1613, when being a *computer* was a skilled profession practised by mathematicians who worked in observatories adding up numbers.

When Charles Babbage invented the precursor of the modern computer he called it an *Analytical Engine*, and when his son improved on the design he called it a *Mill*, on the basis that mills were complicated technical things and that, like his new machine, they took stuff in at one end and spat different stuff out at the other. Then, in 1869, machines that could *compute* the sum of two numbers began to be called *computers*, and slowly, as those machines started to do more and more things, the word spread. When the first modern computer was officially christened ENIAC (Electronic Numeral Integrator And Computer) in 1946, it was already too late.

Early computers were simply calculators, hence the name. Then they got software, which had to be loaded up by the user. Then in the fifties a method was invented whereby a computer would install its own software. The idea was that a single piece of code was loaded, which in turn would load up some more pieces of code, which would load more and more until the computer had ... but first we must explain about Baron von Munchausen in the marsh.

Baron von Munchausen (1720–97) was a real person who had fought as a soldier in Russia. On his return home he told stories about his exploits that nobody believed. These included riding on a cannonball, taking a brief trip to the moon, and escaping from a marsh by pulling himself out by his own hair. This latter feat is impossible, for the upward force on the Baron's hair would have been cancelled out by the downward force on his arm. It's a nice idea, though, and von Munchausen's preposterous principle was later taken up by Americans, but instead of talking about hair, the Americans started in the late nineteenth century to talk of pulling themselves up *by their own bootstraps*.

What's impossible in physics is possible in computing, and a computer that's able to load its own programs is, metaphorically, pulling itself up by its own bootstraps. In 1953 the process was called a *bootstrap*. By 1975 people had got bored with the *strap*, and from then on computers simply *booted up*.

SPAM (not spam)

In 1937 a new product came on to the American market. It was made primarily of pork and potato starch and was originally called *Hormel Spiced Ham* because it was made by Geo A. Hormel & Co. However, a vice-president of Hormel had a brother who was an actor and presumably much better with words, and he suggested that it be shortened from *Spiced Ham* to *SPAM*. Another story says that *SPAM* may stand for *Shoulder of Pork And Ham*. Either way, the Hormel Foods Corporation insists to this day that it should be spelt with capital letters: SPAM, not spam.

Hitler made SPAM a great success. The Second World War caused food shortages in Britain, which caused strict rationing of fresh meat, which caused Britons to turn to tinned meat as it was less tightly rationed. The tinned meat to which the warlike Britons turned was SPAM, and this was shipped from America in gargantuan quantities. After the war, SPAM remained a staple of the British diet, especially in cheap cafés, which is where *Monty Python* comes in.

In 1970 *Monty Python* produced the SPAM sketch in which two people are lowered into a nasty café somewhere in Britain, where almost every dish contains SPAM. After a while, a group of Vikings who also happen to be in the café start singing a song to which the only words are:

SPAM
SPAM
SPAM
SPAM
SPAM
SPAM
SPAM

On and on and on *ad infinitum et nauseam.*

Monty Python is, for reasons best known to nobody, rather popular with computer programmers. There's even a programming language called *Python*, based on their sketches. This leads us, inevitably, to *Multi-User Dungeons,* or *MUDs.*

Multi-User Dungeons are not, as you might have imagined, strange basement rooms in the red light district. Instead they were an early form of internet game that existed in the 1980s. Clever computery fellows would use MUDs to show each other programs that they had written, but the most popular of these programs was a very simple practical joke.

The first command in the joke program was that the computer should print the word SPAM. The second command was to go back to the first command. The result was that the lyrics to the *Monty Python* song would be printed out as a screenful of SPAM. This would scroll down your screen for ever and you couldn't stop it.

By 1990 SPAM had become programmers' slang for anything unwanted on the internet. When the *Monty Python* joke was continued on Usenet in the early 1990s the word *spam* gained wider currency. And that's why, when that Nigerian prince with all the Viagra and the saucy photographs of Britney

Spears started sending his emails, they were called *spam*, or more properly *SPAM*; for you must remember that SPAM is a proprietary name, just like *heroin*.

Heroin

Once upon a time, cough medicines all contained morphine. This made people worried. You see, morphine is addictive, which meant that if you had a bad cold and took the cough medicine for too long, you might cure the cough but wind up physically dependent upon the remedy. The poor cougher of a hundred years ago was therefore faced with a choice: keep hacking away, or risk becoming a morphine addict. Many chose the cough.

So in 1898 a German pharmaceutical company called Bayer decided to develop an alternative. They got out their primitive pipettes and rude retorts, and worked out a new chemical: diacetylmorphine, which they marketed as a 'non-addictive morphine substitute'.

Like all new products it needed a brand name. *Diacetylmorphine* was alright if you were a scientist, but it wasn't going to work at the counter of the drugstore. They needed a name that would *sell*, a name that would make people say: 'Yes! I want to buy that product!'

So Bayer's marketing chaps set to work. They asked the people who had taken diacetylmorphine how it made them feel, and the response was unanimous: it made you feel great. Like a *hero*. So the marketing chaps decided to call their new product *heroin*. And guess what? It did sell.

Heroin remained a Bayer trademark until the First World War; but the 'non-addictive' part turned out to be a little misguided.

And that's why heroines *are* connected to heroin. And it was all because people didn't want to be in thrall to morphine.

Morphing De Quincey and Shelley

Morpheus, from which *morphine* derives, was the Greek god of dreams. He was the son of Sleep and the brother of Fantasy, and he lived in a cave near the underworld where he would make dreams and then hang them upon a withered elm until they were ready to use.

Morpheus was the *shaper of dreams* – his name comes from the Greek *morphe* meaning *shape*. This is why, if you are *amorphous*, it doesn't mean that you're fresh out of *morphine*, but instead that you are *shapeless*.

Drugs and dreams are an easy association. If you smoke a pipe full of opium you will, like as not, fall asleep and have a *pipe dream*. The most famous consumer of opium was a nineteenth-century fellow called Thomas De Quincey, who wrote a memoir called *Confessions of an English Opium Eater*, which contains a wonderful and strange account of his drugged dreams:

> I was stared at, hooted at, grinned at, chattered at, by monkeys, by paroquets, by cockatoos. I ran into pagodas, and was fixed for centuries at the summit, or in secret rooms; I was the idol; I was the priest; I was worshipped; I was sacrificed.

I fled from the wrath of Brama through all the forests of Asia; Vishnu hated me; Seeva lay in wait for me. I came suddenly upon Isis and Osiris; I had done a deed, they said, which the ibis and the crocodile trembled at. Thousands of years I lived, and was buried in stone coffins, with mummies and sphinxes, in narrow chambers at the heart of eternal pyramids. I was kissed, with cancerous kisses, by crocodiles, and was laid, confounded with all unutterable abortions, amongst reeds and Nilotic mud.

De Quincey's opium dreams sound a little less than fun, and much of his biography is about his efforts to give up the drug. The book is much more moving than it is honest.

In fact, when De Quincey wrote his *Confessions*, he was simply out of cash and couldn't afford a fix. Luckily the book was so successful that he was able to maintain himself in top-drawer narcotics for the rest of his life. This life was surprisingly long. While near-contemporaries like Shelley, Keats and Byron fell out of boats, perished of consumption or died feverishly in Greece, De Quincey, drugged up to the eyeballs and beyond, survived them all by 35 years and died of a fever at the over-ripe age of 74. He had been taking opium for 55 years.

During his long and meandering literary career, De Quincey was a master-inventor of words. His opium-fumigated brain was a mint where neologisms were coined at a remarkable rate. The *Oxford English Dictionary* attributes 159 words to him. Many of these, like *passiuncle* (a small passion), are forgotten; yet many survive.

Without De Quincey we would have no *subconscious*, no *entourages*, no *incubators*, no *interconnections*. We would be able neither to *intuit* nor to *reposition* things. He was *phenomenally* inventive, *earth-shatteringly* so. He even came up with the word *post-natal*, which has allowed people to be depressed ever since.

Ante-natal had already been invented by the poet Percy Bysshe Shelley. Shelley wrote an (earth-shatteringly tedious) poem called 'Prince Athenase'. The story goes like this: basically, there's a prince and he's great and stuff, but like every second bloody hero of romantic poetry he's mysteriously sad. Nobody knows why.

Some said that he was mad, others believed

That memories of an antenatal life
Made this, where now he dwelt, a penal hell

Others believed that Shelley had talent, but needed a damned fine editor. Like De Quincey, when Shelley couldn't think of a word he just made one up. By the time he drowned at the age of 29 he had already come up with the words *spectral, anklet, optimistic* (in the sense of a hopeful disposition), and *heartless* (in the sense of cruel). He invented *bloodstain, expatriate, expressionless, interestingly, legionnaire, moonlit, sunlit, pedestrianize* (although not in our sense), *petty-minded, steam-ship, unattractive, undefeated, unfulfilling, unrecognized, wavelet* and *white-hot*.

He even invented the phrase *national anthem*.

Star-Spangled Drinking Songs

A *spangle* is, of course, a little spang: a *spang* being a *small, glittering ornament*. Therefore, to be *spangled* is to be *covered in small spangs*, a fate that befalls the best of us at times.

The word *spangled* crops up in a poem by Thomas Moore – not the famous one, you understand, but the nineteenth-century Irish poetaster. He wrote:

> As late I sought the spangled bowers
> To cull a wreath of matin flowers,

It was one of Moore's translations from the Greek poet Anacreon, who was an ancient boozer and lover and lyric poet. Anacreon's poems (*anacreontics*) are all about getting drunk and making lyrical love in Greek groves. Anacreon was therefore a Good Thing.

Anacreon was, indeed, such a good thing that in the eighteenth century an English gentleman's club was founded in his memory. It was called the Anacreontic Society and was devoted to 'wit, harmony and the god of wine'. It was a very musical affair and two members wrote a society drinking song called 'To Anacreon in Heav'n'. John Stafford Smith wrote the tune and the society's president, Ralph Tomlinson, wrote the words. The first verse ran thus:

> To Anacreon in Heav'n, where he sat in full glee
> A few sons of harmony sent a petition,
> That he their inspirer and patron would be
> When this answer arrived from the jolly old Grecian

'Voice, fiddle, and flute,
No longer be mute,
I'll lend you my name and inspire you to boot,
And, besides, I'll instruct you like me to intwine
The myrtle of Venus with Bacchus's vine.'

Bacchus's vine is, of course, booze, and Venus was the goddess of sex. 'To Anacreon in Heav'n' was a good song with a very catchy tune (which you know). Because it was hard to sing, it became an *ad hoc* test of drunkenness used by the police in the eighteenth century. If you could sing 'To Anacreon in Heav'n' in tune you were sober and free to go. This is, if you think about it, an odd fate for a drinking song. It's also rather unfair on those who can't sing.

Unfortunately the song was so popular that it was usurped and stolen by a chap called Francis Scott Key, who wrote new words that weren't about drink, but about being able to see a flag flying after a bombardment.

Francis Scott Key was an American lawyer. During the war of 1812, he was sent to negotiate with the British fleet for the release of certain prisoners. He dined aboard HMS *Tonnant*, but when the time came for him to leave, the British got worried. Key was now familiar with the British battleships: if he went ashore he could and would pass all this information on to the American forces. This was problematic, as the British were planning to bombard Baltimore first thing in the morning, and if the Americans found out it would spoil the fun. So they insisted that Key remain on board, and he was forced to watch the bombardment from the wrong side (or the right side, if you're thinking about personal safety).

Bang went the guns, but the American flag at Baltimore remained high and visible amid the smoke. Key decided to write a song about it. He stole the tune from the Anacreontic Society, but wrote new words that went:

O, say can you see by the dawn's early light
What so proudly we hailed at the twilight's last gleaming,
Whose broad stripes and bright stars through the perilous
    fight,
O'er the ramparts we watched were so gallantly streaming?
And the rockets' red glare, the bombs bursting in air,
Gave proof through the night that our flag was still there;
O, say does that star-spangled banner yet wave,
O'er the land of the free and the home of the brave?

And the new title that he gave to an old drinking song takes us straight back to *small spangs*.

Torpedoes and Turtles

The conflict between the Royal Navy and the revolutionary Americans also gave us the word *torpedo*, which has nothing and everything to do with being *torpid*.

The Latin word for *tired* or numb was *torpidus*. From this we got the adjective *torpid*, which is still with us today. And that would be the end of the story were it not for electrical fish.

That there are electric eels is commonly known. But there are also kinds of ray that can produce electricity, in fact they can produce 220 volts of the stuff, which is quite enough to knock you out, and therefore render you *torpid*.

In English they were once called *numb-fish* or *cramp-fish*, but the educated Latin name is *Torpediniformes*, with the major family being the *torpedoes*. As Lawrens Andrewe put it in his snappily-titled book of 1520, *The noble lyfe & nature of man, Of bestes, serpentys, fowles & fisshes y be moste knowen*:

> Torpido is a fisshe, but who-so handeleth hym shal be lame
> & defe of lymmes that he shall fele no thyng.

For a long time, therefore, a torpedo was simply *something that rendered you incapable*. For example, there was an eighteenth-century dandy called Beau Nash who was awfully witty but had trouble writing well. 'He used to call a pen his torpedo for whenever he grasped it, it numbed all his faculties.' This is a shame, as Nash was meant to be the wittiest, most charming man of his day and when he died his wife went to live in a hollow tree near Warminster.[7]

But to return to the story: in 1776 the Americans were revolting. The British Navy sailed to New York, but so revolting were the Americans that the Brits decided to stay in the channel and blockade the harbour. The Americans didn't like this, and there was a fellow called Bushnell who invented a submarine with which to attack the blockading British boats in the most unsporting manner.

Bushnell couldn't decide what to call his new submarine: he seems to have been in two minds between the *American Turtle*

---

[7] Yes, really.

and the *Torpedo*. In shape it resembled both. Eventually, he decided on the latter.

The idea of the submarine was that it had a 'magazine or powder' attached to it that it would screw to the hull of the British flagship. A timer would then be set, giving the submarine a few minutes to get clear, and then there would be a big explosion and the British boat would be blown to smithereens and beyond. This didn't happen, as the revolting Americans were foiled by the hulls of the British ships, which were copper-bottomed.

But the Americans were not to be deterred. Another inventor called Fulton took up where Bushnell left off (Bushnell for some reason ran away to the South and took on a new identity). Fulton worked to the same general plan, but he gave the name *torpedo* to the explosive device rather than the submarine itself. He also decided to change it a bit. Rather than the submarine getting right up to the enemy ship, it would instead fire a harpoon at it. The explosive device would be attached to the harpoon by a rope and contain within it a timer. So the submarine would pop up, harpoon the ship, and disappear before the charge went off.

Fulton's torpedoes didn't work either. Decades passed of utterly ineffective torpedo inventing and improvement. The torpedo was fitted with a motor and other such gizmos, but nothing was sunk with a vile torpedo until 1878, when a Russian ship torpedoed an Ottoman one.

And that's how *tired and numb* came to be a name for something *fast and explosive*.

Now, before the next story, what's the connection between Mount Vernon in Virginia, Portobello Road in London, and feeling groggy?

From Mount Vernon to Portobello Road with a Hangover

Relations between the Royal Navy and the Americans were, as we have seen, fraught. However, it was not always thus. The fault lies with George Washington.

But George had an elder half-brother and mentor called Lawrence Washington who had, in fact, been a British soldier. Specifically, he was a marine in the Royal Navy. As a recruit from the British dominions in North America, he served under Admiral Edward Vernon in the Caribbean, and was part of the force that seized a strategically important base called Guantánamo, which has some minor position in modern history.

Lawrence Washington was very attached to Admiral Vernon. So loyal was he that when he went home to the family estate, which had been called Little Hunting Creek Plantation, he decided to rename it *Mount Vernon*. So Washington's house was named after a British admiral.

Admiral Vernon's naming exploits didn't end there, though. In 1739 Vernon led the British assault on Porto Bello in what is now Panama. He had only six ships, but with lots of derring-do and British pluck etc. etc. he won a startling victory. In fact, so startling was the victory that a patriotic English farmer heard the news, dashed off to the countryside west of London, and built Portobello Farm in honour of the victory's startling-ness. Green's Lane, which was nearby, soon became known as Portobello Lane and then Portobello Road. And that's why the London market, now one of the largest antiques markets in the world, is called Portobello Market.

But Admiral Vernon's naming exploits didn't end there, either. When the seas were stormy he used to wear a thick coat made out of a coarse material called *grogram* (from the French *gros graine*). So his men nicknamed him *Old Grog*.

British sailors used to have a daily allowance of rum. In 1740, flushed from victory at Porto Bello and perhaps under the pernicious influence of Lawrence Washington, Vernon ordered that the rum be watered down. The resulting mixture, which eventually became standard for the whole navy, was also named after Vernon. It was called *grog*.

If you drank too much grog you became drunk or *groggy*, and the meaning has slowly shifted from there to the wages of gin: a hangover.

A Punch of Drinks

The etymology of alcohol is as unsteady as one would have suspected. For starters the word *alcohol* is Arabic. This may seem odd, given that Islam is a teetotal religion, but when the Arabs used the word *alcohol* they didn't mean the same stuff that we do. *Alcohol* comes from *al* (the) *kuhul*, which was a kind of make-up. Indeed, some ladies still use *kohl* to line their eyes.

As kohl is an extract and a dye, *alcohol* started to mean the *pure essence* of anything (there's a 1661 reference to *the alcohol of an ass's spleen*), but it wasn't until 1672 that somebody at the Royal Society had the bright idea of finding the pure essence of wine. What was it in wine that made you drunk? What was the *alcohol* of wine? Soon *wine-alcohol* (or *essence of wine*) became the only alcohol anybody could remember, and then in 1753 everybody got so drunk that *wine-alcohol* was shortened to *alcohol*.

Spirits arrived in the drinks cabinet by almost exactly the same root, but this time from alchemy. In *al*chemy (there's the Arabic *the* again) every chemical was thought to contain *vital spirits*, little fairies who lived in the substance and made it do funny things. On this basis gunpowder contained fiery spirits, acid contained biting spirits, and things like whisky and vodka contained the best spirits of all, the ones that got you plastered. It's odd that whisky and vodka get you drunk at all, as, according to their names, they are both water.

Vodka comes from the Russian *voda*, which means *water*, and indeed both words come from the same Proto-Indo-European root: *wodor*.

The word *whisky* is surprisingly recent. It's not recorded before 1715, when it leapt into the lexicon with the sterling sentence: 'Whiskie shall put our brains in a rage.' Philologists, though, are reasonably agreed that it comes from the Gaelic *uisge beatha* meaning *water of life*.

Why the *water of life*? The Scots hadn't made the name up, they merely took it from alchemical Latin. Alchemists, who were trying to turn base metal into gold, could find consolation for their failure in the fact that it's pretty damned easy to distil alcohol, which they called *ardent spirits* or *aqua vitae* (water of life).

It wasn't only drunken Scotsmen who took *aqua vitae* into their own language. The Scandinavians called their home-brew *aquavit*, without even bothering to translate, and the French called their brandy *eau de vie*.

However, the *water of life* is also a delightful euphemism for urine. This should be drunk in moderation. Morarji Desai, who was Prime Minister of India, used to start every day by drinking the liquor brewed in his own internal distillery, which he always referred to as 'the water of life'. Desai claimed that Gandhi had taught him the trick, although the Gandhi Institute denies this vehemently and says that Desai's story is balderdash.

Balderdash used to be a kind of drink as well. Not a very good kind of drink, mind you: it was wine mixed with beer or water or anything else that meant that you could sell it cheap. Balderdash was strange stuff, but not nearly so rum as rum.

Rum was once a thieves' word meaning *good*; but like most thieves' slang the adjective *rum* got a bad reputation and started to mean *queer* or *a little bit fishy*. It's hard to say which of these uses caused the Caribbean spirit previously known as *kill-devil* to be nicknamed *rumbullion*. Or perhaps it was just a variant of *rum booze*, in reference to rum's strong and sugary nature. It might even be something to do with the Devon dialect word *rumbullion* meaning *uproar*, or it could be the dnuora yaw rehto. Or maybe it was a *rum bouillon* or *strange brew*. Either way, *rum* is first recorded in 1654 and by 1683 people were already making *rum punch*.

Vodka, whisky, aquavit, balderdash and rum are just enough to make the sort of punch that will knock you out. Only just, mind you, because *punch* comes from the Hindi word for *five*: *panch*. That's because, technically, a punch should contain five different ingredients: spirits, water, lemon juice, sugar and spice. That's also the reason that the area of India that contains five rivers is called the Punjab.

Panch derives from the Sanskrit for five, *pancas*, which comes from the Proto-Indo-European *penkwe*, which went into Greek as *pent* and gave us a *pentagon*.

But if you want to get properly sloshed you need the queen of drinks: champagne.

The Scampering Champion of the Champagne Campaign

According to legend (the beautiful elder sister of truth), champagne was invented by a Benedictine monk called Dom Pérignon who shouted to his fellow monks: 'Come quickly, I am tasting the stars.'

This is, of course, balderdash. Making sparkling wine is simple; it's bottling it that was difficult. If you put fizzy wine in a normal bottle, it can't take the pressure and explodes. A champagne bottle has to contain six atmospheres of pressure. Even now the caverns of Moët and Chandon lose every sixtieth bottle to explosion. Moreover, it was English glassmakers who perfected the method in order to keep their cider fizzy, and the French simply stole the technology to bottle their bubbly.

Champagne was originally just *vin de campagne*, or *wine from the countryside*. It was only in the eighteenth century that it came to refer to wine from the particular region around Épernay, where many of the worst bits of the First World War happened. That Champagne saw some of the worst trench warfare is no coincidence.

The German advance of 1914 started very well. They stormed across northern France with Teutonic efficiency, until they got to the champagne warehouses. There's something about finding the whole world's champagne supply that can make even a German commander find reasons for pausing, and the pause was all that the French and British needed. The Allies arrived, everybody dug trenches and the rest is War Poetry.

The German campaign took place during the summer. It had to. When winter arrives, armies generally have to find somewhere warm to hole up and wait for the snows and the gales to pass. Then in the spring they can set out into the *campagne* again, which is why an army fights a summer *campaign*: literally *on the countryside*.

Campagne comes from the Latin word *campus*, which meant *field*. The very best soldiers in the field were called the *campiones*, from which we get *champion*. So the champion of a champagne campaign would be the same thing three times over.

You can do a lot of things with a field. You can, for example, build a university on it, in which case you have a university *campus*. But what most campaigning armies do is simply take out their tents and guy-ropes and pitch *camp*.

Actually, there's another thing that armies usually do. Armies are mostly composed of men, young men, without any women to keep them company. This means that the soldiers have every reason in the world to try to sneak out of the camp to seek the solace of sex. Creeping out of camp was called *excampare* by the Romans and *escamper* by the French, but we call it *scampering*.

The ladies towards whom these young champions would be scampering were the *camp followers*, women of more enterprise than virtue, who would follow the soldiers around and rent their affections by the hour.

Camp followers aren't the classiest of broads (a *broad*, by the way, is a woman a*broad*). They tended to wear too much make-up to be truly ladylike, and their dresses were garish and their hair badly dyed. During the First World War, British soldiers started to call such a get-up *campy*. They also referred to such illicit sexual scamperings as *camp*. From here the word *camp* had to make only a short hop before it referred to a man in make-up (and maybe a dress) who had illicit sexual encounters, and that's why tarty men in make-up are, to this day, *camping it up*, often with a glass of pink champagne.

Camp, in the sense of battlefield, also wheedled its way into German as *Kampf* meaning *battle*. So Hitler's book *Mein Kampf* could reasonably be described as rather *camp*.

Insulting Names

It's a funny thing, but Hitler wouldn't have called himself a Nazi. Indeed, he became quite offended when anyone did suggest he was a Nazi. He would have considered himself a National Socialist. *Nazi* is, and always has been, an insult.

Hitler was head of the catchily-named *Nationalsozialistische Deutsche Arbeiterpartei* (National Socialist German Workers' Party). But, like the Cambridge University Netball Team, he hadn't thought through the name properly. You see, his opponents realised that you could shorten **Nationalsozialistische** to *Nazi*. Why would they do this? Because *Nazi* was already an (utterly unrelated) term of abuse. It had been for years.

Every culture has a butt for its jokes. Americans have the Polacks, the English have the Irish, and the Irish have people from Cork. The standard butt of German jokes at the beginning of the twentieth century were stupid Bavarian peasants. And just as Irish jokes always involve a man called Paddy, so Bavarian jokes always involved a peasant called Nazi. That's because Nazi was a shortening of the very common Bavarian name Ignatius.

This meant that Hitler's opponents had an open goal. He had a party filled with Bavarian hicks and the name of that party could be shortened to the standard joke name for hicks. (Incidentally, *hick* was formed in exactly the same way as *Nazi*. *Hick* was a rural shortening of *Richard* and became a byword for uneducated famers.)

Imagine if a right-winger from Alabama started a campaign called **Red** *States for the* **Nex**t *America*. That's essentially what Hitler did.

Hitler and his fascists didn't know what to do about the derogatory nickname *Nazi*. At first they hated the word. Then, briefly, they tried to reclaim it, in roughly the way that some gay people try to reclaim old insults like *queer*. But once they got to power they adopted the much simpler approach of persecuting their opponents and forcing them to flee the country.

So refugees started turning up elsewhere complaining about the *Nazis*, and non-Germans of course assumed that this was the official name of the party. Meanwhile, all the Germans who remained in Germany obediently called them the *Nationalsozialistische Deutsche Arbeiterpartei*, at least when the police were listening. To this day, most of us happily go about believing that the Nazis called themselves *Nazis*, when in fact they would probably have beaten you up for saying the word.

So it all goes back to the popularity of the name Ignatius. The reason that Ignatius was such a common name in Bavaria is that Bavaria is largely Catholic and therefore very fond of St Ignatius of Loyola, founder of the Society of Jesus, better known as the Jesuits.

The Jesuits were set up in the seventeenth century to combat the rise of Protestantism, which had become the state religion of England. They soon gained a reputation for being very clever indeed. But as the Jesuits' cleverness was largely directed against the Protestant English, English Protestants took their name, made an adjective – *Jesuitical* – and used it to describe something that's too clever by half, and that uses logical tricks at the expense of common sense.

This is a tad unfair on the poor Jesuits, who have been responsible for the educations of some of the most famous men in history: Fidel Castro, Bill Clinton, Charles de Gaulle, Cardinal Richelieu, Robert Altman, James Joyce, Tom Clancy, Molière, Arthur Conan Doyle, Bing Crosby, Freddie Mercury, René Descartes, Michel Foucault, Martin Heidegger, Alfred Hitchcock, Elmore Leonard, Spencer Tracy, Voltaire and Georges Lemaître.

And if the last name on that list is unfamiliar, it shouldn't be. Monsignor Georges Lemaître was one of the most important scientists of the twentieth century. His great idea, proposed in 1927, was the theory of the Primeval Atom, which of course you haven't heard of.

That's because the theory of the Primeval Atom, like the *Nationalsozialistische Deutsche Arbeiterpartei*, is a name that never made it. It vanished, usurped by an insult.

The theory of the Primeval Atom asserts that the universe has not been around for eternity, and that instead it started off 13.7 billion years ago with all matter contained in a single point: the Primeval Atom. This point exploded and expanded, space cooled, galaxies were formed, et cetera et cetera.

Many people disagreed with this theory, including the British astronomer Sir Fred Hoyle. He thought that the universe had always been around, and decided to undermine Lemaître's theory by calling it something silly. So he racked his brains and came up with the silliest name he could think of. He called it the *Big Bang Theory*, because he hoped that *Big Bang* captured the childishness and simplicity of the idea.

Names are not earned, they are given. Often the givers don't know what they're doing. Sometimes, it's simply a slip of a child's tongue.

Peter Pan

And sometimes names come out of almost nothing. W.E. Henley (the poet who wrote *Invictus* and not much else)[8] had a daughter named Margaret. Margaret died when she was only five years old, but not before she had met J.M. Barrie. She liked Mr Barrie and tried to call him her *friendy*, but being only five and horribly ill, all she could make of the word was *wendy*.

---

[8] Thank God.

J.M. Barrie then went off and wrote a play about a boy called Peter Pan who takes a girl and her two brothers off to Neverland. He named the heroine Wendy in memory of little Margaret Henley. So he gave her a sort of immortality, for the play was so popular that parents started to name their daughters after the central character. Although, why you would name your daughter after a girl who runs away from home with a strange boy the second the dog's not looking, is a mystery.

Unfortunately, in *Peter Pan*, Wendy is shot with an arrow and dies. However, her death isn't a serious matter, as after a little bit of make-believe she recovers enough to start singing in her sleep. Her song is about how she wants a house, and so Peter and his associates build a tiny cottage around her dormant body. This was, of course, the first *Wendy House*.

Back in London, Mr Darling, Wendy's father, is rather morose about the disappearance of his progeny. He realises that it's all his fault, as he had forced the family dog to sleep out in the kennel. So, as a penance, he takes to sleeping in the kennel himself. In fact, he never leaves the kennel at all and is transported to work in it every day. He is scrupulously polite and raises his hat to any lady who looks inside, but he remains *in the doghouse*. And so popular was *Peter Pan* that Mr Darling's fate became a phrase.

So that's a name, a noun and a phrase: all from one story. But Barrie also took names that had been around already.

The most famous admirer of *Peter Pan* was Michael Jackson, a singer and composer of indeterminate tan, who named his home *Neverland*. This means that Mr Jackson must have been working from the novelisation, because in the original play of

Peter Pan, Peter doesn't live in *Neverland*, but in *Never Never Land*, a name that Barrie got from a thoroughly real place.

The very remotest and most unwelcoming parts of Australia, in Queensland and the Northern Territory, are known as *Never Never Land*, although today this is often shortened by Australians to *The Never Never*. Why give a place a name that refers to time? There have been various explanations for that.

It was claimed in 1908 that it was called *Never Never* because those who lived there *never never* wanted to leave, an explanation so remarkably unconvincing that it deserves a prize. An earlier and more plausible story comes from the *Gentleman's Magazine* of 1862:

> There is in a certain part of Australia a wide and desolate tract of land, a heart-breaking region which has been christened the 'Never-Never' land. It is so called, I believe, from the impression which its drouthy wastes convey to the mind of the traveller on first emerging within its loveless limits that he will never again emerge therefrom.

But the actual origin is a little older and much more racial. A book of 1833 described the strangely peaceful wars of the local aborigines:

> There is certainly more talking than fighting in their battles, and it is, therefore, to be hoped they will some day send over a few of their people as missionaries, to convince civilized nations that it is far worse to cut the throat of a man while alive, than to eat his body when dead.

I was greatly disappointed at not falling in with a tribe on Liverpool Plains, but the stockkeepers informed me that they had gone to war against the Never-never blacks, who are so called because they have hitherto kept aloof from the whites.

So Barrie's imaginary place came from part of Australia named after blacks who would *never never* have anything to do with white-skinned people. This origin is rather odd when you think about Michael Jackson.

Herbaceous Communication

At the time that the Never Never was being named, the British had decided that a warm, sunny country with beautiful beaches was clearly a great spot for a penal colony. If you were caught stealing a loaf of bread in early Victorian Britain you were sent to Australia, where there was less bread but much more sunshine. This system was abolished in 1850 when word got back to Britain that Australia was, in fact, a lovely place to live and therefore didn't count as a punishment. It was decided that lounging on the beach at Christmas did not produce what judges described as 'a just measure of pain'.

Rather than join the colony's work gangs, where they might be forced to do hard labour or, worse, administration, some of the more enterprising of the transportees set off into the Outback, where they obstinately continued to commit crimes. The Australian police would chase after them, hoping to arrest them and deport them somewhere else. However, the population at large tended to prefer the criminal bushrangers to the policemen, and would inform the furtive outlaws about exactly where the long arm of the law was reaching. This irritating and unofficial system of communication became known as the *bush telegraph*.

The *bush telegraph* isn't recorded until 1878, but that's because the telegraph wasn't introduced to Australia at all until 1853. In America, the telegraph had been around since 1844 and it took Americans only six years before they had invented their version of *bush telegraph*.

The *grapevine telegraph* became famous during the American Civil War, but nobody is sure who invented it or why. The Confederate soldiers seemed to think that they had invented the *grapevine* and that it was wonderfully Southern and lackadaisical. This view is backed up by a contemporary Yankee source claiming that:

> We used to call the rebel telegraphic lines 'the grapevine telegraph', for their telegrams were generally circulated with the bottle after dinner.

However, the other story goes that it was the slaves of the South, those who picked the *grapes*, who were the true and original operators of the *grapevine telegraph*. In this alternative version, the grapevine telegraph was the sister system of the metaphorical *Underground Railroad* that took slaves from the South to freedom in the North.

Then, in 1876, Alexander Graham Bell patented the telephone, and the telegraph – bush, grapevine or otherwise

– became old hat.[9] The telephone had a great effect on the English language. For one thing, it made the previously obscure greeting *hello* wildly popular. Before the telephone, people had wished each other *good mornings*, *days* and *nights*; but as the person on the other end of the line might not deserve a *good day*, people needed an alternative. Alexander Bell himself insisted on beginning a phone call with the bluff nautical term *ahoy*, but it didn't catch on and so *hello* rose to become the standard English greeting.

The other effect that the telephone had was that it made *telegraph* sound rather old-fashioned. So unofficial communication became known simply as the *grapevine*, which is why, in 1968, Marvin Gaye sang that he had heard dispiriting news of his beloved's plans *through the grapevine*.

Papa Was a *Saxum Volutum*

Marvin Gaye didn't write 'I Heard It Through the Grapevine'. It was written for him by Norman Whitfield and Barrett Strong, who also wrote the classic 'Papa Was a Rollin' Stone', which is based on another old phrase.

Revolving minerals already had their (movable) place in the Rock and Roll Hall of Fame. Bob Dylan had written 'Like A Rolling Stone' and some students from London had formed a band called The Rolling Stones, named after the Muddy Waters song 'Rollin' Stone'.

---

[9] A dictionary of 1776 defines 'old hat' as 'a woman's privities, because frequently felt'.

All these rock and rollers were referring indirectly to the fact that *a rolling stone gathers no moss*. This was observed in the 1530s by the poet Thomas Wyatt:

> A spending hand that alway powreth owte
> Had nede to have a bringer in as fast,
> And on the stone that still doeth tourne abowte
> There groweth no mosse: these proverbes yet do last.

The phrase also crops up in Erasmus' adages of 1500, where it's rendered in Latin as *saxum volutum non obducitur musco*. But why are all these stones rolling? On the rare occasion that you actually see a stone rolling downhill, it usually gets to the bottom a few seconds later and stops. Its brief trip doesn't tend to knock much moss off, and if it does, then the moss will just grow back later. To keep a stone moss-free, it needs to be rolled *regularly*.

That's why the original rolling stones were not boulders crashing down a hillside. In fact, the sort of rolling stone that gathers no moss is helpfully pinned down in a dictionary of 1611 as a gardening implement used to make your lawn nice and flat. The solicitous gardener who rolls his lawn every weekend will find that his *rolling stone gathers no moss*.

Which means that Mick Jagger, Bob Dylan, Muddy Waters *et al* are all referring to diligent gardening. Moreover, one of the most successful bands of the twentieth century belongs in the garden shed.

The part of the phrase about *gathering no moss* actually predates the gardening implement. In the mid-fourteenth century you can find this observation on stone flooring:

Selden Moseþ þe Marbelston þat men ofte treden.

Which translates loosely as moss doesn't grow on marble that gets trodden on a lot. That line is from a mystic allegorical poem called *The Vision of Piers Plowman*. So before we proceed, what has Piers got to do with a parrot?

Flying Peters

Piers Plowman is a variant of *Peter Plowman* because the farmer in the poem was representative of the ideal disciple of Christ, the chief of the apostles and the first pope, whose real name was not, of course, Peter.

Once upon a time there was a fisherman called Simon. He fell in with a chap called Jesus who nicknamed him 'The Rock' (presumably in preparation for a career in professional wrestling), which in Greek was *Petros*.

And Jesus answered and said unto him, Blessed art thou, Simon Barjona ... And I say also unto thee, That thou art Peter, and upon this rock I will build my church; and the gates of hell shall not prevail against it.

So Simon was – quite technically – *petrified*. And this Jesus chap, not content with renaming his friend, then decided to walk on water and, in contravention of every health and safety rule you can think of, encouraged Peter to do the same. This did not work out well.

And in the fourth watch of the night Jesus went unto them, walking on the sea. And when the disciples saw him walking on the sea, they were troubled, saying, It is a spirit; and they cried out for fear. But straightway Jesus spake unto them, saying, Be of good cheer; it is I; be not afraid.

And Peter answered him and said, Lord, if it be thou, bid me come unto thee on the water. And he said, Come. And when Peter was come down out of the ship, he walked on the water, to go to Jesus. But when he saw the wind boisterous, he was afraid; and beginning to sink, he cried, saying, Lord, save me.

With that story in mind, what do you call a sea bird that appears just before a storm and dips its feet into the water? You call it a *storm peter*. And then you muck about with the letters a bit – just as a *cock* is a *cockerel* – until it's called a *storm petrel*.

Peter went into French as *Pierre*. *Little Peters* are called *Pierrots* and in French sparrows are, for some obscure French reason, therefore called *perots*. For reasons even more obscure, England then imported this word as *parrot*. The word first pops up in the alliterative claptrap that the Tudor writer John Skelton was pleased to call his poetry. Skelton wrote an attack on Cardinal Wolsey called 'Speke, Parrot'. Some fragments of the poem survive, which is a pity.

Parrot got verbed by Thomas Nashe at the end of the sixteenth century in the equally pointless but fantastically titled *Have With You To Saffron Walden*, an inexplicable work of incomprehensible invective.

Parrots are very important linguistically because they preserve the words of the dead. There was an explorer at the beginning of the nineteenth century called Alexander von Humboldt. He was in Venezuela and found an old parrot that still repeated words from the language of the Ature tribe. Nobody else did, because the Atures had been wiped out a few years before. Another tribe had slaughtered every last one of them and returned victorious with, among other things, a pet parrot. This parrot still spoke only words from the tribe that had raised him. So all that was left of a Venezuelan civilisation were the echoes and repetitions of a parrot.

Venezuela and Venus and Venice

The name *Venezuela* has nothing to do with *Venus*, but the chap who thought it up was related to her by marriage.

Amerigo Vespucci was a Florentine explorer with three claims to fame. First, and most obscurely, he was the cousin of a nobleman called Marco Vespucci. Marco married a girl called Simonetta Cataneo, who was possibly the most beautiful woman who ever lived. So beautiful was she, that even after she had died (in 1476) Botticelli still used his memory of her (and the myriad portraits that already existed) as the model for his 'Birth of Venus'.

But to return to Amerigo: not being as noble as his cousin, Amerigo was sent to work in a bank. However, the world of finance couldn't hold him and, at the invitation of the King of Portugal, he set off on an early expedition to the New World. On his return he wrote several accounts of his travels. These accounts were written in Latin and so he signed his name using the Latin form of Amerigo: *Americus*.

One of these accounts fell into the hands of a man called Martin Landseemuller, who, being a map-maker, ran off and made a map with the New World marked on it. He was going to call it *Americus*, but decided that ending a continent name with *–us* simply wouldn't do. *Africa*, *Asia* and *Europa* all ended with the feminine A, so he called it *America* instead.

Finally, Amerigo Vespucci named part of South America *Little Venice*, or in Spanish, *Venezuela*, because lots of the local tribesmen lived in huts that were built out into the water and supported by stilts, making it a sort of ramshackle miniature Venice.

What News on the Rialto?

For all its drainage problems, Venice has given the English language a fair number of words besides *terra firma*. Several parts of the city have entered the language. It was Venice that had the original *Ghetto* and the original *Arsenale*, where the warships were made. The first *regattas* were held on Venice's Grand Canal; and the lagoon in which Venice stands was the original *lagoon* (and is cognate with English *lake* and Scots *loch* and even the bibliographic *lacuna*).

Venice was the first modern democracy, which is why *ballot* comes from the Venetian word *ballotte*, which means *small balls*. Indeed, the word *ballot* arrived on English shores inside *The Historie of Italie* by William Thomas, because the Venetians would cast their votes by placing different coloured *ballotte* in a bag.

The same naming process happened with the voting in ancient Athens. When the Athenians wanted to banish somebody for not being classical enough, they would vote on the question by putting little black or white fragments of pottery in a box. White meant he could stay: black meant banishment. These tiles were called *ostrakons*. Hence *ostracism*. Ostracism has nothing to do with *ostriches* but is distantly related to *oysters* (both words relate to bone).

The method and term survives to this day in *blackballing*. In the gentlemen's clubs of London, an application for membership may be refused on the basis of a single black ball in the *ball*-ot box.

In ancient Syracuse, votes for banishment didn't use shards of pottery. They used olive leaves and so ostracism was called *petalismos*, which is far more beautiful.

Venice was also the first place to introduce what we would now call newspapers. These appeared in the mid-sixteenth century and were little sheets describing trade, war, prices and all the other things that a Venetian merchant would need to know about. They were very cheap and were known as *a halfpenny-worth of news* or, in the Venetian dialect, a *gazeta de la novita*. *Gazeta* was the name for a Venetian coin of very little value, so called because on it was a picture of a magpie or *gazeta*. *Gazette* was therefore a doubly appropriate name: it referred both to the cheapness of the news and to the fact that newspapers were, from the first, as unreliable as the chattering of a magpie, and filled with useless trinkets like the thieving magpie's nest. The Elizabethan linguist John Florio said that gazettes were 'running reports, daily newes, idle intelligences, or flim flam tales that are daily written from Italie, namely from Rome and Venice'.

How different from our own more modern magazines. Now, can you take a guess as to why a *magazine* is a glossy thing filled with news and a metal thing filled with bullets?

Magazines

Once upon a time there was an Arabic word *khazana* meaning *to store up*. From that they got *makhzan* meaning storehouse and its plural *makhazin*. That word sailed northwards across the Mediterranean (*the middle of the earth*) and became the Italian *magazzino*, which then proceeded by foot to France and became *magasin*, before jumping onto a ferry and getting into Britain as *magazine*, still retaining its original meaning of *storehouse*, usually military, hence the magazine in a gun. Then along came Edward Cave.

Edward Cave (1691–1754) wanted to print something periodically that would contain stuff on any subject that might be of interest to the educated of London, whether it be politics or gardening or the price of corn. He cast around for a name for his new idea and decided to call it *The Gentleman's Magazine: or, Trader's Monthly Intelligencer.* So far as anyone can tell (and in the absence of a séance we can only guess at Mr Cave's thought process), he wanted to imply that the information in his publication would *arm* the gentleman intellectually, or perhaps he wanted to imply that it was a *storehouse* of information.

The first edition came out in January 1731. It was largely a digest of stories that appeared in other publications, but it also had its own column of amusing stories from around the world, such as the following:

From *Dijon* in France, 'tis written that a Person having withdrawn himself, his Relations charg'd one who was his sworn Enemy with his murder, and examin'd him with such exquisite tortures that, to shorten them he confess'd the crime: whereupon he was broke alive, and two others as his accomplices were hanged. The Man supposed to be murder'd, soon after return'd home.

Or this pleasant round-up from the courts:

This day one *Tim. Croneen* was, for the murder and robbery of Mr *St. Leger* and his wife at *Bally volane*, sentenc'd to be hang'd 2 minutes, then his head to be cut off, his bowels to be taken out and thrown in his face; and his body divided in 4 quarters to be placed in 4 cross ways. He was servant to Mr Leger, and committed the murder with the privity of Joan Condon the servant maid, who was sentenced to be burnt.

In fact, most of the first issue was taken up with stories of murders and executions,[10] and as the reading public has always loved a good bit of gore, *The Gentleman's Magazine: or, Trader's Monthly Intelligencer* was a big hit. But it was still a bit of a mouthful. So in December 1733 the *Monthly Intelligencer* part was dropped from the title and replaced with the slogan: *Containing more in Quantity, and greater variety, than any Book of the Kind and Price.*

But imagine if Cave had decided to drop the *magazine* bit instead: we might all now be buying *intelligencers*. Cave's

---

[10] I tried to count them all, but gave up.

caprice altered English. If it weren't for him, *porn mags* might now be called *carnal intelligencers* and that, I'm sure, would make the world a Better Place.

Moreover, Cave's *Magazine* gave employment to a young, penniless and unknown writer whose name was Dr Samuel Johnson.

Dick Snary

It's absolutely necessary and fitting that a book such as this should devote a chapter to Samuel Johnson's dictionary. So we won't. After all, Johnson didn't write the first English diction-ary. There were plenty before him and there have been plenty since. The chief recommendation of Johnson's is that he defines a cough as: 'A convulsion of the lungs, vellicated by some sharp serosity.'

Dictionaries had been around for ages before the Doctor. Johnson's dictionary was published in 1755 but the joke name *Richard Snary* was first recorded in 1627. Who was Richard Snary?

A country lad, having been reproved for calling persons by their Christian names, being sent by his master to borrow a dictionary, thought to show his breeding by asking for a Richard Snary.

A word is always older than its pun. The word *dictionary* was invented by an Englishman called John of Garland in 1220. But it wasn't what we would call a dictionary; he had merely written a book to help you with your Latin *diction*.

The first dictionaries that we would recognise were dual-language ones for the use of translators. For example, the *Abecedarium Anglico Latinum* of 1552 is a terribly useful volume if you want to know that the Latin word for *wench always beaten about the shoulders* is *scapularis*. It also contains English words of indescribable beauty like *wamblecropt (afflicted with queasiness)* that have since vanished from the language.

The first dictionary that wasn't just there to help translators was Cawdrey's *Table Alphebetical* of 1604, which is a list of 'hard usual English words' like *concruciate (to torment or vex together)*, *deambulation (a walking abroade)*, *querimonious (full of complaining and lamentation)*, *spongeous (like a sponge)*, and *boat (boat)*.

However, the first English dictionary that actually had *dictionary* in the title was Henry Cockeram's *The English Dictionarie, or, An Interpreter of Hard English Words*, which hit the printing presses in 1623. Again, it's not complete, but it is useful. Before 1623 there were actually people who didn't know that an *acersecomicke* was *one whose haire was never cut*, or that an *adecastick* is *one that will doe just howsoever*. After 1623 they could look up such useful terms, and four years later Dick Snary was born.

Next up was Nathan Bailey's *Universal Etymological Dictionary* of 1721 that contained 40,000 words, which is only a couple of thousand short of Dr Johnson's. The point of Johnson's dictionary is not that it was bigger or more accurate than the others (although it was slightly both); the point of Johnson's dictionary was that it was *Johnson's*. The most learned man in Britain had poured out his learnedness onto the page.

Suppose that you were an early eighteenth-century Englishman and you were arguing with a friend about the meaning of the word *indocility*. You pull out your copy of Nathan Bailey's *Universal Etymological Dictionary*, you flip through the pages and you find:

Indo'cibleness Indo'cilness Indoci'lity
[*indocilitas indocilité indocilità* (L.)]
unaptness to learn or be taught.

You sit back with a smug smile on your face, until your friend asks who this Nathan Bailey guy is anyway? 'Well,' you mumble, 'he's a schoolmaster from Stepney.'

Not that impressive.

But Doctor Johnson, on the other hand, was the foremost scholar of Britain. So his definition of indocility:

Indoci'lity n. s. [*indocilité*, Fr. *in* and *docility.*]
Unteachableness, refusal of instruction.

Well, that had the authority of Dr Johnson behind it. It did not, though, stop Bailey's dictionary outselling Johnson's by a country mile.

Then came Noah Webster, who was an immensely boring man and can usefully be skipped; so that we can get straight on to the OED, which is the greatest dictionary ever. Nor is that opinion a case of anglocentric chauvinism, as the OED was largely the result of the collaboration between a Scotsman and an American. Its story also involves murder, prostitutes, and all sorts of other fun stuff. In fact, those of a weak disposition should skip the following chapter, as the story of the *Oxford English Dictionary* is too scary for most and will probably give you nightmares.

Still here? Right, for those who wish to continue, what is the medical term for slicing off your own penis, and how does it relate to the OED?

Autopeotomy

The *Oxford English Dictionary* is the greatest work of reference ever written, and it's largely the result of a Scotsman who left school at fourteen, and a criminally insane American.

The Scotsman was a former cowherd called James Murray, who taught himself Latin, German, Italian, Ancient Greek, French, Anglo-Saxon, Russian, Tongan ... well, nobody's quite sure how many languages he knew. It's usually estimated at 25. Murray became a schoolteacher and then in the 1860s he moved to London for his wife's health and became a member of the Philological [*word-loving*] Society.

The Philological Society was trying to produce an English dictionary that would be more complete than any other. They eventually did a deal with the Oxford University Press, and James Murray, who at the time was still a teacher, became the editor.

The idea of the *Oxford English Dictionary* was that it would trace the development of every word in the English language. Each word would then have its meanings defined in chronological order with quotations given as evidence. Getting the quotations was a simple business; all that had to be done was to read every book ever written in English.

Even Murray couldn't do that alone, so he advertised for volunteer readers,[11] people who would fight their way through all the books that could be found, copying out significant-looking sentences.

Now, let's leave Murray there for a moment and turn our attention to the island of Sri Lanka in 1834, where we will find a missionary couple from New England who are trying to convert the island's pagan population to Jesus. He is called Eastman Minor, she is called Lucy Minor and has just given birth to a son: William Minor.

The Minors were hyper-religious and at a very early age they decided that little William was much too interested in girls. Maybe they were just being Puritan and repressive, but given subsequent events it's possible that they were on to something.

Either way, the Minors decided that William's fascination with the opposite sex was a) a problem and b) probably something to do with the Sri Lankans. So they packed their son off to a boarding school back in the healthy cold shower that was nineteenth-century America.

There's no record of William Minor's sex life at boarding school, which is a blessed relief. All we know is that he ended up in Yale studying medicine, and that meant that when the American Civil War broke out he signed up in the Union Army as a field surgeon.

Being a doctor is a pleasant business in general. You cure people and that makes them happy. Even if you don't cure them, they are still reasonably grateful that you tried. However,

---

[11] Technically, the adverts went out before Murray was appointed, but we're trying to keep this simple.

Minor was assigned the rather unhippocratic job of branding deserters.

If a chap got caught running away from the Union Army, he would have a big capital D branded on his cheek to inform everybody that he was a deserter and a coward. Minor was the man with the brand. At least one of the people he was forced to disfigure was an Irish immigrant, a fact that will be important later.

After the war, Minor was posted to New York, but he spent so much of his time in the company of prostitutes that the army got embarrassed and transferred him to Florida. It's a rather impressive feat to visit so many prostitutes that you become a scandal in New York. It's also an impressive feat to visit so many prostitutes that the army feels you're overdoing it. William Minor's parents may just have been right.

The next thing Minor did was to go utterly mad, and the army decided to discharge him completely. Minor moved to England to convalesce and settled in Lambeth in London, which was (coincidentally) full of prostitutes at the time. However, the prostitutes weren't the real problem. The real problem was the branding of the deserters, which still preyed on Minor's mind.

One day Minor met an Irishman called George Merret and, for no reason at all, decided that Merret was one of the men he had branded, on a mission of revenge. Minor took out a gun and shot Merret dead. This was unreasonable, as Merret didn't have a D burned onto his cheek. It was also, technically, illegal.

At the ensuing trial it was decided that William Minor was absolutely bloody crazy and he was confined in Broadmoor, the brand-new asylum for the criminally insane. Broadmoor wasn't actually that bad a place. It was a hospital, not a prison, and Minor was rich enough to afford a manservant and all the books he could read. It was at Broadmoor that he came across Murray's advertisement for volunteer readers.

Minor had a lot of time on his hands, and also the advantage of being criminally insane, which is always a plus in lexicography. So he started reading. He read and read and read and took note after note after note, and sent the notes to Murray. He sent Murray hundreds of notes, then he sent him thousands. Minor contributed so much to the *Oxford English Dictionary* that Murray would later say that the whole of the development of the modern English language, from Tudor times to the present day, could have been illustrated using only Minor's examples.

But Minor never said who he was. He seems to have been rather embarrassed about the murder, and Broadmoor Criminal Lunatic Asylum is hardly the most fashionable address in England. All Minor's letters to Murray were signed *W.C. Minor, Crowthorne, Berkshire*, which was technically true, as Crowthorne is the nearest town to Broadmoor.

It wasn't until the 1890s that James Murray discovered that his star contributor, the man on whom his dictionary was based, was an insane murderer. When Murray did find out, he immediately set off to visit Minor, and the two became firm friends. They were rather different people, but by coincidence they looked like brothers. They both had huge beards and flowing white hair, and they both loved words. Murray tried to give Minor emotional support but it didn't really work, as Minor, in 1902, deliberately sliced off his own penis.

This is called an *autopeotomy* and should not be attempted without due consideration. Minor did have a good reason.

He had decided during his confinement that his parents and the army were right and that all his troubles came down to his excessive sexual appetite. Minor may have been correct, but most men intent on curbing their sex drive would have had the good sense to merely chop off their testicles (as the early Christian writer Origen did). The problem with an autopeotomy is that, among other things, it becomes difficult to pee. William Minor was in trouble, and agony.

Murray took up Minor's case and in 1910 persuaded the Home Secretary to have Minor released and deported to America. Minor went back and died in his own country, but he took with him copies of the six volumes of the OED that had so far been completed. Whether these consoled him for the loss of his *membrum virile*, history does not record.

Now, who was the Home Secretary who released Minor, and what weapon did he help to name?

Water Closets for Russia

William Minor was released on the orders of the Home Secretary Winston Churchill. Churchill is remembered by lexicographers as a man of words. He wrote a novel called *Savrola* that appeared in 1899 to reviews that can be given the usual euphemism of 'mixed'. He invented the phrases *out-tray*, *social security* and *V-sign*. He invented the words *seaplane*, *commando* and *undefendable*. He popularised *crunch* in the sense of *the vital moment*; and won the Nobel Prize for literature in 1953. With all these linguistic achievements, it's easy to forget that in his spare time Churchill was also a politician.

As William Minor sailed, *sans* willy, back to America, Europe was getting ready for war. In 1911, Winston Churchill was moved from the position of Home Secretary and became First Lord of the Admiralty, where he was in charge of developing new and more lethal methods of killing the enemy.

One of the ideas that he oversaw was the *landship*. The oceans of the world were, at the time, dominated by the Royal Navy. Britannia ruled the waves. Huge steam-powered gun-ships chuffed around the globe making sure that the Sun never set on the British empire. These ships were covered in iron, so that they were immune to enemy fire, and they had huge guns mounted on them, so that they could destroy others. However, on land Britain was not so invincible. The British army still consisted of men and horses, which are made of flesh rather than iron and could be killed in their millions.

So, under Churchill's supervision, a plan was hatched to take the principle of the iron-clad warship and apply it to land warfare. The British started to design the *landship*. It would be iron, like a warship, it would motorised, like a warship, and it would have guns mounted on it, like a warship. It would be a destroyer, but it would be used in the field and not in the sea.

The idea was pushed forward by an officer called Ernest Swinton. Plans were drawn up and manufacturers approached, but everything was done in deadly secrecy. No mention of *land-ships* was ever made in public, which is why they aren't called *landships* today.

The landship was such a secret that not even the workers in the factory where they were built were to know what they were. By the outbreak of war in 1914, Russia was fighting on the Allied side, so Swinton decided that a good cover story for the new weapons would be to say on all documents that they were *Water Carriers for Russia*, but when Swinton told Churchill about his ruse Churchill burst out laughing.

Churchill pointed out that Water Carriers would be abbreviated to WCs and that people would think that they were manufacturing lavatories. So Swinton had a quick think and suggested changing the name to *Water Tanks for Russia*. Churchill could find no objection to this codename, and it stuck.

Well, it didn't all stick. *Water Tanks for Russia* was a bit cumbersome, so *water* got dropped. Then it turned out that the tanks weren't going to Russia at all. They were going to the trenches on the Western Front, so *Russia* got dropped too. And that's why tanks are called *tanks*. If Winston Churchill hadn't been so careful about lavatorial implications, they might have been called *carriers*. If Swinton hadn't been so careful, they would definitely have been *landships*.

The tank was a very useful weapon of war, but unfortunately the Germans were even then building their own secret weapon, and theirs had a name that was quite ungentlemanly.

Fat Gunhilda

While Britain was developing the tank, Germany was building a gun. To be precise Germany was building an absolutely bloody enormous gun. It weighed 43 tons and could fire 1,800lb shells 2½ miles. Its official name was the *L/12 42-cm Type M-Great Kurze Marine-Kanone*, but that's hardly the catchiest of names. So the designers at Krupp Armaments did a dastardly thing: they named it after their boss. The owner of the company was a fat woman called Bertha Krupp. So the engineers called their new gun *Dick Bertha*, which is German for *Fat Bertha*, or as it came to be known more alliteratively in English, *Big Bertha*.[12]

It's odd to give a cannon a girl's name. You hardly need to be a devoted disciple of Sigmund Freud to see a smidgen of phallic symbolism in a gun. However, history and Freud are at odds: for some reason guns are always girls.

During the Vietnam War, recruits into the US Marine Corps were required to give their rifles girls' names, usually the name of their sweetheart at home; but the practice is much older than that. The standard issue flintlock musket of the British empire was called Brown Bess, and Rudyard Kipling joked that many men had been pierced to the heart by her charms. In Edinburgh castle there's a huge medieval cannon known as Mons Meg, which was probably named after James III of Scotland's wife, Margaret.

Why do guns have girls' names? It's a silly question because *gun* itself is a girl's name. So far as anybody can tell (and theories vary), the very first *gun* in history was a cannon in Windsor Castle. A document from the early fourteenth century mentions *Una magna balista de cornu quae vocatur Domina Gunilda*, which means 'a large cannon from Cornwall which is called Queen Gunhilda'.

Gunhilda is a girl's name and the usual shortening of Gunhilda is *Gunna*. So far as etymology can tell, every gun in the English-speaking world is named after that one *gunna* in Windsor Castle: the Queen Gunhilda.

---

[12] Pity for Bertha Krupp would be misplaced. The Krupp *Berthawerk* was quite officially named after her, and that was the armaments factory attached to Auschwitz.

There actually was a Queen Gunhilda, as well. But what did she have to do with smartphones?

Queen Gunhilda and the Gadgets

Gunhilda was the Queen of Denmark in the late tenth and early eleventh century. She was married to Sven Forkbeard and, as is the way with Dark Age queens, that's all we really know about her. She was the mother of Canute the Great (he of the waves), and presumably she helped her husband out with his beard every morning. She must also have known her father-in-law, King Harald I of Denmark, who lived from 935 to 986 AD.

King Harald had blue teeth. Or perhaps he had black teeth. Nobody's quite sure, as the meaning of *blau* has changed over the years. His other great achievement was to unite the warring provinces of Denmark and Norway under a single king (himself).

In 1996 a fellow called Jim Kardach developed a system that would allow mobile telephones to communicate with computers. After a hard day's engineering, Kardach relaxed by reading a historical novel called *The Longships* by Frans Gunnar Bengtsson. It's a book about Vikings and adventure and raping and pillaging and looting, and it's set during the reign of Harald Bluetooth.

Jim Kardach felt he was doing the king's work. By getting computers to talk to telephones and vice versa he was uniting the warring provinces of technology. So, just for his own amusement, he gave the project the working title of *Bluetooth*.

Bluetooth was never meant to be the actual name on the package. Blue teeth aren't a pleasant image, and it was up to the marketing men at Kardach's company to come up with something better. The marketing men did come up with something much blander and more saleable: they were going to call the product *Pan*. Unfortunately, just as the new technology was about to be unveiled, they realised that *Pan* was already the trademark of another company. So, as time was tight and the product needed to be launched, they reluctantly went with Kardach's nickname. And that's why it's called Bluetooth technology.

Shell

The history of company names is strange and accidental and filled with twists and tergiversations. For example, why is the largest energy company in the world called Shell?[13]

Well, the truth is that in Victorian England seashells were popular. Really popular. Popular to an extent that just looks weird to us. Victorians collected seashells, painted seashells and made things out of seashells. The devouring dustbin of time thankfully means that most of us have never and will never see a whole imitation bouquet of flowers made of nothing other than painted integuments of mortal molluscs. The word *kitsch* doesn't do it justice.

[13] Shell merged with Royal Dutch Petroleum to form the present Royal Dutch Shell.

These seashells had to be supplied by somebody. This is probably the reason that she sold seashells on the sea shore. But the beaches of Britain were not sufficient for the obsessed Victorians, so a lively trade started up importing bigger, shinier shells from all four corners of the Earth.

One man who cashed in on this importing business was Marcus Samuel, who set up shop in Houndsditch in east London and became a shell merchant. It was therefore perfectly natural that he should call his company Shell.

Shell did well and soon expanded into the other areas of the curio market: trinkets, brightly coloured pebbles and the like. Marcus Samuel brought his son (also called Marcus) into the family business and sent him off to Japan to buy gaudy trifles.

It was while on this trip that Marcus Samuel Junior realised that there might just possibly be a little bit of potential profit in, of all things, oil.

Shell did not remain true to its roots. The seashell business on which the company was founded was dropped.[14] Only the name survives, but the Shell logo that stands above all those petrol stations is a mute memorial to what was once the core of the business, and to the fact that oil was only an afterthought.

In a Nutshell

Shells are strewn all over the beaches of the English language. Artillery, for example, can *shell* a town, on the basis that the

---

[14] In a spirit of scholarly enquiry, I tried to find out exactly when this line was discontinued, but the nice lady at Shell customer services thought I was making fun of her and hung up.

earliest grenades looked a little like nuts in their shells. It's difficult to get a nut out of its shell, and it's also difficult to get money out of a debtor. That's why when you do manage it, you have made him *shell out*.

Hamlet said that he 'could be bounded in a nutshell and count myself a king of infinite space, were it not that I have bad dreams', but that's not the origin of the phrase *in a nutshell*, which goes back to a deliciously unlikely story recounted by the Latin writer Pliny.

Pliny was a Roman encyclopaedist who tried to write down pretty much everything he'd ever heard. Some of his writings are an invaluable source of knowledge; others are pretty hard to believe. For example, Pliny claimed that there was a copy of *The Iliad* so small that it could fit inside a walnut shell. The weirdest thing about that story is that it's *probably* true.

In the early eighteenth century, the Bishop of Avranches in France decided to put Pliny to the test. He took a piece of paper that was 10½ inches by 8½ (this book is about 8 inches by 5), and started copying out *The Iliad* in the smallest handwriting he could manage. He didn't copy the whole thing, but he fitted 80 verses onto the first line and therefore worked out that, as *The Iliad* is 17,000 verses long, it would easily fit onto the piece of paper. He then folded the paper, sent for a walnut, and proved Pliny right, or at least feasible.[15]

---

[15] A similar feat was, apparently, achieved in about 1590 by an Englishman called Peter Bales, who did it with the Bible.

The Iliad

The story of Troy (also called *Ilium*, hence *Iliad*) is magnificently grand. The heroes are more heroic than any that have fought since, the ladies are more beautiful and less chaste than all their successors, and the gods themselves lounge around in the background. Winston Churchill once observed that William Gladstone 'read Homer for fun, which I thought served him right'.

However, Homer's words are not nearly as grand as they ought to be. If Ajax – the giant, musclebound hero of the Greeks – had known that he would end up as a popular cleaning product, he might have committed suicide earlier. Hector, the proud hero of the Trojans who would challenge anyone, even Achilles, to a fight, has ended up as a verb, *to hector*, meaning little more than *to annoy with abusive shouting*.

Hector's sister, Cassandra, is now a byword for a moaning, doom-mongering party pooper. Even the great Trojan horse is now a rather irritating kind of computer virus, designed to steal your credit card details and Facebook log-in.

And the phrases? There are very few famous phrases from *The Iliad*. There are a lot of famous lines *about* Troy:

> Is this the face that launched a thousand ships
> And burnt the topless towers of Ilium?
> Sweet Helen, make me immortal with a kiss.

But this is from Marlowe, not Homer. In fact, the only phrase that could be ascribed to Homer that most people know comes from William Cullen Bryant's 1878 translation, where

Agamemnon prays that he'll be able to kill Hector:

> May his fellow warriors, many a one,
> Fall round him to the earth and bite the dust.

Would Homer be proud that his only memorable line was a middling song by Queen?

And the most famous phrase from the most famous Homeric hero isn't Homer's at all. It wasn't until more than two millennia after Homer's death that people started to talk about the *Achilles tendon*. The myth runs that, because of his mother's magic, the only part of Achilles' body that could be wounded was the back of his ankle, hence the expression *Achilles' heel* and the medical term *Achilles' tendon*.

The Trojan War, if it happened at all, happened in about 1250 BC. Homer, if he/she existed, probably scribbled his way to immortality in the eighth century before Jesus. Philip Verheyen wasn't born until 1648 in the unfortunately named Belgian town of Borring, and it was Philip Verheyen who named the Achilles tendon, in the most unfortunate of circumstances.

Verheyen was a very intelligent boy who started out as a cowherd (like the editor of the *Oxford English Dictionary*), but became an anatomist. Verheyen was one of the great dissectors, so when his own leg had to be amputated, it was partly a tragedy and partly a temptation.

Verheyen was an ardent Christian who believed in the physical resurrection of the body. He therefore did not want his leg to be buried separately from the rest of him, as this would be a great inconvenience at the Day of Judgement. So he preserved it using chemicals, kept it with him at all times, and after a few years began to very carefully dissect his own leg.

Carefully cutting up your own body is probably not good for the sanity. Verheyen started writing letters to his own leg, in which he recorded all his new findings. It's in these letters to a limb that we first find the term *chorda Achillis*, or *Achilles tendon*.

Verheyen went mad before he died. A student of his recounted visiting him in the last year of his life. Verheyen was gazing out of the window of his study. Beside him, on a table, was every last tiny piece of his leg laid out and neatly labelled.

The Human Body

The body, by virtue of proximity, is the source of at least a thousand and one words and phrases. There's barely a part of you left that hasn't been made into some sort of verb. Most, like *heading off*, or *stomaching criticism*, are obvious. Some are less so. *Footing the bill*, for example, is a strange phrase until you remember basic arithmetic. You compile a bill by writing down the various charges in a column and then working out the total, which you write at the *foot* of the column. At this point you may find that you are paying *through the nose*, which seems to be a reference to the pain of a nosebleed.

There are phrases based on parts of the body that you probably didn't know you had. The *heart strings*, for example, upon which people so often play and tug are actual and vital parts of your heart. The medical name for them is the *chordae tendineae*, and if anyone ever actually pulled on them it would at least cause an arrhythmia and probably kill you.

There are words that don't appear to have anything to do with the body but do, like *window*, which was originally a *wind-eye*, because, though you can look out through it like an eye, in the days before glass the wind could get in.

There's more in your eye than meets the eye. For a start there are apples. Early anatomists thought that the centre of the eye was a solid that appeared to be shaped like an apple, hence the *apple of your eye*. These days it has an even stranger name. It's called a *pupil*. And, yes, that's the same sort of pupil you have in a school.

In Latin a little boy was called a *pupus* and a little girl was called a *pupa* (which is also where we get *pupae* for baby insects). When they went to school they became school *pupils*. Now gaze deeply into somebody's eyes. Anyone will do. What do you see? You ought to see a tiny reflection of yourself gazing back. This little version of you seems like a child, and that's why it's a *pupil*.

But the part of your body that has the most words named after it is the hand.

The Five Fingers

And there was yet a battle in Gath, where was a man of great stature, that had on every hand six fingers, and on every foot six toes, four and twenty in number.

2 Samuel XXI, v. 20

Human beings count in tens. We say twenty-one, two, three etc. until we get to twenty-nine, thirty. Then we start again with thirty-one, two, three, four until we get to another multiple of ten and the process repeats. The reason we do this is that we have five fingers on each hand, making ten in total. If the three-fingered sloth could count, he would probably do so in groups of six.

Counting on your fingers is such a natural thing to do that the word *digit*, which originally just meant *finger*, now means *number* as well. This also means that when information is stored in the form of numbers it becomes *digital*.

The Old English names for the fingers were much more fun than our own. The *index finger* was once the *towcher*, or *toucher*, because it was used for *touching* things. We call it the index finger, but not because we use it for running through the index of a book. Both *indexes* come from the Latin word *indicare* because an index, whether it's in a book or on your hand, can *indicate* or point you in the right direction. It's the *pointing* finger.

The boringly-named *middle finger* was once called the *fool's finger*. The Romans called it *digitus infamis* (*infamous*), *obscenus* (*obscene*), and *impudicus* (*rude*). This is because they invented the habit of sticking the middle finger up at people they didn't like. The Roman poet Martial once wrote an epigram that went:

Rideto multum qui te, Sextille, cinaedum
dixerit et digitum porrigito medium

Which translates *extraordinarily* loosely as:

> If you are called a poof don't pause or linger
> But laugh and show the chap your middle finger.

The fourth finger has a strange anatomical property that gives it both its ancient and modern names: the *leech finger* and the *ring finger*.

There is a vein that runs directly from the fourth finger to the heart, or at least that's what doctors used to believe. Nobody is quite sure why, as there isn't actually any such thing. Yet it was this belief that made the fourth finger vital in medieval medicine. Doctors reasoned that if this finger connected directly to the heart, then it was probably possible to use it as a proxy. You could cure heart disease and treat heart attacks simply by doing things to the fourth finger of the patient's hand. The medieval word for a doctor was a *leech*,[16] and so this digit used to be known as the *leech finger*.

Who would be so silly as to believe anything like that nowadays? Well, anybody who's married. You see, we put the wedding ring on that finger precisely because of that non-existent vein. If the finger and the heart are that closely connected, then you can trap your lover's heart simply by encircling the finger in a gold ring. Hence *ring finger*.

And the little finger? Well the Old English used to use that for scratching their ears, and so they called it the *ear finger*.

---

[16] Contrary to popular belief, this probably has nothing to do with their sticking leeches on their patients.

Hoax Bodies

Let us finish our tour of the human body with the Latin word for the whole thing: *corpus*. It's pretty obvious how this word gave us *corpse* and *corporal* punishment. It's a lot less obvious how it gave us words for magic and fraud. To explain that we'll have to go back to a certain supper that took place in Jerusalem in around 33 AD.

> And as they were eating, Jesus took bread, and blessed it, and brake it, and gave it to the disciples, and said, Take, eat; this is my body.
>
> Matthew XXVI, v. 26

Funny chap, Jesus. First, it's a little strange to assert that a piece of bread is your body. If you or I tried that we wouldn't be believed. We certainly wouldn't be allowed to run a bakery. Yet, given that Jesus was the son of God,[17] we'll just have to take him at his word.

What's odd is the cannibalistic non-sequitur. If Jesus had said, 'Take, eat; this is plain old bread and not human flesh', then the sentence would make sense. As it is, Jesus tells his disciples, 'This is not bread, this is human flesh. What's more, it's my flesh. Now eat it up like good little cannibals.'

It's enough to make you curious.

Christianity's cannibalism is something so central to Western culture that it often escapes our notice. During the crusades, the

---

[17] This point has occasionally been disputed by people who will burn for ever in God's loving torment.

Muslims got rather worried about it. Nobody was sure how far the Christian's cannibalism went, and rumours spread around the Near East of Muslims being cooked and eaten. When the Christians tried to explain that they only ate God, they just seemed to be adding blasphemy to their sins.

You were meant to take the cannibalism literally, as well. At the time, a Christian could be burnt at the stake for denying the literal truth of transubstantiation. The communion wafer was *actually* turned into Jesus' flesh. All that remained of the original wafer were what theologians called the *accidentals*. The accidentals were those qualities that meant that the wafer still looked, smelled, felt and tasted like a wafer. Other than that it was wholly transformed.

This change was effected by the priest taking the wafer and saying the magic words: '*Hoc est corpus meum*: this is my body.'

And then in the sixteenth century Protestantism happened. This new form of Christianity asserted, among other things, that the wafer did *not* turn into Jesus' flesh but merely represented it.

Rather than behaving like gentlemen and agreeing to differ, the Protestants and Catholics got into an awful spat about whether the wafer was or wasn't the Lord's flesh, and did all sorts of things like burning each other, attaching each other to racks and making jokes at each other's expense.

In the court of the Protestant King James I, there was a clown who used to perform comical magic tricks, during which he would intone the cod-magical words: *Hocus Pocus*. Indeed, the clown called himself *His Majesty's Most Excellent Hocus Pocus*, and the phrase caught on. Where did it come from?

In all probability [says a seventeenth-century sermon] those common juggling words of *hocus pocus* are nothing else but a corruption of *hoc est corpus*, by way of ridiculous imitation of the priests of the Church of Rome in their trick of Transubstantiation.

From the body to cannibalism to religion to magic: *corpus* has come a long way, but it still has a long way to go. *Hocus pocus* got shortened to *hoax*.

The words of Jesus had been translated, parodied, shortened, and now they meant an outright, barefaced con. And it didn't stop there. *Hoax* got changed again: not shortened this time, but lengthened. *Hoax* became *hokum*, an American phrase meaning *nonsense* or *rubbish* or *bunkum*. In fact, it probably gained its *–kum* in order to make it sound more like *bunkum*.

Now, does *bunkum* relate to *bunk beds*, *golfing bunkers*, or *reedy valleys*?

Bunking and Debunking

It's awfully tempting to think that *debunking* has something to do with bunk beds. One imagines that a false idea is found snoozing under a duvet, is woken up and thrown out of his bunk bed by big, burly reason. This is, alas, nonsense.

Debunking is the process of getting rid of an idea that is *bunk* or *bunkum*. *Bunkum*, as we all know, is complete and utter nonsense, but it's also a place in North Carolina. Buncombe County is in the west of the state, a rather pretty and rural area that became a byword for claptrap.

In 1820 the Congress of the United States was debating the Missouri Question. The Missouri Question was to do with slavery and the answer turned out to be the Missouri Compromise. Towards the end of the debate a Congressman called Felix Walker stood up, cleared his throat, began to speak, and wouldn't stop.

He went on and on until people started to get fidgety, and on and on until people started to get annoyed, and on and on until people started to jeer, and on and on until people started to tap him on the shoulder and tell him to stop, and on and on until there was a small crowd round him demanding to know *why* he wouldn't stop.

Felix Walker replied that he was not speaking to Congress, his speech was for the benefit of his constituency back home: he was making 'a speech for Buncombe'.

You see, Felix Walker didn't care about the Missouri Question or the Missouri Compromise: he cared about the press coverage he would get among the voters in his own constituency. It was such an ingenious idea (and such a common practice in all democracies) that the phrase caught on, and *speaking to Buncombe* soon got shortened to *speaking bunkum* and then just plain *bunkum*, which needs to be *debunked*.

It's worthwhile mentioning that though that's the usual story, there's an alternative version in which a Congressman wandered in and found Felix Walker addressing an utterly empty chamber. He asked Walker what the hell he was doing and Walker explained that he was speaking to Buncombe (no doubt a copy of the speech would be mailed home). I prefer this version, but it's less likely to be true. Either way, *bunkum* remains talk that serves no actual purpose, and is definitely down to the place in North Carolina.

Poor Buncombe County! Consigned to the dictionary as a byword for nonsense, Edward Buncombe must be turning in his grave.

Edward Buncombe was a British chap who was born in St Kitt's but moved to America when he inherited a great big plantation in Carolina. He was one of the first fellows in the area to join the pro-independence movement, and when the Revolutionary War broke out in 1775 he joined the Continental Army and was wounded at the Battle of Germantown. He would probably have recovered were it not that one night he got out of bed and sleepwalked to the top of a flight of stairs, toppled down, and died from his re-opened wounds.

In his will he left over two thousand acres of plantation, and ten negroes. He was such a hero that a few years later Buncombe County was named in his honour. So really it's Edward Buncombe whose name is in *debunked*. Or you can go further.

Edward Buncombe must, somehow or other, have been a descendant of Richard de Bounecombe who lived in Somerset in the early fourteenth century. Bounecombe itself means *reedy* (*boune*) *valley* (*combe*). *Combe* is one of the very few words in Old English that comes from Celtic. Why there are so few is a great mystery, and it all depends on how nasty the Anglo-Saxons were.

The Anglo-Saxon Mystery

Once upon a time, two thousand years ago, the British Isles were inhabited by Celts, who, as you might expect, spoke Celtic languages. They also had tattoos. The ancient Greeks called the inhabitants of these foggy islands *Prittanoi* (from where we get the name Britain), meaning *tattooed people*, although this may just have been down to the Celtic habit of painting themselves with woad, which the Greeks thought rather odd.

The important thing for the moment is that Boadicea (died 61 AD) wasn't *English*, even though she lived in what is now England. England didn't exist at the time. Boadicea was a Celtic Briton.

England started to exist only when the Angles began arriving from Denmark in about 400 AD. They referred to their new country as *Angle-land* or *England*. Along with the Angles came the Saxons (from Saxony) and the Jutes (from Jutland) and between them they started to speak Old English.

Soon they had kings and one of these was called Alfred the Great, who was originally the King of the West Saxons but decided to call himself *Rex Angul-Saxonum*, or *King of the Anglo-Saxons*.

So what happened to the Celts? What happened to all the people who had swanned around the island before, covered in woad?

The answer is that nobody's quite sure. There are two arguments: the linguistic one and the historical one.

Whenever one bunch of people conquers another, they pick up a bit of the conquered people's language. You can't help it. Try as you might, the native language is all around you. You may have enslaved the natives, but you still need to be able to order your slaves around. You may not want to learn the language, but there are always new things in a new country that you don't have any words of your own to describe.

Take the example of the British in India. The Brits were there only for a couple of hundred years and yet in that time they picked up *shampoo, bungalow, juggernaut, mongoose, khaki, chutney, bangle, cushy, pundit, bandana, dinghy* etc., etc., etc. And those were only the words that they brought home with them.

So what words did the Angles and Saxons pick up from the Celts?

Next to nothing.

There's *combe*, meaning *valley*, which comes from *cym*. There's *tor*, meaning *rock*, which comes from *torr*, the Celtic word for *hill*. There's *cross*, which we seem to have got from Irish missionaries in the tenth century, rather than from the native Celts. And there's …

Well, there's not much else. It depends on how you count things, really, and it's always possible that words were there but not noted down. The Anglo-Saxons managed to occupy an island for hundreds of years and take almost no words from the people they defeated.

In fact, linguistically, this doesn't look like an occupation, it looks like a massacre. On the surface it would appear to be a pretty crazy massacre as well. Of course, massacres are always pretty bad things, but you'd still expect a *few* more words to have crept into Old English, even if they were only the words for *ouch, no* and *stop it*. In English there's a terrifying absence.

And the historians say that this is absolute hogwash. Where, they ask quite reasonably, are the bodies? There aren't any. No mass graves, no accounts of epic battles. No slaughter recorded. Nothing archaeological. Zero. Zilch. Nil.

So where linguists see a slaughter, archaeologists see peaceful co-existence. It's all rather odd. Although there's a third possibility, which is illustrated by a hill in Herefordshire called Pensax, and a town in Essex called Saffron Walden.

Pensax means *hill (pen) of the Saxons*, and very importantly the *pen* there is a Celtic word. So it would seem that, for a while at least, there were Saxons on the hill and Celts down in the valley. The same goes for the charmingly named Dorset village of Sixpenny Handley. *Sixpenny* is a corruption of *Sex Pen* and is just Pensax with the elements swapped around.

Meanwhile, Saffron Walden is obviously a place where they grew saffron, but the *Walden* is odd. It's an Anglo-Saxon term meaning, literally, *valley of the foreigners*, but *wealh* was a word that was always used to refer to Celts (and, indeed, it gave us the name *Wales*).

So, if you work from the place-name evidence you get a third and very odd picture of a country filled with settlements of Anglo-Saxons and Celts living side by side, but *never* talking. That would mean that they weren't trading, weren't marrying, weren't doing anything at all except naming each other's settlements, presumably as places to avoid.

You might theorise that each people understood the other's language and merely chose to speak their own pure dialect, but it would appear that this wasn't the case. Again it comes down to place-names.

As we have seen, *pen* was a Celtic word for *hill*. Yet when the Old English came across a hill called *Pen*, they decided to name it *Pen hul*, *hul* being the Old English word for *hill*.

The same process was repeated all across England. Names were doubled up, such as *Bredon* (*hill hill*) or the *River Esk* (*river*

river). This would seem to point to a linguistic exchange that didn't go much further than finding out a place-name before driving out anybody who knew what the place-name meant.

It also makes for some very amusing etymologies. *Penhul* became *Pendle* and then a few hundred years later somebody again noticed that it was a hill and changed the name to *Pendle Hill*, which means *Hill-Hill Hill*. This was not a one-off. Bredon Hill in Worcestershire is also *Hill-Hill Hill* on exactly the same pattern of Celtic (*bre*), Old English (*don*) and modern English (*hill*).

We will never know how the Anglo-Saxons and the Celts really got on. Maybe it was a massacre, maybe it was a jolly party. The ages were too dark and history is too forgetful. Nor is it wise to be consumed by sorrow or anger. If you look back far enough everything is stolen and every country invaded. The Celts themselves had conquered the previous people of Britain in around 600 BC, and the Anglo-Saxons were about to get hit by the vicious Vikings, who would bring with them their own language and their own place-names. For example, one Viking found a sedge-covered stream in Yorkshire and decided to name it *Sedge-Stream*, thus spawning one of the world's largest corporations.

The Sedge-strewn Stream and Globalisation

The Vikings were horrid people to whom history has, for some strange reason, been very indulgent. Whether it was the rape, the killing or the human sacrifice that you objected to, it was probably a bad thing when the Vikings arrived at Lindisfarne in 793 and then began to work their way down the north-east coast of England. They quickly got to Yorkshire, and near what is now Harrogate one of them found a sedge-strewn stream and decided to name it *Sedge-Stream*. Except of course he didn't call it that because *Sedge-Stream* would be English; he called it *Sedge-Stream* in Old Norse, and the Old Norse for *Sedge-Stream* is *Starbeck*.

Starbeck is now a little suburb on the eastern edge of Harrogate. The stream is still there, although there's no discernible sedge and it runs quite a bit of its way underground in a pipe next to the railway tracks. The place-name is first recorded in 1817, but, as we've seen, it must go back to the Vikings, and we also know that there were people there in the fourteenth century.

These people had sex (as people almost invariably do) and produced a family. The family were named for the place where they lived, almost. One vowel was changed. The Starbuck family are first recorded living in just the right area in 1379. Since then two things have happened: the Quaker movement was founded and America was discovered.

The result of this double catastrophe was that among the first settlers of Nantucket Island near Cape Cod was a Quaker family whose name was Starbuck. Exactly how much they quaked is not recorded, but they did become big players in Nantucket's biggest trade: whaling.

The Starbuck family took up their harpoons with a vengeance. They were soon the most famous whalers in Nantucket if not the world. In 1823 Valentine Starbuck was chartered by the King and Queen of Hawaii to take them on a trip to England, where the unfortunate royal pair died of measles. Obed

Starbuck discovered Starbuck Island in the Pacific and named it in honour of his cousin.[18]

A little over twenty years later, a man called Herman Melville began to write a novel about whales and whaling. Specifically he wrote about a ship called the *Pequod* setting sail from Nantucket to hunt a white whale known as Moby-Dick. Melville had been a whaler himself and had heard of the famous Starbuck whalers of Nantucket, so he decided to call the first mate of the *Pequod* Starbuck in their honour.

Moby-Dick wasn't a very popular novel at first. Most people, especially the British, couldn't make head or tail of it, though this was largely because the British edition was missing the last chapter. However, in the twentieth century, novels that nobody can make head or tail of became very much the fashion and *Moby-Dick* was taken up by all and sundry, especially American schoolteachers who have been inflicting its purple prose on children ever since. There was one particular English teacher in Seattle who loved the book: his name was Jerry Baldwin.

Baldwin and two friends wanted to start a coffee shop. They needed a name and Jerry Baldwin knew exactly where to find the right one – in the pages of *Moby-Dick*. He told his business partners of his fantastic idea. They were going to call the coffee shop …

Wait for it …

Pequod!

His business partners pointed out (quite rightly) that if you're planning to open a shop selling potable fluids, you

---

[18] History is actually rather bewildered as to who named it in honour of whom first.

probably don't want the name to contain the syllable *pee*. That's just bad marketing. So Baldwin was overruled and the others started looking for something a little more local. On a map of the area they found an old mining settlement in the Rocky Mountains called Camp Starbo. Baldwin's two partners decided that Starbo was a great name. But Jerry Baldwin was not to be defeated. He suggested that they compromise with a little alteration to the second syllable that would make the name match the *Pequod*'s first mate: *Starbucks*. The three of them agreed, and that Viking's name for a little stream in Yorkshire became one of the most famous brands in the world.

The high street might be a different place if Baldwin had remembered that Moby-Dick was based on a real white whale that was said to have fought off over a hundred whaling parties in the Pacific of the early nineteenth century: that whale was called Mocha Dick.

There are no branches of Starbucks on Starbuck Island, but that's probably because there are no people there either, and the occasional seal is unlikely to have the cash for a cappuccino.

Coffee

Balzac once wrote that:

> This coffee falls into your stomach, and straightway there is a general commotion. Ideas begin to move like the battalions of the Grand Army of the battlefield, and the battle takes place. Things remembered arrive at full gallop, ensuing to the wind. The light cavalry of comparisons deliver a magnificent

deploying charge, the artillery of logic hurry up with their train and ammunition, the shafts of wit start up like sharp-shooters. Similes arise, the paper is covered with ink; for the struggle commences and is concluded with torrents of black water, just as a battle with powder.

But Shakespeare never drank coffee. Nor did Julius Caesar, or Socrates. Alexander the Great conquered half the world without even a café latte to perk him up in the morning. The pyramids were designed and constructed without a whiff of a sniff of caffeine. Coffee was introduced to Europe only in 1615.

The achievements of antiquity are quite enough to cow the modern human, but when you realise that they did it all without caffeine it becomes almost unbearable. The words for coffee arrange themselves beautifully into highly-caffeinated spirals. Let's start with *espressos* and consider what they have to do with *expressing* yourself.

An espresso is made in a little machine that *presses* steam *outwards* (*e* in Italian) through tightly-packed grains of coffee. It's exactly the same process by which a cow *expresses* milk, or a sore *expresses* pus, and metaphorically it's the same process by which your thoughts are *expressed* outwards from your brain through your mouth. Thus self-expression.

Those actions that have been thought about are premeditated, intentional and deliberate. If, for example, you have done something *expressly* for a purpose, it's because you have thought about it.

How does this connect to *express* mail? *Expressly* came to mean *for one particular purpose*. A letter can be entrusted either to the tender mercies of the national postal system (who will probably lose it, burn it or deliver it back to you a month later with a fine) or it can be given to a paid messenger who has one *express* job: to deliver that one letter. This is an *express* delivery – one where a postman has been hired *expressly* for the purpose.

And the same is true of trains. Some trains stop at every station; no village halt or stray cow is too small or too irrelevant to slow you down. All this can be avoided, if rather than taking a stopping train you board one that is bound *expressly* for one particular destination. Such trains are now known as *express* trains, and they usually have a little buffet car where you can pay a small fortune for a tiny *espresso*.

Cappuccino Monks

If expressive espressos have a circuitous etymology, it's as nothing compared to the frothy delights of the *cappuccino*.

In 1520, a monk called Matteo Da Bascio decided that his fellow Franciscans were all terrible sybarites who had fallen away from the original calling of St Francis. They did luxurious things like wearing shoes, and Da Bascio decided to start a new order of pure, barefoot Franciscans.

The Old Franciscans were rather hurt by this and tried to suppress Matteo's unshod breakaways. He was forced to flee into hiding with the sympathetic Camaldolese monks who wore *little hoods* called, in Italian, *cappuccios*. Matteo and his brethren wore the cappuccios themselves, just to blend in, but when his breakaway order got official recognition in 1528 they found that they had become so used to the hoods that they decided to keep them on. His followers were therefore nick-named the *Capuchin Monks*.

The Capuchin Monks spread quickly all over Catholic Europe, and their hoods had become so familiar that when, a century later, explorers in the New World found apes with a dark brown patch on the top of their heads that looked like a little monkey-hood, they decided to call them *Capuchin Monkeys*.

What's particularly beautiful about this name is that, so far as anybody can tell, *monkeys* are named after *monks*. You see, most people agreed with Matteo Da Bascio: far from being models of chastity and virtue, medieval monks were all filthy sinners and little better than animals. So what do you call that brown, hairy ape? A *monk*ey.

The habit of the Capuchin Order was, and is, a pretty sort of creamy brown colour. So when the new, frothy, creamy, chocolate-sprinkled form of coffee was invented in the first half of the twentieth century, it was named after their robes: the *cappuccino*.

Mind you, most baristas wouldn't understand you if you ordered a *little hood*. But then again, most *baristas* don't realise that they are really *barristers*.

Called to the Bar

Barista, the chap who serves you your coffee, is a case of English lending a word to Italian and then taking it straight back again. A *barista* is nothing more than an Italian *barman*. The *–ist* suf-fix just means *practitioner*, as in a Marx*ist* evangel*ist*.

A *bar*, as any good dictionary will tell you, is *a rod of wood or iron that can be used to fasten a gate*. From this came the idea of a *bar* as any let or hindrance that can stop you going where you want to; specifically the *bar* in a pub or tavern is the *bar*rier behind which is stored all the lovely intoxicating liquors that only the *bar*man is allowed to lay his hands on without forking out.

We are all, at times, called to the bar, if only in order to pay the bill. But the bar to which *barristers* were called was a lot less alcoholic, even though it was in an inn.

Half a millennium ago, all English lawyers were required to train at the Inns of Court in London. These inns were not the pleasant inns that serve beer, they were merely lodging houses for students of the law, because *inn*, originally, just meant *house*.

The internal arrangement of the Inns of Court was as Byzantine and incomprehensible as one would expect from a building devoted to the law, but basically there were the *Readers*, who were clever folk and sat in an Inner Sanctum separated from the rest of the students by a big *bar*.

The lesser students would sit around reading and studying and dreaming of the great day when they would be *called to the bar* and allowed to plead a case like a proper lawyer. The situation was complicated by the fact that there used to be *outer barristers* and *inner barristers* who had a particular relationship with sheriffs at law, and you would probably have to study for a few years before you understood the bar system even partially, and it wouldn't do you any good anyway, as just when you thought you'd got a grip on things, the meaning of *bar* was changed. That's law for you.

In about 1600 the word *bar* started to be applied to a wooden railing that ran around every courtroom in England, at which prisoners had to stand while the judge ticked them off or sentenced them or fumbled with his black cap. The defendant's *barr*ister would stand next to him at the bar and plead his case.

Meanwhile, the prosecuting lawyer would insist that the prisoner was guilty and that he was ready to prove his case. If he insisted this in French he would say *Culpable: prest d'averrer nostre bille,* but that was a bit of a mouthful so it would be shortened to *cul-prit.*

Then the defendant's fate would be handed over to a jury. If the jury couldn't decide, then they would declare *we don't know,* but they would declare it in Latin – and the Latin for *we don't know* is *ignoramus.*

Ignoramus was thus a technical legal term until a writer called George Ruggle used it as the title for a play in 1615, the main character of which was a stupid lawyer called *Ignoramus.* The usage stuck and now an ignoramus is any old idiot.

This also means that the plural of *ignoramus* is definitely not *ignorami.*

Ignorami

Christians are all cretins, etymologically speaking, and cretins are all Christians. If this sounds unfair, it's because language is much less kind than religion.

The original cretins were deformed and mentally deficient dwarves found only in a few remote valleys in the Alps. These days their condition would be called *congenital iodine deficiency syndrome*, but the Swiss didn't know anything about that. All they knew was that, though these people had a problem, they were still human beings and fellow Christians. So they called them *Cretins*, which means *Christians*.

They meant this in a nice way. It was like calling them *fellow humans*, but of course the word got taken up by bullies and, like *spastic* in modern playgrounds, *cretin* quickly acquired a derogatory sense. So *Christian* became a term of abuse.

The first *idiots* were also Christian, or rather the first Christians were *idiots*. The word *idiot* first appears in English in the Wycliffite Bible of 1382. There, in the Book of Deeds (which we would call Acts), it says that:

> Forsoth thei seynge the stedfastnesse of Petre and John, founden that thei weren men with oute lettris, and idiotis

A verse that was translated in the King James Version as:

> Now when they saw the boldness of Peter and John, and perceived that they were unlearned and ignorant men

But in the Latin of Saint Jerome, the passage ran:

> *videntes autem Petri constantiam et Iohannis conperto quod homines essent sine litteris et idiotae*

St Peter and St John were *idiots* simply because they were *laymen*. They had no qualifications and were therefore their own men, rather than belonging to some professional class. If they had spoken *their own* language it would have been an *idiom*, and if they had been eccentrics with their *own way of doing things* (which they undoubtedly were) they would have been *idiosyncratic*.

Neither *cretin* nor *idiot* was originally meant to be an insult. One was a compliment and the other a simple description, but people are cruel and are always casting about for new ways to abuse others. As fast as we can think up technical terms and euphemisms like *cretin, moron, idiot* or *spastic*, people will take the words and use them to be nasty to others. Consider the poor *moron*. The term was invented in 1910 by the American Association for the Study of the Feeble-Minded. They took an obscure Greek word, *moros*, which meant *dull* or *foolish*, and used it to refer to those with an IQ of between 50 and 70. The idea was that it would be a word reserved for doctors and diagnosis. Within seven years the word had escaped from medical circles and was being used as an insult.

Incidentally, *moron* meant *dull*, but in Greek *oxy* meant *sharp*. Many, many chapters ago we saw how *oxygen* got its name because it *gen*erated acids, and the *oxy* in *oxymoron* has the same root. So an *oxymoron* is a *sharp softness*.

The unkindest twist of the English language is, perhaps, that which happened to John Duns Scotus (1265–1308). He was the greatest theologian and thinker of his day, the *Doctor Subtilis*, the philosopher of the univocity of being, master of the formal distinction and of the concept of haecceity, the essential property that makes each thing this, and not that.

Duns Scotus had a formidable mind which he used to draw the finest distinctions between different ideas. This was, linguistically, his downfall and destruction.

When Duns Scotus died his many followers and disciples lived on. They pursued and expanded on his astonishingly complicated philosophical system of distinctions and differences. One could almost say that they, like their master, were hair-splitters and pedants.

In fact, people did say they were hair-splitters and pedants. When the Renaissance came along, people suddenly got rather enlightened and humanist and were terribly angry when *Duns-men*, as they were called, tried to contradict them with an obscure Aristotelian enthymeme. Duns-men became the enemies of progress, the idiots who would turn the clock back and return to the Dark Ages; and *Duns* started to be spelled *dunce*.

Thus did the greatest mind of his generation become a synonym for *gormless*. This is terribly unfair, as Duns Scotus was full of *gorm*. He was brimming over with the stuff. And if you don't know what *gorm* is, that's because it's a fossil word.

Fossil-less

Do you have any gorm? It's an important question, because if you don't have any gorm it logically follows that you are gormless. *Gormless* is a fossil. Dinosaurs and trilobites once flourished, now only fossils remain, petrified and scattered. The same has happened to *gorm*, *feck*, *ruth* and *reck*. They were all once real words. Now they are frozen for ever in *–less* phrases.

Gorm (spelled all sorts of ways) was a Scandinavian word meaning *sense* or *understanding*. As a twelfth-century monk called Orm put it:

& yunnc birrþ nimenn mikell gom
To þæwenn yunnkerr chilldre

– a sentiment with which we can all, I'm sure, agree. However, poor *gorm* (or *gome*) rarely got written down. It was a dialect word used by Yorkshiremen, and most of the literary action was happening in London.

However, in the nineteenth century Emily Brontë wrote a book called *Wuthering Heights*, in which is the line:

Did I ever look so stupid: so gormless as Joseph calls it?

Joseph is a servant who speaks with a strong Yorkshire accent, and the word *gormless* is clearly being brought in as an example of one of his dialect terms. Joseph would probably have used the word *gorm* as well, but Emily Brontë doesn't mention it. So *gormless* got into one of the most famous novels ever written, while poor *gorm* was left to pine away and die on a lonely moor in Yorkshire.

Once upon a time there was the word *effect*. It was a happy, useful, innocent word until it went to Scotland. Once north of Hadrian's Wall, the word *effect* was cruelly robbed of its extremities and became *feck*.

Indolent, vigourless Scotsmen who had no *effect* on things were therefore *feckless*. This time it was not Brontë but Thomas Carlyle, a Scot, who brought the word into common usage. He used *feckless* to describe the Irish and his wife.

However, it's hard to see exactly what Carlyle meant by *feckless*. This is from a letter of 1842:

> Poor Allan's dust was laid in Kensal Green,—far enough from
> his native Kirkmahoe. M'Diarmid has a well-meant but very
> feckless Article upon him this week.

In another letter Carlyle wrote that the summer had made his
wife feckless, and he even described how living with her in
London had turned the couple into 'a feckless pair of bodies', 'a
pair of miserable creatures'. Anyway, Carlyle used *feckless* but he
never used the word *feck*, and so the one word lived and became
famous, while the other vanished into a Celtic twilight.

Reckless is far simpler and there's more poetry in it, which
is the important thing. *Reck* used to mean *care* (although it's
etymologically far from *reckon*). As Chaucer put it:

> I recke nought what wrong that thou me proffer,
> For I can suffer it as a philosopher.

Shakespeare used *reck* too, yet by his time it already had an
archaic feel. In *Hamlet*, Ophelia chides her brother thus:

> Do not as some ungracious pastors do,
> Show me the steep and thorny way to heaven,
> Whiles, like a puff'd and reckless libertine,
> Himself the primrose path of dalliance treads
> And recks not his own rede.

Rede was an archaic and ancient word for *advice*, and *reck* was
probably already an archaic and ancient word for *take notice of*.
Shakespeare used *reckless* six times in his complete works, as

much as all the other *recks*, *recketh*s and *reckeds* put together. *Reck* must already have been fading, *reckless* rushing headlong to the future.

If something is *true*, it's the *truth*. If you *rue* your actions, you feel *ruth*. If you don't rue your actions, you feel no ruth and that makes you *ruthless*. *Ruth* survived for quite a long time, and it's uncertain as to why it died out in the end. Maybe it's just that there are more ruthless people than ruthful ones.

Language sometimes doesn't have an explanation. Words rise and die for no reason that an etymologist can discover. History is not immaculate, in fact it is *maculate*. We might feel more *consolate* if we could give a span, and even spick, explanation for everything, but to no avail.

And so we come, *exorably*, to the end of our study of fossil words. We could go on, as the language is brimming with them, but you might become listless and disgruntled. P.G. Wodehouse once remarked of a chap that, 'if not exactly disgruntled he was far from being gruntled'. So let us continue by seeing exactly how *gruntling* relates to *grunt*.

The Frequentative Suffix

If a gem frequently sparks, we say that it *sparkles*. If a burning log frequently emits cracking noises, then it *crackles*. That's because *–le* is a frequentative suffix.

With this in mind, let's turn to *grunting*. To *gruntle* is to *grunt often*. If a pig makes one noise it has grunted, if it grunts again you may add the frequentative suffix and call the pig a *gruntler*. A medieval travel writer called Sir John Mandeville[19] described the men who live in the desert near the Garden of Eden thus:

> In that desert are many wild men, that are hideous to look on; for they are horned, and they speak not, but gruntle, as swines do.

But the *dis* in *disgruntled* is not a negative prefix but an intensive one. If the verb already carries negative connotations (and something that makes you keep grunting is probably no good), then the negative *dis* just emphasises how bad it is. *Disgruntled* therefore means almost the same thing as *gruntled*.

Some frequentatives are a little more surprising. The next time you are being *jostled* in a crowd, you may reflect that your fate is rather milder than somebody who is repeatedly being attacked by a *jousting* knight. Medieval lovers used to *fond* each other, and if they did this too often, they began to *fondle*. Fondling is a dangerous business, as sooner or later it leads to *snugging*, an archaic word that meant *to lie down together in order to keep warm*. Repeated incidences of *snugging* will result in *snuggling*, and pregnancy.

Whether you *trample*, *tootle*, *wrestle* or *fizzle*, you are being frequentative. So here's a little puzzle (a *puzzle* being a question that is frequently *posed*). What are the originals of these frequentatives?

---

[19] There never was a Sir John Mandeville, but there is a book by him. That's how authorship worked in the fourteenth century. Moreover, I have modernised the quotation to make it comprehensible. The *gruntle* is spelt *gruntils* in the original.

Nuzzle
Bustle
Waddle
Straddle
Swaddle[20]

Of course, the reason that you can't get all those immediately is that a frequentative often leaves home and starts to be a word in its own right. Take the Latin *pensare*, which meant *to think* and from which we get the words *pensive* and *pansy* (a flower given to a loved one to make them think of you). The Romans thought that thinking was nothing more than *repeatedly weighing things up*. So *pensare* is a frequentative of *pendere*, *to weigh or hang*, from which we get more words than you might think.

Pending

The Latin *pendere* meant *to hang*, and its past participle was *pensum*. *In* meant *not*, *de* meant *from*, *sus* meant *down* …

If you are inde*pend*ent you are not de*pend*ent because the only things that are de*pend*ent are *pend*ulums and *pend*ants that *hang* around your neck. *Pend*ants are therefore *pend*ing, or indeed im*pend*ing. They are, at least, sus*pend*ed, and are therefore left hanging in sus*pense*.

Weighing scales *hang* in the balance. Scales can weigh out gold for paying *pens*ions, sti*pend*s and com*pens*ations in *pes*os (but not *pence*, which is etymologically unrelated).

---

[20] And the answers are: *nose, burst, wade, stride* and *swathe*.

All such dis*pens*ations must, of course, be weighed up mentally. One must be *pens*ive before being ex*pens*ive. You must give equal weight to all arguments in order to have either equi*poise* or *poise*. If you don't give equal weight to all things, your scales will hang too much to one side and you will end up with a pre*pond*erance and pro*pens*ity towards your own *pen*chants. Whether these *pen*chants make you per*pend*icular, I am too polite to ask.

I hope that this section on the *pend*ulous hung together. If it did, it was a com*pend*ium. And though there are a few more words from the same root, to include them all would require the ap*pend*ing of an ap*pend*ix.

An appendix, in either a book or a body, is where you put all the useless crap. However, the bodily tube is more properly known as the *vermiform appendix*, which makes it sound even less pleasant than it is, because *vermiform* means *wormlike*, which is something to consider next time you eat *vermicelli*.

Worms and their Turnings

Worms have a hard time. When not being chased about by early birds or being disturbed in their can, they get trodden on. It's no surprise that Shakespeare records them fighting back against their oppressors:

> The smallest worm will turn, being trodden on,
> And doves will peck in safeguard of their brood.

William Blake, on the other hand, claimed that 'The cut worm forgives the plow', which seems extraordinarily unlikely.

Etymologically, it's hardly surprising that worms turn. *Worm* comes from the Proto-Indo-European *wer*, meaning *turn*, a reference to their bendiness. So a *worm turning* is not just appropriate, it's a tautology.

Worms have come a long way down in the world, as the word *worm* used to mean *dragon*. Then from a huge firebreathing monster they became mere *snakes*, and slowly they declined until they became the little things in your garden being chased around by a blackbird (or sliced up by William Blake). However, the *dragon*-meaning survived for centuries, and as late as 1867 William Morris could still write the wonderful line, 'Therewith began a fearful battle twixt worm and man', with a straight face.

The one constant in the etymological journey of the worm is that man doesn't like worms and worms don't like men. For a long time it was believed that garden worms could crawl into your ear, and as the Old English *wicga* could also mean worm, we get the strange modern formation *earwig*, even though an earwig is technically not a worm but an insect and has nothing to do with the sort of wig you wear on your head.[21]

There are only two places where worms have turned and maintained some of their former greatness. One is a *wormhole*,

---

[21] Although people do wear wigs in odd places. Seventeenth-century prostitutes used to shave their economic areas in order to get rid of lice, and then wear a special pubic wig called a *merkin*. And while we're on the subject of earwigs, ear-hair grows from a place medically known as the *tragus* because *tragos* was Greek for goat, and ear-hair resembles a goat's beard. Ancient Athenian actors used to wear goatskin when they acted in serious plays, which is why the plays came to be known *the songs of the goat*, or *tragedies*.

which used to mean exactly what you might expect until 1957 when the word was hijacked by the Einstein-Rosen Bridge, a theoretical connection between two parts of space-time implied, if not necessitated, by the Theory of Relativity.

The other is the fearsome crocodile, whose name comes from the Greek *kroke-drilos*, which means *pebble-worm*. Pebbles also play a crucial part in *calculus*, which means *pebble*.

Mathematics

Mathematics is an abstract discipline of such austere beauty that it's often surprising to find that its words and symbols have dull, concrete origins. *Calculus* is a formidable word that loses some of its grandeur when you realise that a *calculus* is just a little pebble, because the Romans did their maths by counting up stones.

Oddly, an abacus, which you might reasonably have expected to mean *little pebbles*, comes ultimately from the Hebrew word *abaq* meaning *dust*. You see, the Greeks, who adopted the word, didn't use pebbles; instead they used a board covered with sand, on which they could write out their calculations. When they wanted to start on a new sum, they simply shook the board and it became clear, like a classical Etch A Sketch.

Average has an even more mundane explanation. It comes from the Old French *avarie*, which meant *damage done to a ship*. Ships were often co-owned and when one was damaged and the bill came in for repairs, each owner was expected to pay the *average*.

A *line* is only a thread from a piece of *linen*, a *trapezium* is only a *table*, and a *circle* is only a *circus*. But the best of the mathematical etymologies are in the signs.

People didn't used to write 1 + 1, they would write the sentence *I et I*, which is Latin for *one and one*. To make the plus sign, all they did was drop the *e* in *et* and leave the crossed +. By coincidence, *ET* also gave us &, and you can see how &t became & simply by messing around with the typefaces on your word processor. Type an & and then switch the font to Trebuchet and you'll get &, to French Script MT and you'll get *&*, to Curlz MT and you'll get &, Palatino Linotype and you'll get & and finally, as this book is printed in Minion, you get &.

Most mathematics used to be written out in full sentences, which is why the equals sign was invented by a sixteenth-century Welshman who rejoiced in the name of Robert Recorde. Robert had got thoroughly bored of writing out the words *is equal to* every time he did a sum. This was particularly irritating for him, as he was writing a mathematical textbook with the memorable title, *The Whetestone of Witte whiche is the seconde parte of Arithmeteke: containing the extraction of rootes; the cossike practise, with the rule of equation; and the workes of Surde Nombers.*

But the prolixity of the title was matched by the brevity that the book brought to algebra. Recorde wrote:

… to avoid the tedious repetition of these words: is equal to: I will set as I do often in work use, a pair of parallels, or Gemowe lines of one length, thus: ==, bicause no 2 things, can be more equal.

So $=$ is an equals sign because the two lines are of *equal* length. Robert Recorde published his *Whetstone of ...* (see above) in 1557 and died in debtors' prison the following year, thus demonstrating the difference between good mathematics and good accounting.

Recorde thought that the two lines of $=$ were so similar that they were like identical twins, which is why he called them *gemowe*, meaning *twin*. *Gemowe* derived from the Old French *gemeaus*, which was the plural of *gemel*, which came from the Latin *gemellus*, which was the diminutive of *Gemini*.

Stellafied and Oily Beavers

The *zo*diac is, of course, the little circular *zoo* that runs around the sky. It's a *zoo*-diac because eleven of the twelve signs are living creatures and seven of them are animals. In fact, when the Greeks named the zodiac all of the signs were living creatures. *Libra*, the odd one out, was added in by the Romans.

The zodiac is filled with all sorts of strange word associations. *Cancer* is the *crab* largely because Galen thought that some tumours resembled crabs and partly because both words come from the Indo-European root *qarq*, which meant *hard*. Goats such as *Capricorn* skip about and are generally *capricious*, or *goatlike*. And bulls like *Taurus* get killed by *toreadors*. But let's stick, for the moment, to *Gemini*, the *twins*.

The twins in question are two stars called Castor and Pollux, and how they came to be there is a tender and touching story. Despite what astronomers would have you believe, most of the stars were created not by energy cooling into matter, but by Zeus.

Zeus had a thing for a girl called Leda and decided to turn into a swan and have his wicked way with her. However, later that night Leda slept with her husband Tyndareus. The result was a rather complicated pregnancy and Leda popping out two eggs, which is enough to make any husband suspicious.

The first egg contained Helen (of Troy) and Clytemnestra. The second egg contained Pollux and Castor. Extensive mythological paternity testing revealed that Helen and Pollux were the children of Zeus, and Castor and Clytemnestra were the mortal children of Tyndareus, which can hardly have been much of a consolation for the poor chap.

Castor and Pollux were inseparable until one day Castor was stabbed and killed. Pollux, who was a demi-god, struck a deal with his dad that he could share his immortality with his twin brother, and the result was that Zeus turned them into two stars that could be together for ever in the heavens (well, in fact they're sixteen light years apart, but let's not get bogged down in details).

Castor was the Greek word for *beaver*, and to this day beavers all across the world belong to the genus *Castor*, even if they don't know it. We usually think of beavers as sweet little creatures who build dams, but that's not how a constipated Renaissance man would view them; a constipated Renaissance man would view them as his relief and his cure.

You see, the beaver has two sacs in his groin that contain a noxious and utterly disgusting oil that acts as a very effective laxative. This very valuable liquid was known as *castor oil*.

The name survives, but the source of the liquid has changed. To the delight of beavers everywhere, people discovered in the mid-eighteenth century that you can get exactly the same bowel-liberating effect from an oil produced from the seeds of *Ricinus communis*, also known as the castor oil plant. So though it's still called castor oil, it's no longer obtained from the groin of a beaver.

Several anatomical terms derive from the beaver, but in order to keep this chain of thought decent and pure and family-friendly, let us for the moment consider that *beaver* was once a word for beard.

Beards

The number of hidden beards in the English language is quite bizarre. *Bizarre*, for example, comes from the Basque word *bizar* or *beard*, because when Spanish soldiers arrived in the remote and clean-shaven villages of the Pyrenees, the locals thought that their *bizars* were *bizarre*.

The feathers that were stuck into the back of arrows were known by the Romans as *the beard*, or *barbus*, which is why arrows are *barbs*, and that's ultimately the reason that *barbed* wire is simply wire that has grown a beard.

Barbus is also the reason that the man who cuts your beard is known as a *barber*. The ancient Romans liked to be clean-shaven, as beards were considered weird and Greek, so their barbers plied a regular and lucrative trade until the fall of the Roman empire. Italy was overrun by tribesmen who had huge long beards which they never even trimmed. These tribes-men were known as the *longa barba*, or *longbeards*, which was eventually shortened to *Lombard*, which is why a large part of northern Italy is still known as Lombardy.

The Romans by that time had become effete, perhaps through a lack of facial hair, and couldn't take their opponents on. If they had been more courageous and less shaven, they could have stood *beard to beard* against their enemies, which would have made them objectionable and *rebarbative*.

What the Romans needed was a leader like General Ambrose Burnside, who fought for the Union during the American Civil War. General Burnside had vast forests of hair running from his ears and connecting to his leviathan moustache. So extraordinary was his facial foliage that such growths came to be known as *burnsides*. However, Ambrose Burnside died and was forgotten, and later generations of Americans, reasoning that the hair was on the *side* of the face, took the name *burnside* and bizarrely swapped it around to make *sideburns*.

And it's not only humans that have beards, nor only animals. Even trees may forget to shave, namely the *giant bearded fig* of the Caribbean. The bearded fig is also known as the *strangler tree* and can grow to 50 feet in height. The beards and the height and the strangling are connected, for the tree reproduces by growing higher than its neighbours and then dropping beard-like aerial roots into their unsuspecting branches. The beards wrap themselves around the victim until they reach the ground, where they burrow in and then tighten, strangling the host.

There's an island in the Caribbean that's filled with them. The natives used to call it the *Red Land with White Teeth*, but the Spanish explorers who discovered it were so impressed with the psychotic and unshaven fig trees that they called it *The Bearded Ones*, or *Barbados*.

Islands

Some parts of the English language can only be reached by boat. For instance, there's a small dot in the middle of the Pacific Ocean whose natives called their home Coconut Island, or *Pikini*, which was mangled into English as *Bikini Atoll*.

For centuries nobody knew about Bikini except its natives, and even when it was discovered by Europeans, the best use that anyone could think of for the place was as a nautical graveyard. When a warship had outlived its effectiveness, it would be taken to the beautiful lagoon and sunk.

Bikini Atoll was put on the map (and almost removed from it) by America in 1946 when they tested their new atomic bombs there. *Atom* is Greek for *unsplittable*, but the Americans had discovered that by breaking the laws of etymology they were able to create vast explosions, and vast explosions were the best way of impressing the Soviets and winning the Cold War.

However, the tests at Bikini had a more immediate effect on the French and the Japanese – both, perhaps, illustrative of their national characters.

In 1954 the Americans tested their new hydrogen bomb, which they had calculated would be a little more powerful than the A-bombs they'd previously been mucking around with. It turned out to be an awful lot more powerful and ended up accidentally irradiating the crew of a Japanese fishing boat. Japanese public opinion was outraged, as the Japanese and Americans had a rather awkward military and nuclear relationship. Protests were made, hackles were raised, and a film was made about an irresponsible nuclear test that awoke a sea monster called *Gorilla-whale* or *Gojira*. The film was rushed through production and came out later in the same year. *Gojira* was, allegedly, simply the nickname of a particularly burly member of the film crew. *Gojira* was anglicised to *Godzilla*, and the film became so famous across the world that –*zilla* became a workable English suffix.

A bride-to-be who has become obsessed with every fatuous detail of her nuptials from veil to hem is now called a bride*zilla*, and one of the world's most popular internet browsers is Mo*zilla* Firefox, whose name and old logo can be traced straight back to the tests at Bikini Atoll.

But where the Japanese saw a threatening monster, the French saw what the French always see: sex. A fashion designer called Jacques Heim had just come up with a design for a two-piece bathing costume that he believed would be the world's smallest swimsuit. He took it to a lingerie shop in Paris where the owner, Louis Réard, proved with a pair of scissors that it could be even more scandalously immodest. The result, Réard claimed, would cause an explosion of lust in the loins of every Frenchman so powerful that it could only be compared to the tests at Bikini Atoll, so he called the new swimwear the *bikini*.

So by a beautiful serendipity, it's now possible to log on to the internet and use a Mozilla browser to look at pictures of girls in bikinis, knowing that the two words spring from the same event.

The word *serendipity* was invented in 1754 by Horace Walpole, the son of the first prime minister of England. He was kind enough to explain exactly how he had come up with the word. He was reading a book called the *Voyage des trois princes de Serendip*, which is a story of three princes from the island of Serendip who are sent by their father to find a magical recipe for killing dragons. Walpole noticed that 'as their highnesses travelled they were always making discoveries, by accidents and sagacity, of things which they were not in quest of'. Though the story of the three princes that Walpole read was pure fiction, the Island of Serendip was a real place, although it has since changed its name, first to Ceylon, and then, in 1972, to Sri Lanka. So a *serendipity* is really a *Sri-Lanka-ness*.

Now let us cross the Indian Ocean and head up the Suez canal to Sardinia. In fact, let's not, because the people of Sardinia are a nasty bunch. In ancient times they were considered so waspish and rebarbative that any unfriendly remark would be referred to as *Sardinian*, which is where we get the word *sardonic*. However, Sardinia also gave its name to the little fish that were abundant in the surrounding seas, which are now called *sardines*.

We *could* go to the island of Lesbos, but that wouldn't make us very popular. The most famous resident of Lesbos was an ancient Greek poetess called Sappho. Sappho wrote ancient Greek poems about how much she liked other ancient Greek ladies, and the result was that in the late nineteenth century *Lesbian* became an English euphemism for ladies who like ladies. The idea, of course, was that only people with a good classical education would understand the reference, and people with a good classical education would have strong enough minds not to snigger. In this, *lesbianism* was considered preferable to the previous English term, *tribadism*, which came from a Greek word for *rubbing*.

Before being adopted in the 1890s, *Lesbian* was the name of a kind of wine that came from the island, so you could drink a good Lesbian. Of course, it also was, and is, the name for the inhabitants of the island, not all of whom are happy with the word's new meaning. In 2008 a group of Lesbians (from the island) tried to take out an injunction against a group of lesbians (from the mainland) to make them change the name of their gay rights association. The injunction failed, but just to be on the safe side, let us sail our etymological ship out through the straits for Gibraltar and head for the islands where dogs grow feathers.

The Romans found some islands in the Atlantic that were overrun with large dogs. So they called them the *Dog Islands* or *Canaria*. However, when the English finally got round to inspecting the Canaria a couple of millennia later, all they found there were birds, which they decided to call *canaries*, thus changing dogs into birds (and then into a pretty shade of yellow). Now let's continue due west to get to the Cannibal Islands.

When Christopher Columbus sailed west across the Atlantic, he arrived at the Caribbean Islands, which he rather hopefully called the *West Indies* because the purpose of his voyage had been to find a western route to *India*, which everyone in Europe knew to be a rich country ruled by the Great Khan.

Columbus was therefore terribly pleased when he landed in Cuba and discovered that the people there called themselves *Canibs*, because he assumed that *Cani*bs must really be *Khani*bs, which was a rare triumph of hope over etymology. At the next island Columbus came to, they told him they were *Caribs*, and at the island after that they were *Calibs*. This was because in the old languages of the Caribbean, Ns, Rs and Ls were pretty much interchangeable.

The sea got named the *Carib*bean after one pronunciation. But it was also believed in Europe that the islanders ate each other, and this gastronomic perversity came, on the basis of another pronunciation, to be called *cannib*alism. Whether they did actually eat each other is a subject that is still disputed. Some say they did, others say that it was just a projection of European fears – and it's true that the European imagination was set humming by these stories of far-off islands. William Shakespeare's play *The Tempest* was set on a desert island where a strange half-man half-fish is the only true native. There definitely aren't any men-fish in the Caribbean, but that didn't stop Shakespeare from naming his bestial character *Calib*an after the third possible pronunciation.

But now we sail onwards through the Panama canal[22] to the last of our island chain, Hawaii, after which the world's most popular snack was almost named.

Sandwich Islands

The first European to stand on the shores of Hawaii was Captain James Cook, who arrived there in 1778 and died there in 1779 after an unsuccessful attempt to abduct the king. Captain Cook introduced the words *tattoo* and *taboo* into English, both having been practices that he came across in his Pacific voyages, but there was one name that he couldn't get into the dictionary, or even the atlas.

European explorers loved to name the places that they discovered, a habit that didn't always endear them to the natives,

---

[22] The neatest palindrome in English is undoubtedly: 'A man, a plan, a canal: Panama.'

who felt that they must have discovered the place first as they were already living there. So, although Cook noted down that the locals called his new discovery *Owyhee*, he knew which side his bread was buttered and decided to rename the place in honour of the sponsor of his voyage. Captain Cook was, of course, thinking of his future career (something that he should probably have considered when abducting the king), for Cook's sponsor was, at the time, the First Lord of the Admiralty: John Montagu, 4th Earl of Sandwich.

But the name *Sandwich* didn't stick, and Cook died before his sponsor could even hear of the attempt. The poor Earl of Sandwich has had to make do with the South Sandwich Islands (an uninhabited chain of rocks near the South Pole), Montague Island (an uninhabited island near Alaska), and every *sandwich* shop, *sandwich*-maker, and *sandwich* filling in the entire world. And he managed that latter feat without ever going near a breadknife.

The Earl of Sandwich was a gambler, and not just any sort of gambler. He was an addict who lost money hand over fist over hand over fist. Even by the British standards of the time he was considered a bit odd, and the British were famous for gambling. The first and only account of the origin of the world's favourite snack comes from a French book of 1765 about what terrible gamblers the English are. It runs thus:

The English, who are profound thinkers, violent in their desires, and who carry all their passions to excess, are alto-gether extravagant in the art of gaming: several rich noble-men are said to have ruined themselves by it: others devote their whole time to it, at the expense of their repose and health. A minister of state passed four and twenty hours at a public gaming table, so absorbed in play, that, during the whole time, he had no subsistence but a bit of beef, between two slices of toasted bread, which he eat without ever quitting the game. The new dish grew highly in vogue, during my residence in London: it was called by the name of the minister who invented it.

The author didn't mention the name of the minister, because he was a Frenchman writing for a French audience in French;[23] so there would be no point in his explaining the origin of an English word. It's therefore a delicious twist in the tale that *sandwich* is now one of the few English words that everybody in France knows too.

There's a myth that the Earl of Sandwich *invented* the sandwich. He did not. He had servants and chefs to actually make his food for him. Sandwich simply made sandwiches cool. People have almost certainly been stuffing things between two slices of bread since the stuff was invented around the end of the last ice age. What the Earl of Sandwich did was to take a humble little snack that you wouldn't think twice about, and give it associations of aristocracy, power, wealth, luxury and 24-hour gambling.

Great men and women do not busy themselves in the kitchen hoping to achieve the immortality that can be conferred by a recipe book. They simply wait until a food is named after them. Take Margherita Maria Teresa Giovanna, Queen of

---

[23] In case you were wondering, the quotation reproduced here comes from a 1772 translation. From the fact that it doesn't even feel the need to mention sandwiches, we can assume that everybody in England now knew the name.

Italy and wife of Umberto I. She never climbed Mount Stanley, but Mount Stanley's highest peak still bears her name. She certainly never cooked any pizzas: they were made for her, and they had to be fit for a queen.

Italian aristocrats of the nineteenth century didn't eat pizza. It was peasant food, flavoured with that peasant favourite: garlic. However, in the 1880s, European royalty, wary of revolution, were all trying to be nice to the common men whom they ruled. So when King Umberto and Queen Margherita visited Naples, the home of the pizza, a man named Raffaele Esposito decided to make a pizza fit for the lips of the queen.

Esposito was the owner of the Pizzeria di Pietro e Basta Così, and he got over the garlic problem by simply not using any garlic, an idea that was previously unheard of. He then decided to make the pizza properly patriotic and Italian by modelling it on the colours of the flag: red, white and green. So he added tomatoes for the red (nobody had done this before), mozzarella for the white, and herbs for the green. He then named it *Pizza Margherita* and sent it, in June 1889, to the queen.

To be honest, Queen Margherita probably didn't deign to eat the first margherita, but she did have one of her servants write a note saying thank you. Thus has her name become immortal, and a coded version of the Italian flag is on the menu of every pizza restaurant in the world.

The Italian flag consists of three vertical stripes. This design is based on *le Tricolore*, the flag of the French Revolution.

The French Revolution in English Words

When the world changes, language changes. New things need new words, and the new words of a period betray the inventions of the age. The Vietnam War gave American English *bong* and *credibility gap*.

You can follow the history of the English-speaking world by watching the new words flow by. The forties gave us *genocide, quisling, crash-landing, debrief* and *cold war*. The fifties gave us *countdown, cosmonaut, sputnik* and *beatnik*. The sixties gave us *fast food, jetlag* and *fab*. And so on through *Watergate, yuppie, Britpop* and *pwned*.

But nothing has ever been as new as the French Revolution, which was essentially a mob of new ideas armed with pitchforks and intent on murder. Every new event, every new idea, had to be rendered for the English-speaking world in new words that were being imported from the French. Each twist, turn, beheading and storming was reported a few days later in Britain and the course of history can be seen in the words that were imported from French.

1789 *aristocrat*
1790 *sans culottes*
1792 *capitalist, regime, émigré*
1793 *disorganised, demoralised* (meaning *made immoral*), *guillotine*
1795 *terrorism* (meaning *government by terror*)
1797 *tricolore*

And the *tricolore*, as we know, would survive both as a flag and a pizza topping. Moreover, the French contribution to the English language, which had been going on for centuries, would continue for centuries more.

About 30 per cent of English words come from French, though it depends, of course, on how you're counting. This means that, though English is basically a Germanic language, we are, at least, one third romantic.

Romance Languages

French is a *romance* language, because the French are, by definition, *romantic*.

Once upon a time there was a thing called the Roman empire that was ruled by Romans in Rome. However, the language they spoke was not called Roman; it was called Latin.

The Roman empire was a grand affair. They had lots of great authors, like Virgil and Ovid, who wrote books in Latin. They also had a frighteningly efficient army that spread death and Latin to every part of the known world.

But empires fall and languages change. Six hundred years ago, Chaucer could write 'al besmotered with his habergeon', but it's difficult today to make out what he meant, unless you've studied Chaucerian English.

The same thing happened to the Romans and their Latin. There was no sudden break, but little by little their language changed, until nobody in Rome could understand the great Roman authors any more, unless they had studied Latin at school. Slowly, people had to start distinguishing the old Latin from the language that people were speaking on the streets of Rome, which came to be known as *Romanicus*.

The Dark Ages darkened and the difference between Latin and Romanicus grew larger and larger. Latin was preserved in a way. Classical Latin, or something very like it, became the language of the Catholic Church and of academic discourse. If you wanted to write something that would be taken seriously by a pope or a professor you had to do so in Latin. Even as late as 1687, Isaac Newton still needed to call his great work *Philosophiae Naturalis Principia Mathematica* and publish it in Latin.

Yet in the Middle Ages, most people didn't want to read books about theoretical theology. They wanted stories about knights in shining armour and beautiful damsels in distress. They wanted fire-breathing dragons, enchanted mountains and fairylands beyond the oceans. So such stories got written by the bucketful, and they were *romanice scribere*, that is to say they were *written in Romanic* (the *–us* had been dropped by this stage).

Not all versions of Romanic were the same. There was the Romanic that had developed in Rome, another one in France, another in Spain, another in Romania. But *Romanic* became the catch-all term for all these languages and then for all the stories that were written in them.

Then lazy people stopped pronouncing the *i* in *Romanic* and the stories and the languages in which they were written stopped being *Romanic* and started to be *romances*.

And that's why, to this day, stories of brave, handsome knights and distressed damsels are called *romances*; and when somebody tries to reproduce the atmosphere of such a tale by taking moonlit walks, or lighting candles at dinner, or remembering birthdays, they are being *romantic* or *Roman*.

Peripatetic Peoples

One word that has absolutely nothing to do with *Roman*, *romance* or *Romania* is *Romany*. The people who have for centuries travelled around Europe in caravans have had an awful lot of names, and all of them are insanely inaccurate. The most common name given to them by suspicious house-dwellers is *gypsy*, a name that derives from the utterly false idea that they are from E*gyp*t.

Gypsy and *Egyptian* used to be completely interchangeable words. Shakespeare, in *Antony and Cleopatra*, refers to Cleopatra's 'gypsy lust' in the very first speech. So where did this idea come from?

The Romany ended up being called Egyptians because of a single event in 1418, when a band of them arrived in Augsburg claiming to be from 'Little Egypt'. What exactly they meant by this is unclear, but they wanted money and safe conduct, which was given to them by the authorities and then denied them by the people. The Egyptian idea caught on, and a legend grew up that the Roma were cursed to wander the Earth because when Joseph, Mary and Jesus were obliged to escape the wrath of Herod by fleeing to Egypt, a local tribe had denied them food and shelter. The gypsies, it was reasoned, were the descendants of this tribe, condemned to suffer the same fate for all eternity.

In fact, the Roma are not from Egypt but from India. We know this because their language is more closely related to Sanskrit and Hindi than to anything else. The word *Roma* comes from *Rom*, their word for *man*, which derives ultimately from *domba*, a Sanskrit term for a kind of musician.

That hasn't stopped the legends of their origin spreading, though. The Egyptian mistake has been perpetuated in Hungary, where they were known as *Pharaoh-Nepek*, or *Pharaoh's people*. But different countries have different legends and names, all of which are untrue. In Scandinavia they were thought to be from Tartary and were called the *Tatars*, in Italy it was Walachia and *Walachians*.

The Spanish believed that the Romany were Flemish Belgians. Why they thought this is something of a mystery. Most of the other European mistakes were at least based on the idea that the Roma had come from somewhere eastern and exotic. Indeed, one theory runs that the Spanish were only joking. Whatever the reasoning, the Spanish started to call both the Roma and their style of music Flemish, or *Flamenco*.

The French thought that they must come from Bohemia (now the Czech Republic) and called them *Bohemians*. Then, in 1851, a penniless Parisian writer called Henri Murger came to write about life in the city's Latin Quarter. He decided that the scorn that most of his fellow artists felt for convention made them social Bohemians. So he called his novel *Scènes de la vie de bohème*. The word caught on. Thackeray used it in *Vanity Fair*, and Puccini took Murger's book and turned it into an opera called *La Bohème*. And that's why unconventional and insolvent artists are known to this day as *Bohemians*.

From Bohemia to California (via Primrose Hill)

Bohemia holds a special place in literary geography. The third scene of the third act of Shakespeare's *The Winter's Tale* occurs upon the shores of Bohemia. Indeed, the first line makes sure of it:

> Thou art perfect, then, our ship has touched
> Upon the deserts of Bohemia?

What is so special about that? Well, let's jump forward by a century and quote *Tristram Shandy*:

> … and there happening throughout the whole kingdom of
>   Bohemia to be no sea-port town whatever—
> —How the deuce should there, Trim? cried my uncle Toby; for
>   Bohemia being totally inland, it could have happened no
>   otherwise.
> —It might, said Trim, if it had pleased God.

Whether or not it pleased God, the fallacious notion that Bohemia isn't landlocked pleased Shakespeare, and Bohemia gained in fiction what it never had in fact. Never? Well, almost never. Uncle Toby doesn't seem to know that Bohemia did get a tiny bit of territory on the coast of the Adriatic for a short period in the late thirteenth century, and again in the early sixteenth.

Shakespeare almost certainly didn't know that Bohemia had ever been anything other than landlocked. Shakespeare

didn't give a damn about geography. In *The Tempest*, Prospero
is abducted from his palace in Milan and bundled down to the
docks under cover of darkness. Seventy-four miles overnight is
a good bit of bundling in the days before the Ferrari. Not that
that bothered the Bard. He had people sailing from Verona and
a sail-maker working in Bergamo, an Italian town that's over a
hundred miles from the nearest port.

Writers these days devote their time to research, Shakespeare
devoted his to writing. He set a whole play in Venice, apparently
unaware that there were any canals there; at least he never mentions any, and whenever the city pops up he refers to it as a *land*,
even though it's in the sea.

Shakespeare seems never to have consulted a map, and anybody who feels too sniffy about that can, like Cleopatra, go and
hang themselves from the top of the pyramids. After all, fiction
is only fact minus time. If the polar ice caps keep melting the
sea will, eventually, come to Verona, to Milan and finally to
Bergamo. Then the Sun will expand and the Earth, in a few
billion years' time, will be a parched and burning rock, and the
charred bones of Shakespeare, resting in their grave, will be
vindicated because all the canals in Venice will be dry.

The poet A.E. Housman took the same attitude with his
poem 'Hughley Steeple'. In a letter to his brother he wrote:

> I ascertained by looking down from Wenlock Edge that
> Hughley Church could not have much of a steeple. But as
> I had already composed the poem and could not invent
> another name that sounded so nice, I could only deplore
> that the church at Hughley should follow the bad example
> of the church at Brou, which persists in standing on a plain

after Matthew Arnold said [in a poem called 'The Church at Brou'] that it stands among mountains.

A French playwright called Alfred de Vigny once wrote a play set in London about the doomed poet Chatterton. Apparently it's a rather good play if you're French, but any Londoner is bound to snigger when Chatterton's friends set off to hunt wild boar on Primrose Hill, which is a small park in a rather leafy little suburb. However, Primrose Hill adjoins London Zoo, so it would only take a loose railing or two to render de Vigny right, and Londoners endangered.

Under the tutelage of time, nonsense becomes geography. The Greeks believed in a country called *Amazonia* filled with fierce female warriors that never existed. Then, a couple of thousand years later, an explorer called Francisco de Orellana was attacked by angry women during a voyage up a big South American river, so he called it the *Amazon*. Or take the case of the utterly fictional island of *California*.

California

The first description of California was written in Spain in about 1510, which is odd because, at the time, no European had been to the western coast of the Americas. But fiction usually beats fact to the punch.

The description was written by Garci Rodriguez de Montalvo, and the reason that he was able to write it with such authority was that California was an entirely fictional place.

Montalvo wrote and compiled stories of high and wonderful chivalry. He had knights in gleaming armour, dragons, sorcerers, maidens in distress, and wonderful exotic locations that he populated with fantastic creatures. In his fourth book, the *Exploits of Esplandian*, he invented a strange island that was near to the lost Garden of Eden.[24]

Montalvo wrote:

> Know that on the right hand from the Indies exists an island called California very close to a side of the Earthly Paradise; and it was populated by black women, without any man existing there, because they lived in the way of the Amazons. They had beautiful and robust bodies, and were brave and very strong. Their island was the strongest of the World, with its cliffs and rocky shores. Their weapons were golden and so were the harnesses of the wild beasts that they were accustomed to domesticate and ride, because there was no other metal in the island than gold.

This gives you some idea of Montalvo's imagination, and also of why the promise of these strong-bodied, sex-starved ladies might have appealed to the lusty Spanish explorers who were sailing off to the New World. We know that Christopher Columbus' son owned a copy of Montalvo's work, and Cortés, the first European to enter the Pacific, referred to it in a letter of 1524. What's more, the place we now call California was thought to be an island at the time.

---

[24] Just to keep you informed, the Garden of Eden, being perfect, was assumed not to have been destroyed in Noah's flood, but to have been washed far away to some inaccessible place where it could no longer be found.

Of course, California was never actually an island, but owing to a mistake by an exploratory monk, European map-makers believed that it *was* an island from the sixteenth century up until about 1750. How the explorers got it so wrong is unclear,[25] but as late as 1716 an English geographer was able to write:

> *California*
> This Island was formerly esteem'd a peninsula, but now found to be intirely surrounded by Water.

Which is good enough for me, and it was good enough for the Spaniards who were deciding what to name this temperate paradise. The explorers decided to name it after the magical land of ferocious (and attractive) women who had appeared in Montalvo's chivalric fantasy.

Montalvo called his island *California* because it was ruled by a beautiful queen called *Calafia*. In the *Exploits of Esplandian*, Calafia has been persuaded to bring her army of ferocious (and attractive) women, plus some trained griffins, to fight alongside Muslims and against Christians at the siege of Constantinople. However, Calafia falls in love with Esplandian, is defeated, taken prisoner and converts to Christianity. Then she returns to the island of California with her Spanish husband, and her trained griffins.

There are several theories as to why Montalvo chose the name *Calafia*, but by far the most convincing is that, as she was fighting alongside Muslims, her name was chosen to suggest or

---

[25] I refer the curious reader to Seymour Schwartz's *The Mismapping of America*, whose detailed account of the mistake I have tried, and failed, to compress.

echo the title of the Muslim leader: the *Caliph*. So California is really, ultimately, etymologically the last surviving *Caliphate*.

The Caliphate, a sometimes factual and sometimes formal union of all Islamic states, was abolished by the Young Turks of Turkey in 1924. Recently there have been strenuous and violent attempts to revive the Caliphate by Al Qaeda. However, if a troop of crack etymologists could be sent into terrorist strongholds, they could gently explain that the Caliphate never disappeared: it's alive and well and is, in fact, the most populous state in America.

The Hash Guys

Even without California complicating the matter, the question of who should be Caliph and what counts as the Caliphate has been a tricky one ever since the Prophet Mohammed died. The first *khalifa* was a fellow called Abu Bakr who had been one of the first converts to Islam. However, after a few years, some folk decided that it shouldn't have gone to him and that the position should, instead, have been handed down to Mohammed's son-in-law and thence to his grandson and so on and so forth from one eldest son to the next. These people were called the Shia, and the others were called the Sunni.

However, heredity in principle always leads to dispute in practice, and so in 765 AD, when one of the descendants of Mohammed disinherited his eldest son, Ismail, the Shias themselves split into two. There were those who agreed that Ismail should be passed over and there were those who didn't. These latter were called the Ismailis.

The Ismailis did rather well for themselves. They managed, in the ninth century, to conquer most of North Africa and they sent out lots of undercover evangelists to the rest of the Islamic world. These evangelists converted people in secret until there was a huge network of secret Ismailis who were, perhaps, going to help to establish an Ismaili Caliphate once and for all.

But they didn't, because the Sunnis invaded North Africa, burnt all the Ismaili books and converted everybody straight back to the first form of Islam at the point of a scimitar. Now all the Sunnis needed to do was to root out the Ismaili converts in their home territory and everything would be fine and dandy.

So the Ismailis had a hard time of it. They were tracked down and persecuted and fined and put to death and all the other lovely things that mankind likes to do to his neighbour. They couldn't fight the persecution because, though there were a lot of them, they were scattered about here and there and couldn't raise an army. Then an Ismaili called Hasan-i Sabbah had a brilliant idea.

He seized one single, solitary castle near the Caspian Sea. It wasn't a strategically important castle, as it was at the top of a remote mountain at the end of a remote mountain valley in a remote region. But for all these reasons the castle of Alamut was essentially invincible and unattackable. From this base Hasan let it be known that if any Ismailis got persecuted he would respond: not by fighting the soldiers or taking territory or anything like that – he would simply send one of his disciples out to kill the one man, the senior official who had ordered the persecution; and what's more, the killing would be done with a golden dagger.

And they did. The first chap they killed was the Vizier of the Caliphate himself, and then they picked people off left, right and centre. Two things (other than the gold dagger) made them utterly terrifying. The first was that they would get into their target's entourage as sleeper agents and were prepared to work for years as stable boy or servant just to get close enough to the victim. You could hire bodyguards, but how did you know the bodyguards weren't killers themselves? The second was that they were quite prepared to suffer death afterwards, indeed they saw it as a bit of a bonus. They would kill their targets and then kill themselves, confident in the promise of paradise.

Nobody knew what to make of them, but the general opinion was that they were all on hashish. This is almost certainly untrue, but the name stuck. They were the *hash guys*, or in the colloquial Arabic plural, the *hashshashin*.

Religious fervour fades but gold always gleams, and when the Crusaders arrived in the Middle East they made contact with the Syrian branch of the Ismailis, in a second mountain fortress that was run by the Old Man of the Mountain. The Old Man agreed to hire out the services of his disciples to the Christian invaders, who were immensely impressed by their fatal fanaticism and discipline. Stories of the hashshashin got back to Europe, where the Arabic H was dropped and the hash-guys became the *assassins*.

It wasn't long before *assassin* had been verbed into *assassinate*, and then all you needed was William Shakespeare to invent the word *assassination* for his play *Macbeth*:

If it were done when 'tis done, then 'twere well
It were done quickly: if the assassination

Could trammel up the consequence, and catch
With his surcease success …

But, etymologically speaking, assassination will always be the *cannabisation* of the victim, or the *marijuanafication* or the *potification*, or whatever synonym you want to use for dope.

Drugs

Dope is a terrible thing, and is particularly bad for racehorses. Drug a racehorse just a little bit and you ruin his performance, which is why it's absolutely necessary for a betting man to know in advance which horses have been doped and which are clean-living and ready to win. Such a gambler is said to *have the dope on* a race: the inside knowledge of which runner has *gone to pot*.

Pot itself has nothing to do with pots and pans, but comes from the Mexican-Spanish word *potiguaya*, which means marijuana leaves. And *marijuana* is a Mexification of *Mary Jane* for reasons that everybody is much too stoned to remember. Another Mexican part of drug language is *reefer*, which comes from *grifo*, a word for a drug addict south of the border.

In fact, the vocabulary of drugs is as exotic as their origins. The assassins would, if they did smoke hashish, have done so through a *hookah*, a small pot through which the intoxicating vapours are allowed to bubble. When American troops took up doing the same thing during the Vietnam War, they took the local Thai word for a hookah, *buang*, and turned it into *bong*.

Of course, the terminology of drugs is a matter of dispute, legend and stoned supposition. Nobody is *utterly* sure whether a joint is something smoked in an opium *joint*, or whether it's something that's shared and therefore is *jointly* owned. Nor does anybody have any idea why people from 1920s New Orleans called joints *muggles*, but it sheds an interesting new light on the Harry Potter novels (another of Rowling's characters is called *Mundungus*, which is an archaic word for low-grade tobacco). Whoever invented the word *spliff* didn't bother to write down why.

Dope itself was originally a kind of thick sauce called *doop* into which Dutch people would *dip* pieces of bread. The sense transferred over to drugs only when people started smoking a thick and gloopy preparation of opium. Given that Amsterdam's dope cafes have now become famous throughout the world, it's a little disappointing that any high you might receive from the original Dutch *doop* would be a placebo effect.

Pleasing Psalms

Placebo is Latin for *I will please*, and its origins are not medical, but religious.

From the beginning of the nineteenth century a *placebo* has been a medical term for a 'medicine adapted more to please than to benefit the patient'. Before this, a *placebo* was any commonplace cure that could be dreamt up by a barely qualified medic. The point was not that that pill would please, but that the doctor would. For long before *placebo* medicines there was *Dr Placebo*.

In 1697, a doctor called Robert Pierce recalled rather bitterly how he was always being beaten to new business by a charming and talentless medic whose name he was either too polite or too scared to write down. He called him instead *Doctor Placebo*, and noted with tragic jealousy that Placebo's 'wig was deeper than mine by two curls'.

Whoever the original Dr Placebo was, his nickname was taken up by various other embittered doctors of the eighteenth century, until *placebo doctors* had given *placebo pills* with *placebo effects*.

At this point things get a little misty, because although *placebo* does mean *I will please*, the word was originally associated not with cures, but with funerals. There's nothing so much fun as a good funeral, and anybody who's truly fond of a good party will tell you that the death rate is much too low, even though it adds up to 100 per cent in the end. The drink doled out at a wake has a certain morbid lavishness to it that is rarely or never found at christenings.

People probably still do turn up at the funerals of those they never knew, just in order to get their hands on some booze, but the practice was much more common in medieval times. People would put on their best clothes and turn up to the funerals of the rich, taking part in the service in the hope of joining in the wake.

This meant that they would all stand silent while the first nine verses of Psalm 114 were sung. Then, as it was an antiphon, and as they all wanted to seem particularly enthusiastic about the deceased, they would lustily sing the ninth verse back to the presiding priest:

Placebo Domino in regione vivorum

Which means:

I will please the Lord in the land of the living

In the *Ayenbite of Inwit* ('The Prick of Conscience') from the mid-fourteenth century, the author observes that 'the worst flattery is that one that singeth placebo'. Chaucer chimes in by saying that 'Flatterers [are] the Devil's chaplains that singeth ever Placebo'.

So the psalm led to the funeral, which led to the flatterers, which led to the flattering doctors, which led to the placebo pill.

This may all seem rather unlikely, and some etymologists are more inclined to go straight to the Latin *I will please*, but the psalms were much more important in the Middle Ages than they are today, and they have given us all sorts of words that we might not expect. *Memento* became famous because it was the first word of Psalm 131:

Memento Domine David et omnis mansuetudinis eius

Lord, remember David and all his afflictions

Even more obscure is the connection between the psalms and the phrase *to pony up* or pay.

Consider that 25 March is the end of the first quarter of the year, and was thus the first pay day for those who were paid quarterly. 25 March was therefore a good day for everybody except employers, and nobody likes them anyway.

People would wake up on 25 March, toddle along to church for Matins, and sing the psalm with avaricious expectation in their heart. The psalm for that day is the fifth division of Psalm 119, which is the longest psalm in the Bible and needs to be broken up into bite-size chunks. The fifth division begins with the words:

> Legem pone mihi Domine viam iustificationum tuarum et exquiram eam semper

> Teach me, oh Lord, the way of thy statutes; and I shall keep it unto the end

Legem pone therefore became a slang word for a down-payment, because in the psalm-obsessed medieval mind it was the first two words of pay-day. In the centuries since then, the *legem* has been dropped, but that doesn't mean that the phrase has disappeared. If you have ever been asked to *pony up*, it's only a corruption of *legem pone* and a reference to the praises of pay.

Biblical Errors

Some people say that the Bible is the revealed word of God, which would imply that God spoke English. There's even a society in America that believes the King James Version was given to mankind by divine revelation, and it has a big ceremony once a year in which other versions of the Bible are piled up and burnt.

It's certainly true that the King James Version was a lot more accurate than Myles Coverdale's attempt of a hundred years before. Myles Coverdale was an early Protestant who believed in principle that the Bible should be translated into English. He decided that, as nobody else seemed to be doing it, he had better get on with the job himself, and he didn't let the tiny detail that he knew no Latin, Greek or Hebrew get in his way. This is the kind of can-do attitude that is sadly lacking in modern biblical scholarship.

Coverdale did know a bit of German, though, and the Germans, who had invented Protestantism, had already started preparing their own translation. Coverdale threw himself into his work and produced a Psalter that is still used in Church of England services today. It is, though, much more beautiful than it is accurate. For example, he has the line:

> The strange children shall fail: and be afraid out of their prisons.

It's beautiful and mysterious. Who are the strange children? What's so strange about them? And what on earth are they doing in prison? The answer is that the line should be translated as:

> The foreign-born shall obey: and come trembling from their strongholds.

But the best of Coverdale's mistranslations is about Joseph, whose neck, we are told in Psalm 105, was bound in iron. The problem is that Hebrew uses the same word for *neck* as it does for *soul*. The word is *nefesh*, and it usually means *neck* or *throat*, but it can mean *breath* (because you breathe through your neck), and it can also mean *soul*, because the soul is the breath of life. (You have the same thing in Latin and English with *spirit* and *respiratory*.)

If Coverdale had made only one mistake, English would have been given the phrase, *His soul was put in iron*. But Coverdale was never a man to make one mistake when two would do; so he mixed up the subject and the object and came up with the wonderfully inappropriate and nonsensical: *The iron entered into his soul*.

And yet somehow that phrase works. It may have nothing to do with the original Hebrew, but Coverdale's phrase was so arresting that it caught on. Nobody cared that it was a mistranslation. It sounded good.

Even if the translation of the Bible gets it right, English-speakers can still get it wrong. *Strait*, these days, is usually used to describe a narrow stretch of water like the *Bering Straits* or the *Straits of Gibraltar*, but, if you think about it, other things can be *strait*. *Straitjackets* are small jackets used to tie up lunatics. People who are too tightly laced-up are *strait-laced*. If a gate is hard to get through, then it's a *strait gate*, and the hardest gate to pass through is the gate that leads to heaven:

Because strait is the gate, and narrow is the way, which leadeth unto life, and few there be that find it.

Which is why it's not *the straight and narrow* but *the strait and narrow*.

Finally, *the salt of the earth* is a biblical phrase that has managed to almost reverse its meaning. These days, the salt of the earth are the common folk, the working men and women, the ordinary Joes on the Clapham omnibus; but if that were the case, then the earth would be much too salty to taste good.

When Jesus invented the phrase *the salt of the earth*, he meant exactly the opposite. The world was filled with sinners and pagans, and the only reason that God didn't destroy it utterly was that the few people who believed in Him were like salt to earth's stew.

> Ye are the salt of the earth: but if the salt have lost his savour, wherewith shall it be salted? it is thenceforth good for nothing, but to be cast out, and to be trodden under the foot of men.

This is strange, as Jesus was later crucified by a bunch of Roman *salt-men*.

Salt

Nobody is certain where the word *soldier* comes from, but the best guess is that it has to do with salt. Salt was infinitely more valuable in the ancient world than it is today. To the Romans, salt was white, tasty gold. Legionaries were given a special stipend just to buy themselves salt and make their food bearable; this was called the *salarium* and it's where we get the English word *salary*, which is really just *salt-money*. The Roman writer Pliny the Elder therefore went so far as to theorise that *soldier* itself derived from *sal dare*, meaning *to give salt*. There's nothing intrinsically wrong with this theory, but as Pliny the Elder was a little bit of a nutjob, it should probably be taken with a *pinch of salt*, which, like the salt of the earth, makes something easier to swallow.

Mainly, though, salt is not military but culinary. Salt gets into almost every food, and into an awful lot of food words. The Romans put salt into every single one of their sauces and called them *salsa*. The Old French dropped the L and made this *sauce*, and they did the same with Roman *salsicus*, or salted meats, that turned into *saucisses* and then into *sausages*. The Italians and Spanish kept the L and still make *salami*,[26] which they can dip into *salsa*, and the Spanish then invented a saucy dance of the same name.

So necessary is salt to a good meal that we usually put it on the table twice. The Old French used to make do with a *salier* or *salt-box* on the table at mealtimes. The English, who are always trying to work out how the French make such delicious food, stole the invention and took it back home. However, once the *salier* had been removed from France, people quickly forgot the word's origin and how it should be spelt. So we ended up changing *salier* to *cellar*. Then, just to be clear what was in the cellar, we added *salt* onto the beginning and called it a *salt cellar*, which is, etymologically, a *salt-salier* or *salt-salter*.

The Romans would have used a *salt-salter* to season their vegetables and make *herba salata*, which we have since short-ened to *salad*. This brings us to a strangely salty coincidence involving the good old days. In *Antony and Cleopatra* the Egyptian queen talks of her

salad days,
When I was green in judgment …

---

[26] The Spanish call theirs *salchichón*, which clearly shows the link to *salsicus*.

And the phrase has now taken up residence in the language. We use *salad days* as a synonym for *halcyon days*, which by an odd coincidence also means *salty days*.

Halcyon Days

People talk nostalgically of the halcyon days. They hanker and pine, and in the midst of their hankering they ask if we shall ever see such halcyon days again.

We shall.

The Halcyon Days begin each year on 14 December and last until the 28th, and like the salad days they are, etymologically, very salty. This time the salt is Greek, and so the prefix we're looking for is *hal–*, the same *hal* in fact that you find in the salt-producing chemicals known as *halo*gens.

Indeed, halcyon and halogen are etymologically almost identical: the one gives birth to salt, the other is a salty conception. That's because *halcyon* is another word for the kingfisher, and kingfishers lay their eggs at sea.

For a full and accurate explanation of all this, we shall have to turn to the Roman poet Ovid who explained it all in his *Metamorphoses*. Once upon a time there was a boy called Ceyx and a girl called Halcyon who fell madly in love. Unfortunately, Ceyx had to go away to sea and Halcyon would wait for him every day on the beach, gazing at the horizon and longing for her lover's return.

Halcyon continued this vigil until she was informed, by the utterly reliable medium of a dream, that Ceyx's ship had sunk and he had been drowned. At this news she got so upset that she fell ill and died a couple of days later; or, as Chaucer put it in one of his most beautiful couplets:

Alas! She said for very sorrow
And died within the thridde morrow.

Everybody was very upset by the whole business including the gods, who got together and decided that the least they could do for the poor couple was to turn them into birds. So Ceyx and Halcyon were raised from the dead and covered in feathers, and that's where kingfishers come from.

Because Halcyon had spent so long gazing out to sea, that's where she now lays her eggs in a little floating nest; and, just to make sure she's not disturbed, the gods have arranged that the winds should be light during her nesting season, which lasts through the second half of December. This fortnight of good weather is therefore known as the Halcyon Days.

Of course, modern biologists scoff at Ovid's story and dismiss it purely on the basis that it isn't true. However, poetry is much more important than truth, and, if you don't believe that, try using the two methods to get laid.

Dog Days

The Dog Days, like the Halcyon ones, are a precisely defined part of the year, or at least they were once. The second brightest star in the sky (after the Sun) is Sirius, the Dog Star, so called because it's the largest star in the Great Dog constellation, Canis Major. However, during the height of summer you can't see the Dog Star because it rises and sets at the same time as the Sun. The ancient Greeks worked out that this happened from 24 July to 24 August, and they noticed that this was also the most unpleasantly hot time of the year. So they, quite logically, decided that it must be the combined rays of the Sun and the Dog Star that were causing the trouble. They also thought a lot about how to cool down. The ancient Greek writer Hesiod has this advice:

In the season of wearisome heat, then goats are plumpest and wine sweetest; women are most wanton, but men are feeblest, because Sirius parches head and knees and the skin is dry through heat. But at that time let me have a shady rock and wine of Biblis, a clot of curds and milk of drained goats with the flesh of an heifer fed in the woods, that has never calved, and of firstling kids; then also let me drink bright wine, sitting in the shade, when my heart is satisfied with food, and so, turning my head to face the fresh Zephyr, from the ever-flowing spring which pours down unfouled, thrice pour an offering of water, but make a fourth libation of wine.

It's well worthwhile memorising that passage and reciting it to a waiter on the first of the Dog Days. However, you must be careful, as, owing to the precession of the equinoxes, the Dog Days have slowly shifted over the last two thousand years and now begin around 6 July, although it depends on your latitude.

None of this has anything whatsoever to do with the notion that every dog will have his day, which comes from *Hamlet*:

Let Hercules himself do what he may,
The cat will mew and dog will have his day.

We call it the Dog Star, the Romans called it *Canicula* (meaning *dog*)[27] and the Greeks called it *Sirius*, which meant *scorching*, because of the heat of the Dog Days. However, the Greeks also sometimes referred to it as *Cyon* (the Dog), and the star that rises just before Sirius is still called *Procyon*; and that same Greek word for dog – *cyon* – also gave the English language the word *cynic*.

Cynical Dogs

The Cynics were a school of ancient Greek philosophy, founded by Antisthenes and made famous by his pupil Diogenes.

Diogenes was, by any standards, an odd chap. He lived in a barrel in the marketplace in Athens and used to carry a lamp about in broad daylight, explaining that he was trying to find an honest man. His one worldly possession was a mug that he used for drinking. Then one day he saw a peasant scooping water up with his hands and immediately threw his mug away. Accounts of his death vary, but one story is that he held his breath.

Cynic meant *doglike*. But why was Diogenes' school known as *the dogs*?

There was a *gymnasium* near Athens for those who were not of pure Athenian blood. A gymnasium in ancient Greece wasn't exactly the same thing as a gymnasium today. For starters, it was

---

[27] The French still call a heatwave *une canicule*.

an open-air affair. It was more of a leafy glade than a building filled with parallel bars and rubber mats. People did do their physical training at the gymnasium, in fact they did it naked. The word *gymnasium* comes from the Greek *gymnazein*, meaning *to train in the nude*, which itself comes from *gymnos*, meaning *naked*. But if you could take your mind off the naked boys (which many Greek philosophers found difficult), gymnasiums were also places for socialising and debating and teaching philosophy. Diogenes' gymnasium was known as the Gymnasium of the White Dog or *Cynosarge*, because a white dog had once defiled a sacrifice there by running away with a bit of meat.

Diogenes, not being a native Athenian, was forced to teach in the Dog's Gymnasium, which is how one hungry and ownerless canine gave his name to a whole philosophical movement. A fun little result of this is that any cynical female is, etymologically speaking, a bitch.

Greek Education and Fastchild

If Cynics are dogs, the Stoics were the *porch philosophers* because their founder Zeno taught in the painted porch or *Stoa Poikile* of the Great Hall in Athens. If you didn't like either the Stoics or the Cynics you could go out to a grove that was named after a hero of the Trojan War called *Akademos*. It was in the grove of *Akademeia* that Plato taught, and all *academies* since are named after it, which means that the *Police Academy* films are all named after a hero of the Trojan War via Plato.

The Athenians, as you can tell, were jolly philosophical chaps. This was largely because they had a wonderful education system in which the Greek children, or *paedos*, were taken through the whole cycle, or *cyclos*, of learning. Their knowledge was therefore *en-cyclo-paedic*.

The Romans were so impressed with the way Greek children were taught all these different subjects that they started writing books called *encyclopaedias* that were meant to contain articles on every topic there was. Then, two thousand years later, the internet was invented.

The internet works on computers, and computers work on all sorts of different programming languages. These programming languages tend to be rather complicated things that are hard to learn and, even for initiates, slow to use. So in 1994 a chap called Ward Cunningham developed a system of making related webpages that would be very simple and very fast. Because it was so quick, he called it *wikiwikiweb*, because *wiki* is Hawaiian for *fast* and the reduplication *wikiwiki* therefore means *very fast indeed*.

Soon, though, people decided that *wikiwiki* was a bit of a mouthful, and so it was colloquially shortened to *wiki*. That was the state in which Larry Sanger found the word in 2001, when he had the idea of a collaborative, web-based encyclopaedia that would use the wiki system. He took the words *wiki* and *encyclopedia* and mashed them together to form *Wikipedia*, which is now the seventh most visited website in the world. However, few among its 365 million readers know that *Wikipedia* means *Fastchild*. Fewer still will have considered the fact that anyone who likes Wikipedia is technically and etymologically a *Wikipedophile*.

Cybermen

These days, if you aren't *wiki* or *cyber* or *virtual*, you are nothing. You might as well give up and make do with real life, which mankind has been trying for thousands of years without success.

Cyberspace is out of control and filled with cybersquatters having cybersex with cyberpunks. This would make more sense if anybody actually knew what *cyber* meant, and the answer may come as a shock to cyberpunks, because *cyber* means *controlled* – indeed, it comes from the same root as *governed*.

Back in the 1940s there was a man called Norbert Wiener who was studying how animals and machines communicated with and controlled each other. He decided to call his field of study *cybernetics* after the Greek word for a steersman. A steersman controls the boat that he's in: in Greek, he *cubernans* it. From this the Romans got the idea that a governor who steers the ship of state *gubernans* it. Even though the B has been replaced by a V in the modern *governor*, things that belong to the governor are still *gubernatorial*.

Meanwhile, *punk* was an early twentieth-century American term for a homosexual, specifically the young and pliable companion of an elderly and implacable hobo. From there, *punk* turned into a generalised insult and then was taken as a badge of honour by noisy rockers in the 1970s. However, an etymologist can still look at the term *cyberpunk* and wonder what these well-governed homosexuals are up to.

Another word that has switched its meaning entirely is *virtual*. Virtual reality, in case you didn't know, is reality that isn't real. It's *virtually real*, though that's not much better than being *virtually pregnant*. But what really bothers the etymologist is that very few of the things that happen in virtual reality are in the slightest bit *virtuous*.

If one thing is *virtually* another, it's because it shares the same *virtues*. Of course, *virtues* here don't have to be moral virtues, they can be physical ones. If I'm virtually asleep, then I'm not asleep but possess the same physical virtues as somebody who is. A virtue doesn't have to be good: a *virtu*oso torturer isn't a good man, he's just good at his job. It's the sense of virtue that survives in the phrase *by virtue of*.

Even though you can now achieve things *by virtue of dishonesty*, *virtue* used to be a much better thing. Courage, strength, honesty and generosity all used to be virtues, although few of those survive in virtual reality. In the ancient world, a virtue was anything that was commendable in a person. Well, I say person, but I mean man.

Women can't be virtuous. A virtue is *that which is proper to a man*. The Latin for *man* was *vir*, and *virtus* was the Latin word for *manliness*. *Virtue* is basically the same thing as *virility*.

So if a woman were to be virtuous she would become a manwoman, which is a terrible idea. A man-woman might be so bold as to have her own opinions. She might even express them, at which point she would become a *vir*ago.

To be fair, *virago* was originally a word for a heroic woman; but that's still rather sexist, as it implies that heroism is a purely manly quality. In fact, language is irredeemably sexist; but that's not my fault, it's the Romans'. Look at their attitude to women in the workplace.

Turning Trix

Meretricious is an odd little word that lots of people get wrong. It sounds a little like *merit* and, as merit is a good thing, you would take a guess that *meretricious* means, well, *meritable*.

It doesn't. *Meretricious* means *showy*, *gaudy* and *contemptible*. However, the *meret* in *meretricious* is the same Latin root that you find in *merit*. The only difference is that it's women who are doing the meriting.

When the Romans wanted to point out that somebody was female, they would put a *trix* on the end on the word. It's a habit that has largely died out, but you still find it occasionally. A female aviator is sometimes an *aviatrix*, a female editor can be an *editrix*, and a lady who is paid to dominate men is a *dominatrix*.

There used to be more trixes – a *tonstrix* was a female hairdresser – but they slowly died out. Back in ancient Rome, though, they didn't like women having jobs at all. In fact, almost the only women who had jobs in Rome were the women who stood in front of brothels looking for customers. The Latin for *standing in front* of things is *pro-stitutio*.

It was a way of earning a living, almost the only one for a girl, and the Latin for earning was *merere*. When a man earned a living he *merited* it, and became *meritable*. A veteran soldier who had retired to spend his money could proudly call himself *emeritus*, meaning that he had *earned* all he needed and retired, which is where we get Emeritus Professors.

That's because a soldier was a man. But when a girl earned a living she was a *meretrix*, and *meretrix* could mean only one thing: tart. And that's why *meretricious* still means *tarty*.

Amateur Lovers

The opposite of *meretricious* can be found hidden away in the game of tennis, where the true nature of love can also be discovered. But first, a brief note on the word *tennis*. It's not called that, you know. The proper term for the game played at Wimbledon is *sphairistike*.

The rules of tennis as we know them were set down by a man called Major Walton Clopton Wingfield back in the 1890s. Tennis had been played before, of course – Shakespeare refers to the game several times – but it had always been played by kings and princes in the courtyards of palaces. It wasn't until the invention of the lawnmower in the nineteenth century that people were able to play on lawns. Major Walton Clopton Wingfield wanted to distinguish his new game from the old tennis, which came from the French word *tenez*, meaning *hold!* So he lighted on the name *sphairistike*, which is ancient Greek for *ball-skill*.

Sphairistike became wildly popular, but there was one hitch: nobody knew how the hell to pronounce it. Did it rhyme with *pike*? Or with *piquet*? In fact, it rhymed with *sticky*; but nobody knew that. So rather than make fools of themselves by getting it wrong, people just decided to call it *lawn tennis* and to hell with Major Walton Clopton Wingfield and his Greek.

Wingfield did keep the scoring system of the old tennis, though, and it's there that we may find the true nature of love. You may have heard that *love* in tennis is a corruption of the French *l'oeuf*, meaning *egg*, because an egg looks a bit like a zero. This is a myth.[28] *Love* is *nothing* because those who do something for the love of it do it for nothing. For example, people either marry for money or connections, or for love. Love therefore became a synonym for nothing, because if you do something purely for love, you get nothing. By 1742 this notion of *love* being *zero* had been taken across to games and sports. In fact, the first known reference is to the score in whist.

Love in tennis is therefore the exact opposite of prostitution. It's the celebration of the *amateur*. *Amare* is the Latin for *love*, from which we get *amiable*, *amorous* and *paramour*. And if you were doing something for your paramour, you wouldn't charge for it, would you? As late as 1863, a man could still write that he was 'not an amateur of melons', which simply meant that he didn't like them.

The distinction between amateur and professional is merely a distinction between those who love what they do, and those who do it because they are paid. Unfortunately this means that all lovers are rather amateurish. They can't help it, it's built into the etymology.

Love is much better than money. You should be afraid of money – that's what *money* means.

---

[28] It is, though, true in cricket, where a zero was referred to as a *duck's egg*, which then got shortened to *duck*.

Dirty Money

Money is a monster, etymologically speaking. It all comes down to the Latin word *monere*, and even though the connection is accidental it's probably still significant.

Monere was Latin for *warn*, and if you have a pre-*monition* you are forewarned. In the ancient world they believed that horrible beasts were omens of disasters. The idea was that just before the fall of an emperor or the loss of a great battle, centaurs, griffins and sphinxes would come out of wherever they were hiding and roam around in full view. These unnatural creatures, composed of the parts of other animals, were therefore called *warnings*, or *monsters* (*monstrum*, from *monere*).

However, if you need a warning and can't afford a centaur, geese will do just as well. People still keep guard geese because they kick up a fearsome racket if they spot an intruder and they can also be pretty vicious. You should never say boo to a goose, not unless you're prepared for a fight. The Romans kept guard geese on the Capitoline Hill. This came in useful when Rome was attacked by the Gauls in 390 BC, so useful in fact that the Romans put up a temple in thanksgiving. But being ungrateful sods they didn't dedicate it to geese, they dedicated it to Juno, the goddess of warnings, or *Juno Moneta*.

Next door to the temple of Juno Moneta was the building where all the Roman coins were produced. In fact, the coins may have been made in part of the temple itself. Nobody is quite sure, and the sources are rather vague. What is certain is that the coin-producing building got named after the temple. It was the *Moneta*, and though we've changed all the vowels, we still call such a building a *mint*.

In the Moneta, they produced *moneta*: literally *warnings*. The French took the word and dropped the T so that it was already *money* when it arrived in English. However, our adjective *monetary*, meaning *related to money*, keeps the reference to the temple and the angry geese alive and well.

It's only by an accident of propinquity that *money* is a *monster*. Perhaps you shouldn't worry about it at all. Money's not that bad. You shouldn't be so frightened. Go on, take out that *death-pledge*. Sorry: *mortgage*.

Death-pledges

Anyone who has ever taken out a mortgage will be unsurprised to learn that it is, literally, a *death-pledge*. However, it's the sort of thing you would only usually notice if you were taking out a mortgage on a *mort*uary. *Mort* is death, and *mort*al man has nothing else waiting for him. Nothing is certain in this life except death and mortgages.

The reason a mortgage is called a death-pledge is that it can die in two ways. You can pay off the whole thing, in which case the deal dies and you own your house. However, that happy ending is far from certain in these troubled and impoverished times. The other possibility is that you fail to make a payment, the deal dies, and your house is repossessed. The whole thing was spelt out in *mort*ifying terms in the *Institutes and Laws of England* in 1628:

It seemeth that the cause why it is called mortgage is, for that it is doubtful whether the Feoffor will pay at the day limited such summe or not, and if he doth not pay, then the Land which is put in pledge vpon condition for the payment of the money, is taken from him for euer, and so dead to him vpon condition, etc. And if he doth pay the money, then the pledge is dead as to the Tenant, etc.

There are a lot of hidden deaths in English. Many people will have noticed the similarity between the words *executive* and *executioner*, but what have the two got in common? Is it that an executioner is just somebody who executes the sentence, just as an undertaker is someone who undertakes to bury you? No. The original legal term for execution was *execute to death*, from the French *exécuter à mort*. So you execute the sentence until they die.

Another hidden *mort* comes in the word *caput*. Monks used to remind themselves of their own mortality by contemplating a skull. This was called a *death's head* or *caput mortuum*, and the original owner of a *caput mortuum* was definitely *caput*. It's enough to make you scream *blue murder*, which is a direct translation of the French phrase *mort bleu*, which itself is a non-blasphemous form of *mort dieu*, or *death of God*.

The *gage* in *mortgage* is much more cheerful. It means *pledge* and is exactly the same *gage* that you find when you fall in love and get *engaged*. It's also very closely related to *waging* war.

Wagering War

You can't really *wage* anything other than *war*. You can try, but it sounds rather odd. Indeed, the phrase *waging war* gets stranger the more you look at it. Does it have anything to do with wages, or wage disputes, or maybe freeing the wage slaves? There's a connection between all these different *wages*, and indeed to *wagers*. But you have to go back to the fourteenth century.

A *wage* was, originally, a *pledge* or *deposit*. *Wage* is simply a different way of pronouncing the *gage* in mort*gage* and en*gage*-ment.[29] A wage was something given in security. From this *wage* you quite easily get to the modern *wager*: it's merely the stake, or deposit, thrown down by a gambler. It's also reasonably simple to see how *money given in security* could end up meaning *money given as pay*. But waging war? That involves trial by combat.

In medieval law it was considered quite reasonable to settle a legal dispute by duelling to the death. Though somebody had to die in this system and there was no guarantee of justice, lawyers' fees were at least kept to a minimum.

A wronged medieval man would throw down his *gage/wage* (or pledge), and challenge his opponent to trial by combat. In Latin that was *vadiare duellum*; in French it was *gager bataille*; in English you *waged* [pledged yourself to] *battle*.

Not war. *Battle*. It was, after all, a technical legal term for the violent resolution of individual arguments. You *wagered* your body in mortal combat. However, it's easy to see how the sense

---

[29] The medievals often mixed up their Gs and Ws, which is why another word for *guarantee* is *warranty*.

of *waging battle* extended from the promise of violence to the act of violence.

In the end, when two countries couldn't agree, they started *waging war* against each other. This last shift in meaning could reasonably be described as *wage inflation*.

Strapped for Cash

Why are people so often *strapped for cash*?

Being strapped for cash is actually a good thing. If you're falling down and you need something to hang on to, a strap is good. If you fall overboard, it's a good thing if somebody throws you a strap. And if you've fallen from the ship of solvency and are drowning in a sea of debt, then you very much want somebody to throw you a strap. Of course, it means that you're currently in debt, but to be strapped for cash is better than to have no cash at all.

Oddly, the same metaphor has been invented twice. These days, when a bank is about to go bankrupt, the government throws them a *lifeline*. This means that the bank survives, although they are still strapped for cash.

Incidentally, *bank* comes from an old Italian word for *bench*, because money-lenders used to sit behind a bench in the marketplace from which they would do their deals. If a money-lender failed to make good on one of his arrangements, his bench would be ceremonially broken, and the old Italian for a broken bench was *banca-rotta* or *bankrupt*.

Fast Bucks and Dead Ones

So almost every form of money involves death, danger and destruction. A frightened word-lover might start to wish that the stuff had never been invented at all. It is, after all, possible to run a society without any money. America, which is now the land of the *fast buck*, had no money until European colonists arrived.

Well, almost. On the coasts of the North-East they used clam shells called *wampums* that could be threaded together into necklaces, and in Mexico they used coffee beans as a standard by which to barter; but the point, essentially, stands. There were no coins, no notes, no green and folding pictures of presidents.

This presented a problem to those colonists who wanted to trade. The natives looked on coins and banknotes with a mixture of scorn and confusion. What were they meant to do with that? You couldn't wear it round your neck, you couldn't even make a nice cup of coffee from it.

Early attempts at trading involved tobacco. Tobacco made a lot more sense than coins. With tobacco the peace pipe could be pulled out, and if you combined it with the coffee beans of Mexico you might feel almost civilised. But of course tobacco needs to be weighed out, and it's rather bulky. The harvests go up and down, causing sudden inflation and deflation, and you need a warehouse to store it in.

So the traders eventually gave up on tobacco and moved to another staple item that everybody knew and valued: deerskins. A deerskin can be slapped over the saddle of a horse, it's thin and light, and when you're not spending it you can use it to keep warm. Buckskins soon became the standard unit of barter in North America, and a standard unit of barter is, in effect, money. So it was buckskins, or *bucks* for short, that were used for trade.

With this in mind, let us turn to Conrad Weiser, the first man ever to *make a buck*. He was born in Germany in 1696, but his family, being Protestant, were forced to flee to Britain in 1709. There they were held in a refugee camp just outside London before being sent to populate the colonies on the Hudson River. In 1712, when Conrad was sixteen, his father took the rather extraordinary step of sending his son to live with the Mohawk tribe for half a year. Conrad learnt the language and the customs of the Iroquois and started an illustrious career as a diplomat for the British among the native tribes of America.

Despite having fourteen children, Conrad still found the time to negotiate most of the significant treaties between the British and the disgruntled tribes and convince them that their real enemies were the French. In 1748 Conrad was sent into Ohio to negotiate with the tribes of the Five Nations. His mission had several purposes. One was to make peace and seek amends after the murder of some colonists. In this he succeeded. The tribal council told him that:

> … what was done we utterly abhor as a thing done by the Evil Spirit himself; we never expected any of our People wou'd ever do so to our Brethren [the British]. We therefore remove our Hatchet which, by the influence of the Evil Spirit, was struck into your Body, and we desire that our Brethren the Gov. of New York & Onas may use their utmost endeavours that the thing may be buried in the bottomless Pit.

… which is one of the earliest references to *burying the hatchet*. The next item on the agenda, though, was rather more tricky. It involved rum. Specifically, it involved a request that the British would stop selling rum to the Ohio Indians. To this Weiser replied that:

> … you never agree about it—one will have it, the other won't (tho' very few), a third says we will have it cheaper; this last we believe is spoken from your Hearts (here they Laughed). Your Brethren, therefore, have order'd that every cask of Whiskey shall be sold to You for 5 Bucks in your Town, & if a Trader offers to sell Whiskey to You and will not let you have it at that Price, you may take it from him & drink it for nothing.

And that is the very first reference to a *buck* as a unit of American currency. The deal was then finalised with a belt of wampum.

This was good news for American trade, but bad news for American deer. However, it was all about to get much worse for the American buck. Not content with their skins, the Americans were about to make a phrase out of their horns.

The Buck Stops Here

You might assume that *passing the buck* has something to do with passing a dollar to the person next to you. This is not so. After all, passing a dollar would hardly shift responsibility to someone. The only thing that these two *bucks* have in common is a dead deer.

Not, of course, that you pass a whole animal. That would be ridiculous. The phrase *to pass the buck* simply involves another part of the buck's corpse.

Deer don't have a good time in language. Their entrails are put into pies and their skins are used in lieu of currency; one of the few parts of the buck deer that remains is the horn. Waste not, want not.

A buck's horn makes a very pleasant-looking knife handle, and a knife has many uses. You can cut up venison with a knife, or you can skin another deer and make a fast buck. You can also use a knife to mark the dealer in a game of poker by stabbing it into the table in front of whoever currently has responsibility for handing round the cards.

This isn't done much by people who value their furniture, but in the Wild West life and woodwork were cheap, and the first reference to *passing the buck* comes from the diary of a 'border ruffian' during the fight for Kansas in 1856. On approaching a place called Buck Creek, he says that 'we remembered how gladly would we "pass" the Buck as at "poker"'.

This is odd because the dealer usually has a slight advantage in poker. However, among the border ruffians of the Wild West the dealer probably stood a good chance of being shot, as, if you suspect there's cheating going on, the dealer is the first chap you should murder.

So bucks were passed without cease until the 1940s when they finally stopped in a prison in El Reno, Oklahoma. The prison governor had decided that all responsibility ended with him. He dealt, and the prisoners received. So he had a sign put up in his office saying that 'THE BUCK STOPS HERE'.

Of course, the buck didn't really stop there. The prison governor had to answer to the state government and then to the federal government and then to the President, with whom the buck would grind to a final and undeniable halt. This point was not lost upon an aide to Harry S. Truman who visited the prison and saw the sign. He liked it so much that he had a replica made. He gave it to President Truman, who put it up in his office and made the phrase famous.

So are all bucks really deer? Almost.

Back to Howth Castle and Environs

So the humble buck-deer is the source of all things *buck*, with one exception. *Buckwheat*, which looks like it should be the wheat that bucks eat, has nothing whatsoever to do with deer.

The leaves of buckwheat look very similar to the leaves of a beech tree. The German for *beech* is *Buche* and so *buckwheat* is really *beechwheat*.

Beech trees were important to the ancient Germans. Beechwood is thick-grained and not splitty (to use woodworking terminology), so it's easy to carve things in it, and that's exactly what the Germans used to do. Beech, *buche* or *bok*, as it was called in Old High German, was the standard material for writing on. Even when wood was finally overtaken by the newfangled invention of parchment, the Germans kept the name, and so did the English. *Bok* became *boc* became *book*.

This is a book. The glorious insanities of the English language mean that you can do all sorts of odd and demeaning things to a book. You can cook it. You can bring a criminal to it, or, if the criminal refuses to be brought, you can throw it at him. You may even take a leaf out of it, the price of lavatory paper being what it is. But there is one thing that you can never do to a book like this. Try as and how you might, you cannot turn up for it. Because a *turn-up for the books* [continued on page 1]

Quizzes

In Lewis Carroll's book *Through the Looking Glass, and What Alice Found There* (often erroneously referred to as *Alice Through the Looking Glass*), Humpty Dumpty tells Alice: 'There's glory for you.'

'I don't know what you mean by "glory,"' Alice said.

Humpty Dumpty smiled contemptuously. 'Of course you don't – till I tell you. I meant "there's a nice knock-down argument for you!"'

'But "glory" doesn't mean "a nice knock-down argument",' Alice objected.

'When I use a word,' Humpty Dumpty said, in rather a scornful tone, 'it means just what I choose it to mean – neither more nor less.'

'The question is,' said Alice, 'whether you can make words mean so many different things.'

However, as the greatest joy a human being can achieve in this sorrowful world is to get one up on his or her fellow man or woman by correcting their English, and as I have spent far too long consulting dictionaries, here's a list of some common English words and what the dictionaries say they actually mean:

Burgeon – To bud
Blueprint – The absolutely final plans that are sent to the factory
Backlash – The small period of inactivity when a system of cogs is reversed

Celibate – Unmarried

Compendium – Brief summary

Condone – Forgive

Coruscate – To glow intermittently

Decimate – To reduce by 10 per cent

Enormity – Crime

Effete – Exhausted

Fulsome – Over the top

Jejune – Unsatisfying

Noisome – Annoying

Nauseous – Causing nausea

Pleasantry – Joke

Pristine – Unchanged

Refute – To utterly disprove

Restive – Refusing to move (obviously)

Scurrilous – Obscene

Swathe – The area of grass cut with one stroke of a scythe

As you will have learnt from the preceding stroll through the English language, it's almost impossible to guess where a word has come from or where it's going to go to. So here, just to puzzle you, are a series of quizzes in which you have to guess where a word has come from or where it's going to go to.

We shall start with some names of famous people. Except that I haven't given you the names, I've given you the etymological meaning. So, for example, if I were to write *God of war and man of peace*, the answer would be me, Mark Forsyth, because *Mark* comes from *Mars*, the Roman god of battles, and *Forsyth* is Gaelic for *man of peace*. Got that? Good. Let us begin. (Answers below.)

Politicians of the last hundred years

1. Blessed, handsome and crooked (US President)
2. Courageous cabbage (European politician)
3. Noble wolf who lives in a hut (Second World War)
4. God loved the ugly-face (US President)
5. Blessed one from Mosul (Second World War)

Music

1. God loves a mud-caked, travelling wolf (composer; clue: *wolves*)
2. My little French lady (female pop star; clue: *my lady*)
3. Loud war in the vegetable garden (composer; clue: *he wouldn't have heard it anyway*)
4. Tattooed javelin-thrower (female pop star; clue: *another word for javelins*)
5. The dwarf in the priest's garden (male rock star; clue: *middle name Aaron*)

Glamour

1. Victorious goatherd (actress; clue: *baby goat*)
2. Christmas councillor (actress; clue: *odd name as she's Israeli*)
3. Cruel twin (actor; clue: *a kind of missile*)
4. The moon at the ford of blood (supermodel; clue: *----ford*)
5. He who listens among the cows (TV; clue: *cow---*)

Writers

1. Little Richard's husband (nineteenth-century novelist)
2. Good Christian (twentieth-century novelist)
3. Virile wonder (seventeenth-century poet)

4.   Pants-maker in a peaceful land (fourteenth-century poet)
5.   Tiny foreign snake (twentieth-century novelist)

And the answers are:

Politicians of the last hundred years

1.   Blessed, handsome and crooked = **Barack Hussein Obama**
      Barack is Swahili for *blessed. Hussein* is Arabic for *handsome. Obama* is Dholuo for *crooked.*

2.   Courageous cabbage = **Helmut Kohl**
      Nobody is quite sure what the *hel* means, but *mut* is definitely *brave* and *kohl* is *cabbage.*

3.   Noble wolf who lives in a hut = **Adolf Hitler**
      Adolf is *edel wolf,* which means *noble wolf,* and so far as anyone can tell, a *hitler* is just somebody who lives in a *hut.*

4.   God loved the ugly-face = **JFK**
      John comes from the Latin *Johannes* which comes from the Hebrew *y'hohanan,* which means *Jahweh has favoured. Kennedy* comes from the Irish *O Cinnéide,* which means *ugly head.*

5.   Blessed one from Mosul = **Benito Mussolini**
      Benito means *blessed* and *Mussolini* means *muslin,* because his ancestor was probably a merchant who dealt in muslin. However, *muslin – mussolina* in Italian – gets its name from Mosul in Iraq, where it was believed to be made.

Music

1. God loves a mud-caked, travelling wolf = **Wolfgang Amadeus Mozart**

    Wolf gang is German for a *travelling wolf*, *Amadeus* is Latin for *loved* (*ama*) by *god* (*deus*), and *Mozart* comes from the Allemanic *motzen* meaning *to roll about in the mud*. It was originally an insulting term for somebody dirty.

2. My little French lady = **Madonna Ciccone**

    Ma donna is Italian for *my lady*. *Ciccone* is an augmentative of *Cicco*; but *Cicco* is a diminutive of *Francesco*. So it means *little Francis*, and *Francis* means *French*.

3. Loud war in the vegetable garden = **Ludwig van Beethoven**

    Lud means *loud*, *wig* means *war*, and a *beet hoven* is a *garden* that grows the vegetable *beet*.

4. Tattooed javelin-thrower = **Britney Spears**

    Britney was a surname meaning *British*. *Britain* comes from *prittanoi*, which means *the tattooed people*. *Spears* is a shortening of *spearman*.

5. The dwarf in the priest's garden = **Elvis Presley**

    So far as anybody can tell, *Elvis* comes from *Alvis*, a dwarf in Viking mythology. *Presley* is a variant of *Priestly* and means *one who lives in land belonging to a priest*.

Glamour

1. Victorious goatherd = **Nicole Kidman**

    Nicole is the feminine of *Nicholas*. *Nicholas* is from the Greek *nike laos*. *Nike* means victory (as in the trainers) and *laos* means people. A *kidman* is a man who looks after the *kid goats*.

2.   Christmas councillor = **Natalie Portman**
     Natalie is related to *natal* and comes from the day of Jesus' birth, or *dies natalis*. A *portmann* in Old English was a townsman elected to administrate the affairs of a borough.

3.   Cruel twin = **Tom Cruise**
     Thomas comes from the Semitic *toma* meaning *twin*, and *Cruise* comes from the Middle English *crus* meaning *fierce* or *cruel*.

4.   The moon at the ford of blood = **Cindy Crawford**
     Cindy is a variant of *Cynthia*, which was an epithet of Artemis and meant *moon*. *Craw* or *cru* was Gaelic for *blood*, and *ford* is *ford*.

5.   He who listens among the cows = **Simon Cowell**
     Simon is often and justifiably confused with the identical ancient Greek name *Simon*, which meant *snub-nosed* (as in *simian*). However, our Christian *Simon* comes from a different root: *Symeon*. It's from the Bible and the Hebrew *shim'on*, which means *listening*. *Cowell* is just *cowfield*.

Writers

1.   Little Richard's husband = **Charles Dickens**
     Charles is from the German *karl*, which meant either *man* or *husband*. *Dickens* is a diminutive of *Dick*, which is short for *Richard*.

2.   Good Christian = **Agatha Christie**
      Agathos was ancient Greek for *good*. *Christie* means
      Christian.

3.   Virile wonder = **Andrew Marvell**
      Andreios was ancient Greek for *manly*. *Marvell* means
      marvel.

4.   Pants-maker in a peaceful land = **Geoffrey Chaucer**
      Geoffrey comes from the Latin *Gaufridus*, which in turn
      comes from the Old German *gewi*, land, and *fridu*, peace-
      ful. *Chaucer* is from Old French *chaucier* meaning *man
      who makes chausses*. *Chausses* could refer to almost any-
      thing worn on the lower half of the body.

5.   Tiny foreign snake = **Evelyn Waugh**
      Evelyn is a double-diminutive of *Eve*, so it's *tiny Eve*. In the
      Bible, *Eve* – *hawah* – is said to come from Hebrew *havah*,
      she who lived; however, this looks rather like a folk etymol-
      ogy and the word is suspiciously similar to *haya*, which is
      Aramaic for *serpent*. *Waugh* probably comes from *wahl*,
      which is the Old English for *foreigner*.

Now, a quick trip around the capital cities of the world. Can
you make out the modern names from the original meanings?
For example, if I were to say *Place of the Bad Smell*, you would
immediately realise that I was referring to the Objibwa *Shika
Konk*, which developed into our *Chicago*. To make it guessable,
we shall stick to capital cities.

Europe
Merchant harbour
Place by an unfordable river
Wisdom
Smoky bay
Black pool

Africa
Three cities
Victorious
New flower
The place of cool waters
End of an elephant's trunk

Asia
Muddy confluence
Modern
Garden
Anchor
Father of a gazelle

The Americas
Good winds
I saw a mountain
Peace
Place of many fish
Traders

And the answers are:

Europe
Merchant harbour – Copenhagen
Place by an unfordable river – London
Wisdom – Sofia (although Athens is named after Athena, goddess of wisdom, so give yourself half a pat on the back for that)
Smoky bay – Reykjavik
Black pool – Dublin

Africa
Three cities – Tripoli
Victorious – Cairo
New flower – Addis Ababa
The place of cool waters – Nairobi
End of an elephant's trunk – Khartoum

Asia
Muddy confluence – Kuala Lumpur
Modern – Tehran
Garden – Riyadh
Anchor – Ankara
Father of a gazelle – Abu Dhabi

The Americas
Good winds – Buenos Aires
I saw a mountain – Montevideo
Peace – La Paz
Place of many fish – Panama

Traders – Ottawa

And for those familiar with London, can you guess the Tube Station from its origin?

Forge
Horse pond
Beer gate
Lace collar
Skin farm
Road to Ecgi's weir
Padda's farm
Dominican monks
Stream in a sacred wood
Sacred place that welcomes strangers

Forge – Hammersmith
Horse pond – Bayswater
Beer gate – Aldgate (ale gate)
Lace collar – Piccadilly
Skin farm – Hyde Park
Road to Ecgi's weir – Edgware Road
Padda's farm – Paddington
Dominican monks – Blackfriars
Stream in a sacred wood – Waterloo
Sacred place that welcomes strangers – Walthamstow

And finally, some multiple choice. What is the true derivation of each of these words?

Clue

a) A ball of yarn
b) A skeleton key
c) A love letter

Karaoke

a) Japanese for *singing under water*
b) Japanese for *howling*
c) Japanese for *empty orchestra*

Slogan

a) An Algonquian prayer
b) A Celtic war-cry
c) Russian for *repetition*

Boudoir

a) French for *sulking room*
b) French for *gun room*
c) French for *Peeping Tom*

Grocer

a) One who buys in gross
b) One who grows his own
c) One who is grossly fat

Hotbed

a) A medieval form of torture
b) A Victorian medical treatment
c) A covered flowerbed

Bollard

a) Tree trunk

b) Cricket ball

c) Dr Cornelius Bollard

Kiosk

a) Aztec word for *umbrella*

b) Turkish word for *palace*

c) Burmese word for *hut*

Quarantine

a) Forty days

b) Asking time

c) Pseudo-prison

Bigot

a) Old English for *By God*

b) Old French for *thorn*

c) Old German for *stone wall*

Thesaurus

a) A riddling lizard from Greek mythology

b) A treasure chest

c) The book of Theseus

Beetle

a) Little biter

b) Little bean

c) Little bee

Aardvark

a) Swahili for *grandmother*

b) Dutch for *earth pig*

c) Croatian for *Jesus*

Pundit

a) Hindi for *wise man*

b) Irish for *counsellor*

c) Eskimo god of riddles

Winging it

a) Flying when the engine has failed

b) Eating only the chicken wings (and not the breast)

c) An actor learning his lines in the wings

Quiz

a) Latin for *who is?*

b) Hindi for *unclaimed property*

c) Chinese for *escape*

The answers:

Clue

a) A ball of yarn

Karaoke

c) Japanese for *empty orchestra*

Slogan

b) A Celtic war-cry

Boudoir

a) French for *sulking room*

Grocer

a) One who buys in gross

Hotbed

c) A covered flowerbed

Bollard

a) Tree trunk

Kiosk

b) Turkish word for *palace*

Quarantine

a) Forty days

Bigot

a) Old English for *By God*

Thesaurus

b) A treasure chest

Beetle

a) Little biter

Aardvark

b) Dutch for *earth pig*

Pundit

a) Hindi for *wise man*

Winging it

c) An actor learning his lines in the wings

Quiz

a) Latin for *who is?*

The Cream of the Sources

A book like this would need a bibliography at least twice its own size; so in the interests of paper preservation, there isn't one.

I can, though, assure you that everything in here has been checked, mainly against the following works:

The Oxford English Dictionary
The Oxford Dictionary of Place Names
The Oxford Dictionary of English Surnames (Reany & Wilson)
The Dictionary of Idioms by Linda and Roger Flavell
The Dictionary of National Biography
Brewer's Dictionary of Phrase and Fable

And online:

The Online Etymology Dictionary
Phrases.org.uk

And (with vast circumspection):

Dear old Wikipedia (or *Fastchild*)

Unfortunately, there are many points on which these sources disagree. Usually, rather than take you carefully through all of the arguments and counter-arguments, I have simply picked the one that I believe is most likely and recounted that.

All other things being equal, I have trusted them in the order in which they are listed above. However, if a good citation is produced then I am quite prepared to side with the underdog.

Occasionally, I've given citations that you won't find in any work of reference because I've found them all by myself. So for confused scholars who suspect me of making things up as I go along:

'Draw a blank': *The History of Great Britain*, Arthur Wilson (1643)

'Blank cheque': *An Inquiry into the Various Systems of Political Economy*, Charles Ganilh (1812)

'Talk cold turkey': *One of Three*, Clifford Raymond (1919)

'Crap' and 'Number one': *Poems in Two Volumes*, J. Churchill Esq. (1801)

'Dr Placebo': *Bath Memoirs*, Robert Pierce (1697), quoted in *Attempts to Revive Antient Medical Doctrines*, Alexander Sutherland (1763) and elsewhere

'Pass the buck': *The Conquest of Kansas*, William Phillips (1856)

Published in November 2012:

The Horologicon

– which means 'a book of things appropriate to each hour' – follows a day in the life of unusual, beautiful and forgotten English words.

From the moment you wake to the second your head hits the pillow, there's a cornucopia of hidden words ready for every aspect of your day.

From encounters with office *ultracrepidarians*, lunchtime *scamblers* and six o'clock *sturmovschinas* to the post-work joys of *thelyphthoric grinagogs* and *nimtopsical nympholepsy*, Mark Forsyth unearths words that you didn't even know you needed.

ISBN 978-184831-415-3

£12.99

THE
HOROLOGICON

THE
HOROLOGICON

A Day's Jaunt
Through the Lost
Words of the English
Language

MARK FORSYTH

ICON

Published in the UK in 2012 by
Icon Books Ltd, Omnibus Business Centre,
39–41 North Road, London N7 9DP
email: info@iconbooks.net
www.iconbooks.net

Sold in the UK, Europe, South Africa and Asia
by Faber & Faber Ltd, Bloomsbury House,
74–77 Great Russell Street,
London WC1B 3DA or their agents

Distributed in the UK, Europe, South Africa and Asia
by TBS Ltd, TBS Distribution Centre, Colchester Road,
Frating Green, Colchester CO7 7DW

Published in Australia in 2012
by Allen & Unwin Pty Ltd,
PO Box 8500, 83 Alexander Street,
Crows Nest, NSW 2065

ISBN: 978-184831-415-3

Typeset in Minion by Marie Doherty

Printed and bound in the UK by Clays Ltd, St Ives plc

Contents

About the author

Mark Forsyth is a writer, journalist, proof-reader, ghostwriter and pedant. He was given a copy of the *Oxford English Dictionary* as a christening present and has never looked back. In 2009 he started the Inky Fool blog, in order to share his heaps of useless information with a verbose world. He is also the author of the *Sunday Times* No. 1 bestseller *The Etymologicon*, published in 2011 by Icon Books.

The author would like to thank Jane Seeber and
Andrea Coleman for their judicious advice,
sensible suggestions and peculiar patience.

This book is the papery child of the Inky Fool blog, which was started in 2009. Though almost all the material is new, some of it has been adapted from its computerised parent. The blog is available at http://blog.inkyfool.com/ which is a part of the grander whole www.inkyfool.com.

Therefore doth Job open his mouth in vain;
he multiplieth words without knowledge.
Job 35, verse 16

For my parents

Preambulation

Tennyson once wrote that:

> Words, like Nature, half reveal
> And half conceal the soul within.

This book is firmly devoted to words of the latter half. It is for the words too beautiful to live long, too amusing to be taken seriously, too precise to become common, too vulgar to survive in polite society, or too poetic to thrive in this age of prose. They are a beautiful troupe hidden away in dusty dictionaries like *A glossary of words used in the wapentakes of Manley and Corringham, Lincolnshire* or the *Descriptive Dictionary and Atlas of Sexology* (a book that does actually contain maps). Of course, many of them are in the *Oxford English Dictionary* (OED), but not on the fashionable pages. They are the lost words, the great secrets of old civilisations that can still be useful to us today.

There are two reasons that these words are scattered and lost like atmic fragments. First, as already observed, they tend to hide in rather strange places. But even if you settle down and read both volumes of the *Dictionary of Obsolete and Provincial English* cover to cover (as I, for some reason, have) you will come across the problem of arrangement, which is obstinately alphabetical.

The problem with the alphabet is that it bears no relation to anything at all, and when words are arranged alphabetically they are uselessly separated. In the OED, for example, aardvarks are 19 volumes away from the zoo, yachts are 18 volumes from the beach, and wine is 17 volumes from the nearest corkscrew. One cannot simply say to oneself, 'I wonder whether there's a word for that' and turn to the dictionary. One chap did recently read the whole OED, but it took him a year, and if you tried that every time you were searching for the perfect word, you might return to find that the conversation had moved on.

The world is, I am told, speeding up. Everybody dashes around at a frightening pace, teleconferencing and speed-dating. They bounce around between meetings and brunches like so many coked-up pin-balls, and reading whole dictionaries is, for busy people like you, simply not feasible. Time is money, money is time, and these days nobody seems to have much of either.

Thus, as an honourable piece of public service, and as my own effort to revive the world's flagging economy through increased lexical efficiency, I have put together a Book of Hours, or *Horologicon*. In medieval times there were books of hours all over the place. They were filled with prayers so that, at any time of day, the pious priest could whip out his horologicon, flip to the appropriate page and offer up an orison to St Pantouffle, or whoever happened to be holy at the time. Similarly, my hope with this book is that it will be used as a work of speedy reference. 'What's the word?' you will think to yourself. Then you will check your watch, pull this book from its holster, turn to the appropriate page and find *ante-jentacular*, *gongoozler*, *bingo-mort*, or whatever it might be. This is a book of the words appropriate to each hour of the day. Importantly, as I have noted, it is a reference work. You should on no account attempt to read it cover to cover. If you do, Hell itself will hold no horrors for you, and neither the author nor his parent company will accept liability for any suicides, gun rampages or crazed nudity that may result.

Of course, there is a slight problem with attempting to create an efficient reference work of this kind, namely that I have to know what you are doing at every moment of the day. This isn't quite as hard as it sounds. I've consulted all of my friends and both of them have told me much the same story: they get up, they wash, they have breakfast and head off to work in an office. Neither of them is quite clear what they do there, but they insist that it's important and involves meetings and phone calls, work-shy subordinates and unruly bosses. Then they pop to the shops, eat supper and, as often as not, head out for a drink. It is on this basis that I have made a game attempt at guessing your hypothetical life.

Some things I have, quite deliberately, ignored. For example, there are no children because they are much too unpredictable. I have included a chapter on courtship for reasons explained at the time. I haven't quite been able to decide whether you are married – sometimes you are and sometimes you aren't – although I am sure that you must possess a firmer opinion. Throughout, I have taken the liberty of imagining you as being half as lazy, dishonest and gluttonous as I am. You have to write about what you know. If you are a piece of virtue into whose wipe-clean mind sin and negligence have never entered, I apologise. This is not the book for you and I hope you have kept the receipt. And of course the nature of your job is a bit of a mystery and a sticking point.

Though most of this is being written in the British Library, as that is where the dictionaries are, the British Library is in fact very like an office, except that nobody is allowed to talk. It has all the usual usualnesses – i.e. the lady on my left has spent the last hour on Facebook, occasionally chortling quietly – and it has all the usual eccentricities – i.e. the chap on my right has all sorts of behemothic tomes on the theories of post-Marxist historiography out on his desk, but is in fact reading *Sharpe's Revenge* under the table, and thinks nobody has noticed.

I mean, I assume you work in an office, but I suppose I may be wrong. Though I have drawn on all the knowledge I could, I can never be quite sure that I've got you down to a T. You might not work in an office at all. You might be a surgeon, or a pilot, or a cattle rustler, or an assassin, taking a little break between hits to find out the lost gems and *hapax legomena* of the English language before heading out for a hard day's garrotting.

You could do anything, anything at all. Your life might be a constant welter of obscenity and strangeness. For all I know, you could spend all day inserting live eels into a horse's bottom. If you do, I must apologise for the arrangement of this book, and the only consolation I can offer is that there is a single eighteenth-century English word for shoving live eels up a horse's arse. Here is the definition given in Captain Grose's *Dictionary of the Vulgar Tongue*:

FEAGUE. To feague a horse; to put ginger up a horse's fundament, and formerly, as it is said, a live eel, to make him lively and carry his tail well; it is said, a forfeit is incurred by any horse-dealer's servant, who shall show a horse without first feaguing him. Feague is used, figuratively, for encouraging or spiriting one up.

There are three instructive points to be taken from that

definition. First, you should never trust an eighteenth-century horse dealer. Especially if you're a horse. Or an eel.

Second, the English language is ready for anything. If you were to surprise a Frenchman in the act of putting a conger up a mare's bottom he would probably have to splutter his way through several sentences of circumlocutory verbocination. However, ask an English-speaker why they are sodomising a horse with a creature from the deep and they can simply raise a casual eyebrow and ask: 'Can't you see I'm feaguing?'

The ability to explain why you're putting an eel up a horse with such holophrastic precision is the birthright of every English-speaking man and woman, and we must reclaim it.

Thirdly, and finally, you will notice that that definition is not from the *Oxford English Dictionary*. Though the OED is the greatest and heaviest reference work yet devised by man, it does not necessarily touch the sides of the English language. In the case of feaguing, the OED does actually quote Grose, but rather coyly mentions only the stuff about ginger. Other words have been grabbed from rural dialects and criminals' dens. Any dictionary that I could find, I have used; from Cab Calloway's *Hepsters Dictionary: Language of Jive* (1944) all the way back to the rainswept miseries of Old English. I shall probably slap together a list of all the works used and stick it at the back, just in case anybody reads that far.

If I have found a word in a dictionary, any dictionary, then it has merited inclusion. Wise and learned professors have asked what makes a word truly a word. I neither know nor care. Such questions I leave to my betters. I must be content to tootle my lexicographic kazoo and dance my antic hay near, but not in, the sacred grove of Academe.

Chapter 1

6 a.m. – Dawn

*Alarm clocks – trying to get back to sleep
– feigning illness*

☙❧

There is a single Old English word meaning 'lying awake before dawn and worrying'. *Uhtceare* is not a well-known word even by Old English standards, which were pretty damn low. In fact, there is only one recorded instance of it actually being used. But uhtceare is there in the dictionaries nonetheless, still awake and waiting for dawn.

Uht (pronounced *oot*) is the restless hour before the dawn, when Aurora herself is loitering somewhere below the eastern horizon, rosying up her fingers and getting ready for the day. But for now, it is dark. And in the *antelucan* hush you should be happily slumbering and dreaming of pretty things.

If you are not, if you are lying there with your eyes wide open glaring at the ceiling, you are probably suffering from a severe case of uhtceare.

There's an old saying that the darkest hour comes just before the dawn. However, that's utter tosh. If you get out of bed and peek through the window, you will see a pale glow in the east. But don't, whatever you do, actually get out of bed. It's probably chilly and you'll never get your posture in bed (technically called your *decubitus*) quite right again. You'll just have to lie there and try not think about how horrid it all is.

Ceare (pronounced *key-are-a*) was the Old English word for care and sorrow, emotions that have an annoying habit of striking during the uht. For some reason these early hours are the time when you remember all your sins and unpaid bills and, perhaps, the indelicate thing you did last night, and as each of these creeps into your mind your uhtceare grows more and more severe.

For an affliction so common, uhtceare is a very rare word. It is recorded only once in a poem called *The Wife's Lament*, which, surprisingly, isn't about how awful and messy her husband is, but about how he has been exiled to a far country and left her here with her uhtceare and her vicious in-laws. Old English poetry is almost universally miserable, and Old English poets should really have bucked up a bit, but they did give us *uhtceare* and for that we should be grateful.

The Old English used to cure their uhtceare by going to listen to the monks singing their uht song. But the monks are long since gone and you have nothing to distract you except for the possible chirruping of an insomniac songbird or the gentle sound of the dustman.

One qualification remains, though, before you self-diagnose with uhtceare. Are you sure you're awake?

Many is the time that I have lain awake before dawn thinking that I would be able to get back to sleep if only this giant squirrel would stop chasing me round the dentist's surgery. These strange half-dreamful, half-conscious delusions and illusions have a technical name – they are *hypnopompic*. *Hypno* from the Greek for sleep and *pompic* from the word for sending.

Nor should you be too keenly *oneirocritical*. Oneirocritical means 'of or pertaining to the interpretation of dreams'. If your dream has a meaning it is probably obscene, and best forgotten, something that will happen in a couple of minutes anyway.

So best to suffer your uhtceare in silence and wait for the *day-raw*, which is the first streak of red in the dawn sky. Aside from being terribly pretty and a warning to shepherds, the day-raw will also decide whether today is a *high* or *low dawn*. Low dawn is when the sun appears straight over the horizon, high dawn is when it is, at first, obscured by clouds and then pops out suddenly in its glorious nuclear-fusive majesty farther up in the sky.

Whatever happens, this is the *dayening*, the *greking*. An eighteenth-century highwayman would have called it the *lightmans*, for some reason, and would probably have decided that this was the time to go home to bed, making way for the eighteenth-century farmers who would have called it, rather charmingly, the *day-peep*. Exhausted chorus girls in 1940s New York would have called it *early bright*. But for you it is simply the end of your usual uhtceare and the cue, one suspects, for your *expergefactor*.

Alarm clocks

An expergefactor is anything that wakes you up. This may simply be your alarm clock, in which case it is time to hit the snooze button. But it may be a dustman or a milkman or a delivery van, in which case it is time to lean out of your window and shriek: 'Damn you all, you expergefactors!' This ought to keep them quiet until one of them has at least found a good dictionary.

You may, though, not have opted for the alarm clock. Many people, for reasons that baffle, make the radio their expergefactor of choice. If this is the case, you will be horribly awoken by news of far-off massacres, earthquakes, plagues, elections etc., or by voices of anxious politicians explaining exactly why they were utterly blameless and how the money or mistress was simply resting in their account or bed.

The technical term for a dishonest politician is a *snollygoster*. Well, all right, it may not be the technical term, but it is the best one. The OED defines *snollygoster* as 'A shrewd, unprincipled person, esp. a politician', although an American journalist of the 1890s defined it more precisely (if less clearly) as:

> ... a fellow who wants office, regardless of party, platform or principles, and who, whenever he wins, gets there by the sheer force of monumental talknophical assumnacy.

Unfortunately, the American journalist didn't stop to explain what *talknophical* or *assumnacy* meant. I can't see why snollygoster has fallen out of use, unless perhaps politicians have all become honest, in which case the rest of us owe them an apology.

If you feel that snollygoster is too ridiculous a way to refer to a dishonest man who holds public office, you may always refer to that voice on the radio by the name *throttlebottom*.

Either way, you shouldn't use the radio news as a means to wake you up, as it is liable to irritate or depress or both. Also it may distract you from the correct method of expergefaction: an *aubade*.

Turn off the radio.

Turn off the alarm clock.

Listen carefully.

Do you hear an aubade?

An aubade is a song sung at dawn by your lover beneath your bedroom window. Providing that your lover can carry a tune, a good aubade is enough to put you in a merry mood until at least breakfast. However, if you cannot, at present, hear an aubade there are only two sad possibilities: I am sorry to have to break this to you so early in the day, but either your lover is a lazy, *lollygagging* shirker of his/her duties; or you have no lover at all.

In the olden days they had a much better system of waking people up. There was a chap called a *knocker-up* who would wander around the village tapping on people's bedroom windows with a special stick. This was actually considered a proper job and was probably a lot safer than its alternative: the *weaver's larum*.

A weaver's larum was an odd device that worked like this. Take a reasonably heavy object like a stone or a small child and tie two pieces of string to it. Both these pieces of string should then be fed through a single hook. One of them should be attached to the wall, so that the string is taut and the stone/baby dangles. The second piece of string, which is loose, should be tied to your finger.

Got that? Heavy object attached by a taut string to the wall and by a loose string to your finger.

Right, now get a tall, thin candle and put its base right next to the taut bit of string. Now light the candle and drift off to sleep. During the night the candle will slowly burn down and down until the flame gets to the piece of string, which is incinerated.

The stone/baby falls to the floor and your finger gets a vigorous yank to pull you rudely from your slumbers.

The final possibility is a *reveille*. This is the drum roll or bugle-blast that's meant to waken a whole barracks full of soldiers. It's thus a term that can usefully be applied to the noise of dustmen, children or any of the other inconveniences and natural expergefactors of modern life.

Zwodder

Uhtceare is now officially over; however, that does not mean that you feel great. There is a word for people who are breezy and bright in the morning: *matutinal*. In fact, there are a bunch of words, but most of them are rude. As Oscar Wilde observed, only dull people are brilliant at breakfast. And, anyway, breakfast is still a long way off.

For the moment, you can lie there in a *zwodder* cursing the arrival of a new day. The rather racy lexicographical classic *Observations on some of the Dialects in the West of England, particularly Somersetshire* (1825) defines a zwodder as: 'A drowsy and stupid state of body or mind.'

This would, in and of itself, make zwodder a useful word. But the really important thing is how it sounds. Say it. *Zwodder*. It's the sort of word that can and should be mumbled from the refuge of your bedclothes. *Zwodder*. It's the drowsiest word in the English language, but there's also something warm and comfortable about it.

Alternatively, you could be addled, stupefied and generally speaking *philogrobolized*, a word that should be said at about an octave beneath your normal speaking voice and reserved for the morning after the carnage before. As responses to 'How are you this morning?' go, 'Philogrobolized' is almost unbeatable. Nobody will ever have to ask you what you mean as it's all somehow contained in the syllable *grob*, which is where the stress should always be laid. It conveys a hangover, without ever having to admit that you've been drinking.

Another rather more religious way of doing this is to speak enigmatically of your *ale-passion*. Passion here is being used in its old sense of suffering, as in the Passion of Christ. (That a word for suffering became a synonym for romantic love tells you all you need to know about romance.) Ale-passion is mentioned in the 1593 book *Bacchus Bountie* in the following context:

> Fourthly, came wallowing in a German, borne in Mentz, his name was Gotfrey Grouthead; with him he brought a wallet full of woodcocks heads; the braines thereof, tempered with other sauce, is a passing preseruatiue against the ale-passion, or paine in the pate.

In fact, you should probably keep a small aviary of woodcocks next to your bed, just in case. If not, you will lie there feeling awful. You will suffer from *xerostomia*, the proper medical term for dryness of the mouth through lack of saliva. But there will be nothing you can do about it unless you actually get out of bed. You're also liable to have slumbered in the wrong decubitus and found that your arm has fallen asleep, a condition that the medical world refers to as *obdormition*. The only way to cure this is to wave the said limb about frantically, like a string-puppet having a fit, until the *prinkling* starts and your blood slowly, reluctantly resumes its patrol.

Alas that such sufferings should invade your bleary-eyed *lippitude*. Now is the zwoddery time when you wish that you'd invested in thicker curtains, for the sun is insistent, and you are one of those *lucifugous* creatures that avoids sunlight like a vampire, or a badger. Lucifugous (or light-fleeing) is a word that is usually applied to sins and demons, but it can just as well refer to somebody making a tactical retreat beneath the duvet because they cannot endure the gaze of heaven.

The final suffering of dawn is *pissuprest*. A horse-keeper's manual from 1610 says: 'Pissuprest in a horse, is when a horse would faine stale, but cannot.'

And that's you, comfortable in your covers, with this *micturition*, this intense desire to urinate, that can only be relieved if you actually get out of bed and stumble to the lavatory. But not yet, not yet. All my possessions (as Queen Elizabeth almost said) for one more moment in bed. Perhaps if you lie here the micturition will magically vanish.

It is time for procrastination and *cunctation* and generally putting off the inevitable. There's nothing wrong with that. This is, after all, life in miniature. We know that death and going to the lavatory are inevitable, but that doesn't mean we have to do it cheerfully or leap enthusiastically into the grave. Hold out! Enjoy the brief moment that you have. Treasure and savour your *grufeling*, which is defined in *Jamieson's Etymological Dictionary of the Scottish Language* (1825) thus:

> **To be grufeling**: To lie close wrapped up, and in a comfortable-looking manner; used in ridicule.

The Scots are clearly a nation devoid of pity, or indeed of medical knowledge. Don't they realise that you may be suffering from undiagnosed *dysania*? Dysania is extreme difficulty in waking up and getting out of bed, and there may be a secret epidemic of it.

Slightly better known is *clinomania*, which is an obsessive desire to lie down. But that doesn't quite answer, does it? Perhaps you'd be better off with Dr Johnson's word *oscitancy*, which he defined as 'Yawning or unusual sleepiness'. The first recorded usage of the word back in 1610 mentions 'such oscitancie and gaping drowsiness' in describing the effects of a dull sermon in church. You can accompany your oscitation with *pandiculation*, which is the stretching of the arms and body characteristic of this mournful yawnful time.

If you were king in the dawns of old, this would be the moment to hold your *levee*. A levee was a funny sort of formal occasion when you would lie in bed while all your social inferiors came to congratulate you on your superiority. Unfortunately the system of levees got out of hand in the eighteenth century. There were so many of them, and so many degrees of society, that those at the top were forced to remain in bed until early afternoon. The novelist Henry Fielding described it thus in 1742:

> ... early in the morning arises the postillion, or some other boy, which no great families, no more than great ships, are without, and falls to brushing the clothes and cleaning the shoes of John the footman; who, being drest himself, applies his hands to the same labours for Mr Second-hand, the squire's gentleman; the gentleman in the like manner, a little later in the day, attends the squire; the squire is no sooner equipped than he attends

the levee of my lord; which is no sooner over than my lord himself is seen at the levee of the favourite, who, after the hour of homage is at an end, appears himself to pay homage to the levee of his sovereign. Nor is there, perhaps, in this whole ladder of dependance, any one step at a greater distance from the other than the first from the second; so that to a philosopher the question might only seem, whether you would chuse to be a great man at six in the morning, or at two in the afternoon.

During a levee you should know that your favourite courtiers are allowed to stand in the *ruelle*, which is the space between the bed and the wall where your shoes and socks are probably lying. Everybody else must make do with milling around at the foot of the bed or even by the door.

If you are conducting a levee, I wish you well. But these days the closest thing to a levee is the early-morning phone call to your boss to *egrote*.

Egrote is a fantastically useful word meaning 'to feign sickness in order to avoid work'. If it has fallen out of use, the cause must be that workers have lost their cunning. So here are some instructions for a beginner.

Wait until your boss has answered the phone and then start to *whindle*. Whindling is defined in a dictionary of 1699 as 'feigned groaning'. It's vital to whindle for a while before giving your name in a weak voice. Explain that you are a *sickrel* and that work is beyond you. If asked for details, say that you're *floccilating* (feverishly plucking at the bedclothes) and *jactating* (tossing around feverishly).

If your boss insists that you name your actual condition, don't call it dysania. Go instead for a severe case of *hum durgeon*. Unless your boss is fluent in eighteenth-century slang he'll never suspect that:

HUM DURGEON. An imaginary illness. He has got the hum durgeon, the thickest part of his thigh is nearest his arse; i.e. nothing ails him except low spirits.

Unfortunately, you cannot use hum durgeon every day. Your employer will suspect. You can probably get away with it at most twice a week, and the second time you should probably just shriek 'My thighs! My thighs!' down the telephone until they hang up.

No. You have been lying here too long and too languorously. Seven o'clock is upon us. Throw off the duvet! Toss away the sheet! And crawl out of bed.

Chapter 2

7 a.m. – Waking and Washing

Slippers – looking in the mirror – self-loathing – lavatory – shower – hair – shaving – brushing your teeth

∽∼∾

Exodus

That's it. You're out of bed. Like Adam and Eve expelled from Eden.

First, grope for your slippers, or to give them their much merrier name: *pantofles*. Pantofles are named after Saint Pantouffle who is as obscure as he is fictional. He (or she, or it) appears to have been invented in France in the fifteenth century. Nobody knows why the French would have invented a saint, or indeed why slippers should be named after him, but they were and that's that. Robert Burton's great medical work *The Anatomy of Melancholy* describes how Venus, the goddess of love, was so enraged with her blind son Cupid making people fall in love willy-nilly that:

> … she threatened to break his bow and arrows, to clip his wings, and whipped him besides on the bare buttocks with her pantophle.

And any slipper that can double up as a weapon with which to spank godlings has to be a good idea.

Once your toes are snugly pantofled, you can stagger off to the bathroom, pausing only to look at the little depression that you have left in your bed, the dip where you have been lying all night. This is known as a *staddle*.

The bathroom

Part I: The looking glass and what you saw there

There are a lot of synonyms for mirror – everything from *tooting-glass* (Elizabethan) to *rum-peeper* (eighteenth-century highwayman), but the best is probably the *considering glass*. That is, after all, what you do with the thing. But first, before you even peek in the considering glass, take a *gowpen* of water – i.e. a double handful – and throw it over your face. After all, nobody but an angel is beautiful before eight o'clock.

The word *pimginnit* may be necessary here. It's a seventeenth-century term meaning 'a large, red, angry pimple'. This is a particularly fine definition as it implies that pimples have emotions, and that some of them are furious. Pimginnits are much more wrathful than, for example, *grog-blossoms*, which are those spots that pop up the morning after one has indulged in too much grog, or rum. Grog-blossoms are more sullen than angry, like a resentful letter mailed overnight from your liver.

But enough of your *furuncles*. Let us just say that you are *erumpent*, which is a jolly-sounding way of saying spotty (nicer than *papuliferous* and infinitely more pleasant than *petechial*, a word that Dr Johnson defined as 'pestilentially spotted'). There are too many other sorrows for us to get hung up on spots.

First, there are the *elf-locks*. It is, or was, a well known fact that elves sneak into your bedroom during the night with no better motive than to tangle up your hair. The sad result, which you will see reflected, is elf-locks.

Then there are the wrinkles and, in extreme cases, *wrines* (these are the big ones); the crows' feet, the *frumples*, the *frounces*, the lurking *lirks* and a million other synonyms for the lines on your face, which are, after all, merely signs of how thoughtful and wise you are.

There's also the *culf*, which is the name for the bed fluff that has lodged in your navel. There are the red *ferret-eyes* through which you're looking. There's the *ozostomia* and *bromodrosis*, which is what a doctor would call your stinking breath and sweat, because doctors have a lovely habit of insulting you in Greek, which softens the blow. Almost anything sounds softer in a classical language. For example, if a fellow were to suggest that you stank of horse piss, you would probably take offence, but if he merely said that you were *jumentous*, you might imagine that the chap was telling you that you were *jubilant* and *momentous*, or something along those lines. You might even thank him.

All in all, though, you are *idiorepulsive* (you disgust even yourself) and something really ought be done about it soon. However, I fear that things must get worse before they can get better.

On particularly bad mornings, this may be the time to attempt a *through cough*. These aren't easy. I have tried it myself and consistently failed. If you can cough and fart at precisely the same instant then you have achieved what was known – two hundred years ago – as a through cough, and can therefore continue the rest of the day with a feeling of secret satisfaction.

Anyway, a through cough is only the preface to the lowest part of the day – that part when you are no better than a beast and no worse than a monarch: the lavatory.

Part II: The Spice Islands

In the Book of Samuel, as the whole history and future of salvation is being worked out between Saul and David, everything comes to rest upon Saul's popping to the lavatory. Not, of course, that they had proper lavatories in those days. Salvation was not that far advanced. But as Saul with his army hunted for David beside the Dead Sea, he found that his dinner was, like his kingship of Israel, a fleeting thing that he would be forced to relinquish.

> Then Saul took three thousand chosen men out of all Israel, and went to seek David and his men upon the rocks of the wild goat. And he came to the sheepcotes by the way, where was a cave; and Saul went in to cover his feet: and David and his men remained in the sides of the cave. And the men of David said unto him, Behold the day of which the LORD said unto thee, Behold I will deliver thine enemy into thine hand, that thou mayest do to him as it shall seem good unto thee. Then David arose, and cut off the skirt of Saul's robe privily.

What concerns us here is not the question of who was truly the Lord's anointed, nor the symbolism of the king's cloak, nor even the necessity of checking your lavatory carefully for rival claimants to the throne; but the delightful phrase *to cover his feet*, which is a literal rendering of the ancient Hebrew meaning to do the necessities of nature.

If the Bible teaches us one thing, it's that you should never be so vulgar as to call a spade a spade or a lavatory a lavatory. Even if you choose not to cover your feet (which should already have pantofles on them), you can disguise your baseness with all sorts of lovely phrases. The Victorians would visit *Mrs Jones*, or *my aunt*, or *the coffee shop*, although that last phrase may be too suggestive for those of a liquid disposition. Others have been more exotic. In the thirteenth century they would visit *a chamber foreign*, or in the eighteenth century you could take *a voyage to the Spice Islands*, these being the most exotic place imaginable, and particularly appropriate for the morning after a curry.

However, these references to exoticism may be inappropriate to something that is often so troubling in foreign lands. The great actor David Garrick took a trip to Europe in 1764 and wrote to his brother saying:

> … I never, since I left England, till now, have regal'd Myself with a good house of Office, or as he calls it, a *Conveniency* – the holes in Germany are generally too large, & too round, chiefly owing I believe to the broader bottoms of the Germans […] We have a little English Gentleman with us who Slipt up to the Middle of one of the holes & we were some Minutes before we could disengage him. – in short you may assure Townley, (Who loves to hear of the state of these Matters) that in Italy the People *do their Needs*, in Germany they *disEmbogue*, but in England (& in England only) they *Ease* themselves.

House of office has a pleasing grandeur to it, although some of Garrick's contemporaries would have called it a *House of Commons*, which is good for the politically-minded. Medieval fellows would *go to siege*, which has a fine martial ring and is particularly appropriate for the constipated. And militarism was still present in the Victorian *scraping castle*. In fact, there are a million and one variants and euphemisms, all of which mean that since the thirteenth century nobody has had to be so vulgar as to *do their filth-hood*.

While actually on the *gong-hole* one should take care about one's precise actions. For example, in a house with thin walls it is a little rude to *squitter* or 'void the excrement with a noise'. Your *purgation*, *exoneration*, *dejection* or whatever you choose to call it should be performed pianissimo and the *tantadlin tart* baked in silence.

When it is all over you may turn your attention to the necessary paperwork, and if you think that the English language may fail you here, then you haven't read Sir Thomas Urquhart's 1653 translation of Rabelais, which has this tantalising little tip:

> I say and maintain, that of all torcheculs, arsewisps, bumfodders, tail-napkins, bunghole cleansers, and wipe-breeches, there is none in the world comparable to the neck of a goose, that is well downed, if you hold her head betwixt your legs. And believe me therein upon mine honour, for you will thereby feel in your nockhole a most wonderful pleasure, both in regard of the softness of the said down and of the temperate heat of the goose …

Bumfodder has had a rather curious history in the English language, for though it is now a very obscure word for loo roll, it still survives in a shortened form. *Bumf* is, to this day, a rather derogatory term for large, but necessary, amounts of paperwork. And necessary it certainly is, if you want to avoid what were once called *fartleberries*.

However, in the dire circumstance that you have neither paper nor a back-up goose, you can always resort to a corner of your cloak, provided David hasn't crept up on you and cut it off, privily.

Part III: For all the water in the ocean/Can never turn the swan's black legs to white,/Although she lave them hourly in the flood

Benjamin Franklin invented the lightning conductor, bifocal glasses, the chair-desk and the *cold air bath*. This last innovation he described in a letter of 1768. The crux of it was that he didn't like water:

> The shock of the cold water has always appeared to me, generally speaking, as too violent, and I have found it much more agreeable to my constitution to bathe in another element, I mean cold air. With this view I rise almost every morning, and sit in my chamber without any clothes whatever, half an hour or an hour, according to the season, either reading or writing.

In the interests of water conservation, Franklin's invention could be usefully revived, although it is hard to see what effect it would have on dirt and smell. So we of the twenty-first century are probably stuck with water; and, such is the pressure of time, we are probably going to use a shower. The best thing about taking a bath is that you get to use the 1950s American slang term *make like a fish*.

However, before launching rashly into the waters, you should prepare. Sod's Law states that you'll be halfway through showering before you realise that there's almost no shampoo left in the bottle; so you should *duffifie* it now. Duffifie is an old Aberdeenshire verb meaning 'to lay a bottle on its side for some time … that it may be completely drained of the few drops remaining'. It's therefore much more compact than the English equivalent of *making the bottle confess*. Either way, a bit of duffifying will save you much annoyance later on.

As you set the waters running you might wish to notice the *shower curtain effect*, which would doubtless have interested Benjamin Franklin. When the shower starts, the curtain will be sucked in towards you, and though several theories have been proposed, modern science is still uncertain as to why this happens.

Even as the curtains are being pulled in around you, you will probably experience the *curglaff*, which is another old Scots term, this time for the feeling you get when you're hit with cold water. Your heart gallops, your blood rushes, and, if you're Benjamin Franklin, you don't like it one little bit.

Anyway, there's nothing to be done about that. It is time to *buddle* (scrub in water) all that is not *illutible* (unwashawayable). Baudelaire said that humans were deluded if they thought they could wash away all their spots with vile tears, but Baudelaire was French and therefore knew nothing about hygiene or shower gel.

There are funny words for almost all the parts of the body, but the important ones in the shower are these:

Oxter – armpit

Popliteal – behind the knees

Dew-beaters/beetle-crushers – feet (depending on your usual use for them)

Inguinal – relating to the groin

Everywhere else is optional. After all, if you spend too long in there you'll end up with the skin on the ends of your fingers *quobbled*.

Part IV: Stare, stare in the basin/And wonder what you've missed

Hair

The Scots used to have a terrible reputation for lice. Whether this was justified, I don't know. I deal in dictionaries, not Scotsmen. However, *the Scots Greys are in full march* once meant that lice were crawling all over your head. And a dictionary of 1811 defines *clan* thus:

> A family's tribe or brotherhood; a word much used in Scotland. The head of the clan; the chief: an allusion to a story of a Scotchman, who, when a very large louse crept down his arm, put him back again, saying he was the head of the clan, and that, if injured, all the rest would resent it.

All of which should explain why a comb used to be called a *Scotch louse trap*. So reviving this term will enrich the language and enrage the Scots, which is a double benefit.

In fact, one can continue to enrage the Celtic fringes of the hair by dispensing with your comb and instead using your fingers to get your hair into some semblance of order. The Welsh had no reputation for lice, but they did once have a reputation for using cheap substitutes. So a *Welsh diamond* is a crystal, a *Welsh carpet* is a pattern painted on the floor, and a *Welsh comb* is your five fingers.

The things people do to their hair are so weird and varied that the English language is brimming with useful words on the subject, most of which contain the element *trich-*, which was the ancient Greek word for the stuff. For example, smooth-haired people are *lissotrichous* and wavy-haired people are *cymotrichous*, and *trichotillomania* is a manic desire to pull out all your hair.

If dictionaries are to be believed then the best possible thing you can do is cultivate dangling curls. Even Dr Johnson's dictionary called a woman's curls *heart-breakers*, and the Victorians called them *bow-catchers*, on the basis that they would catch handsome young men, or *beaus*. And Victorian women, in a rare fit of equality, would run after men who sported *bell-ropes*, which brought *belles* to ruin with their curly charms.

Shaving

Let us now turn our attention to the chins of men and unfortunate ladies. Let us turn to *shavery*, which the OED solemnly defines as 'subjection to the necessity of being shaved', although the poet Robert Southey used it better when he observed in 1838:

> Oh pitiable condition of human kind! One colour is born to slavery abroad, and one sex to shavery at home! – A woman to secure her comfort and well-being in this country stands in need of one thing only, which is a good husband; but a

man has to provide himself with two things, a good wife, and a good razor, and it is more difficult to find the latter than the former.

Slavery has been abolished but shavery survives. This latter is rather a shame, as it lessens the need for all of the technical beard words, of which there are many. They all involve the Greek root *pogo*, which is pronounced in exactly the same way as the stick (although the two are etymologically unrelated). So there's *pogonology* (the study of beards), *pogonate* (having a beard), *pogoniasis* (a beard on a lady), and *pogonotomy* (shaving). As we live in an essentially misopogonistic society of beard-haters, most men must start the day by taking a razor from the *pogonion* or tip of the chin up to the *philtrum*, which is the name for the little groove between your nose and your upper lip. Then you have to work carefully to avoid a neckbeard, which the Victorians called a *Newgate fringe*. Newgate was the name of a London prison where people were hanged. So a Newgate fringe was meant to resemble the rope that was slipped around the felon's neck before he took the plunge into eternity.

Teeth

In the first century BC, the Roman poet Catullus wrote these lines about a man called Aemilius:

Non (ita me di ament) quicquam referre putaui,
utrumne os an culum olfacerem Aemilio.
Nilo mundius hoc, niloque immundius illud,
uerum etiam culus mundior et melior:
nam sine dentibus hic.

It is impossible to capture the solemn beauty of the original in English, but a loose translation might go:

> I really cannot tell between
> His mouth above and arse beneath;
> They are identically unclean,
> The only difference: one has teeth.

Nothing else is known about filthy-breathed Aemilius beyond Catullus's poem. For two thousand years that has been his sole posterity. From this we may learn two lessons: don't get on the wrong side of poets, and keep your teeth clean.[1]

So open your mouth wide and say *oze*. It's a lovely, long, wide-throated word and means 'a stench in the mouth'. The good thing about oze is that merely by saying it, you distribute it.

When toothpaste manufacturers talk about the small amount of toothpaste that fits on the end of your toothbrush, they call it a *nurdle*. Why they should do so is lost in the oze of time, but it's been the word since at least 1968, and a recent court case between two of the largest manufacturers was centred entirely around who was allowed to depict which nurdle on their packaging. Not only was the nurdle said to chase away oze, it could also whiten your teeth (or, to be more technical about it, stop your being *xanthodontic*).

However, the greatest advance since the days of Catullus is the introduction of mouthwash, which was, unfortunately,

---

[1] In fact, Catullus wrote another poem about a chap with shiny white teeth, claiming that they only got that way because he drank piss. There's no pleasing some poets.

introduced after the words *squiggle* and *gleek* had died out. Squiggle was an old Norfolk dialect word meaning 'to shake and wash a fluid about in the mouth, with the lips closed'. Squiggling is a lovely word because it sounds exactly like what it is, as does gleek. To gleek is to squirt liquid from your mouth. This should be done from as far from the basin as possible, just for the challenge.

Done

That's it. You're done. There may be other things you should take care of, but I'm much too shy to enquire. Instead, I shall ask what God asked your forebears in the garden of Eden: Who told you you were naked?

Chapter 3

8 a.m. – Dressing and Breakfast

Clothes – make-up – breakfast – preparing to depart

∽∾

Naturism is all very well, but it gets chilly after a while. So it is time to become what nudists refer to as a *textile*, i.e. one of those poor fools who wears clothes. You're ready to get togged up, to become the *concinnate* (finely dressed) and consummate gentleman; or if you are of the womanly persuasion, to become a *dandizette*, the nineteenth-century term for a female dandy. Certainly you cannot remain starkers or, as a witch would put it, *sky-clad*.

In the second century AD a group of Christian fanatics called Adamites practised Adamism, or holy nudity, but only in church, and even there they had to have central heating. St Epiphanius described Adamism thus:

Their churches are stoves, made warm for the reception of company by a fire underneath. When they come to the door they pull off their clothes, both men and women, and enter naked in to the place of meeting. Their presidents and teachers do the same, and they sit together promiscuously. And so they perform their readings and other parts of worship naked.

The theory of Adamism, if you can believe it, was that by exposing themselves to such temptation they actually strengthened their wills and conquered lust. But though God may have approved of the Adamites (He has remained silent on the subject), the police and most employers take a dim view. So let us dress.

We begin with what the Victorians coyly referred to as one's *abbreviations*, which in these coarse times is simply called underwear. In Herefordshire, capacious and roomy knickers used to be known as *apple-catchers* on the basis that they were large enough to serve a useful purpose in a late-summer orchard.

Moving to other unmentionables, the English language is weirdly wanting in slang terms for the brassiere. The only fun to be had is with padded bras, which were known in the 1940s as *gay deceivers*. As you can imagine, this was before the word gay had become widely used as slang for homosexual, and when a gay old man could still be lusting after members of the opposite sex. Such gays could be deceived by the use of rubber falsities, which, because pure rubber is a trifle smelly, would be flavoured with chocolate. It might be worthwhile to bring back the gay old terminology, but not the technology.

There's a curious little entry in *A New Dictionary of the Terms Ancient and Modern of the Canting Crew* (1699):

Sir Posthumus Hobby, one who Draws on his Breeches with a Shoeing-horn, also a Fellow that is Nice and Whimsical in the set of his Cloaths.

It's curious for two reasons. First, it doesn't mention whether the shoeing-horn is necessary because the fellow is fat, or because he wears terribly tight trousers to show off his lovely legs. Secondly, there really was a chap called Sir Posthumus Hoby who had lived a hundred years before that dictionary was written. He was a famous Puritan and may well have been the model for the stern and strict Malvolio in Shakespeare's *Twelfth Night*. But that Sir Posthumus (so named because he was born after his father's death) was neither particularly fat nor particularly dandyish. Indeed, the only really notable things about him were his humourlessness and the fact that he matriculated at Oxford at the age of eight. Nonetheless, it seems unfair to deny him immortality at that awkward moment when you try to slip into the clothes of last year's slimness.

It is at this point that you're bound to notice a *grinnow*. A grinnow is a stain that has not come out in the wash and that you probably haven't seen until this vital moment. For a word that useful, it's astonishing that grinnow is only recorded as an obscure Shropshire dialect word in a dictionary of 1879, where they provide the helpful sample sentence: 'I canna get the grinnows out if I rub the piece out, they'n bin biled in so many times.'

One must be wary of grinnows; too many grinnows and you end up looking like a *tatterdemalion*. A tatterdemalion is a chap (or chappess) whose clothes are tattered and torn. It is the same as a *tatter-wallop*, a *ragabash*, or a *flabergudgion*; and, given the threadbare state of modern fashion, it is an eminently useful word.

Tatterdemalion has the lovely suggestion of dandelions towards the end (although pronounced with all the stress on the *may* of malion) and should be immediately comprehensible even to the uninitiated, because everybody knows what *tatter* means, and the *demalion* bit was never anything more than a linguistic fascinator. More wonderfully still, there are spin-off words: *tatterdemalionism* and *tatterdemalionry*, the latter meaning tatterdemalions considered as a group.

Once you are *snogly geared* (as they said in the eighteenth century), *dressed to death* (nineteenth century) or simply *togged to the bricks* (twentieth-century Harlem), it is time, if you are a lady, to apply some auxiliary beauty.

Make-up

Everybody remembers the line 'Alas, poor Yorick', but fewer recall the final lines of Hamlet's skull speech. 'Now get you to my lady's chamber, and tell her, let her paint an inch thick, to this favour she must come; make her laugh at that.' Which shows that Hamlet was not the sort of person to help you choose a lipstick.

It is tempting to bring back all the winsome words that Shakespeare would have known for make-up. In his time there would have been no brutal application of foundation, as ladies would *surfle* instead. They would then apply *ceruse* as a blusher, the eyes would have been touched with *collyrium* and the eyelids with *calliblephary*. But as the whole process back then was called *fucation*, it's probably best not to get carried away with Elizabethan vocabulary. It could become awkward if your husband called, 'What's taking so long?' and you accidentally replied: 'I just need to fucate, darling. Won't be a minute.' To which your significant other might reasonably reply: 'Eight?'

So we must content ourselves with a few 1940s terms for auxiliary beauty such as *pucker paint* for lipstick. The 1940s also provide the splendid phrase *preparing bait*, which takes in the whole process of lustrification. It imagines the prinked paintress and perfumeress as a fisherlady, her lips as the hooks, and men as mere fish.

The *ante-jentacular* part of the day is almost over. Ante-jentacular is simply an immensely clever-sounding adjective meaning 'before breakfast'. It is best applied to strenuous exercise or Bloody Marys.

Breakfast

The Greek for breakfast was *ariston*, so the study of breakfast is *aristology*, and those who devote their lives to the pursuit of the perfect morning meal are *aristologists*. The subject had a brief vogue in the mid-nineteenth century and there was even a book published called *Cookery for the Many*, by *an Australian Aristologist*; but it is now a forgotten art. This is a shame, as breakfast presents a wide buffet to the enquiring mind. Who but an aristologist would be able to tell you that a *ben joltram* was 'brown bread soaked in skimmed milk; the usual breakfast of ploughboys', that a *butter shag* was 'a slice of bread and butter', or that *opsony* was strictly defined in the OED as 'any food eaten with bread' (plural: *opsonia*).

The disciplined student of aristology must begin their studies nearly three millennia ago with Homer, as there is a whole book of the *Iliad* – the nineteenth – devoted to the subject of whether or not to eat breakfast.

Essentially, Agamemnon gives a long speech commanding the Greeks to *jenticulate* (which is the posh way of saying eat your breakfast). Achilles, though, is having none of it and gives an even longer speech pointing out that they are late for work (i.e. killing Trojans) and really ought to get on with it. Odysseus then weighs in with an even longer speech that essentially says, 'It's the most important meal of the day. You may not feel like it now, but when you're bathing in the blood of your enemies you'll regret it.' Achilles says that really, he'd rather not, especially as his breakfast always used to be made by his best friend Patroclus, whose mangled body now lies in his tent with its feet towards the door. He then turns to the corpse and gives a rather lovely little speech that goes:

> 'Thou,' said he, 'when this speed was pursued
> Against the Trojans, evermore apposedst in my tent
> A pleasing breakfast; being so free, and sweetly diligent,
> Thou madest all meat sweet.'

And that would have been that, except that the gods themselves are very keen that Achilles should have a hearty breakfast, so, at Zeus's direct order, Athena descends from heaven and magically instils 'heaven's most-to-be-desired feast' directly into his body, thus allowing him to set off to work. Then there's a brief incident with a talking horse and the book ends.

Had Achilles been a more reasonable man he might have settled for a quick *chota hazri*, which is a brief breakfast that is just enough to keep you going till elevenses. The term comes from the British empire in India and is simply Hindi for 'little breakfast', but it has much more history and glamour to it than that. It's the sort of snack that you eat after spending the night up a tree with a tiger. So, when a chap in 1886 did just that, he returned at dawn and:

> … he was hailed by his friends amid a perfect shower of ejaculations; all the answer they got was a wail of hunger and a cry for 'chota hazri,' after which Brown promised to relate his adventures faithfully and truly.

It reminds one of the sort of world where a gobbled energy bar or brief banana was not an indignity, it was simply something that you wolfed down because you were in a hurry to conquer the earth.

If you have time on your hands and a hole in your stomach you can cook yourself a proper breakfast, not quite as proper as 'heaven's most-to-be-desired feast', but a damned good second place. Achilles, for example, would never have seen a chicken or a hen's egg, as they weren't imported to Europe until the fifth century BC. So familiar are eggs to us, however, that in the eighteenth century they were referred to as *cackling farts*, on the basis that chickens cackled all the time and eggs came out of the back of them. Unlike Achilles, we can have them fried, boiled, scrambled, coddled, poached, devilled, Benedict or Florentine.

A much grander eggy word is *vitelline*, which means 'of or pertaining to egg yolk'. The seventeenth-century poet Robert Herrick once wrote:

> Fain would I kiss my Julia's dainty leg,
> Which is as white and hairless as an egg.

Which shows an unsettling erotic fascination with breakfast, and also misses the point that though egg whites sustain you, it is the vitelline parts that yield the true glory. It is the vitelline yumminess into which you can dip what Mr Herrick's contemporaries would have called *ruff peck*, which to us is merely a rasher of bacon.

The earliest explanation for why it's called a rasher comes from John Minsheu's *Ductor in Linguas* of 1612 where he explains that it gets 'rashly or hastily roasted'. Modern etymologists are much less fun and think rasher relates vaguely to razor. Nonetheless, a rashly roasted rasher can easily end up *brizzled*, or 'scorched near to burning'. Brizzled is a lovely word, onomatopoeic of the sound that pigmeat will make as it burns and sizzles its way to deliciousness.

All of this can be washed down with a glass of *yarrum* (thieves' slang for milk), or, if you are feeling rakish, a *whet*, an early-morning glass of white wine, popular in the eighteenth century but terribly hard to find in these drier and duller days. In fact, in the Age of Enlightenment they would often breakfast on a thing called *conny wabble*, which was 'eggs and brandy beat up together', although sadly no more precise recipe than that survives.

In fact, there are an almost infinite number of possible breakfasts and this brief book cannot contain them all. One would need a seasoned aristologist to look into all the nooks and crannies. For example, there was once such a thing as a *Spitalfields breakfast* that crops up in a dictionary of Victorian slang:

Spitalfields breakfast, at the East end of London this is understood as consisting of a tight necktie and a short pipe.

Which I assume means dressing hurriedly and valuing tobacco over food. If you go further back through the slang dictionaries things get more gruesome. Back in the seventeenth and eighteenth centuries, when the death penalty was punishment for almost anything (this is before the invention of Australia and deportation), there were a million and one artful phrases and euphemisms for being hanged. You could *dance upon nothing with a hempen cravat* or *caper in the wind* or, if the hanging were at dawn you could:

Have a hearty choke and caper sauce for breakfast – To be hanged

There was even a euphemism for this euphemism, mentioned in an article of 1841 called *Flowers of Hemp; or the Newgate Garland*. The author is searching for a particular criminal and is told by an informant that:

'He died last Wednesday morning of a vegetable breakfast, that did not altogether agree with his digestive system.'

'A vegetable breakfast! What do you mean?'

'Mean! well now, the like of that! And so you do not perceive, that this is what Dr Lardner calls a delicate form of expression for "a hearty choke with caper sauce."'

'As we live and learn, sir; I am much beholden to you for the information,' I replied, hardly able to repress my disgust at the brutal jocularity of the wretch.

So it's worthwhile remembering as you sweep the crumbs from the table that it could all be a lot worse.

Once upon a time, back in ancient Greece, they had a special slave called an *analecta* whose job was to gather up the breadcrumbs after a meal. *Ana* meant 'up' and *lectos* meant 'gathered'. That's why the gathered up sayings of Confucius are called *The Analects*, and that's also why Henry Cockerham's *English Dictionarie* of 1623 has the entry:

Analects, crums which fall from the table.

Conge

A *conge* (pronounced *kon-jee*) is a formal preparation to depart. It's the sort of thing medieval kings did before processing around their kingdom or that beautiful princesses performed before being shipped off to marry a distant emperor. However, conges today tend to be much more disorganised affairs as you realise that you're running late, haven't got your phone, haven't charged your phone, can't find your car keys and have forgotten to put on your trousers. You are much more likely to end up running around in circles (or *circumgyrating* as Dr Johnson would have put it). The conge of today consists of grabbing everything that you possibly can into an *oxter lift*, an old Scots term for as much as you can carry between your arm and your side.

Now charge for the door, and with a quick cry of 'Abyssinia' (which was the hepcat way of saying 'I'll be seein' ya'), you are off to work.

Chapter 4

9 a.m. – Commute

Weather – transport – car – bus – train – arriving late

ᥬᵒᵔᥬ

The weather

When a death sentence is commuted to life imprisonment, it's a good thing. However, commuting is uniformly awful. The connection between them, since you ask, is that both involve a *commutual* exchange. The noose is exchanged for the cell, small debts can be commuted for one large debt, and in nineteenth-century America individual purchases of railway tickets could be exchanged for one *commutation ticket* at a slightly reduced rate, that was valid for a year.

However, you are still at your front door. It is said that every journey begins with a single step, but in my experience, every journey begins with a single step followed by a disorderly retreat once I realise that I'm sporting the wrong clothes for the weather or have forgotten my wallet or hipflask or crossbow. So let us begin with a *cellivagous* (or 'heavenward-wandering') glance.

The worst form of weather is a *pogonip*, which is a word we stole from the Shoshone Indians (along with the rest of their possessions) to describe a fog so cold that it freezes into ice crystals in mid-air. Actual pogonips are quite rare, as air needs to get down to about −40°C before the water in it crystallises, but reality should never get in the way of talking about the weather. Real pogonips tend to be very localised affairs, occurring in deep Alaskan valleys and the like, so you can always claim that there was a sudden pogonip on your street, and nobody will be any the wiser.

Non-Alaskan commuters are much more likely to find the weather *swale*. Swale is recorded in the indispensable *A Collection of English Words, not generally used* (1674), where it is defined as:

Swale: windy, cold, bleak.

It barely needs to be mentioned that swale is a north-country word, but nor do you even really need the definition. Swale is already a windy, cold, bleak word. It sways between *wail* and *windswept*, and is irresistibly suggestive of rain, misery and Yorkshire.

And more miserable even than the skies of northern England are the skies of Scotland, where they actually have the word *thwankin*, which is dismally defined in a dour dictionary of Scots as:

Thwankin: used of clouds, mingling in thick and gloomy succession.

If it is swale and the clouds are thwankin, you should probably turn back and grab your umbrella. But no! Etymologically speaking, an umbrella is something that shades you. The Latin for shade is *umbra*, and *ella* is just a diminutive. So *umbrella* is 'a little shade' – the same as a *parasol* or 'defence against the sun' – and as the clouds are already thwankin and swale you'll need a *bumbershoot*.

A bumbershoot is exactly the same as an umbrella, but it's a much better word. The *bumber* bit is a variant of brolly, and the *shoot* is there because it looks a little bit like a parachute. Bumbershoot is first recorded in America in the 1890s and, for some reason, never made it across the Atlantic, which is a crying shame as it's a beautiful word to say aloud.

If you have no bumbershoot, you will have to make do with a *Golgotha*, which was the Victorian slang term for a hat, on the basis that, as it says in Mark's Gospel:

> And they bring him unto the place Golgotha, which is, being interpreted, The place of a skull.

So with a Golgotha on your head, and bumbershoot in hand, you may now *hurple* onwards, hurple being a verb defined in an 1862 glossary of Leeds dialect as:

> To shrug up the neck and creep along the streets with a shivering sensation of cold, as an ill-clad person may do on a winter's morning. 'Goas hurpling abart fit to give a body t'dithers to luke at him!'

However, there remains the possibility that you open the door to discover that the skies are blue, the sun has got his Golgotha on, and it's a lovely day. This is unlikely, especially in Leeds, but possible. If it is a hot day, then the English language allows you to use almost any word beginning with the letters SW. *Sweltering*,

swoly, swolten, swole-hot, swullocking, swallocky will all do; however, it should be noted that swallocky means that a thunder-
storm is on the way, so you should still have your bumbershoot
to hand.

The very best sort of morning, though, is the *cobweb morning*. This is an old Norfolk term for the kind of morning
when all the cobwebs are spangled with dew and gleaming in
the misty hedgerows. On such mornings, when the world is
dewbediamonded, you can almost forgive your expergefactor
for waking you and your work for compelling you out from
your house. Dew is a beautiful thing, often said to be the tears
of Aurora, goddess of the dawn, although what she's crying
about is never specified. If you are of a scientific bent, you can
measure dew using a *drosometer*. If you are of a poetic bent, you
can contemplate what Browning called the 'sweet dew silence'. If
you are of a practical bent, you can worry about getting your feet
wet, for morning moisture can have calamitous consequences,
such as *beau traps.*

Have you ever trodden upon an innocent-looking pav-
ing stone, only to find that there is a hidden hole full of water
beneath it? The stone tilts down under your weight and the disgusting dirty rainwater (once known as *dog's soup*) spurts up all
over your ankles and into your shoes. There is a name for this.
It is called a beau trap, on the basis that it destroys the leggings
of the finely dressed beau about town. Grose's *Dictionary of the
Vulgar Tongue* from 1811 demonstrates that some annoyances
are eternal:

Beau Trap A loose stone in a pavement, under which water
lodges, and on being trod upon, squirts it up, to the great

damage of white stockings; also a sharper neatly dressed, lying in wait for raw country squires, or ignorant fops.

And the worst possible consequence of a beau trap is to have your shoes filled with water so that you can actually hear it sloshing and squeezing between your toes. There is a word for making this noise: *chorking*, as in this Scots poem of 1721:

Aft have I wid thro' glens with chorking feet,
When neither plaid nor kelt cou'd fend the weet.[1]

In fact, it may be best to set off to work on *scatches*, which are defined in a dictionary of 1721 as stilts to put the feet in to walk in dirty places, and it would certainly show a sense of balance and altitude that would make you the envy of your neighbours. Also, scatches would allow ladies to be sure that their skirts were never *daggled*, which is to say muddied at the hemline. However, walking on scatches would, I imagine, require an awful lot of practice and they would be hard to stow away at work, so you could instead go for *backsters*, which are the planks of wood laid out over soft mud used by people who want to wander around on the seashore without getting their boots or their clothes dirty.

That's it. The door has closed behind you. So it's time to check whether you've got your keys and your phone and your purse or wallet. This is done by *grubbling* in your pockets. Grubbling is like groping, except less organised. It is a verb that usually refers to pockets, but can also be used for feeling around in desk drawers that are filled with nicknacks and whatnot. It can even have a

---

[1] Scots dialect was invented by poets who couldn't think of a rhyme.

non-pocket-related sexual sense, although this is rare and seems only ever to have been used by the poet Dryden, as in his translation of Ovid's *Ars Amatoria* where he rather wistfully arranges to meet his lover thus:

> There I will be, and there we cannot miss,
> Perhaps to Grubble, or at least to Kiss.

Having established beyond doubt that you've forgotten your keys, that your wallet/purse is empty and that your phone is not charged, you can now decide that it's too late to do anything about it and instead *incede* (advance majestically) to work. Or, if inceding is beyond you, you may *trampoose* to your chosen mode of transport.

Transport

There are so many methods of getting to and from your place of labour that the lexicographically-minded may simply drown in words. Pliny the Elder records that in the days of Augustus Caesar a boy managed to train a dolphin to carry him to school every morning, a story that resulted in the English word *delphinestrian*. However, in default of a dolphin you may make do with a *cacolet*, which is a comfortable basket affixed to a mule for the benefit of Pyrenean travellers. You could even *brachiate* to work, brachiate being the technical term for the way that Tarzan swings through the jungle. This gives a fantastic workout to the upper body, but requires that you have a continuous line of trees between your house and your office. If you have enough horses and too little sleep, you could opt for a *besage*, which is a bed carried on the backs of four horses. I would say that a besage was the finest form of transport that I've ever heard of, except that I can't see how the horses would know which way to go if their passenger were snoozing. And it's a cruel thing to put somebody in a bed and not allow them to sleep. If there was a solution to this problem of the besage, it is not, alas, recorded in the *Dictionary of Obsolete and Provincial English*.

Cars

But to return to the more prosaic methods of transport, let us begin with the motorcar. In the Second Book of Kings, God decides that he doesn't like Ahab one little bit. In fact, he wants to 'cut off from Ahab him that pisseth against the wall'. This is actually a relatively common ancient Hebrew phrase meaning 'every man jack of them'. Anyway, the chosen instrument of God's off-cutting will be a chap called Jehu (pronounced *gee who*). So Jehu jumps into a chariot and heads off to kill the king. The king's watchman sees the approaching chariot and dashes down to tell the monarch that 'the driving is like the driving of Jehu son of Nimshi; for he driveth furiously.' This one clause in the Bible was all that the English language needed to import his name and immortalise Jehu as a noun for a furious driver.

A *jehu* is a particularly bad (or good) thing if you are driving down *jumblegut lane*, which was an eighteenth-century term for a bumpy road too obvious in its origin to require any explanation at all. However, jehus and jumbleguts aside, you are much more likely to get caught in a *thrombosis* of traffic, wherein the veiny and arterial roads of the metropolis are blocked by the embolism of roadworks and by clots that have broken down.

Thus Jehu sits immobile in his chariot and gazes enviously at the bus lane.

Bus

The plural of bus is, of course, *buses*. But it's a curious little point of history that, etymologically, the plural of bus would be *bus*. The *voiture omnibus*, or 'carriage for everybody' was introduced in Paris in 1820, and the plural would be *voitures omnibus*, which wouldn't affect the shortening at all. (The same, incidentally, would apply to the *taximeter cabriolet*.)

The central problem with buses is that you wait for ages and then none come along. This waiting (or *prestolating*) is a miserable affair as it's usually raining, and you huddle up in the bus shelter, which starts to feel rather like a *xenodochium* or hostel for pilgrims, inhabited by people who peer optimistically down the road for the approaching Godot.

When your bus does arrive, it is all too likely to be *chiliander*, or containing a thousand men, at which point you have to barrel onto the monkey board like a spermatozoa trying to get into the egg. Once within, you have no choice but to *scrouge*, which is helpfully defined in the OED thus:

> To incommode by pressing against (a person); to encroach on (a person's) space in sitting or standing; to crowd. Also, to push or squeeze (a thing).

But scrouge you must, and furiously, while at the same time looking out for *chariot buzzers*. Chariot buzzers are pickpockets who work on buses, but as the term is Victorian, you ought to be able to recognise them by their antiquated attire.

Margaret Thatcher never said 'Anybody seen in a bus over the age of thirty has been a failure in life.' However, the poet Brian Howard (1905–58) did. It's a rather snobby-sounding comment, but given that Brian Howard published only one serious book of poems, and given that the one biography of him is titled *Portrait of a Failure*, one must assume that he spent a lot of time on buses himself.

Nonetheless, the over-thirty-year-old who wishes to be thought a success, but has no access to an automobile or jetpack, should probably opt for a sub- or superterranean train.

Train

Trains present their own problems. For starters you need to fight your way singlehanded through a railway station just to get on one. This involves dodging a lot people with heavy, bruising suitcases who are all milling around like an illustration of Brownian motion.

The people who design guided missiles refer to a *balladromic course*, which is the path that a rocket takes towards its target, ignoring everything else and moving at speeds in excess of Mach 3. This is probably the best way to approach a station concourse: know where your platform is and be ready to explode at the slightest provocation. Keep it balladromic.

If you are of a more pacifist and peacenik disposition, you could always *gaincope*, which is 'to go across a field the nearest way', and is a word more suited to the pastures and meadows of Olde Englande. But what you really need is a *whiffler*.

There are very few whifflers today, if any; and I've never understood this, as a whiffler for hire at a station entrance could make an awful lot of money during rush hour. A whiffler is, according to the OED:

> One of a body of attendants armed with a javelin, battle-axe, sword, or staff, and wearing a chain, employed to keep the way clear for a procession.

Of course, a full-time whiffler (if you could afford one) would be useful at all sorts of events such as Christmas shopping or cocktail parties. But at rush hour, a whiffler is not merely useful, but necessary. Without your whiffler you may well be reduced to a state of *hemothymia*, which is what psychiatrists call an impulse to murder, or, more literally, bloodlust.

If you are ever reduced to such a helpless state of violent anger that you want to set about your fellow commuters with a bow and arrow, you should be comforted that the English language already has a phrase in place for you. Grose's *Dictionary of the Vulgar Tongue* (1811) says:

> **Have among you, you blind harpers**; an expression used in throwing or shooting at random among the crowd.

This constitutes some usefully enigmatic final words before the ticket inspector wrestles you to the ground.

If you ever do make it to the train, then you can settle down with your coffee and newspaper and spend your journey chuckling over the obituaries. Incidentally, the thing round the coffee cup that stops you burning your fingers is a *zarf*, and a newspaper is much more fun when referred to as a *scream sheet*.

None of this applies of course if the train is so *thringed*, thronged and crammed that you cannot get a seat. Whether this is better or worse than being scrouged in a bus or clotted in a traffic thrombosis is a question that I cannot answer; all I can tell you is that the standard unit of measurement for pain is a *dol* and is measured with a *dolorimeter*.

Clocking in

By the time you arrive anywhere near your place of work you ought to be exhausted, bruised, battered, frustrated and generally broken in to twenty-first-century life. Nothing from here on in can be as bad as the commute, so things are looking up. You may celebrate this fact with a sly *dew drink*, which is a beer taken before the working day begins. This will delay you still further, but as you are almost inevitably the *postreme* (one who is last) as it stands, and as your tardiness is hardly your fault but can be blamed on the traffic/trains/bus driver/vengeful God or whatnot, a dew drink seems to be exactly what you need and deserve.

Once refreshed you can stride into the *barracoon*, or slave depot, refreshed and ready to do a passable impression of a day's work. Of course, you don't stride into the barracoon: the correct method for entering the workplace is to *scuddle* in, which Dr Johnson defined as:

Scuddle: To run with a kind of affected haste or precipitation.

It doesn't matter how slowly you ambled up the front steps. Or how you paused to admire the pretty clouds in the sky: the actual entrance to the office should be done at a scuddle. The correct method is to hyperventilate a few times to make yourself out of breath. Once gasping, give both cheeks a firm pinch and then hurl yourself at the doors, slamming them loudly as you shoot through and stagger to a halt in the middle of your office. Try to speak. You can't. You're too out of breath, swallowing air like a man who has nearly drowned. At last, gazing around you with wild innocent eyes, and with your scuddle complete, you finally manage to ask with perfect seeming-sincerity, and as though you don't already know the answer to the question: 'Am I late?'

Chapter 5

10 a.m. – The Morning Meeting

Staying awake – listening – arguing – yes, no, who cares?
– mugwumps – keeping quiet

ᴄᴀᴀᴄ

Offices are peculiar places and nobody is ever quite sure what happens in them, least of all the people who work there. But the day tends to begin with a morning meeting, in which everybody decides what they will fail to do for the rest of the day. This is usually held around a little table, or, in a particularly modern office, standing up or even walking, a strangely nomadic habit known as *pedeconferencing*. Indeed, if trends continue, the offices of the future will hold their morning meetings at an all-out sprint, with the winner getting to be boss for the day.

Medieval guilds would call this a *morn-speech*, the ancient Greeks a *panegyris*, the medieval church a *synod*. In Turkey a council of state was called a *divan*, after which the item of furniture is named – so in Milton's *Paradise Lost*, when all the demons of Hell are 'rais'd from their dark divan', it has nothing to do with comfy seating arrangements. However, the best word for a meeting is a *latrocinium*.

A latrocinium is, technically speaking, a robber-council. So, when deciding what to thieve next, Ali Baba and his 40 thieves would have held a 41-strong latrocinium in their magical cave. It is up to the conscience of the individual office-worker to decide whether it is a latrocinium that they attend, but as the word is incomprehensible and sounds pleasantly similar to latrine, it should be used at all possible opportunities. Moreover, latrocinium has a great and significant history. The word was first applied to the Second Council of Ephesus, a grand meeting of the fifth-century church to decide upon the exact nature of Christ and who should therefore be burnt. It was so riotous, raucous and disagreeable that the Pope declared the whole thing null and void, called it a latrocinium, and then held another council at Chalcedon, which reversed all of its decisions. As most morning meetings, like most mornings, will someday be thought better of, latrocinium has resonance.

So, everybody here? When you read the minutes of a meeting, whether it's a board-meeting, an AGM or an orgy, you will find near the top the cumbersome phrase 'apologies for absence', or in some particularly verbose cases 'apologies for non-attendance'. This can be done away with. You see, there is a single (and singularly suitable) word for that: *essoinment*.

Essoinment is the act of *essoining*, and essoining is (OED):

> To offer an excuse for the non-appearance of (a person) in court; to excuse for absence.

So all that the minutes of the meeting really need is 'Essoinments' followed by a list of names. Once the essoinments are given, the *constulting* (or being stupid together) can begin.

Eutychus in the boardroom

At any given meeting somebody is bound to go on too long, and it's usually the first speaker. It doesn't really matter if the speaker is St Paul himself, as is clear from the Book of Acts, Chapter 20:

> And upon the first day of the week, when the disciples came together to break bread, Paul preached unto them, ready to depart on the morrow; and continued his speech until midnight. And there were many lights in the upper chamber, where they were gathered together. And there sat in a window a certain young man named Eutychus, being fallen into a deep sleep: and as Paul was long preaching, he sunk down with sleep, and fell down from the third loft, and was taken up dead.

This is a story to remember if anybody ever tells you about the enthusiasm and ecstasy of the early Christians. Indeed, if there were any justice in this world or the next, Eutychus would by now be the patron saint of people who doze off during sermons.

There are all sorts of precise and technical words for exactly how somebody might bore you. For example, Henry Cockeram's *English Dictionarie* of 1623 has the word *obganiate*, which he defines as 'to trouble one with often repeating of one thing', and which comes from the Latin for 'growl'. So once the same point has been made for the umpteenth time in the umpteenth different way, you can nod and murmur 'Obganiation' as though it weren't rude.

If the obganiation comes down to the repetition of a particular word – like 'teamwork', 'delivery', or 'chryselephantine' – it becomes *battology*. Battology is named after an ancient

Greek king called Battus, who founded the city of Cyrene but is remembered in the English language only for the fact that he had a stammer. A word can be battologised so often that it relinquishes all meaning or significance and becomes a pure series of sounds that flutter around the meeting table. This is called *semantic satiation*, or 'lapse of meaning'.

But it is not merely repetition that annoys: there's some talk that is pointless in the first place. One can, for example, speculate with neither fruit nor point about how a client might react to something that will never happen, or where the company will be in twenty years' time. Such pointless speculation is technically known as *mataeology*, and such speculators as *mataeologians*.[1] And though this term of abuse is usually applied to theologians, it is as rife in the corporation as the cathedral.

Listening

In all this, the important thing is to look as though you're listening. If you are actually listening, that's even better, but let us start with simple goals. Evelyn Waugh, in his later years, used to have an ear trumpet. It probably wasn't even necessary, but he would hold it conspicuously to his shell-like during conversations, and, when he was bored, would just as conspicuously put it back in his pocket, sometimes while you were in midsentence. This is a Bad Tactic, unless you own the company.

---

[1] *Mataeology* comes from the Greek *mataios*, meaning pointless, and *logia*, meaning words. This same root also gave the English language *mataeotechny*, which means 'an unprofitable or pointless science, skill or activity'.

Much better is the method adopted by the actor Peter Lorre when he had fled the Nazis and managed to get a meeting with Alfred Hitchcock in London. Lorre knew no English, but as Hitchcock was remarkably enamoured of the sound of his own voice this was not a problem. When Lorre had to speak, he said 'Yes'. For the rest of the time:

> I had heard that [Hitchcock] loved to tell stories and so I watched him like a hawk and when I was of the opinion he had just told the punch line of a story I broke out in such laughter that I almost fell off my chair.

If you take this method and replace laughing with nodding, you have achieved all you really need to do in the morning meeting: you have become *nod-crafty*.

Nod-crafty is defined in the OED as 'Given to nodding the head with an air of great wisdom'. And once you notice nod-crafties, they're everywhere. Those who are paid to interview people on television are notoriously nod-crafty. Indeed, as many interviews are conducted with only one camera, which is pointed at the interviewee, they then have to set everything up again for a second series of shots that show nothing but the interviewer nodding. In the trade, these are called *noddies*. W.H. Auden pointed out in 1969 that a lot of doctors are nod-crafty, that's despite the fact that the OED doesn't record any uses after 1608. But the best place to observe the nod-crafty is in an art gallery. Here the nod-craftiest will approach a picture, pause, tilt up their aesthete chins for a few seconds of apprecia-tion and then finally, with a small smile, nod. The pictures rarely nod back.

In an office meeting, being nod-crafty can be combined with *pectination*. This is when the fingers are interlaced like two combs (the Latin for comb was *pectin*). Well-pectinated fingers and a head like a rocking horse should be enough to get you through the meeting unscathed, especially if you are also wise enough to keep your mouth shut and play at *mumbudget*, a lovely old phrase for keeping quiet.

I should warn you that Sir Thomas Browne observed in his *Pseudodoxia Epidemica* (1646) that:

> To set cross leg'd, or with our fingers pectinated or shut together
> is accounted bad, and friends will perswade us from it.

It's at times like this that you know who your real friends are.

Argument

There are times, though, when good people have to take a stand, even at the morning meeting. Sometimes you can no longer sit there in silent *longanimity*, but must stand up and speak out for what you believe in, such as comfier chairs and a new printer. At such times you should remember Cicero before the Senate, Socrates before the Athenians, Jesus before Pilate, and that they all ended up dead. So it's probably better to follow the example of Lord Copper's underling in Evelyn Waugh's *Scoop*:

> When Lord Copper was right he said 'Definitely, Lord Copper';
> when he was wrong, 'Up to a point.'

You must not simply *ding* people, ding being an eighteenth-century term for telling a chap what he really doesn't want to hear. If you tell your opponent that they're an idiot and that you'd no more take their advice on innovative teamwork than you would ask a rabbi whether to go for streaky or back, it may cause a scene. Far better to start off with the words: 'Permit me to *discept*.' And then, before anybody has a chance to grab a dictionary and discover that *discepting* means 'disagreeing utterly', you can continue with: 'I see what you're saying and it's *ultra-crepidarian*.' Be careful here to put the stress on *ultra*, as words with *ultra* always sound cool.

Ultracrepidarianism is 'giving opinions on subjects that you know nothing about', and is thus a terribly useful word. Ultracrepidarian was introduced into English by the essayist William Hazlitt, but it goes back to a story about the great ancient Greek painter Apelles.

The story goes that Apelles used to leave his new paintings out on public display and then hide behind a pillar to hear people's reactions. One day he overheard a cobbler pointing out that Apelles had painted a shoe all wrong. So he took the painting away, corrected the shoe and put it out on display again the next day.

The cobbler came back, saw that Apelles had taken his advice and was so proud and puffed up with conceit that he started talking loudly about what was wrong with the leg; at which point Apelles jumped out from his hiding place and shouted: '*Ne sutor ultra crepidam*',[2] which approximately translates as 'the

---

[2] Apelles was Greek, but the only version of the story we have is in Latin.

cobbler should go no further than the shoe'. Thus *ultracrepidarian* literally means 'beyond-the-shoe'.

Providing that nobody else at the table knows that little story, you can use *ultracrepidarian* with impish impunity.

Though this may not provide a *sockdolager*, or winning point in an argument, it will nonetheless give you a certain gravitas and mystery that will unsettle any dictionaryless meeting. Nor should your attack end here; it should be pressed home with all the ferocity of a Vandal sacking Rome. In fact, this may be the moment to get all Cab Calloway on your colleagues' sorry bottoms.

Yes, No, Who cares?

Cabell Calloway was one of the great big-band leaders of the 1930s and 40s. He succeeded Duke Ellington at the Cotton Club, made 'Minnie the Moocher' a hit, travelled around America in a private train in which he kept his green Lincoln car, and, when not drinking and womanising his way around New York, he wrote a dictionary.

Cab Calloway's Hepsters Dictionary: Language of Jive went through six editions between 1938 and 1944, and even includes a test section and translation essays. The idea was that the lonely American, exiled in the Mid-West, Deep South or Nameless North, could prepare himself for the lingo of the Big Apple. It can also be used in the office of the present day to startling effect.

A little preparation is required. Physically, you can only speak in hepster jive if you are sitting in the correct posture:

slouched in your chair, eyelids half-down, legs stretched languidly under the table. If you have a toothpick, that's good. If you have a canary yellow suit and a tommy gun, that's better (although here you should consult the HR department about dress codes and office conduct). Now, suppose you wish to tell the speaker that you thoroughly concur and that you wish to progress their proposals proactively. Click your fingers, show some teeth and say, in the deepest voice you can: 'I dig your lick, baby, I dig your lick.'

A *lick* here is, of course, an ostinato phrase played upon the brass or the piano forte, transferred metaphorically to the office, and *dig* means ... well, digging means liking for reasons that nobody is really sure of. In fact, you can go one further than digging and simply exclaim: 'That's shovel city, man!'; although this phrase should not be used without careworn consideration, particularly of gender discrimination policies.

You can even be lukewarm and still keep things jive-assed. For example, if somebody is droning on and on about stuff that everybody at the meeting already knows, lean forward intently, stare threateningly into their face and say, 'We're all breathin' natural gas', thus implying by analogy that the information they thought they were revealing for the first time is already as common as air.

Downright disagreement can be properly imparted with the simple words, 'I don't go for that magoo', and that should put an end to the subject.

So that's 'Yes', 'No' and 'Who cares?', which is all you really need in life, and usually more than you need in the office where two of those will do. You can, if you like, take this principle further. Why stop at 1930s New York when you can go back to

Victorian London and act like a sweet-faced orphan or under-nourished Dickensian crossing sweeper? Of course, the costume is more demanding, but if your meeting room does have a chimney then you can burst out of it at the vital moment and register agreement by shouting 'That's screamin', mister!' And 'I'm breathin' natural gas' has its equivalent in the words 'I've seen the elephant, chum', a reference to the fact that the travelling circuses of Victorian England had made elephants commonplace to all but the most bumpkinish of rustics. 'No' can be rendered by the enigmatic expression 'Saw your timber'.

Mugwumpery

Whatever age or idiom you elect to use, the truth remains that if an argument breaks out everybody will start piling in. It's what schoolboys at Winchester College would have called a *Mons* (whereby everybody jumps on top of one boy for reasons that remain suspicious). You are no longer a *conventicle* of thoughtful professionals, you are *Dover Court*: all speakers and no listeners.[3] And it is time for a *mugwump* to step in.

A mugwump is a derogatory word for somebody in charge who affects to be above petty squabbles and factions. So when your boss tries to make peace at the meeting table like an impartial angel, he is being a mugwump.

---

[3] The church at Dover Court in Essex once contained a speaking crucifix, which may be the origin of this expression. Apparently, the crucifix insisted that the church doors were never shut, and it was therefore filled with chattering pilgrims, which may also be the origin. Unfortunately, the cross was burnt to ashes by Protestants in 1532, so we can no longer ask its opinion.

Mugwump is therefore an eminently useful word. It has a preposterous sound: the *ug* and the *ump* get across the idea of plodding stupidity, and context can give it meaning.

The origin of the word is rather extraordinary and involves the first American Bible.

There was a seventeenth-century chap called John Eliot who was a Protestant, a Puritan and a colonist in America. He wanted to convert the local natives – the Wampanoag – to Christianity and to do so he needed a Bible in their language. He learnt Massachusett, the language of the Wampanoags, and then had to invent a writing system to get it down on paper. The result was Eliot's Massachusett Bible of 1663: the first Bible ever printed in America.

Eliot had the perennial translator's problem of finding words for concepts that don't exist in a language. The Wampanoags had no centurions, no captains, no generals, and so what was he to do when such fellows cropped up in the Bible? He decided to translate all of them using the Wampanoag word for war leader: *mugquomp*.

Mugwump then disappeared for 150 years. There is neither citation nor quotation until the early nineteenth century when it reappears as a comical and derisive term for a boss.[4]

---

[4] So long is the silence that some say John Eliot's *mugquomp* has nothing to do with the nineteenth-century *mugwump*. The OED avers that there is no reason to connect the two. I might believe the OED, were it not that the first modern *mugwump* it cites is from Vermont in 1828. Vermont is only just to the north of the Wampanoag homeland. This alone would test coincidence to the limit. The second citation is from Rhode Island in 1832 and Rhode Island is slap bang in the middle of Wampanoag territory. Had *mugwump* reappeared in California or Dorset, I might credit it as an independent coinage. But geography being what

Mugwumpery can be dealt with in two ways. You can return to hepcat jive-talking and shout 'Get off the fence, Hortense!' This is an example of the mid-century American craze for throwing in a rhyming word at the end of a sentence, e.g. 'See you later, alligator', or 'What's on the agenda, Brenda?' or 'The figures from the third quarter are disappointing but we're confident that we have the sales team in place to make progress in this exciting sector, Hector'.

The other way to deal with mugwumpery is to accept it and switch to *log-rolling*, which is an American term derived from the phrase 'You roll my log, and I'll roll yours'. Log-rolling can therefore refer to the mutual and excruciatingly boring exchange of praise and plaudits, as everybody agrees that everybody else is just super. There's even a specialist term, *literary log-rolling*, that refers to authors writing complimentary reviews of each other's dreary tomes. There should be an example on the back.

Discretion

And now, once the *contekors* have stopped quarrelling, the dust has settled and everybody has resolved on a course of *aboulia* (indecisiveness) and *periergy* (needless caution), the morning meeting can finally be wrapped up. Anything further would be *supervacaneous*. Most importantly, we should leave now before anybody mentions the *tacenda*. Tacenda are those things that must never be mentioned, like the fact that the company is effectively bankrupt or overstaffed or in breach of child labour

---

it is, I am as certain as certain can be that *mugwump* is *mugquomp*, and that the first American Bible produced a fine American insult.

laws, or all three. In fact, the tacenda is the absolute opposite of the agenda: those *nefandous* words that the tongue of man should never utter in front of his colleagues, but must instead be dedicated in reverent hush to Harpocrates, the ancient and terrible god of silence.

So take your harpocratic oath, gather up your things and dash out of the meeting room. You may even have time for a quick *earnder*, which is an old Yorkshire term for a morning drinking session.

Chapter 6

11 a.m. – Taking a Break

Coffee – gossip – incredulity – cigarette

ᘖᘖᘖ

Since mankind first mastered the concept of the time, eleven o'clock has been the sacred hour of the mid-morning break. It is the holy hour of tea or coffee, and possibly a biscuit. At the eleventh chime of the clock, spring into inaction.

Even bears hold this *undecimarian* hour to be a time of eating and idleness, as is witnessed in the first book of *Winnie the Pooh*, Chapter 2:

> Pooh always liked a little something at eleven o'clock in the morning, and he was very glad to see Rabbit getting out the plates and mugs; and when Rabbit said, 'Honey or condensed milk with your bread?' he was so excited that he said, 'Both,' and then, so as not to seem greedy, he added, 'But don't bother about the bread, please.'

There are all sorts of words for this snack: *elevenses* (Kentish dialect), *dornton* (northern), *eleven hours* (Scottish), *eleven o'clock* (American) and *elevener* (Suffolk). An elevener is best, as it includes the possibility of a drink or tipple, whereas all the rest are teetotalitarian.

Of course, you mustn't be lazy. It is important to work ener-
getically at your coffee- or tea-making.[1] You may bustle around
with the mugs and spoons while the kettle *thrumbles* (makes
that rumbling noise just before it boils). And that thrumbling
will act as a summons to all the office gossips.

The word for a person who always wants to know the
latest gossip and scandal is a *quidnunc*, which is Latin for
'what now?' The practice of being a quidnunc is called either
quidnuncism or, slightly more delightfully, *quidnuncery*. There's
even an alternative term, *numquid*, which means exactly the
same thing: 'now what' instead of 'what now'. So as the tea
brews, the water cools or the coffee percolates, it is time to drop
your voices and *quother*, or speak in low tones of firings, hirings,
of bonks and rumours of bonks.

Even if you don't want to know 'what now', you will probably be told anyway. The following is from a dictionary of late
eighteenth-century slang, but it rings terribly true today:

> FIRING A GUN, Introducing a story by head and shoulders.
> A man wanting to tell a particular story, said to the company,
> Hark! did you not hear a gun? – but now we are talking of a
> gun, I will tell you the story of one.

Now they all come out: the rumours, *furphies* and strange tid-
ings – the pure joy of being a *rawgabbit* and a *spermologer*. A
rawgabbit, just in case you were wondering, is somebody who
speaks in strictest confidence about a subject of which they

---

[1] In the eighteenth century they used to mix tea and coffee together and call it
twist. In the interests of scholarship I tried this myself and do not recommend
that anybody else does.

know nothing. A rawgabbit is the person who pulls you aside and reveals in a careful whisper that the head of Compliance is having an affair with the new recruit in IT, which you know to be utterly untrue because the head of Compliance is having an affair with you, and the new recruit in IT hasn't started yet. Nonetheless, as a careful spermologer you mustn't reveal that you know too much. Being a spermologer isn't nearly as mucky as it sounds. Though it does come from the Greek for seed-gathering, spermologer's use in English is a metaphorical one for a gatherer of gossip and a seeker after scurrilous rumours.

You may begin to feel that you are in what Second World War soldiers called a *bind*.

> **Bind**. This must be the most used of all Air Force slang expressions. It may describe a person who bores with out-of-date news or who is always in the know.

Hence:

> **Binding rigid.** The act of continually retailing stale information.

Disbelief

Actually, though we are beside the kettle, most of the best rumours are started in the lavatory. The technical term for a story started in the lavatories is *latrinogram*, from *gram* being writing in Greek and *latrine* being, well, a latrine. Latrinogram is first recorded in 1944 as a British military term and was probably where guesses as to the date of D-Day were exchanged.

So popular were wartime lavatories as a source of gossip that there's a similar and slightly earlier version of latrinogram: *Elsan gen*, which is defined in a 1943 dictionary of services slang thus:

> **Elsan gen**: News which cannot be relied upon. [Literally, 'news invented in the gentlemen's toilet', Elsan being the trade name of the excellent chemical lavatories with which bombers are equipped.]

I'm not sure exactly how you would fit two people into the lavatories of an RAF bomber, or why indeed you would wish to do so. The rumble and thrumble of the engines might also make it hard to exchange the juiciest furphies in an appropriate quother. It therefore looks to me as though *Elsan gen* was a circumlocutory manner of saying that the information (or gen) was equivalent in quality to the stuff physically produced in such a cubby hole, and therefore fit only to be flushed out over Axis territory.

Soldiers of the Second World War seem to have spent as much time gossiping as fighting, if their slang is anything to go by. Aside from Elsan gen, they had *duff gen* (bad), *pukka gen* (good) and the *gen king* (the chap who knew all of the gossip before it had even happened).

All of the best rumours are false. The more that you yearn to believe a good yarn, the more likely it is that that yarn is mere *flim-flam*, *flumadiddle*, *fribble-frabble*, *effutiation*, *flitter-tripe*, *rhubarb*, *spinach*, *toffee*, *waffle*, *balductum* and *bollocks*.

This leaves the question of how you should respond to the Elsan gen. The politest method would be to tell your interlocutor that they are a *controver*, an obsolete word for an 'inventor of false gossip'. Though it's recorded in a dictionary of 1721 the word, for some reason, never caught on or even made it into any subsequent dictionaries. This strange vanishing means that you can call somebody a controver to your heart's content and they'll never know what you mean. Thus the cogs of office society can remain oily.

Alternatively, you can exclaim, as the Victorians would have done, that a story is 'all my eye and Betty Martin'. The origins of this phrase are rather peculiar. The story goes that a British sailor happened to wander into a church in some foreign and Roman Catholic country. There he heard a prayer which of course sounded like nonsense to him because it was in Latin. So far as the sailor could tell, they were saying something along the lines of 'All my eye and Betty Martin'. The original prayer was probably *Ora pro mihi, beate Martine* or 'Pray for me, blessed Martin', Saint Martin of Tours being the patron saint of innkeepers and reformed drunkards. Alternatively, it could have been *Mihi beata mater* or 'For me blessed Mother', making Betty Martin the Virgin Mary. So if you want to be sure not to blaspheme, you could just call your story-teller a *blatherskite* or *clanjanderer*. Or you could take a lesson from this singular dictionary entry:

DICK That happened in the reign of queen Dick, i.e. never: said of any absurd old story. I am as queer as Dick's hatband; that is, out of spirits, or don't know what ails me.[2]

This is my personal favourite, as it usually takes the other party a couple of seconds to figure it out.

---

[2] The second half of that entry is irrelevant, but much too much fun to leave out.

Honesty is as under-represented in the dictionary as in life. It makes occasional appearances, such as:

> BUFFING IT HOME is swearing point-blank to anything, about the same as bluffing it, making a bold stand on no backing.

But that's taken from an 1881 dictionary of New York criminal slang, so it doesn't fill you with confidence. The best you can do is a *corsned*, which was a part of ancient English law:

> **Corsned**, Ordeal bread, a Piece of Bread consecrated by the Priest for that Use, eaten by the Saxons when they would clear themselves of a Crime they were charged with, wishing it might be their Poison, or last Morsel, if they were guilty.

As we are having elevenses, you may simply reach for the nearest chocolate biscuit.

Finally, there is the gossip that has neither the virtue of truth nor the fun of falsehood, and is merely old. A standard riposte to hearing old news is to say 'Queen Anne is dead'. The phrase is first recorded in 1798 (Queen Anne having died in 1714), but it's still used in British journalistic circles. It's a slightly out of date expression for being out of date, but it does have the virtue of finality. And having informed your colleagues of the monarch's demise, you may sneak off for a cigarette.

Cigarettes

James VI of Scotland and I of England was a *misocapnist*, i.e. he didn't like smokers or smoking one little bit. In 1604 he wrote a pamphlet about how much he didn't like smokers called *A Counter-Blaste to Tobacco*. A few years later the Bishop of Winchester translated *Counter-Blaste* into Latin. Why anybody would have bothered translating an anti-smoking tract into Latin is beyond me, but that didn't stop the Bishop of Winchester. He called the translation the *Misocapnus*, which is Latin for 'against smoke', and the word blew gently into the English language as *misocapnist* (the noun) and *misocapnic* (the adjective).

The primary reason that James I didn't like tobacco was that it was a habit newly imported from the American Indians, whom he thought simply horrible. He asks his subjects:

> ... shall we, I say, without blushing, abase our selves so farre, as to imitate these beastly Indians, slaves to the Spaniards, refuse to the world, and as yet aliens from the holy Covenant of God? Why doe we not as well imitate them in walking naked as they doe? in preferring glasses, feathers, and such toyes, to golde and precious stones, as they do? yea why do we not denie God and adore the Devill, as they doe?

Does that put you off your ciggy? No? Then off we go to our fag break (or *smoko* as the Australians call it). But first, it would be only polite for you to ask some of your co-workers if they wish to come along for a puff. The best way to word such an invitation can be found in a dictionary of highwayman's slang from 1699:

Will ye raise a Cloud, shall we Smoke a Pipe?

It's best to ask this in a raspy, piratish voice and, if possible, to carry a blunderbuss. But you can't smoke here. The misocapnic ghost of James I still haunts us all with smokeless restrictions and rules, and so you will probably not be able to raise a cloud at your own desk and must instead retreat to a designated smoking area, an indignity that was never suffered by highwaymen.

'Designated smoking area' is an unnecessarily wordy and official name for a *fumatorium* or even better, a *coughery*, which is a place where people go to cough. Sir Thomas Urquhart wrote that before a service, priests:

> … dunged in the dungeries, pissed in the pisseries, spit in the spiteries, coughed in the cougheries and doted in the doteries, that to the Divine Service they might not bring any Thing that was unclean or foul.

Even though Urquhart wasn't being thoroughly serious about that, coughery is still as good a name as any for the little yard by the office's back door where a forlorn but persistent *tabagie* still holds out like the last remnants of a dying Amazonian tribe. A tabagie, by the way, is the technical term for a group of smokers, although the collective noun (as in a *pride of lions* or a *murder of crows*) is a *parliament of smokers*. Both words emerged in the nineteenth century, the high-point of fumious vocabulary. For the Victorian, a smoker was not merely a smoker, he was a *tobacconalian* or a *nicotinian.* So if you don't feel like using 'coughery' and 'raising a cloud' you could always escape from the misocapnists by taking 'a voyage to the Land of the Nicotinians'.

The Land of the Nicotinians would be a fabulous place: shrouded in impenetrable clouds and dotted with naturally occurring humidors. There the obedient Nicotinians would do homage before their goddess Nicotia, and no, I didn't just make her up. Nicotia too is an invention of Victorian poetry. The American poet James Russell Lowell even wrote in the 1860s about her divine lineage. She was, according to him, the daughter of Bacchus, god of revelry, and her mother was the daughter of Morpheus, god of dreams.

> Now the kind nymph to Bacchus born
> By Morpheus' daughter, she that seems
> Gifted upon her natal morn
> By him with fire, by her with dreams,
> Nicotia, dearer to the Muse
> Than all the grape's bewildering juice,
> We worship, unforbid of thee …

But the goddess can't even protect her poor worshippers who, persecuted by the malevolent misocapnists, are forced to raise their clouds in distant pavement cougheries in the wind and the rain.

And why? Because smoking is considered unhealthy (and Red Indian). But it was not always thus! Once upon a time there was no great divide between the sporty and the smoky, because smoking *was* a sport. There was such a thing as a *smoking match.* It is recorded in Joseph Strutt's *Sports and Pastimes of the People of England* (1801) in an entry between 'Grinning Matches' and 'Hot Hasty-Pudding Eaters'.

> **Smoking matches** are usually made for tobacco-boxes, or some other trifling prizes, and may be performed two ways: the first is a trial among the candidates who shall smoke a pipe full of tobacco in the shortest time: the second is precisely the reverse; for he of them who can keep the tobacco alight within his pipe, and retain it there the longest, receives the reward.

Smoking matches were filled with twists and turns and yellow-nail-biting excitement. Consider this match report from 1723, when men were men and smoking was a competitive sport:

> Oxford, a scaffold being built up for it just at Finmore's, an ale-house. The conditions were, that anyone (man or woman) that could smoak out three ounces of tobacco first, without drinking or going off the stage, should have twelve shillings. Many tryed, and 'twas thought that a journeyman taylour, of St Peters in the East, would have been victor, he smoaking faster than, and being many pipes before, the rest; but at last he was so sick, that 'twas thought he would have dyed; and an old man, that had been a souldier, and smoaked gently, came off conquerour, smoaking the three ounces quite out, and he told one, (from whom I had it,) that, after it, he smoaked four or five pipes the same evening.

In the seventeenth century smokers were even given the ridiculously romantic title of *fume gallants*, conjuring an image of white knights with yellow teeth. There used to be none of this nonsense about smoking being bad for you. In fact it was once generally recognised (but since covered up by misocapnist spoilsports) that smoking cures you (a fact that has always been known to salmon). Hence a medical dictionary of 1859 contains this fascinating entry:

INSUFFLATION (*in*, in; *sufflo*, to blow). The act of blowing a
gas or vapour into a cavity of the body, as when tobacco smoke
is injected into the rectum, or air blown into the lungs, &c.

I don't know how useful that word will be to you; but if the necessity ever arises, you will at least know what to call it.

Anyhow, having arrived in the tabagie, you must now obtain a cigarette (the cost these days being such that nobody at all buys their own). The correct 1950s way to ask for a smoke is 'Butt me', which works very well unless you're talking to a ram. If you are among particularly generous company, somebody may even offer you a cancer stick without being asked, in which case they should, if they wish to be equally 1950s, accompany their generosity with the kind words, 'Have a firework'.

Of course, the problem with accepting cigarettes from others is that they may smoke a different kind of coffin nail to you. For example, you may be offered a *straight*, or manufactured cigarette, when what you were really after was a *quirly* which you roll yourself. And even if you and your patron are in agreement that smoking should be an arts and crafty type of affair, their favourite tobacco may be to you little more than *mundungus*, which is 'bad, or rank tobacco', also called *old rope*.

Now that you have something tobaccical, look around for a *salamander*, or 'red hot iron used for lighting tobacco'. If none has been provided, you may settle for an entry in

Dr Johnson's dictionary:

> **Sponk**. A word in Edinburgh which denotes a match, or any
> thing dipt in sulphur that takes fire: as, *any sponks will ye buy?*

Once you have a sponk you may *cock your organ* (light your
pipe) and begin to *funk*. Funk was the standard term for smoking from the late seventeenth century through to the early nineteenth, when it suddenly started to mean a panic attack, and
then in the twentieth century it became a kind of music. Funk
was also, by association, a term for tobacco smoke, which means
that you are currently smelling rather *funky*.

Ashcan used to be a slang term for wasted time. So unfortunately you must funk as fast as you can and then remember the
poor of the parish. This from a dictionary of Victorian slang:

> HARD-UPS, cigar-end finders, who collect the refuse pieces
> of smoked cigars from the gutter, and having dried them, sell
> them as tobacco to the very poor.

So don't whatever you do stamp out your stub. Remember the
hard-ups, and remember those devilish Red Indians that James
I hated. But why rely on his misocapnist claptrap? Instead we
can use an actual account of tobacco in the New World: the very
first written record of the human smoking. It's from Gonzalo
Fernandez de Oviedo, who visited Hispaniola in 1535 and
recorded how the native chieftain would smoke until he passed
out and then 'his wives, who are many, pick him up, and carry
him to his hammock'.

But not for you! Back to your desk, and pretend to work.

Chapter 7

Noon – Looking as Though You're Working

Effortlessness – sales and marketing – emails – approaching bankruptcy – asking for a raise

ᘏᗢᘏᗢ

Sprezzatura, or the nonchalance of the perfect office worker

It is probably time to do some work, or at least appear to. Work, like justice, must not only be done, it must be seen to be done. Appearances are everything, reality an inconvenience.

In the Renaissance, there was an exquisite idea named *sprezzatura*, the nonchalance of the perfect courtier. It was the newest and most fashionable thing once. You see, all through the medieval period, knights had known what they had to do: they had to be knights in armour. They had to be chivalrous to ladies of course, but they also had to be warlike and violent and bloodthirsty. When the Renaissance came along the bar was raised somewhat. Skill at arms was still valued, but suddenly a man was expected to stop being medieval and be Renaissance, which meant learning to do all sorts of things like read, write, paint, play a few instruments, speak Latin, appreciate sculpture and whatnot.

These new requirements were handily laid out in a sort of textbook by Baldassare Castiglione. Castiglione was the very model of a modern courtier and peregrinated around Italy being a friend of Raphael and the Medicis. He was an ambassador, a classicist, a soldier and a sonneteer. And he wrote a book about how you too could be like him. It was called *The Book of the Courtier*, was translated into every language anyone could think of, and for centuries afterwards was the European definition of the Perfect Man. However, there was one word in it that could never quite be translated properly: *sprezzatura*.

Sprezzatura sort of means nonchalance, but more precisely it means the appearance of nonchalance – the effort made to disguise the fact that you're making an effort. So you should be a brilliant musician, for example, but nobody should ever see or hear you practise. Thus you take your flute or lute or whatever and disappear well out of earshot and work at your musicianship in secret. Then when somebody says, 'Hey, Baldassare, do you play the lute at all?', you can reply, 'The lute? Hmm. I've never tried but pass it here … Oh, like this?' – and then knock off a little virtuoso performance while looking bored. Everybody gasps in astonishment at your effortless ability, and you appear much better than you would have done had the whole court heard you plink plonk plunking for months on end.

This Great Untranslatable, graceful nonchalance hiding discreet diligence, simply had to be imported into the other European languages including English, where the OED defines it as 'studied carelessness'.

But the Renaissance is dead and done, and with it sprezzatura has wandered nonchalantly from the language. It has been replaced, though, by that most horrible of ideas: *presenteeism*, the belief that you should be the first in and the last to leave and do nothing in between because it's not work but the appearance of work that is rewarded.

But imagine, just imagine, if sprezzatura were brought back to the modern office. Gone would be those dreary press releases saying 'Flumshoe Incorporated are really excited about this new acquisition! John Splunkington, Head of Mergers, said: "I want to thank everybody on the team who have put in the long hours over the last year to make this deal happen."' Instead, you would have: 'Flumshoe Incorporated is filled with languorous indifference at this new acquisition. John Splunkington, who lolls gracefully around the mergers department, murmured: "It was nothing. A trifle really", and continued to play his lute.'

Earning a living

But sprezzatura is gone, and it is time to actually sit down at your desk and *quomodocunquize*. Quomodocunquizing is 'making money in any way that you can', and was used in this glorious phrase by Sir Thomas Urquhart in 1652: 'Those quomodocunquizing clusterfists and rapacious varlets.'

A *clusterfist* is, as you might imagine, somebody who keeps a tight grip on his cash. Quomodocunquizing can be used of governments, football clubs, famous people who advertise things, and of course yourself. For we are quomodocunquizing animals. It is the chief symptom of *plutomania*, which is 'the frenzied pursuit of money'.

In case you were wondering, the planet Pluto is named after the god of the underworld. As gold and silver and diamonds are always found underground, the ancients decided that Pluto was also the god of money, hence plutomania, *plutocracy* (government by the rich), *plutography* (written descriptions of the lives of the rich) and *plutolatry* (worship of wealth).

The best course for the aspiring plutomaniac is to become a *plutogogue*, which can mean either somebody who speaks only to the rich or somebody who speaks only for them. The former is commonly known as sales, and the latter advertising, but plutogogue is a much more impressive word to put on your business card or CV.

If you would prefer, though, to have a more rough-and-ready feel to your job description in sales, you could always describe yourself as a *barker*, which was the Victorian term for somebody who stood outside a shop shouting its virtues into the smoggy air. Unfortunately, Victorian slang dictionaries also contain this entry:

> CHUFF IT, *i.e.*, be off, or take it away, in answer to a street seller who is importuning you to purchase.

A useful phrase for dealing with cold callers.

Email

These days, the telephone is used less and less and email more and more. It's enough to bring back the noble business of *screeving*. A screever is a professional writer of begging letters.

These letters would not be sent, rather they would be given to somebody else who would use them as a sort of certificate of authenticity as they told their hard luck story. Luckily for historians of strange trades, a typical Victorian screever's price list survives:

Friendly letter 6d
Long ditto 9d
Petition 1s
Ditto with signatures 1s 6d
Ditto with forged names 2s 6d
Ditto 'very heavy' (dangerous) 3s
Manuscript for a broken-down author 10s
Part of a play for ditto 7s 6d

It is somehow comforting to know that there were broken-down authors even then.

There's something rather nasty about the sound of the word *screever* that makes it less than wholesome. It's a mixture of *scream* and *grieve* and would not look good on the résumé. If you want a more high-flying term for a writer of begging letters, the Victorians also called them *high fliers*.

Once you have screeved and flown high, the matter is up to the *answer jobber*, who is, as you may have guessed, a professional writer of answers. This is the way most of us spend at least the first half hour of our day at the desk, picking through the emails that have accumulated like dew in the night.

It's a shame that there are not, as yet, any particularly beautiful names for kinds of email. In the days of pen and paper, a little letter could be called a *notekin* or a *breviate* or a *letterling*, but a short email is a short email and nobody seems to be doing much about it. Some of the terms for letters can be saved, though. For example, an *omnibus letter* – one intended for several recipients – could easily become an 'omnibus email' and replace the tedious 'group email'. In fact, here is a list of the possibilities, in which I have simply replaced 'letter' with 'email' and provided the old definition.

Bread and butter email – one saying thank you.

Cheddar email – one to which several people have contributed, just as several dairies contribute to a single cheddar cheese.

Email of comfort – one that assures a creditor that a debt will be paid, without being legally binding.

Journal email – one that talks about what you've been up to lately.

Email of placards – one that grants permission.

Email of marque – one that allows you to behave like a pirate. These should be sent sparingly. (Letters of marque would be sent out to ships' captains when war was declared, allowing them to plunder the merchant ships of the enemy nation.)

Laureate email – one announcing victory.

Email of Uriah – 'A treacherous email, implying friendship, but in reality a death warrant', thus (almost) *Brewer's Dictionary of Phrase and Fable*. I send a lot of these. The name refers to the Second Book of Samuel: 'And it came to pass in the morning, that David wrote a letter to Joab, and sent it by the hand of

Uriah. And he wrote in the letter, saying, Set ye Uriah in the forefront of the hottest battle, and retire ye from him, that he may be smitten, and die.'

Once the emails are finished with, there are all sorts of jobs for a busy *jobler* to do (a jobler is somebody who does small jobs). You could rearrange the stuff on your desk, update your status on the interweb, or you could work hard as a *nephelolater* (one who admires passing clouds). Whatever you do, though, don't look at the accounts unless you have *audit ale*.

Audit ale was a specially strong and tasty kind of ale to be drunk only on the day of an audit. You can't buy it any more. You couldn't even buy it back in 1823 when Byron wrote 'The Age of Bronze', lamenting the fallen state of modern Britain and asking:

Where is it now, the goodly audit ale,
The purse-proud tenant never known to fail?

And you can't do an audit without an audit ale, because you should never look at your finances without a good strong drink in your hand. Bankruptcy looks so much better through the bottom of a bottle. If ale-sodden insolvency does beckon, all that you can do is grab what you can while you can. A pleasant little word for this is *deaconing*. A dictionary of Americanisms from 1889 has this helpful definition:

To deacon land, to filch land by gradually extending one's fences or boundary lines into the highway or other common property.

So move that pile of papers just a little onto your podmate's desk, and dream of slow victories and distant laureate emails.

Deaconing can also mean 'putting the most attractive goods on the top of a pile' or 'watering down liquor' or 'killing a calf the second it is born'. Why it should mean this nobody knows, but all the phrases are American and nineteenth-century, so one must imagine that nineteenth-century American deacons were all dishonest, acquisitive, calf-murdering scoundrels.

Asking for a raise

If you have been deaconing for long enough and have acquired enough territory, it may even be time to ask for a raise. This must be done with tact and discretion. Begin by approaching your boss in a *sardonian* manner. A sardonian is, according to the OED, 'one who flatters with deadly intent'. The reason for this odd and unusually precise word is not a person but a plant. The *herba sardonia* was said to cause horrible facial convulsions that resembled laughter, followed by death.

You don't need to kill your boss, of course, but a bit of calculated *glavering* and flattery will take the bitter edge off any *rogitating* you happen to do (to rogitate is to ask again and again for the same thing, in the manner of a child who wants a biscuit). You could try the other route, and just call your paymaster a miser and a *sting-bum* every time they walk past, but people don't like being called a sting-bum and it could all end up being counterproductive.

Then there's the Indian custom of *Dharna*. In east India, if somebody hasn't paid their debt to you, you go and sit on their doorstep and refuse to eat. You stay there until a) the person pays up or b) you starve to death. Dharna should not be attempted with somebody who lives in an out of the way place, or who takes long holidays. But in a workplace where there are lots of other people wandering around, sitting by the door of your boss's office growing slowly thinner and thinner is bound to produce some sort of effect.

You may not get a real raise today, but you might at least get a *brevet*, which is a military term for a rise in rank without a rise in salary. Brevets are usually accompanied with a nice wodge of *Spanish money*, which is an old term for 'fair words and compliments'. And that should be enough to keep you going till lunch. Until then, you may simply *fudgel*:

To Fudgel, to make a Shew of doing somewhat to no Purpose, to trifle.

Chapter 8

1 p.m. – Lunch

*Where to eat – who pays – The Free Lunch – eating
– eating turtles – indigestion*

☙

It is the *amell*, which is to say the hour between one and two o'clock when all right-thinking creatures rush joyously from their labours to their lunch. You hardly need a clock to know that this grand hour is at hand, as your own belly will chime with impatient *borborygmi*, the rumbling noises produced by an empty stomach. H.G. Wells once wrote that:

> … few creatures seem to have found their 'perfect' food or, having found it, are able to keep to it: elephant hunters say they can tell the proximity of a herd by the borborygmic (see dictionary) noises the poor brutes emit, and Glasfurd describes a tiger's life as an alternation of uncomfortable hunger and uncomfortable repletion.

Better, as the saying goes, to live one day as an uncomfortable tiger, than a hundred years as a borborygmic elephant. The human is a *famelicose* (or constantly hungry) creature. And so to lunch!

But where? It seems a shame to visit the same sandwich shop every day, and anyway, you might be taking somebody out to lunch on expenses. Even if you are denied this fundamental right of luncheon by fate or your boss, you may simply be struck with a sudden case of *allotriophagy*, which is 'the desire, – the morbid longing, – to devour extraordinary substances commonly regarded as inedible, innutritious, or even hurtful'. It is thus a suitable term for anybody who suggests going to a kebab shop. Etymologically, though, it simply means a desire to eat other things, and it can therefore be used to break away from the old haunts rather than go to the same old *slap-bang shop*:

> **Slap-bang shop**, a petty cook's shop where there is no credit given, but what is had must be paid down with the ready slap-bang, i.e. immediately. This is a common appellation for a night cellar frequented by thieves, and sometimes for a stage coach or caravan. (1785)

If you want to go to a grander grubbery, you'll have to either find the cash, credit or, if possible, a *Sir Timothy*. Sir Timothy (sometimes known as *Sir Timothy Treat-All*) was a mythical figure recorded from the late seventeenth to the early nineteenth century who bought lunch. It was, and still can be, the title of 'One that Treats every Body and pays the Reckonings every where'.

The politer and more recondite term for such a saviour is *gastrophilanthropist*. That's from the Greek *gastro* meaning stomach (as in a gastropod that walks on its tummy) and *philanthropist* which means lover of men (but not in that way). Gastrophilanthropy is a sadly forgotten art, as people these days tend to give their money to feed the starving on the other side of the earth, rather than the peckish on this, and have thus substituted charity for kindness.

If you can find a suitably pliable Sir Timothy then you can settle down to some serious *scambling*. A scambler is defined in Dr Johnson's dictionary thus:

Scambler: A bold intruder upon one's generosity or table. [Scottish]

By which he didn't of course mean that all scamblers are Scottish, only that enough of them are for the word to have become necessary in that country first. A scambler is the only sensible eater of lunch, for the exquisite cost of most restaurants destroys the palate, whereas the knowledge that you are dining on the gastrophilanthropy of a careless Sir Timothy allows you to fill your belly without evacuating your pocket.

One way to enter into a career as a scambler is to *groke*, which is to stare wistfully at somebody while they are eating in the hope that they will give you some of their food. Groking was originally applied only to dogs, who have this habit down to a wide-eyed T. But it can just as well be applied to the hopeful scambler or anybody who sidles over to your desk when you're eating a biscuit.

But back to lunch, or more precisely, to the preparations and *precibals* thereto and of. A precibal, by the way, is another way of saying preprandial, but which can be applied to any meal including breakfast, elevenses and midnight snacks. And speaking of preprandials, what are we having to drink? In the eighteenth century the idea of not having a drink with lunch was considered so bestial that it was referred to as a *horse's meal*: as dry as straw and fit only for an animal. So it is probably best to bid adieu to any hopes for afternoon productivity now.

Actually, alcohol is the founder of that elusive snark known as the Free Lunch. People have been insisting since the 1930s that the Free Lunch does not exist in the wild, and would lock it up in that chimerical menagerie where are stored the unicorn, the phoenix and the bunyip. But the Free Lunch is not mythical, though it may be extinct. It was observed in its natural habitat by Rudyard Kipling. In 1891 Kipling visited San Francisco and observed the Free Lunch hiding behind a bunch of spittoons.

> In a vast marble-paved hall, under the glare of an electric light, sat forty or fifty men, and for their use and amusement were provided spittoons of infinite capacity and generous gape. Most of the men wore frock-coats and top-hats – the things that we in India put on at a wedding-break-fast, if we possess them – but they all spat. They spat on principle. The spittoons were on the staircases, in each bedroom – yea, and in chambers even more sacred than these. They chased one into retirement, but they blossomed in chiefest splendor round the bar, and they were all used, every reeking one of them … By instinct I sought refreshment, and came upon a bar-room full of bad Salon pictures in which men with hats on the backs of their heads were wolfing food from a counter. It was the institution of the 'free lunch' I had struck. You paid for a drink and got as much as you wanted to eat. For something less than a rupee a day a man can feed himself sumptuously in San Francisco, even though he be a bankrupt. Remember this if ever you are stranded in these parts.

Perhaps the Free Lunch is perished for ever like the dodo – too delicious to live long; or perhaps like the shy coelacanth it lurks forever unchanged and unchanging in some cold ocean canyon that we do not know. The only way to test for its existence is to order a drink and see what happens. And remember: you're not drunk if you can still read the menu.

Mrs Beeton (1836–65) was the tragic goddess of the British kitchen. She had four children, wrote a book containing 900 recipes, and dropped down dead at the age of 28. In her authoritative gospel *Mrs Beeton's Book of Household Management* she recommends the following light luncheon:

> The remains of cold joints, nicely garnished, a few sweets, or a little hashed meat, poultry or game, are the usual articles placed on the table for luncheon, with bread and cheese biscuits, butter, &c. If a substantial meal is desired, rump-steaks or mutton chops may be served, as also veal cutlets, kidneys, or any dish of that kind.

It may be best to simply cut that paragraph out of the book and calmly hand it to your one o'clock waiter. Then the eating can begin.

Mastication

The traditional cry announcing that those at the table should start eating is 'Fall-a-bord!' At which point you, and all your trenchermates, may start to gobble, gourmandise and *guttle*. The last of these words, meaning 'eat greedily', is the solid food companion to the more liquid *guzzle*. It seems a terrible shame that one of these should have died out, especially as they make such a pretty couple. Indeed, if you want to make the twins near-identical you can *guttle* your food and *guddle* your drink. It is especially convenient for the enthusiastic *gutguddler* that both words can be pronounced with your mouth full or while swallowing.

In fact, there's something just a little bit greedy about the letter G. For a gourmand who gluttonously guttles and guddles too much will end up as a *gundy-guts*, which is a pleasantly eighteenth-century way of saying 'lard-arse'.

Of the seven deadly sins only three are enjoyable: gluttony, sloth and lust balance their lethality with fun. If somebody could only think of a way of combining the three, humanity would go to Hell quite happily. The procession would be accompanied by *tooth music*, which is the sound of jolly eating that serenades all the best lunches.

Another term for thorough chewing is *Fletcherism*. Horace Fletcher (1849–1919) wrote hugely influential books on how the whole human condition can be improved by chewing. He recommended 32 chews per mouthful, and even took the seemingly unnecessary precaution of chewing his drinks. He thus became, according to him, one of the fittest men alive, and earned the grand title of 'The Great Masticator'. Such was his fame and the power of his jaws that a movement sprang up known as Fletcherism, whose adherents were called *Fletcherites* and who didn't just chew their food, but *Fletcherized* it. Thus Henry James could write to his brother: 'It is impossible, save in a long talk, to make you understand how the blessed fletcherism – so extra blessed – lulled me, charmed me, beguiled me.'

He even once commented that Fletcher had so improved his bowel movements that he 'saved my life, and what is more, he improved my disposition. By rights he should receive all my future royalties.' P.G. Wodehouse, on the other hand, merely used the word *fletcherize* in a description of a mongrel attacking a terrier.

It should perhaps be noted here that Gladstone was also a proponent of chewing every gobbet 32 times, and a sly onlooker at dinner once reckoned that he averaged 70 mastications per mouthful. However, if you look up Gladstone in the dictionary, you will find that he only gave his name to a bag and to cheap French wine, on which he reduced the importation taxes. So it may now be time to order another bottle.

But perhaps you have no appetite. Rather than being an *esquire trenchant*, you merely *pingle* your food, which is a sure prognosticator of melancholy. To pingle is to push food around your plate without really eating much of it. It's an old word, and an obscure one at that, which appears in an 1823 dictionary of Suffolk dialect (vital if you ever find yourself in Long Melford with a time machine).

> **PINGLE**. To eat a little, without appetite. 'I heen't no stummach for my wittels. I jest *pingle* a bit.'

Pingle should not be confused with *pinguid*, which means greasy, though if the food is too much the latter, it may cause the former. So if you were stuck with a bad cook in Antarctica you might pingle a pinguid penguin.

A bad cook is a crime against lunch and a sin against nature's bounty. The cow and the cabbage die for us, and the least a cook can do to reward their selfless sacrifice is to cook them well and give to their corpses an honourable marinade. To do otherwise is to be the very devil, and as the devil used to be known as *ruffin*, the old term for a bad cook was therefore:

COOK RUFFIN: The Devil of a Cook; or a very bad one. (1723)

A cook ruffin can turn the noblest beast in nature into a mere *kickshaw*, which was ruefully defined in Dr Johnson's dictionary as 'A dish so changed by the cookery that it can scarcely be known'. The word kickshaw is, in fact, a garbled version of the French *quelque chose*, which simply means 'something'. The worst restaurants of old London Town had heard the French term, wished to appear fine and Frenchified; but one must imagine that their food was as bad as their pronunciation. Some scholars take a reversed view and believe that kickshaw was a contemptuous term for French food, which was effete and enfeebled, as opposed to proper British fare, which was filled with roast beef and vigour.

Those who are, like the French, very particular about what they devour, have all sorts of lovely names. They are the *gastolaters* or stomach worshippers, they are the *ingurgitating belly-gods*. They are the *goinfres*, the *gullet-fanciers* and *golofers*. However, the finest phrase in the dictionary for such epicures is *turtle-eater*.

Turtles were well known to be the best food available to mankind before they became endangered and hard to find in the supermarket. But even in the eighteenth century to eat a turtle required a lot of money. First, you had to import the creatures alive and then have a special room built in your house to keep them in. You had to feed them on a leg of mutton every day. Then you had to have a special oven capacious enough to fit a whole turtle, and cooks specially trained in their execution and preparation. Then, of course, you had to have special turtle-eating clothes. In fact, it would be best at this point to turn to an account of a turtle feast written in 1755:

> Upon hearing the clock strike, he [the immensely wealthy host] rung his bell, and asked if his turtle cloaths were aired. While I was meditating on this new term, and, I confess unable to divine what it could mean, the servant brought in a coat and waistcoat, which my friend slipped on, and, folding them round his body like a nightgown, declared that, though they then hung so loose about him, by that time he had spoke with the turtle, he should stretch them as tight as a drum.

And once the turtle is on the table and the guests have arrived, those closest to it forget all good manners in order to obtain the finest parts. And those at the other end of the table?

> In vain did they send their plates, and solicit their share; the plunderers, who were now in possession of both the shells, were sensible to no call but that of their own appetites, and, till they had satisfied them, there was not one that would listen to anything else.

The taste of the turtle was so fine that it conquered all good manners, drained fortunes and jaded appetites. Even those who could not afford a turtle of their own could at least pretend that they were at a turtle feast. Thus the invention of *mock turtle soup*, which was simply a boiled calf's head. Those who were not obscenely rich were assured that this was the closest they would ever get to the true heaven of turtle-eating.

From all this, it should be easy to see why *turtle-eater* became a byword for those of the finest and most luxurious palate. It is, anyway, better than a *petecure*, which is modest cooking, or *rypophagy*, which means 'the eating of filth'. Rypophagy is actually a terribly useful word for insulting somebody's cookery without letting them know that you're doing it, as in: 'Thank you for such a large, and may I say rypophagous, meal. No, I mean it. I don't think I've ever eaten a meal of quite that quality before. You're a regular cook ruffin.'

Aftermath

There is a single word in the English language meaning 'a person given to remaining at table'. It is *residentarian*, and, so far as I can tell, it has been used only once, in 1680 by the writer of a rather dull religious tract who was complaining about those who sing hymns without really meaning them:

> The daily feaster, such as the Residentarians, whose legs can scarce bear about his Gross Corpulent Body, he sings, *My knees are weak through Fasting, and my Flesh faileth of Fatness.*
>
> Satan's Captive, who wallows in the Mire and Puddle of Sin and Iniquity, he sings, *O Lord, truly I am thy servant.*

But the mire and puddle of sin and iniquity is such a comfortable place, and good for one's digestion. It is a good place for belching, or *eructation*, to give it its more genteel name, and without a little after-lunch lounging one is liable to end up *wamblecropt* for the rest of the day.

Wamblecropt is the most exquisite word in the English language. Say it. Each syllable is intolerably beautiful.

Wamblecropt.

Wamblecropt gets its first mention in the *Abecedarium Anglico Latinum* of 1552, which you have doubtless read. It's a sort of early English-to-Latin dictionary. So if you were wondering what the Romans would call a 'Siege, jacques, bogard, or draught', it tells you that they are all *latrina*. It also tells you:

Wamble cropped *Stomachichus*
Wamble stomaked to be *Nauseo*
Wamblyng of stomake, or disposition, or will to vomit. *Nausea*

That ought to give you some idea, but if you want something more precise (or less Latinate) then the OED has *wamble* as 'a rolling or uneasiness of the stomach' and *wamblecropt* as being afflicted with and incapacitated by such wambling. So wamblecropt means queasy, only slightly stronger.

The odd thing about the word is that after a little citation from 1616 the wamblecropt goes into hiding and doesn't reappear until 1798 in America, where it remained. The *Massachusetts Spy* has the line, 'I feel a good deal womblecropped about dropping her acquaintance'. And that is almost the end of wamblecropt. It was revived here and there but always as a joke, an example of a dialect word, a mickey-take. For example, there was a humorous Canadian writer called Thomas Chandler Haliburton who wrote a (rather good) series of sketches in the persona of Sam Slick, who says of marriage that:

> The difference atween a wife and a sweetheart is near about as great as there is between new and hard cider: a man never tires of puttin' one to his lips, but makes plaguy wry faces at t'other. It makes me so kinder wamblecropt when I think on it, that I'm afeared to venture on matrimony at all.

Sam Slick uses the word, but I doubt that Haliburton did. It was fast disappearing down the chute of quaint dialect and all future uses are of the '"By jiminee I'll be wamblecropt", averred the blacksmith quaintly' variety.

Wambling, of the uncropt kind, survived far longer on these shores. Indeed, wambling was a standard activity of British stomachs right up to the late nineteenth century. Here are my three favourite examples:

> [My soul] can digest a monster without crudity, a sin as weighty as an elephant, and never wamble for it.
> Thomas Middleton, *A Game At Chess* (1624) (because I like the sin as big as an elephant)

> Vast fires subterranean … work and wamble in the bowels of the earth
> John Goad, *Astro-Meteorologica* (1686) (because I like the idea of the earth having indigestion)

> Yes faith have I [been in love], and have felt your flames and fires, and inclinations and wamblings.
> Thomas Betterton, *The Revenge* (1680) (because it's beautiful)

Incidentally, wamble can by extension mean to roll or stumble around and can be spelled with an O, making *womble*.

And nothing is so inclined to crop your wambles as the arrival of the bill. This is the dread moment when you hope that Sir Timothy Treat-All is a good residentarian. Otherwise, it may fall to you to waste yourself in *abligurition*. Abligurition is 'extravagant spending on food and drink' and is a terribly valuable word when it comes to filing expenses claims, especially as it has a rather legal ring to it. The wily business traveller could happily say that they had spent ten thousand pounds on conveyancing and abligurition without anybody in HR being any the wiser. It comes from the Latin word *abligurire* which meant 'to squander on dainties', and thus has the justification of antiquity.

The Romans were greedy fellows, but the ancient Greeks had no word for squandering money on long and luxurious lunches. They knew what to spend their ancient cash on. Instead of *abligurire*, they had the word *katapepaiderastekenai*, which meant 'squander your money on the love of beautiful boys'.

Chapter 9

2 p.m. – Returning to Work

Nap – phoning family members

ᢀᢀᢀ

Thank God for modern medicine. It was not until 1905 that *ergophobia* (the morbid fear of returning to work) was first identified and reported in the *British Medical Journal*. As yet there is no known cure, but doctors have been working on it, and may get back to working on it sometime soon.

There is something about a good lunch that quite cures one of the delusion that toil is ennobling. It frees one from the temptation to strive, to seek, to find and not to yield. Instead, one sees the immediate and practical necessity for a *nooningscaup*, which was the rest granted to the farm labourers of Yorkshire after a particularly laborious lunch. One might have imagined that a nooningscaup would occur at noon, and though that's correct, it should be noted that noon has moved backwards over the years. Noon was originally the ninth, or in Old English *non*, hour after dawn, which averages it out as three o'clock. Nobody is quite sure why noon moved backwards, but it did, leaving some odd words behind, one of which appears to be nooningscaup, which probably originally meant noon-song. Midday was therefore, of course, the sixth hour or *sexta hora* in Latin, from which we get *siesta*.

The world being what it is, appearances must be maintained and you ought to show your face back at the office before discreetly dozing off in your cubicle. This may be difficult, especially if your lunch hour ended up being *sesquihoral*, or an hour and a half long.

You could delay your return to work and just wander about. You could even go out for a *doundrins* or afternoon drinking session. But your absence might be noticed, and the Scots have a word for that sort of thing (or at least they did in Victorian Aberdeenshire):

> **CAUSEY-WEBS** A person is said to make *causey-webs*, who neglects his or her work, and is too much on the street.

An efficient way to make causey-webs is to *gongoozle*. Gongoozling has the benefit of being a ridiculous-sounding word that manages to contain *gone*, *goose* and *ooze* all in one. In fact, it's probably a portmanteau of two ancient dialect terms: *gawn* meaning 'stare curiously' and *gooze* meaning 'stare aimlessly'; but its technical meaning, set for eternity in the OED, is to stare at canals. This is one of those words that must cause even the most avid dictionary reader to stop and wonder to himself: Why?

The term gongoozler is first recorded in a glossary of canal terminology:

> **Gongoozler**, an idle and inquisitive person who stands staring for prolonged periods at anything out of the common. This word is believed to have its origin in the Lake District of England.

There is still a small canal in Ulverston, but it is closed, which must render the lives of the true and native gongoozlers even less eventful than before. Nonetheless, it is as pleasant a way of spending an afternoon as any, and there are always the ducks.

But if canals don't interest you, the thing to do is to head back to your workplace for a nap. The best way to do this is to *snudge* along to your desk. Everybody snudges along now and then, even if they don't know that they're doing it. Nathan Bailey's *Universal Etymological Dictionary* (1721) defines it thus:

> **To SNUDGE along**: to walk looking downward, and poring, as though the Head was full of Business.

Nobody will interrupt you if you snudge, especially if you use the modern prop of the mobile phone, which can be studied with undistractable intensity. Indeed, a really good snudger could probably just snudge around the office for years without being caught and end up drawing a handsome pension, all for having learned how to furrow his brow in just the right way. However, permanently snudging along would probably work havoc with your feet and so it's best to get back to your desk where you can have a good *rizzle*.

Rizzle is a mysterious word that had a sudden vogue in late nineteenth-century America and then disappeared. It appeared in several terribly respectable medical journals and might have had the same success as ergophobia, as doctors of that lost and lovely era were clearly civilised chaps and not the stern fun-spoilers who prowl around the hospitals of today telling you not to smoke or eat turtles. Here is a description of *rizzling* taken from the American *Medical Bulletin* of 1890:

Do you rizzle every day? Do you know how to rizzle? One of the swell doctors in town says that it is the most wonderful aid to perfect health.

'I masticate my food very thoroughly at dinner,' he says, 'and make sure to have my family or friends entertain me with bright talk and plenty òf fun. After dinner it is understood that I am going to rizzle. How do I do it? I retire to my study, and having darkened the room, I light a cigar, sit down and perform the operation.

'How to describe it I don't know, but it is a condition as nearly like sleep as sleep is like death. It consists in doing absolutely nothing.

'I close my eyes and try to stop all action of the brain. I think of nothing. It only takes a little practice to be able to absolutely stifle the brain.

'In that delightful condition I remain at least ten minutes, sometimes twenty. That is the condition most helpful to digestion, and it is that which accounts for the habit animals have of sleeping after eating. I would rather miss a fat fee than that ten minutes' rizzle every day.'

People are liable to notice if you pull down all the blinds and start smoking a cigar at your desk, and if they don't you can be sure that you are working in a very superior sort of office. However, in the late Victorian world it would have been considered, quite rightly, a medical necessity.

Sometimes, though, rizzling is not enough. Emptiness of the mind may be fine for the enthusiast of meditation, but what of those who really need a good nap and don't have a cigar to hand? These people may now *sloom*.

Sloom is a beautiful word because you almost know what it means without needing to be told. The *Oxford English Dictionary* defines it as a 'gentle sleep or slumber', inadvertently letting us know that all the best sleeping words begin with SL. This was a point not lost upon the alliterative poets of Middle English, who could write lovely lines like:

Slipped upon a sloumbe sleep

There was even a proper set of rules on how to have your after-dinner medieval sloom. The fourteenth century was teeming with courtesy books, which were rather like self-help manuals for nervous knights. These would tackle all of the important subjects like how to make your armour shine, how to address a dragon, and how to have a nap after lunch.

Whole men of what age or complexion so ever they be of, should take their natural rest and sleep in the night: and to eschew meridial sleep. But and [if] need shall compel a man to sleep after his meat: let him make a pause, and than let him stand and lean and sleep against a cupboard, or else let him sit upright in a chair and sleep.

Sleeping against a cupboard is nearly impossible, and, worse, much more likely to get you noticed. So sit in your chair and *streke*, which is to say stretch out all your limbs. Now, rest some worthy-looking file of papers with one end on your stomach and the other on the edge of the desk, let the tip of your chin rest upon your neck and very subtly sloom, and dream of being a knight errant.

Intermission

Feeling refreshed? Splendid. You may draw the curtains and extinguish your cigar, for rizzling and slooming are over and there may be nothing for it but to do some work. What are your *facienda*? Your list of things that you must get done? They must be tackled one faciendum at a time, of course; you wouldn't want to strain something. But facienda there must be. Otherwise somebody will notice and you'll be out of a job and forced to gongoozle all day, which would probably become rather dull, canal traffic being so much reduced from its day of hey.

A quick phone call

Perhaps you should turn to your personal facienda, especially as you've only just woken up, and perform your familial duties by calling a relative. Relatives like to be telephoned. Nobody knows why, but they do. Now seems as good a time as any, and you never know when people will be drawing up their wills. So, just to be helpful, here are all the words you'll need to love your family.

Uxorious: Excessively fond of one's wife. It should be noted that wives rarely put any stress on the *excessively* part of that definition, feeling correctly that whatever fondness they get is too little. Uxorious also has the splendid little cousin word *uxorilocal*, which means 'of a husband living in the vicinity of his wife's relatives'. Whether this is a good or bad thing is disputed.

Maritorious: Excessively fond of one's husband. This is, for some reason, a much rarer word than uxorious. Indeed, few people have ever heard of it. This may be because its only notable appearance in English literature is in the pithy statement: 'Dames maritorious ne'er were meritorious.'

Philadelphian: Loving your brother. Alternatively this can mean from the city of Philadelphia, which was named after the virtue of brotherly (*adelphian*) love (*philos*). This should not be confused with *philodelphian*, which would mean loving dolphins.

I have never found a word for loving your sister. This may be significant.

Matriotic: This is a usefully abstract word for doting on your mother, although it can also simply mean nostalgic love for one's old school or university. There are other words for loving one's mother, but they generally have some connection to an uncouth fellow called Oedipus who was unlucky and is dead.

Philopater: One who loves his father or his country. The true philopater can be recognised by their tendency to *patrizate*, or to take after or imitate one's father (again, not like that evil Oedipus).

Philoprogenitive: Loving one's offspring. This was, originally, a phrenological term and referred to a philoprogenitive bump on the skull.

Materteral: Relating to an aunt. Amazingly this word never appears in the works of P.G. Wodehouse.

Avuncular: Relating to an uncle, more specifically a maternal uncle. There's an even more curious and useless term:

the *avunculate*, which means maternal uncles considered as a group.[1]

It's a little thing, but a phone call to a loved one can make all the difference. Think of how much pain could have been avoided if King Lear had only called Cordelia from the blasted heath, or if Odysseus had texted Penelope to say that he would be late, or had Romeo picked up the phone to hear the sweet sound of his wife's voice saying, 'Hi, I'm in the crypt'.

If you are to use Alexander Graham Bell's product, which is to say the blower, you should, in all courtesy, use it as he would have wished; and Dr Bell insisted that all phone calls should begin with the words 'Ahoy, ahoy'. Nobody knows why he insisted this – he had no connection to the navy – but insist he did and started every phone call that way. Nobody else did, and it was at the suggestion of his great rival Edison that people took to saying 'Hello'. This seems unfair.

Telephones improved greatly over the course of the twentieth century and went, in terms of the reproduction of sound, from a distorted and distant voice to a clear and ringing intimacy. Such was the improvement that we all decided we needed a new challenge and switched to mobile telephones, which give you the splendidly retro feeling of crackly lines, broken connections and Too Few Bars.

Soldiers and pilots have been dealing with such precarious lines for years and have developed a thing they call Voice Procedure that eliminates all sorts of annoyances. For example,

---

[1] And, in case you need them, the words for murdering all these would be *uxoricide*, *mariticide*, *fratricide*, *sororicide*, *matricide*, *parricide* and *filicide*.

if you are a coastguard radioing the captain of a sinking ship you don't want to spend ten minutes having a conversation that goes 'Can you hear me?' 'I can hear you, can you hear me?' 'I can't hear what you said. Did you say you could hear me?' Quite aside from the fact that a hundred souls might be lost beneath the angry waves, it's just plain annoying. So, instead of saying 'So sorry, I can't quite make you out. Could you repeat that?', coastguards just go: 'Say again.' This is a practice that could usefully be applied to modern mobile communications that are cursed with a Bad Line. Here are the important ones:

Roger means 'I can hear you perfectly well, granny'. This is because 'roger' and 'received' both begin with an R. Incidentally, *roger* can also mean 'have sexual intercourse', which makes the technical terms *roger that* and *roger so far* rather amusing. (*Roger* can also mean 'an itinerant beggar pretending to be a poor scholar from Oxford or Cambridge' but nobody knows why.)

Wilco (short for **wil**l **co**mply) means 'Absolutely, granny, I shall remember to wrap up warm'.

Copy means 'Yes, I heard what you just said. There's no need to repeat it.'

Reading you five: 'Yes, the line is perfectly good from my end.'

Wait out means 'I've no idea, can I call you back sometime?'

And, most importantly, all chitchat about the weather or instructions on which bus to take to the pub tonight should be prefixed with *Securité!*, which means 'I have important meteorological, navigational or safety information to pass on'.

Got all that? Good. So a typical phone call to your dear old mother might go something like this:

> 'Ahoy, ahoy! Just feeling matriotic and thought I'd give you a call.'
> 'Darling! So lovely to copy that.'
> 'Roger that. How are things?'
> 'Securité! Securité! We've had such glorious weather this morning that I was out in the garden, but then Securité! Securité! it began to drizzle a bit so I came inside. Now, when are you going to come up and visit us?'
> 'Wait out.'
> 'It's been five years.'

Click. Phone call finished. Family obligations and filial piety complete. As it says in the Ten Commandments: 'Honour thy father and thy mother that thy days may be long in the land of the Lord.' It's the only commandment with a promise.

Chapter 10

3 p.m. – Trying to Make Others Work

Finding them – shouting at them

∽∾∾

If you follow learning you shall learn more each day. If you follow the Way you shall do less each day. You shall do less and less until you do nothing at all. And, if you do nothing at all, there is nothing that is left undone.

The Tao Te Ching of Lao Tzu, fifth century BC

So far I have been assuming that you are a subordinate, a mere Israelite slaving and sweating for some cruel taskmaster, and have provided you with the words necessary for workshy *lollygagging*. This is, perhaps, unfair, and I may have underestimated you. You could well be a captain of industry, a tycoon, a big shot, a *buzz-wig*, a *king-fish*, a *mob-master*, a *satrapon*, a *celestial*, a *top-hatter*, a *tall boy*, or a Fat Controller. If you are any or all of these, work avoidance is exactly the other way round: you must prowl around your business empire finding people to whom to delegate your toils, and you require the words with which to do it.

You must get your lazy *lolpoops* and *loobies* – your staff who are not operating as productive units of humanity – and scream

Imshi! at them, a Second World War expression meaning 'Get to work!'

Finding them

But first you must find them, and this is going to be a problem if your staff are *michers*, a micher being, according to Dr Johnson's dictionary, 'A lazy loiterer, who skulks about in corners and by-places, and keeps out of sight; a hedge creeper'. A *hedge creeper* is, of course, 'A hedge-thief, skulker under hedges, pitiful rascal' – according to Farmer's *Slang and its Analogues,* anyway.

The first thing to do is check under all the hedges in the office, a brief pursuit unless you manage a hedge fund. Having dealt with the hedge creepers, you must then turn your attention to the *latibulaters*, latibulate meaning 'hide in a corner'. In fact, you could save yourself some time by merely posting signs in every corner of the office saying NO LATIBULATION in big red letters. This may not solve the problem completely, though, as hardened latibulaters deprived of their corners may *incloacate*, or conceal themselves in a lavatory. Incloacation is not a common problem, but it was on the charge sheet of a seventeenth-century outlaw who was said to have 'incloacated himself privily'. Incloacaters are probably the hardest michers to deal with, and the best way to flush them out is to make the lavatories as unpleasant as possible. This is easily and subtly achieved by spraying the necessary room with *mercaptans*, one or more of the several stinking compounds in the sulphydryl group, or, to put it another way, the thing that smells in shit.

Shouting at them

Once all your *chasmophiles* – or lovers of nooks and crannies – have been beaten back to their desks and cubbyholes, you should give them a good earful. However, your reprimands must be chosen with the care befitting the dignity of an executive like you. You may be stern or soft, so long as you are memorable enough that your rockets stick in their memory, as it were. That way you shouldn't have to admonish anybody more than once a week or so. There was a don at Oxford University in the seventeenth century whose insults were considered so exquisite that they merit a whole paragraph in Aubrey's very brief *Brief Life* of him. His name was Dr Ralph Kettell and his …

> … fashion was to goe up and down the college, and peepe in at the key-holes to see whether the boyes did follow their bookes or no […] When he scolded at the idle young boies of his colledge, he used these names, viz. *Turds, Tarrarags* (these were the worst sort, rude raskells), *Rascal-Jacks, Blindcinques, Scobberlotchers* (these did no hurt, were sober, but went idleing about the grove with their hands in their pocketts, and telling the number of trees there, or so).

These might seem to be enough, but they clearly weren't, as Aubrey also mentions that:

> Upon Trinity Sunday he would commonly preach at the Colledge, whither a number of the scholars of other howses would come, to laugh at him.

So you must, in your scolding, rise above even the invention of
Dr Kettell. You could try resorting to John Florio's 1598 *Worlde
of Wordes* and go for:

A shite-rags: an idle, lazie, loobie fellow

... but this may get you in trouble. To be honest, there are any
number of words for layabouts, loafers, lingerers and *lurdans*.
You might want to save time by just shouting at all of them at
once, in which case you will need to know that the correct collective noun is a *lounge* of idlers. However, it might be more
interesting to up the philosophical stakes by bringing in the
concept of the *drogulus*.

The drogulus was invented as a purely theoretical concept
by the British philosopher A.J. Ayer. Ayer is a chap who deserves
everybody's respect and time, if not for his thought, then at
least for the fact that he once, at the age of 77, stopped Mike
Tyson from attacking a young model called Naomi Campbell.
It was at a party in New York, and when Ayer got in the way
Mike Tyson asked him: 'Do you know who the fuck I am? I'm
the heavyweight champion of the world.' To which Ayer replied:
'And I am the former Wykeham Professor of Logic. We are both
pre-eminent in our field. I suggest that we talk about this like
rational men.' Meanwhile, Miss Campbell had slipped away.

But to return to the drogulus: this fascinating little speculative creature was invented in a less glamorous argument in
1949 when Ayer was debating with a priest about meaningful
and meaningless statements. Ayer contended that a statement
could be meaningful only if you could state what would prove
that it was true or false. So 'God exists' would be a meaningful

statement only if you could say definitively what would make you believe or disbelieve it. Ayer invented the idea of the drogulus, which is a creature that has no discernible effect whatsoever on anything.

> And you say, 'Well how am I to tell if it's there or not?' And I say, 'There's no way of telling. Everything's just the same if it's there or it's not there. But the fact is it's there.'

Drogulus has remained a term of speculative epistemological philosophy, but it could easily be imported into the repertoire of management-speak. For what better insult to a lazy employee than 'You drogulus!' It sounds a bit like *dog* and a bit like *useless*, but if your subordinate went crying to an employment tribunal, they would probably be rather impressed with your erudition and say with A.J. Ayer: 'Everything is just the same if you're there or you're not there. But the fact is you're there.'

All this, of course, assumes that there is Something To Be Done. And if there is not something to be done then it is your duty as manager to cover the fact up. This has been the central point of leadership since leadership began and there are all sorts of cunning and inventive manoeuvres. For example, on 1 April junior employees used to be sent out to buy *pigeon milk* for their masters. Every shopkeeper would direct them onwards to somewhere just round the corner and they could wander around town all day on this *sleeveless errand*.

On exactly the same basis, modern recruits to the British Army are often sent by their commanding officer to get *the keys to the indoor tank park*. Indeed, the futility of war is as nothing to the futility of basic training, where the old rule is that if it doesn't move you should paint it and that if it does you should salute it.

Even once you have sent your employees running around milking pigeons, you must still watch them like hawks in case they are merely *eye-servants* and *lip-labourers*.

> EYESERVANT. n.s. [*eye* and *servant*.] A servant that works only while watched …
>
> Servants, obey in all things your masters; not with *eye-service*, as men pleasers, but in singleness of heart. Cor. I ii.22

> LIP-LABOUR. n.s. [*lip* and *labour*.] Action of the lips without concurrence of the mind; words without sentiments.
>
> Christ calleth your Latyne howres idlenesse, hypocresye, moche bablynge, and *lyppe-laboure*. Bale, *Yet a Course &c* (1543)

Eye-servants are even worse than those incloacated chasmophiles mentioned earlier, because you think they're working when in fact they are napping, phoning their friends, tweeting, texting, booking their faces, indulging their *oniomania* (or compulsion to buy stuff) on the Internet, or otherwise *ploitering*, which is to say pretending to work when they are not. Such people are leeches upon the healthy limbs of business and must be salted accordingly.

Dressing down

At this point, you may be called upon to summon them to *a meeting without coffee*. This is an immensely useful term invented in the British Ministry of Defence. It combines gentleness of phrasing with a subtle and malevolent menace. On the international stage the Ministry of Defence will go and organise naval manoeuvres or missile tests right next to whatever impish country they want to intimidate. Internally, they achieve exactly the same effect by mentioning a meeting without coffee. It works like this. The permanent secretary's secretary will phone up a subordinate to arrange a meeting. The subordinate will say something along the lines of, 'Oh, that's splendid. I'm terribly excited about our new initiatives on installing tea-makers in British Army tanks,[1] and I'd like to discuss the possibility …' But here the secretary will cut them off with the dread words: 'Actually, this is a meeting without coffee.'

It's an easy and friendly thing for the secretary to say, but the subordinate knows what it means. Their opinion will not be asked. They will not be smiled at. They will not even be allowed to sit down and sip a thoughtful cup of the brown stuff. They will stand there and be shouted at until their feet are sore and their ears *tintinnabulate*. A good, proper military carpeting. And the beauty of it is that the dread felt on the part of the subordinate as they pencil the meeting meekly into their diary, as they fail to sleep the night before, as they spend all morning fretting and practising excuses – that dread is the real punishment. It is psychological trench warfare.

But should you be so cruel? Would it not be better to organise a caring and sharing office environment where everybody feels valued? No, it would not. I refer you to Machiavelli.

---

[1] I am, of course, making this example up. British Army tanks all contain tea-making facilities as it stands. Really.

It has been asked whether it is better to be loved than feared, or feared than loved. I am of the opinion that both are necessary; but as it is not an easy task to unite them, and we must determine on one or the other, I think the latter (to be feared) is the safest. Men, it must be allowed, are generally ungrateful, fickle, timid, dissembling, and self-interested; so much so, that confer on them a benefit they are entirely yours; they offer you, as I have already said, their wealth, their blood, their lives, and even their own offspring, when the occasion for any of them is distant; but should it present itself, they will revolt against you.

Any questions? Good. Now that your meeting without coffee has been arranged with the eye-serving drogulus, the next step is to work out exactly what you are going to say. It's always good to start with something ear-catching, and, as the executive self-help books suggest, to learn from history's greatest managers. When Ghengis Khan seized Bukhara he gathered all the city's most prominent citizens to kneel before him and began his pep talk thus:

I am the punishment of God. If you had not committed great sins, God would not have sent a punishment like me upon you.

Change 'punishment' to 'line manager' and you have your opening. Ghengis could have saved a lot of time by using the word *theomeny*, which means wrath of God, but we will let that pass. Now that you've softened them up and established the tone of the meeting (and hidden any stray cafetieres) you can press home your advantage by shrieking the dread words: 'You are a *purple dromedary*!'

Pause for a while to let this sink in; it is a terrible thing for anyone to learn that they are a purple dromedary. The pain is particularly acute if you have not read *A New Dictionary of the Terms Ancient and Modern of the Canting Crew*, where they translate:

> You are a purple Dromedary – You are a Bungler or a dull Fellow

If you're feeling particularly alliterative you can add *drumbledore* to dromedary, for, although the former is usually applied to a clumsy insect, it can also mean a clumsy, incompetent individual.

Now that their dromedarian nature has been exposed, you can pin them down with any of the other words that English has produced for the incurable incompetent: *maflard, puzzlepate, shaffles, foozler, juffler, blunkerkin* or *batie-bum*. Or if you feel that the work of selecting words is beneath the dignity of a director like you, you can just copy Shakespeare, who provided a handy cut-out-and-memorise passage in *King Lear*, where Kent calls Oswald:

> A knave; a rascal; an eater of broken meats; a base, proud, shallow, beggarly, three-suited, hundred-pound, filthy, worsted-stocking knave; a lily-livered, action-taking knave, a whoreson, glass-gazing, super-serviceable finical rogue; one-trunk-inheriting slave; one that wouldst be a bawd, in way of good service, and art nothing but the composition of a knave, beggar, coward, pandar, and the son and heir of a mongrel bitch: one whom I will beat into clamorous whining, if thou deniest the least syllable of thy addition.

Shakespeare saw that simply piling up personal abuse is much more effective than trying to be clever. And, in case you were wondering:

Finical = excessively fastidious
Super-serviceable = Officious
Action-taking = litigious

Incidentally, the OED lists this as the very first citation for 'son of a bitch', demonstrating what a debt we owe to the Bard.

Your employee is probably now weeping and quivering and appealing for mercy. Show none. If they plead and beg, just say in a deep and dismal voice 'Gabos', and shake your head.

Gabos (or G.A.B.O.S.) is an acronym for Game Ain't Based On Sympathy. The game in question is the frolicsome world of gangland Miami, where the enthusiastic and endearingly territorial *narcotraficantes* refer to their lives, their code of conduct, their retail activities and occasional tiffs as The Game. Unlike cricket, this game has no central authority, book of laws, professional umpires, or even an equivalent of *Wisden*. In fact, nobody is quite sure what The Game is based on at all, yet all agree that the Game Ain't Based On Sympathy, and that kicking a gangster when they're down, or indeed popping a cap into their ass while so prostrated, is thoroughly licit. It would appear that the term is merely the beginning of a long process of elimination that will eventually lead to the discovery of firm foundations for The Game and thus clear up all the confusion.

This lack of sympathy with the plucky underdog was shortened into an acronym some time in the early years of this century and then made popular by rappers and documentaries.

Thus it is no longer the preserve of Miamians, and is now, I am told, part of the common parlance of the British House of Commons. The use of the word gabos in the office will give you a rakish, gangstery air that is bound to increase the productivity of your terrified subordinates or 'soldiers' as you may now call them.

You may finish off your carpeting by threatening to *rightsize* them. Rightsizing is the euphemistic way of saying *downsizing* which is the euphemistic way of saying *streamlining* which is the euphemistic way of saying that you'll sack the whole sorry lot of them any day now. This saves on confusion because the verb 'to sack' has several different meanings listed in the dictionary, including

> **Sack**: To put (a person) in a sack to be drowned.
> 1425 *Rolls of Parl.* IV. 298/2 Ye said Erle lete sakke hym forthwith, and drounyd him in Thamyse.

Oh for the heady days of real line management. Once you have herded everybody to their desks, shouted at a few people, and put the fear of God and unemployment into every purple dromedary, there is nothing much more for a good manager to do beyond playing golf and drawing a salary. And, besides, it's time for tea.

Chapter 11

4 p.m. – Tea

∽∾

There's an odd thing that though an English lord might have a cup of *tea*, the working classes are as likely to have a cup of *cha*. In this they are correct. 'Cha' is the original aristocratic Mandarin name for the infusion of *Camellia sinensis*, 'tea' is merely the term used in Fuchau, the coastal province from which the stuff was shipped to Europe. So it should be cha if you're feeling posh, and tea only if you're feeling particularly raffish and filled with *nostalgie de la boue*.[1]

The first great treatise on tea, by the eighth-century writer Lu Yu, was called the *Ch'a Ching* or Classic of Cha. The name *cha*, along with the plant, was imported into Japan, where the true lover of a good cuppa is not merely a tea enthusiast, but a follower of *Chado*: the Way of Tea (*do*, pronounced *doh*, is the word for 'way').

Chado is the mystic and magical practice of drinking tea in order to achieve spiritual enlightenment, and is a lot more fun than fasting or self-flagellation. Any particular instance of Chado is called *chanoyu*, which translated literally means 'tea's hot water'. However, it is difficult for our debased Western

---

[1] This is a French term meaning 'homesickness for mud', which refers to those of the upper classes longing for the gritty suffering of the lower.

minds, filled with the cheap spiritual gratification of the teabag and electric kettle, to appreciate the obscure Oriental mystery of tea.

It is a common piece of wisdom in the lands of the rising sun that 'Zen and tea are one and the same'. This may lead you to believe that you can practise zen merely by sipping at a cup of Rosie Lea, but this is not so. The great tea-master Shuko taught that you could not drink tea unless your mind was completely pure, a proposition I have disproved by experiment.

The greatest master of Chado was Rikyu, in the sixteenth century, whose skill with a teapot was so great that his overlord became jealous and ordered him to commit *seppuku*, or ritual suicide. Rikyu made what is meant to have been the finest damn cup of tea in history, after which he broke the teacup and obediently fell upon his sword.

In English we do have some equivalents to the idea of Chado. The poet Percy Bysshe Shelley was expelled from Oxford for writing a tract called *The Necessity of Atheism*, signed 'Thro' deficiency of proof, AN ATHEIST'. But in private he freely admitted that he was a *theist*, by which he meant nothing in the way of religion, only that he was addicted to tea (French *thé*). Theism became as popular a religion as England has ever known. In 1886 an article appeared in *The Lancet* saying:

> America and England are the two countries afflicted most with the maladies arising from the excessive consumption of tea. Individuals may suffer in a variety of ways. It is customary to speak of acute, sub acute, and chronic 'theism' – a form that has no connection with theological matters. It is possible to be a 'theic' by profession, or a 'theic' by passion [...] There is

hardly a morbid symptom which may not be traceable to tea as its cause.

Given that the love of tea is both a religious rite and a narcotic need, it is unsurprising that all sorts of terrible names have been invented for badly made tea. For example, tea that is too weak may be cursed with the name of *cat-lap*, *husband's tea*, *maiden's pee*, and *blash*. Indeed, one who has made the tea too weak may be said to have *drowned the miller* for reasons that nobody is quite sure of.

The opposite of such watery nonsense is strong tea, tea that blows your mind and wakes you up. Thus British servicemen of the Second World War would refer to good strong tea as *gunfire*, on the basis that it had the same enlivening effect upon the senses as coming under attack from the enemy.

Nor is this caffeinism a recent development. According to an utterly reliable Japanese legend, there was a monk named Bodhidharma who had sworn to spend nine years staring at a blank bit of wall. Why he would want to do this is not recorded, but it was considered terribly holy and nobody seems to have mentioned to him that it might be a waste of time. The story goes that after a mere five years he got tired and dozed off. When he woke up the wall was still very much there but, nonetheless, Bodhidharma felt awfully ashamed and, to make sure that it never happened again and he wouldn't miss a moment of the fun, he cut off his own eyelids and chucked them on the ground. The eyelids germinated and sprouted and from them grew the very first tea plant. Bodhidharma decided to make an infusion from the leaves (presumably without taking his eyes off the wall – I've never been able to get this point clear) and thus was made the first cup of tea. The caffeine contained in it was enough to keep him alert for the next four years.

So let us get to the making. While the kettle is thrumbling away you must first choose your brew. Here is a quick reference guide to the various etymologies of tea.

Charles Grey, 2nd **Earl Grey**, was a great man. He became an MP at the age of 22, seduced the Duchess of Devonshire, was Prime Minister of Britain from 1830 to 1844, and passed the Great Reform Act and the abolition of slavery. But he is chiefly remembered for being fond of tea flavoured with bergamot oil, a fondness that was leapt upon by tea merchants eager to associate their wares with such a chap. Lady Grey is a figment of a tea merchant's caffeinated imagination. There was, of course, a real Lady Grey, but she was too busy having sixteen children to bother about bergamots.

Lapsang Souchong (or *lāpǔshān xiǎozhǒng*) means 'small plant from Lapu Mountain'. A rather unreliable story says that an army arrived and wanted their tea, but as the crop was still damp it was dried quickly over fires built from pine trees, hence the smoky flavour.

Ceylon was the old name for the island of Sri Lanka. It comes from the Sanskrit *Sinhala*, which means 'blood of a lion', which is odd as there are no lions in Sri Lanka.

Assam means either 'unequal' or 'unequalled'. If the former, then it's probably due to the mountainous terrain of this far north-eastern state of India; if the latter, then it's due to the ancient rulers of the area who thought themselves peerless.

Darjeeling comes from the Tibetan *dojeling*, which means 'diamond island'. This is down to the practice there of Vajrayana Buddhism. *Vajra* can mean diamond and so *Vajrayana* is often translated as 'diamond vehicle'. However, there is another story that Darjeeling is named after a particular stone that people used to meet at to gossip, called the *Taji-lung* in the native language. This latter etymology is rather appropriate as tea has always been intimately connected with gossip, even in English. Some used to call it *chatter broth*, others *scandal broth*, as in this lament of a pious farmer in 1801:

> ... we never have any tea but on Sundays, for it will not do for a hardworking family, and many of our neighbours call it *Scandal broth*.

The Victorians, in a rare fit of simplicity, just had:

> BITCH, tea; 'a bitch party,' tea drinking.

Anyway, the kettle should have boiled now and the tea should be drawing. It must not do so for too long or it will be *overdrawn* and *potty* – which is to say, tasting of the teapot. So grasp the handle of the teapot (technically called the *boul*, which is also the name for the little finger holes in scissors) and pour the bitch into a teacup.

Skeuomorphs

The handle of the common or garden teacup is a classic example of a *skeuomorph*. In the nineteenth century, when photography was still in nappies, exposure times were so long that people who were walking would be blurred. They would have ghosts flowing out behind them. It was this that introduced the idea in paintings and drawings that movement could be indicated by lines flying out behind a moving object. Photography changed our visual ideas and that changed representations in other mediums. The viewer looks at a blurred drawing and thinks: 'Ah, the chap's running. I know that because of the technological failings of photography.' Think about it: have you ever actually seen a runner with lines coming out of their back?

There's a technical term for this: it's *skeuomorphic*. A skeuomorph is a technological limitation that is deliberately imitated even when it's no longer necessary. My digital camera has a little loudspeaker that emits a clicking noise when I take a photograph, just like an old mechanical camera.

Once upon a time there were teacups whose handles you might reasonably fit your fingers through. They were handles that you could, well, handle. But now they remain purely as skeuomorphic decoration, a mere memory of usefulness.

Now that the tea is ready and piping hot, it's time to summon your fellow *thermopotes* (or drinkers of hot drinks). You could do this with the rather dull shout of 'Tea's up', but for a bit of tropical allure there's nothing like this entry in an eighteenth-century dictionary:

> CONGO. Will you lap your congo with me? Will you drink tea with me?

You may add some *moo juice*, but as Fielding said: 'Love and scandal are the best sweeteners of tea.'

Reading your future

And once the day's gossip is done, and the cha is all gone, it remains only to check the tea leaves to see what the future holds. Tea-leaf reading is called *tasseography* and there is, so far as I can tell, only one major work on the subject: *Tea-Cup Reading and Fortune-Telling by Tea Leaves* by 'A Highland Seer' (1920). It contains a dictionary, or at least a table of 'Symbols and significations', which is practically the same thing. The idea is to look at the tea leaves left in the cup and see if you can discern any familiar shapes. Here is a brief selection of the ones I consider most urgent:

AIRCRAFT, unsuccessful projects.

BADGER, long life and prosperity as a bachelor.

CANNON, good fortune.

CAR (MOTOR), and CARRIAGE, approaching wealth, visits from friends.

DONKEY, a legacy long awaited.

GRASSHOPPER, a great friend will become a soldier.

KANGAROO, a rival in business or love.

KETTLE, death.

PARROT, a sign of emigration for a lengthy period.

UMBRELLA, annoyance and trouble.

YEW-TREE indicates the death of an aged person who will leave his possessions to the consultant.

ZEBRA, travel and adventure in foreign lands.

Chapter 12

5 p.m. – Actually Doing Some Work

*Panicking – deadlines – giving up – stealing from
your employer – leaving*

ᔐᔑᔐᔑ

We are now approaching the end of the working day, and I don't
mean to sound beastly, but it may be time to stop fudgeling and
ploitering and actually do some work.

As five o'clock strikes you may well think wistfully of how
you are missing out on your *cinqasept*. This French term may
usefully be pondered (if only from a distance) for the light it
throws on the French nation and their working practices as a
whole. A cinqasept is literally a 'five till seven', but in French
reality it means:

> A visit to a mistress or a brothel, traditionally made between
> five and seven p.m.

It's that word 'traditionally' that tells you all you need to know
about Gallic morals. Oh, to be French! But it's too late now –
you have an hour left at work and, so far as I can recall, you
have achieved next to nothing. You must therefore attempt to
fit a whole *dieta* (or day's work) into one measly hour of insane,
betwattled toil. The end times are upon us.

Theologically speaking, we are in work's *eschaton*, which is the correct term for the rumpus that precedes the end of the world. If you're being very strict about things an apocalypse is not the end of the world, it is merely a *vision* of the eschaton. So The Apocalypse of Saint John the Divine, commonly known as the Book of Revelation, is just that: a revelation, or apocalypse, of what will happen when God finally calls time on this sorry mess we call existence. Viewed from this rigorous linguistic perspective, *Apocalypse Now* is a much less worrying title.

So to work! Time is ticking away and if we're going to get anything done we can't think about cinqasepts and revelations. We must get down to a proper *fit of the clevers*, as Sir Walter Scott's maids allegedly described a sudden burst of activity.

The Russians have a particularly wonderful word for such a work schedule: they call it *shturmovshchina*, and it is a word so useful that it might even be worthwhile remembering how to spell it. It is the practice of working frantically just before a deadline, having not done anything for the last month. The first element means 'storm' or 'assault', the second is a derogatory suffix.

Shturmovshchina originated in the Soviet Union. Factories would be given targets and quotas and other such rot by the state, but they often weren't given any raw materials. So they would sit around with their feet up and their tools down waiting until the necessaries arrived, and it was only when the deadline was knocking at the door and the gulag beckoned that they would panic, grab whatever was to hand, and do a really shoddy, half-arsed heap of work, or *shturmovshchina*. It's an excellent and easily usable word that should be included in the Special Skills section of any good CV.

Hermann Inclusus, or Hermann the Recluse, could be said to have engaged in a Satanic shturmovshchina. Hermann lived in the thirteenth century in Podlazice in the middle of Bohemia (which is now the Czech Republic, approximately). But Hermann was not like other monks praying and fasting and living a life of virtuous virginity. Hermann could never quite get the hang of virtue. Hermann the Recluse was an Evil Monk.

Nobody knows how evil Hermann was or in what particular specialities of evil he excelled, but it was quite enough to attract the notice of the other monks in the monastery, who decided that he was quite beyond any normal redemption or punishment and decided to *immure* him, which is to say that they put him in a room and then built a wall where the door had once been. This done they settled down, like good Christians, to let him starve to death.

Of course, Hermann Inclusus didn't want to die; he had all sorts of extra evil things he wanted to do and felt that he was being cut off in the prime of his sin. So he did a deal that involved writing a book to expiate his sins, although nobody seems to be very clear on how the deal was done or with whom.

This notion of writing as repentance was considered less odd at the time than it now appears. Atonement before the Lord is not included in modern publishing contracts, not even the very generous ones, but in the Middle Ages it was considered a practically automatic part of the system of royalties. For example, Oderic Vitalis (1075–1142), in his *Historia Ecclesiastica*, recounts a story about a monk who was surprisingly sinful, but also a very devoted scribe. When he died they counted up all the words that he had ever written and found that they outnumbered all the sins that he had ever committed, by a total of one. He therefore went to heaven.

So, Hermann the Recluse struck a deal whereby he could expiate his guilt by writing the biggest book in the whole wide world in a single night. He set to work, but like many writers who signed their contract thinking that it would be easy, he discovered the deadline charging towards him like a herd of elephants. He then struck a second deal, this one with the Devil (I told you that Hermann the Recluse was an evil monk). The Devil agreed to help him write the book, but only in exchange for Hermann's soul. Deal done, the book was produced in a single night, after which Hermann tried to strike a third deal giving him forgiveness and salvation, this time with the Virgin Mary, who, I suppose, happened to be around. However, just before he could sign on the dotted line, he died and went to Hell.

There are historians and cynics who question the absolute accuracy and veracity of the stories above, but no writer who has ever worked to a deadline would doubt a word of it.

Anyway, the book that was produced survives to this day. It's called the Codex Gigas and is kept in the National Library of Sweden. It's just under a metre tall, half a metre wide, and twenty centimetres thick. It weighs slightly more than I do, and its parchment reputedly contains the skins of 160 donkeys. All this shows what can be achieved if you leave everything until the last possible minute and then work like stink.

Shturmovshchina has, for some unjust reason, never made it into an English dictionary, though we do have the equivalent term of a *charette*. Charettes began in Paris in the nineteenth century among students of architecture. Unlike most of the other university disciplines, architects were often made to build little models of the buildings they were designing, using very large pieces of paper. This was a difficult and time-consuming activity, and it also meant that the work was so cumbersome and bulky that it was very hard to hand in.

Consequently, on the day that the work was to be handed in, Parisian architecture students would be forced to hire a cart to transport all their designs and models across Paris to be given to their examiners. Architecture students were not actually so different to their peers in other disciplines, in that they tended to leave their work till the last possible minute. The difference with them was that the last possible minute was spent in a cart, and once a year the would-be Haussmanns could all be seen parading through Paris in their carts still adding little details to their designs and fixing inelegant parts of their models. These were said to be working 'in the cart' or, in French, *en charette*. Somehow the term charette ended up on the other side of the Atlantic with a sense given by the OED of:

A period of intense (group) work, typically undertaken in order to meet a deadline.

It is somehow comforting to know that whether immured in Bohemia, Soviet Russia, Belle Époque Paris or modern America, everybody procrastinates until the deadline is almost upon them. Even in the Second World War in Britain, with Nazi invasion looming and freedom and civilisation at stake, soldiers would still work in what was known as a *panic party* in an attempt to remedy a week of rest with an hour of intense labour.

Though a panic party was usually a soldiers' shturmovshchina, another military definition is recorded in the *Sydney Sun* (1942):

A route march is an organised shemozzle, while any rush move is a panic party.

And, just in case you were wondering, this is from *Soldier and Sailor Words* (1925):

Shemozzle, to, to make off: to get out of the way – e.g., 'We saw the M.P.'s (Military Police) coming, so we shemozzled.'

Between your shturmovshchina, charette and panic party, you should now be as busy as a one-legged tap dancer. You will be *very throng*, as they said in rural eighteenth-century England. Indeed, you may lose all respectability and self-control and begin to *fisk*, which once meant 'to run about hastily and heedlessly'. Fisking is best done with a sheaf of papers in each hand and a mobile telephone jammed between your head and shoulder. This is also the best time of day to have a heart attack, should you be so inclined. And even if you aren't, you can liven up the office by pretending. It would be rather apt, as there's a lovely little definition in Grose's *Dictionary of the Vulgar Tongue*:

GRAVE DIGGER: Like a grave digger; up to the a-se in business, and don't know which way to turn.

You may even lose all sense of perspective and forgo your *seven beller*, which is a naval term for a cup of tea taken exactly half an hour before the end of a shift. This is on the basis that a watch in the Royal Navy used to last for four hours, with a bell tolling every thirty minutes. So eight bells signified completion and seven bells meant near-completion and a cup of tea.

This is also, incidentally, the reason that you can still *beat seven bells* out of somebody in a fistfight. If you were to beat eight bells out of a fellow sailor it would mean that they were dead, that their watch on this watery earth was finally over. But seven bells means Not Quite Dead, or a nice cup of tea, depending on your propensity to violence.

But there is no nice cup of seven bells for he who is *festinating* (that is hurrying) to get everything done before the clock strikes six. In fact, you may be forced to do whatever it is you're doing *frobly*, which is to say indifferently well. If a job is worth doing it is, after all, worth doing badly. There is a splendid journalistic term for this: the *quality of doneness*. This term originated in an editorial meeting of the American magazine *The Weekly Standard* in 2005. The staff were debating whether to use an article that wasn't quite up to snuff or scratch. Everybody felt that it could have been written rather better until the executive editor pointed out its one vital advantage. It might not have the highest quality of writing, but it did have the most important quality of any article: *the quality of doneness*.

If something has the quality of doneness you can forgive its having been done half-arsed or *crawly-mawly* or *frobly-mobly*. It is *upwound, perimplenished, perfurnished, expleted* and ended.

And if it isn't, it can always be put off till tomorrow, which is the precise and technical meaning of the word *pro-* (for) *crastinate* (tomorrow). Indeed, why put off till tomorrow what you can put off till the day after tomorrow? The technical term for this is to *perendinate* a task – a rare word for a common action.

At this late hour you are probably seized with *eleutheromania*, or 'a crazed desire for freedom'. Thomas Carlyle mentioned it in his *History of the French Revolution* but it hasn't been found much since. This is a crying shame, as it can be used in all sorts of situations. You can get out of any dull social event by explaining ruefully to your host that you'd love to stay but just happen to be suffering from a touch of eleutheromania and must be excused. And eleutheromania bites hardest when the working day is nearly done.

So if everything is neatly perendinated, give up and go. But before you leave the office, it may be wise to claim any *estovers* that you may need. Estovers are those parts of your lord's estate to which you, as a faithful serf, are entitled. You may take wood from your lord's forest to repair your cottage, or water from your lord's well, or milk from your lord's fridge, or biros from your lord's stationery cupboard, or loo rolls from your lord's lavatory. Nobody will object, especially if nobody notices. And who would notice a mere *niffle*? A niffle is a Yorkshire term for a trifle or thing of little value. As a verb, *niffling* is the practice of 'not doing very much' or 'stealing a little at a time'. A niffle here and a niffle there and you end up with an awful lot of biros.

This is all nearly legal and utterly natural. Biologists even have a word for it: *lestobiosis*, which comes from the Greek *lestos* meaning 'robber', and *biosis* meaning 'way of life'. It's defined in the OED as:

> A form of symbiosis found among certain social insects in which a small species inhabits the nest of a larger one and feeds on the food stored there, or on the brood of the larger species.

And it would seem remarkably unfair to deny office workers a privilege that is accorded to the humble ant. So grab a good handful of biros and maybe a couple of chairs and head for the *vomitoria*.

A vomitorium is *not* a room in which ancient Romans would throw up halfway through a banquet in order to make room for the next course. That's a myth. A vomitorium is simply a passage by which you can exit a building, usually a theatre. But the word can happily be applied to any building, and it is rather poetic and lovely to imagine all these personified office blocks puking their merry workers out into the evening air.

Chapter 13

6 p.m. – After Work

Strolling around – arranging your evening

ᴄᴀᴄᴀᴏ

It is the violet hour, the crepuscular, twilit hour when (on average) the sun drops into the western bay and night comes. If you are reading this in midsummer in the Arctic Circle, my apologies – I can deal only in averages.

It is, as I was saying, *cockshut*, the 'close of evening at which poultry go to roost'. The sky *obnubilates* (or darkens) and all sorts of words beginning with *vesper-* come out to play in the twilight.

When the planet Venus shines at dusk, it becomes Hesperus, the evening star. And if you pronounce the H as a V you get the evening service of the church: *vespers*. From that you get *vespertine* (belonging to the evening), *advesperate* ('to wax night'), *vesperal* (a song to be sung in the evening), and *vespertilionize* (to convert into a bat). I'm not sure if that last word is truly useful for those who aren't of the vampiric persuasion; but, for those that are, it is invaluable.

The best vesper word, though, is *vespery*. Vesperies were the exercises and disputations practised in the evening by scholars at the Sorbonne University in Paris. The word made it into a couple of English dictionaries back in the seventeenth century but has since pretty much vanished. This is a shame, as it's a splendid catch-all term for whatever it is that you do after work. Your vesperies might consist of a visit to a gym (if you are *exergastic* or 'tending to work out'), a supply run into a supermarket, or a stroll or a sprint to the nearest bar. All are vesperies, and each person chooses their own.

If you do go to the gym, you are liable to be *tread-wheeled*, which is, according to the OED, a transitive verb meaning 'to inflict the discipline of the treadmill upon'. This refers, of course, to the use of treadmills as a punishment in Victorian prisons. This was viewed, even at the time, as a barbaric practice[1] and was abolished in 1898. It was then slyly reintroduced in the twentieth century for those who wanted to experience the misery of a nineteenth-century prison without the necessity of committing any crime.

Over in nineteenth-century France, they had a much better idea for how to pass this twilit hour: *flânerie*.

Flânerie

Flânerie is often cited as one of those French words for which there can never be a true English translation. People harp on about how neither strolling nor loitering nor lingering nor promenading can ever express what flânerie really is. Such

---

[1] I refer any defenders of gym-culture to a plea for prison reform written in 1824: 'The labour of the tread-mill is irksome, dull, monotonous, and disgusting to the last degree. A man does not see his work, does not know what he is doing, what progress he is making; there is no room for art, contrivance, ingenuity and superior skill – all which are the cheering circumstances of human labour.'

people cannot have checked the OED, as they would have noticed that we don't need to translate the word: we have simply nicked it, along with the related verb *flâner* and the noun *flâneur*, one who indulges in flânerie.

Even though the word has been kidnapped by English, it is still very hard to define exactly what it is. The OED does a reasonable job with 'A lounger or saunterer, an idle "man about town"'. But this doesn't get to the true essence of the business, for which we will have to turn, reluctantly, to the French.

Put simply, the flâneur is the average French citizen raised to the level of a spiritual ideal. They wander about talking to nobody and doing very little. You can see what the OED is getting at, but it's so much more than that. The concept was promulgated best by Charles Baudelaire:

> The crowd is his domain, as air is that of a bird, or water that of a fish. His passion and his profession, it's to become one with the crowd. For the perfect flâneur, for the ideal idler, for the impassioned observer, it is a vast joy to be at home among the passers-by, in the swirl of people, in the movement, in the fugitive and the infinite. To be away from his home, but to be at home everywhere; to see the world, to be at the centre of the world, but to be concealed from the world; such are the smaller pleasures of these independent, impassioned and impartial souls, which language can only clumsily define.

Flânerie is an idea that was expanded and refined through the nineteenth and early twentieth century. It is the practice of sitting alone in a café observing the world hurrying past and trying to read a life in each face. It is the practice of wandering through narrow streets and seeing people on their balconies or children hurrying home from school. It is the practice of smoking endless moody cigarettes as you *scamander* through the city.

Scamander, by the way, is the sister verb of *meander*. The river Maeander winds, by a preposterously curly-whirly route, through Izmir in Turkey. The ancient Greeks were very taken with the twistings of the Maeander, and their chief geographer, a fellow called Strabo, declared that 'its course is so exceedingly winding that anything winding is called a meander'. Of course he declared that in Greek, but the term was nonetheless carried over into English, so that we moderns may meander around as much as we like. If you feel that the Maeander isn't the river for you, you may pick the Scamander, another Turkish watercourse now known as the Karamenderes. The Scamander wound mazily across the windy plain before the walls of Troy, and is where Achilles did some of his best killing.[2] The Scamander made a brief go of ousting its fellow river, and a dictionary of the street slang of Victorian London defines scamander as:

To wander about without a settled purpose.

There is, though, no need for the terms to fight. They rhyme so well that one can happily meander and scamander in the same sentence. By a process of alliteration we may add in here the *scoperloit*, an old north-country word for 'the time of idleness' when weary labourers would lounge around beneath a vespertine tree, which they would have called the *mogshade*. They might even, in their rustic way, have indulged in a spot of

---

[2] Just after his paranormal breakfast described in Chapter 3.

sauntry, which is the act of sauntering, and perhaps the closest native equivalent to flânerie.

Evening arrangements

As the *dimpsy murkens* and the sky obnubilates into night's blackness it is time to sort out exactly what you are going to do with yourself this evening. You may, of course, settle down to watch the gogglebox for the rest of the night. I can't stop you, but if you do, I fear that there are few arcane medieval words to help you in your glaze-eyed channel hopping. So instead, I shall blithely assume that you will spend the evening out on the town with your friends. Should you stay in, this reference work will cease to function.

However, trying to arrange a good evening's *compotation* and *commensation* is always a tricky task. All societies are *commensal*, to some extent or another, which is the anthropologist's term for the rules of who you can and cannot sit down to dinner with. In the ancient Near East commensality was considered immensely important, to the extent that if you sat down to have a nice supper with a sinner, that made you a sinner too. It is this strict principle of commensality (from *com* meaning 'with' and *mensa* meaning 'table') that makes Jesus's sitting down with the wine-bibbers and tax collectors such a prickly point in the gospels. A man could be judged by the company he kept at table.

Even the Messiah, trying to arrange a nice jolly before he got riveted to a plank, had to go through all sorts of weird shenanigans just to get a table:

And he sent Peter and John, saying, Go and prepare us the passover, that we may eat. And they said unto him, Where wilt thou that we prepare? And he said unto them, Behold, when ye are entered into the city, there shall a man meet you, bearing a pitcher of water; follow him into the house where he entereth in. And ye shall say unto the goodman of the house, The Master saith unto thee, Where is the guestchamber, where I shall eat the passover with my disciples? And he shall shew you a large upper room furnished: there make ready.

Jesus also had the tricky task of picking the guests for his fare-well bash, and he seems to have managed eleven chums and one stinker. There always seems to be what a British soldier of the Second World War out on leave would call a *constable*:

The Constable. Unwanted person who attaches himself to another; a hanger-on who refuses to take the hint.

American servicemen had their own equivalent rank to con-stable, described in the same dictionary of Second World War slang:

Heel. This is an Americanism for a hanger-on, and in the ser-vice it means a fellow who seeks your company for the sake of a free drink. Thus HEELING, paying a heel for something.

Constable seems to me a much more useful word, as it can be used without the person in question having any idea of what you mean. 'Hello, Constable', you can say with an amicable smile, and they may even assume that the word is a mark of respect. You can go further and explain to the others that so-and-so is the Constable for the evening. Thus everybody can be set to leap out of the window and hare off down the street the moment their back is turned. Judas Iscariot, however, was definitely a *heel*.

The question of how to avoid unwanted friends is one that has been bothering English-speakers for centuries. At Cambridge University in the late eighteenth century they had four distinct ways of not bumping into an old chum on the street:

> TO CUT: (Cambridge.) To renounce acquaintance with any one is to cut him. There are several species of the cut. Such as the cut direct, the cut indirect, the cut sublime, the cut infernal, &c.
>
> The CUT DIRECT, is to start across the street, at the approach of the obnoxious person in order to avoid him.
>
> The CUT INDIRECT, is to look another way, and pass without appearing to observe him.
>
> The CUT SUBLIME, is to admire the top of King's College Chapel, or the beauty of the passing clouds, till he is out of sight.
>
> The CUT INFERNAL, is to analyze the arrangement of your shoe-strings, for the same purpose.

The cut infernal is the most effective, and, while you're down there, do you see the little plastic bits on the ends of your shoe-laces? They're called *aglets*. Jesus, I suppose, would have had to practise the cut sublime. How different theological history would have been if, in the Garden of Gethsemane, when Judas came to *judasly* (yes, that's a real word) kiss Him, Jesus had simply pretended not to notice and just stared up at the Temple Mount.

He could also have been helped by two little-known negatives. To recognise a chap is to know (*cognise*) him again (*re*). However, if you cease to recognise a fellow you *decognise* him. This is, to be fair, a rare word, and so far as I can tell it has only ever been used in a parliamentary debate about the position of Charles II,[3] but it is still useful in phrases such as: 'I'm so sorry, old chap, I must have decognised you.' You can even formalise things by sending somebody you really don't like a *devitation*, an obsolete and rare word that is the exact opposite of an invitation. So maybe a nice formal thing written on card with your name in curly letters at the top requesting the pleasure of _____'s absence.

Some people just keep popping up and clapping you on the shoulder when your shoulder least needs to be clapped (incidentally, a *shoulderclapper* is a term for somebody who is unnecessarily friendly). Old acquaintances you thought consigned to the dustbin of your address book sometimes appear with an almost rasputinish obstinacy. Such people are known as *didappers*. A didapper was, originally, a name for the Little Grebe or *Podiceps minor*, a kind of water bird that dives for its food and, just when you think that it must have been eaten by a pike, pops up again on the other side of the pond looking sleek and well fed. The English libertine Charles Colton, in the same book in which he coined the phrase 'Imitation is the sincerest form of

---

[3] Not in a Nell Gwynn way.

flattery', wrote of John Wilkes that:

> There are some men who are fortune's favourites, and who,
> like cats, light for ever up their legs; Wilkes was one of those
> didappers, whom, if you had stripped naked, and thrown over
> Westminster bridge, you might have met on the very next day,
> with a bag-wig on his head, a sword by his side, a laced coat
> upon his back, and money in his pocket.

But even as you try to dodge heels and constables and are busy
hurling shoulderclapping didappers naked from Westminster
Bridge, other people are attempting to do the same to you.

What about your friends, your *makes*, *marrows*, *sociuses*,
sociates, *compadres*, *consociators*, *belamies* (from the French *bel
ami*, beautiful friend), *friars*, *familiars*, *inwards* and *tillicums*?
You may send out your invitations by text and telephone, but
they may remain mere *pollicitations* – an offer made but not
yet accepted – while your so-called friends wait around for a
slightly better prospect. Damn those tillicums (*tillicum* or *tili-
kum* is, by the way, the Chinook word for people, which then
came to mean a member of the same tribe, and then got taken
up by English-speakers to mean chum).

Rather than being picky about it, it may be time to run back
after all those didappers and constables and hoist the *gin pennant*. The gin pennant is a real flag used by the British Navy to
invite people round for a drink. It is first recorded (or at least
remembered) in the 1940s as a small green triangular pennant
with a white wine glass in the middle. If it is hoisted then the
officers of any accompanying ships are invited on board for
drinks. However, it is very, very small.

You see, the officers of the Royal Navy were attempting, as the old phrase goes, to *have their mense and their meat*. 'Mense' means politeness and 'meat' meant food, so trying to have your mense and your meat was trying to earn a reputation for hospitality without actually giving any food away. So this tiny gin pennant is hoisted very quietly at sunset in the hope that nobody will notice. But it must be hoisted occasionally, just so you can say that you did, and didn't you see it? What a shame! We were so hoping to give you our whole allowance of rum.

In fact, several traditions have arisen concerning the gin pennant, which these days is green at each end with a white centre and green glass upon it. You can, for example, when aboard somebody else's ship, attempt to hoist their gin pennant and thus force them to give you free booze. However, if you are caught doing this then you have to invite them back to your ship for the same. Gin pennants can even be flown privately above the bar, just to show those already present that the drinks are on you for the evening. It therefore seems to me that the Royal Navy has a splendid piece of English ready to be taken up by us landlubbers, as in: 'I had nothing whatever to do, so I just hoisted the gin pennant, phoned everyone, and had a splendid evening.'

But before hoisting your gin pennant, you should make sure that you actually have some gin worth flagging up. You'll probably need tonic and lemons and perhaps even some food as well. And for all those you will need not just a market, but a supermarket.

Chapter 14

7 p.m. – Shopping

Disorientation – ecstasy in the supermarket

∽∾∽

Gruen transfer

It is about time that you popped to the shops. Man cannot live on bread alone, but it's a good start. Sadly, these days, none but the most fastidious potter from little shop to little shop buying their beef at a butcher, their bread at a baker and their *costards* (large apples) from a costermonger. No. Our markets must be super or even hyper: cloud-capped palaces of commerce. Places that quite deliberately blow your mind even as you walk in the door in a process called the *Gruen transfer*.

Victor Gruen was born Victor Greenbaum in Austria in 1903. In 1938 he fled the Nazis and arrived in America with 'an architect's degree, eight dollars and no English'. It was with the first of those that he created something wonderful: the modern shopping mall. Gruen is the acknowledged originator and master of the mall, as he designed over fifty of them in the USA and accidentally gave his name to the strange mental effect they have on you.

Shopping malls rarely have any windows on the outside. There is a good reason for this: if you could see the world beyond the window you would be able to orientate yourself and might not get lost. Shopping malls have maps that are unreadable even to the most skilled cartographer. There is a good reason for this: if you could read the map you would be able to find your way to the shop you meant to go to without getting lost. Shopping malls look rather the same whichever way you turn. There is a reason for this too: shopping malls are built to disorientate you, to spin you around, to free you from the original petty purpose for which you came and make you wander like Cain past rows and rows of shops thinking to yourself, 'Ooh! I should actually go in there and get something. Might as well, seeing as I'm here.' And this strange mental process, this freeing of the mind from all sense of purpose or reason, is known to retail analysts as the Gruen transfer.

The term Gruen transfer does not seem to have appeared until a decade after Victor Gruen's death in 1980, but it is now an essential part of planning a shop. It is the combination of sensory overload and spatial amazement that means you buy many more things than you meant to and thus keep the whole place profitable. It is what turns you from *traffic* – the people passing a shop – to *footfall* – the people entering the shop. And, oh, what linguistic beauties are within!

The ecstasy of the supermarket

To the uninitiated, supermarkets can seem rather boring places; places, indeed, that you just go to buy things in. But to the initiated they are palaces of poetry.

For starters, do you see those lines of free-standing, two-sided shelves that divide the aisles? They are not called free-standing, two-sided shelves, because that would be much too dull for the race of poets that manage supermarkets. They are called *gondolas*, because to the romantic mind of the retail manager they resemble nothing so much as a Venetian punt.

This marine motif is taken up with the standalone displays, the little tubs of crisps or tights or whatever is on offer, which are called *islands*, lapped by waves of customers like a consumer ocean. And look up! Those strings and bars suspended from the ceiling are the *aisle-leapers*, strange sure-footed godlings who jump above us, laughing at the mortals below. And their role in the great mythology is to support the *danglers* – the pennants that advertise Twenty, Thirty and Forty Percent Off Selected Products! If the danglers are made of such a material that they may sway in the soft zephyrs of the air-conditioning they are *wobblers*, which are thus the supermercantile equivalent of cherubim.

Nothing is too fantastical for the inherently magical mind of the retail manager. The *Light Thief*, a creature never imagined by the Brothers Grimm, is their name for a display that has no illumination of its own but, painted in merry fluorescent colours and bejewelled with reflective surfaces, steals the light of others and shines itself. In traditional supermarket folklore the Light Thief is the eternal enemy of the *Shelf Miser*, that little tray affixed to the side of the gondola that sticks out a bit into the aisle and thus contains more goods than tradition or equality would allow.

The Shelf Miser beetles o'er the *price channel*, the thin strip where the costs of items and their Every Day Low Price are shown, and casts his niggardly shadow upon the *kick band*, that little strip a few inches high at the base of the gondola that is darkly coloured so as not to show the marks of scuffing shoes or the drips from an unruly mop.

There is high and low. Those cardboard thingies around the top of a bottle? They're *bottle glorifiers*. Those hard plastic packs that contain the product in a little bubble and are absolutely impossible to open? They're *blister packs*.

Nothing in the supermarket is what it seems to the dreary crowds who know not its glories. They pass by discounts that are for a limited period only, without realising that they are standing next to an *exploding offer*. Where two products compete for shelf-space, or *facing* as it is anthropomorphically called, they fight to the death. And if those two products are manufactured by the same parent company, this fight is known to bloodthirsty retail outlets as *cannibalism*. So when Coca-Cola competes with Sprite, Magnum with Cornetto, or Tampax with Always Ultra, the retail manager sees brother eating the body of brother. No mere Venetian gondola, idle up its sleepy canal, ever held such scenes of anthropophagy, where sibling devours the flesh of sibling while the offers detonate below.

And at the checkout you suddenly find love. For when you are given a store-card or collect points towards a future purchase this is known as *romancing the customer*. Of course, the romance is really just someone making calculations and offering you what they can afford to give in exchange for your favours, but all romance is like that really, and it's best to go along with it.

With fluttering heart, it's little wonder the impulse buys you whimsically commit to at the point of sale! For humankind cannot bear very much supermarket. It is too grand and too terrible, too tempting and too fantastical. When you are on the street again and looking around at this blank world, you will know that it can never match the dreams and nightmares that lie beyond the Gruen transfer. When Faustus asks Mephistopheles how he has escaped from Hell, the fallen angel replies:

> Why, this is Hell, nor am I out of it.
> Think'st thou that I, who saw the face of God
> And tasted the eternal joys of Heaven,
> Am not tormented with ten thousand hells
> In being deprived of everlasting bliss?

And so it is with supermarkets. Be not afraid. You will return, if only for the romance. But for now, it is time for supper.

Chapter 15

8 p.m. – Supper

*Dietary requirements – seating arrangements
– making conversation – avoiding conversation
– hogging the wine – finishing supper – avoiding the bill*

∽∼∾

It is time to sidle *supperward* (a pleasant little word that gets its own entry in the dictionary), although before we do, we ought to sort out the difference between *supper* and *dinner*. Supper is, according to the OED, the last meal of the day. (It goes on to contradict itself by mentioning a *rere supper*, which is a second supper consumed after the main supper; but we'll let that pass.) Dinner is the main meal of the day. Supper can therefore sometimes be dinner, and dinner can sometimes be supper. It all depends on the size of your lunch, or indeed breakfast. It's such a thorny question that the OED makes a rare venture into sociology for *dinner*'s definition:

> The chief meal of the day, eaten originally, and still by the majority of people, about the middle of the day (cf. German *Mittagessen*), but now, by the professional and fashionable classes, usually in the evening.

So assuming that you are professional or fashionable, and perhaps both at once, we shall hereinafter refer to this meal as supper, except when we don't.

Another useful word here is *tocsin*, meaning a bell rung as an alarm, but only because you need it to understand Lord Byron's supperish lines:

> That all-softening, overpowering knell,
> The tocsin of the soul, the dinner bell.

This is an example of *coenaculous*, or supper-loving, poetry. Coenaculous (deriving from the Latin *cenaculum* (meaning dining room) but somehow obtaining an unnecessary O) is a curiously obscure word, when you consider that man is a uniformly coenaculous creature. Indeed, the rest of the day can often seem like a long preprandial tease. As Sir Francis Bacon said: 'Hope is a good breakfast, but it is a bad supper.'

Once the dinner bell has sounded and the guests are gathered, whether at a restaurant or at home, the first thing to do is to try to work out whether this is a *Dutch feast*, 'where the entertainer gets drunk before his guest'. Having established that your host is, indeed, *bumpsy*, you can get on with the usual chit-chat and introducing yourself to people who remember you.

At this point, there's usually a panic as it turns out that one person is a vegetarian, another kosher, another is halal and a fourth wants to check that the ingredients were all humanely and sustainably sourced. At this point you can apologetically admit to being a *halalcor*. You can even try making a big fuss about it, provided, that is, that nobody looks in the OED and discovers:

Halalcor One of the lowest and most despised class in India, Iran, etc., (lit.) to whom everything is lawful food.

If caught out like this, you should simply change tack and insist that you *only* eat food that is inhumanely and unsustainably sourced, as it tastes better. Anything for a little trouble.

Once everybody's dietary foibles have been established, along with the host's drunkenness, everybody can sit down and prepare to eat.

Marshalling

People are *marshalled* to their places at the supper table. This meaning of the verb predates the 'marshalling-your-troops' sense by seventy years. Mind you, before that it meant to look after horses, which shows how much respect people had for their dinner guests in the fifteenth century.

The place that you shall be marshalled to is the *cenacle*, the proper word for the chamber in which supper is to be taken (from the same Latin root as coenaculous above). Indeed, the word cenacle originally referred only to the mysterious room in which the Last Supper was taken by Jesus and co-dinnerists. Once in the cenacle, Jesus encountered the same problem that faces any supperist, namely where to sit everybody. He had had this problem before; in Matthew Chapter 20:

Then came to him the mother of Zebedee's children with her sons, worshipping him, and desiring a certain thing of him. And he said unto her, What wilt thou? She saith unto him, Grant

that these my two sons may sit, the one on thy right hand, and
the other on the left, in thy kingdom. But Jesus answered and
said, Ye know not what ye ask.

This sort of thing can indeed be tiresome and it's probably why
he ended up at the Last Supper with one chap's head on his lap
and another annoyingly trying to dip bread at exactly the same
time. Nor are those of us with lesser parentage exempted from
these tribulations. Who shall sit where? Who, as they would say
in medieval times, should *begin the board* and take precedence
at table?

Technically, the host of the meal should *hold the dais*, but
as we've established that they're drunk, it's time to sit *at one's
reward*, or in a much better place at table than you deserve.

It would have been much easier in Roman times when everybody *discumbed*, which is to say that they ate lying down on a
triclinum that ran around three sides of the table. That meant
that if two people particularly wanted the same place they could
just lie on top of each other. However, discumbency may cause
indigestion. So it is best to merely grab your seat and *lollop* or
'lean with one's elbows on the table'.

Making conversation

Seventeen centuries ago, a chap called Athenaeus of Naucratis
wrote a book about the perfect conversation over supper. The
ideal subjects for conversation were, according to Athenaeus,
absolutely bloody everything, with a particular focus on homo-
sexuality and lexicography.

Neither of these subjects need detain us (except perhaps to note that the 'Celts, although they have very beautiful women, prefer boys'), for what concerns us here is not the content of the book, but the title. Athenaeus called his book the *Deipnosophistae*, which means, literally, the 'kitchen-wisemen' but is more usually translated as those who talk wisely over supper. From this we get the English word *deipnosophist*, first recorded in 1581, which means 'a chap who talks wisely at supper' or alternatively 'a master of the art of dining'.

The Greek word *deipnon* has given English a couple of other interesting little words: *deipno-diplomatic*, which means 'of or pertaining to dining and diplomacy', and *deipnophobia*, which is a 'dread of dinner parties', an emotion more often felt than named. But both those words have been used only once, whereas deipnosophism has survived and endured as a recondite yet necessary art. Only a true master of deipnosophism can tell the difference between a *colloquist*, one who takes part in a conversation, and a *colloquialist*, one who excels in conversation.

For my own part, knowing that I lack the qualifications to speak wisely, I have instead learned to excel at the art of *rhubarbing*, which is the last refuge of the failed deipnosophist. To rhubarb is to say the word 'rhubarb' over and over again in a low, indistinct voice. The reason that this strange verb has made the dictionary is that rhubarb is the standard word that actors use in a crowd scene when they wish to mimic the sound of general conversation. So when Mark Antony comes out on stage all the actors are rhubarbing, and when he shouts 'Friends, Romans, countrymen, lend me your ears', they cease to rhubarb.

Nobody knows why rhubarb was picked for this purpose, or

exactly when, but it's etymologically perfect. 'Rhubarb' comes from the ancient Greek *Rha Barbaron*, which literally means 'foreign rhubarb', because rhubarb was a strange oriental delicacy imported to the classical world via Russia from Tibet. 'Barbaron' was Greek for foreigner because foreigners were all *barbarians*. But the important thing was that the barbarians were called barbarians because they spoke a foreign and unintelligible language, which sounded to the Greeks as though they were just saying 'bar-bar-bar-bar' all the time (roughly in the way that we say 'blah-blah-blah' or 'yadda-yadda-yadda'). Therefore, the ancient word for unintelligible mumbling has, after a journey of several thousand years, come straight back to its original purpose.

Rhubarbing is particularly useful if you want to disguise the fact that nobody wants to talk to you, although you must remember not to use it when the waiter comes to take your order.

Avoiding conversation

Society is now one polished horde
Formed of two mighty tribes, the bores and bored.

Lord Byron

Better to be a rhubarber than a *bromide*. Bromide used to be used as a sedative and was therefore taken up as a nineteenth-century American term for a fellow who can put you to sleep, with the efficiency of good Valium, merely by talking. A dedicated bromide moves through his subject with the same tortoise-speed as a drill boring its way through granite, hence the more usual term: a bore.[1]

However, in this I feel (as an inveterate and ambitious bore myself) that bromide is not quite the right word. Boredom is not merely the lack of stimulation, it is an active property. Sit somebody in an empty room or in front of the proverbial drying paint and they will be quite content for a while, musing on something or another, and, provided that they are over the age of ten, restlessness may not set in for quite a while. But a Class-A bore can have you frantic within seconds. I personally have merely to say the words, 'Ah, I'm glad you asked me that …' to observe a terrified, hunted light come into my interlocutor's/victim's eyes. The only way to stop me is immediate *kittle pitchering*, which is amply described in a late eighteenth-century dictionary.

> KITTLE PITCHERING. A jocular method of hobbling or bothering a troublesome teller of long stories: this is done by contradicting some very immaterial circumstance at the beginning of the narration, the objections to which being settled, others are immediately started to some new particular of like consequence; thus impeding, or rather not suffering him to enter into, the main story. Kittle pitchering is often practiced in confederacy, one relieving the other, by which the design is rendered less obvious.

Why is it called kittle pitchering? Ah, I'm glad you asked me that. Well, *kittle* is an old word for tickling, and a *pitcher* is somebody who loads hay onto a cart, and hay, being dry, is proverbially

---

[1] The French *bourre*, meaning padding, may also be responsible. I could go on.

boring (Thomas Gray once commented that trying to read Aristotle was like eating dried hay).

And what do you call the rhetorical act of asking a question and then answering it yourself? Ah, I'm glad you asked me that. It is called *anthypophora*, and was a practice much beloved of the ancient Greeks. And what do you call it when you keep doing this again and again and again? That's *dianoea*. And why do I keep using these tiresome techniques? Quite simply because it disguises the fact that nobody is interested and that nobody can get a word in edgewise anyhow.

In fact, once I've got a good rhythm going with my dianoea, the only thing to do is to attack directly by interrupting. However, it is of no use simply asking, 'May I interrupt?', as such polite proposals are rarely accepted. The best thing to do in this situation is to use a particularly obscure and puerile synonym of the word 'interrupt'. So lean forward, look the speaker in the eyes, and say in a deep and loud voice: 'I would like to *interjaculate*.'

A long silence may be left after the use of this phrase before asking somebody to pass the salt. The Latin *jaculari* only means 'throw', so interjaculate means 'throw in between'. Put an E on the front and you have throw out. There's even a related word *interjaculatory*, which is defined as 'expressed in parenthetical ejaculations'. For example, a writer in *Blackwood's Magazine* in 1827 mentions how the arrival of the host's child 'smites a large dinner-party mute, or into interjaculatory admiration of its hereditary beauties'.

Thus can the monologue be turned to a *duologue*, and thence to a *tetralogue* (there is, for some reason, no English word for a conversation between three people), and hence into a free-for-all *collocation*.

Who skinks?

With the conversation resting in an uneasy truce, it is possible to get down to matters truly *cenatory* (or 'related to supper') such as eating and drinking. The first thing to ask is 'Who *skinks*?', which is an old-fashioned way of asking who the hell is meant to be pouring out the drinks.

Often, though, there is no designated skinker and the bottle is simply wandering around the table. It will usually be seen cowering at the far end and out of reach, which means that you'll have to get somebody to pass it along – clockwise.

In our modern, fallen age the practice of passing things clockwise around the table is confined to only the poshest and most hidebound of dinners, and even there only to the port and snuff, but it was once universal. Everything had to be done in the direction of the sun.

If you spend a whole day standing still and staring southward you will see the sun rise upon your left and then trot across the sky in front of you before setting to the right. If you stand facing northward all day you will see the shadow of your head doing the same thing on the other side, making you the living *gnomon* of a sundial.

You will only face south, though, if you're in the northern hemisphere, where the sun spends most of its time more or less slightly south of you. Botswanans, New Zealanders and other occupants of the southern hemisphere will look north for the sun. (I must refer Equitorialists to previous comments about the average.) Clocks were built to imitate sundials in the northern hemisphere, and that is why clockwise is sunwise. If clocks had been invented in Australia, they would go the other way.

Once upon a time it was considered right and proper to do everything in the direction of the sun, i.e. clockwise. If you were, for example, to walk around a church, you would do so sunwise. If a group of peasants were passing around their lunchtime loaf of bread, they would do so sunwise, since to pass the other way would be terribly bad luck – this is called doing something *withershins*. In fact, a standard way for a witch to curse you was to walk nine times about your house withershins; and when witches danced in a circle, they did (and do) so withershins. Everything good had to be done clockwise.

This sensible precaution against the Arch-Fiend did have some drawbacks. You could find yourself in a seventeenth-century tavern gazing longingly at a bottle but unable to reach for it. So all sorts of phrases were invented to hint to whoever had the bottle that they should get a bloody move on. 'Remember Parson Malham', 'Who is Peter Lug?', 'Who has any lands in Appleby?' were all cries that would come from the droughty end of the table. All of these phrases are, so far as anyone can tell, completely meaningless.[2]

Today, the belief that doing anything withershins is bad luck is confined to the high table of Oxbridge colleges, where they know that it's all true. And the current standard phrase to get the bottle moving is: 'Do you know the Bishop of Norwich?'

However, it is vital to remember that, technically, the port should always be passed to the right if you are in the southern hemisphere.

---

[2] Although there is something odd that I noticed. Do you remember the mysterious Sir Posthumus Hoby in Chapter 3? No? Oh well. He was MP for Appleby and, as a Puritan, would probably be against drinking. Peter Lug was also a name for someone who hogs the bottle.

Finishing off

A fine strategic brain is required when passing the wine around, as you must try to predict who will be left with the *swank*, a dialect word recorded in an early eighteenth-century dictionary:

> Swank [at Bocking in Essex] that remainder of liquor at the bottom of a tankard, pot or cup, which is just sufficient for one draught; which is not accounted good manners to divide with the left hand man, and according to the quantity is called either a large or little swank.[3]

If you have managed to obtain the swank, guzzle it down as fast as you can and explain about Essex later. If somebody else has it, then you may suggest that you do the decent Victorian thing and *buz*, which is:

> To share equally the last of a bottle of wine, when there is not enough for a full glass for each of the party.

But what of the food? As the dinner draws to a close it is vital, in the interests of good manners, that you remember to leave a *tailor's mense*. In the days when a tailor came to fit you in your own home, it was customary to provide him with a light meal. This he would eat lightly. If he finished it all off, you would be left with the awkward feeling that perhaps you hadn't provided

---

[3] A hundred years later the term was still going, although this time it had moved across the county to Braintree where, in 1813, 'A pint of beer is divided into three parts or draughts; the first is called Neckum, the second Sinkum, and the third Swank or Swankum'.

enough food for the poor tradesman. To pre-empt such worries the tailor would always nearly finish his meal but leave a little bit on the side of the plate to show that he was stuffed and couldn't possibly eat another bite if his life depended upon it. As we've seen, mense was another word for tact or politeness, so this tactful gobbet of food was called a tailor's mense. Thus:

> *Tailor's mense*, the morsel of meat which a country tailor leaves at dinner, when working out, that he may not be charged with indecently eating all up.

In the late nineteenth century, people got very precise as to exactly how much you should leave as a tailor's mense. One book of 1872 specifies that:

> A 'tailor's mense,' ration, or allowance, is, according to an old saying, a small portion of a meal left for good manners, only one-ninth part of the quantity required for a man.

The recommended daily food intake for a man is usually 2,500 calories, and so dividing that up into three equal meals a day, we can conclude that a tailor's mense is 93.6 calories, which is about the same as one large fried egg.

Even with a fried egg gleaming on the side of your plate, though, you may for reasons purely of comfort adjust your belt to the most expansive setting. This is called the *yule hole*, and is meant to be used only after Christmas dinner. However, in *A Complete Collection of Scottish Proverbs Explained and Made Intelligible to the English Reader* (1818) the author notes that telling your host that you have 'Set the bag to the old stent [stretch], and the belt to the yule hole' is terribly polite as it implies that 'we eat as heartily as we did at Christmas'.

If, though, you are only using the yule hole out of politeness, it's a good thing to remember this before standing up.

Thanking your host

Now all that remains (aside from the tailor's mense) is the duty of thanking whoever has *bedinnered* you, bedinnering being providing with dinner. Obviously, this should only be done if you actually thought that the supper was up to snuff. If it wasn't, you could say 'Thank you for that collation', and it would only be much later, when your host was flicking through Dr Johnson's dictionary, that they would find that you meant it was 'a treat less than a feast'.

My own standard phrase here is to say that I have been *golop-shusly* (or deliciously) bedinnered, before calmly handing over the bill. This has the desired effect on all but the most impudent, in which case you must simply agree to having a *blind man's dinner*, which is one where you run away without paying. If your supper has been taken in a private dwelling then the same thing applies to the washing up. Simply explain that you are awfully sorry but you cannot stay a moment longer as you see by your watch that it is *quafftide*.

Chapter 16

9 p.m. – Drinking

Persuading others to – choosing a bar
– opening the door – approaching the bar – ordering
– drinking – the results of drinking – empties
– forms of drunkenness

ༀༀ

Picking your ale-knights

You are fed, but you are not yet sufficiently watered, and man cannot live on supper alone. Indeed, the main purpose of supper is to make sure that you are not subjecting your body to the indignity of *dry-drinking*, which is to say, in a seventeenth-century way, boozing on an empty stomach.

However, there are various tasks that must be performed before you can declare with confidence that it is *quafftide*, which is a lovely old term meaning the time of drinking (rather like eventide or morningtide, but a lot more damaging to the liver). First, you will have to explain to your co-supperists that they want a drink too. A lot of people are strangely ignorant of the fact that they are yearning to stay up all night deliberately impairing their mental faculties. However, you must get them along, as if you drink alone it is much harder to avoid buying your round.

A few people will concede immediately that they are up for a *small go*. The definition of this phrase (in a dictionary of Second World War services slang) is not very promising:

A Small go. A reasonable night out with everybody happy and nobody drunk.

But a small go is easily enlarged, and can be considered the Trojan Horse of an evening's entertainment. A little *compotation* (drinking together) can open the gates for a *perpotation* ('the act of drinking largely' according to Dr Johnson). So to those who insist on a small go, you can insist that that was what you had in mind yourself, and you were only planning to have one little tipple. Such little lies, or *taradiddles* as they used to be called, are merely truths that aren't yet true.

However, there may be others who insist that they don't want a drink at all. With these people there is no gentle cajoling to be done; all you can do is hurl insults at them. 'You *drink-water*!' you can shout. '*Nephalist*! *Hydropot*! *Wowser*!' All that these words really mean is teetotaller, but hydropot, even though it's only Latin for 'water drinker', has a lovely ring to it; and only the Australians could have come up with wowser, which the OED defines as 'a fanatical or determined opponent of intoxicating drink'.

It is the old war between the *antithalians* and the *apolaustics*, and everybody has to pick which side they're on right now. Thalia is the Muse of Comedy, the Grace of Plenty and the ancient deity of good fun. If you are against her, you are antithalian, a word that, admittedly, has only one documented use in 1818. On the other side are the apolaustics, from the Greek *apolaustikos* meaning enjoyment. The war between these two armies is the eternal conflict of humanity. The antithalians are better organised, but the apolaustics have all the camp followers.

At this point the obstinately funless will probably just scamper home. Good riddance. All that are left are *owlers*.

Owler One who goes abroad at night, like an owl.

Choosing a drunkery

Anyone who thinks a bar is a bar is a bar has not read enough dictionaries. There are myriad distinctive subtleties to be observed. For example, Dr Johnson, who occasionally interrupted his lexicography with night-long boozing-bouts, insisted:

Alehouse. n.s. [Sax. ealhus.] A house where ale is publickly sold; a tipling house. It is distinguished from a tavern where they sell wine.

Each drink has its proper purveyor. There are whisky-houses, rum-holes, gin-joints or occasionally -palaces, wine-lodges, punch-houses, and beer-halls, -gardens, -cellars, -parlours and, inevitably, -bellies.

You must choose your *potation-shop* wisely, for not all *sluiceries* are equal. For example, you might be tempted to visit a *speakeasy blind tiger* (if you were in nineteenth-century USA). A newspaper of 1857 records:

> I sees a kinder pigeon-hole cut in the side of a house, and over the hole, in big writin', 'Blind Tiger, ten cents a sight.' … That 'blind tiger' was an arrangement to evade the law, which won't let 'em sell licker there, except by the gallon.

And as a gallon is really pushing it for what was meant to be a small do, a blind tiger (or *blind pig*, as they were also called) would be a bit much. Inexperienced drinkers should instead attend a *fuddling-school*, where the fine arts and crafts of fuddling may be explained to them by a competent teacher.

Fuddling is a recondite verb that lies behind the common adjective *befuddled*, which technically means drunk. Fuddling is drinking. Nobody knows quite where the word comes from. It is not, alas, a frequentative, as *sparkle* is of *spark* or *gobble* is of *gob*. There is a word *fud*, but it's a noun and means either buttocks or a woman's pubic hair. No, fuddle is an orphan of mysterious ancestry, but it does produce the lovely word *fuddler*.

The *Gentleman's Magazine* of 1756 condemned people who 'fuddle away the day with riot and prophaneness', which is doubtless the result of the fact that fuddling-schools have been undocumented since 1680.

You could be dull and go for some all-purpose *bibbery* (drinking establishment), or you could be ambitious and choose a *drunkery* (a place where people get drunk). But it is vital that you start the evening with precision, even though you will in the end arrive at that dread place written of in the *Western Canadian dictionary and phrase-book: things a newcomer wants to know* (1912):

Snake-room, a side room of a basement where saloon-keepers accommodate doped or drunken people until they recover their senses, presumably a place where they 'see snakes'.

In fact, it may be worthwhile to enquire about the facilities in the snake-room before you even go through the door with your *snecklifter*.

Lifting the sneck

A *lanspresado* is (according to a 1736 dictionary of thieves' slang):

He that comes into Company with but Two-pence in his Pocket.

You either know a lanspresado, or you are one. I have taken the latter course.

Lanspresados are everywhere. They have usually forgotten their wallets or can't find a cashpoint (did you know that in Wisconsin cashpoints are called *time machines*?) or some intensely complicated thing has happened with their rent, which means that they're skint till Thursday.

A lanspresado was originally a *lancepesato* or broken lance, who did the work of a corporal without getting a corporal's pay. However, if you want a more English-sounding term you may turn to the snecklifter.

You see, a lanspresado has to prowl around. He goes to the pub, but of course he can't approach the bar unless he sees a friend already there. So he lifts the latch of the pub door, pokes his head in, sees if there's someone who'll buy him a drink, and if there isn't he walks calmly away.

An old word for a latch is a *sneck*, and so a snecklifter is a person who pokes his head into the pub to see if there's anyone who might stand him a little drink.

Called to the bar

Once in the door, sprint straight for the bar, if necessary employing your whiffler (see Chapter 4). Having clubbed your way through the throng, gesticulate wildly and shriek for service. The best way of getting noticed by the bar staff is to call them by unusual names. A man might positively resent being called 'barkeep' but hurry to serve somebody who addressed him as *Squire of the Gimlet* (1679) or *Knight of the Spigot* (1821). Similarly, a lady of the bar may be called (and apparently was called in the eighteenth century) a *pandoratrix*, on the basis that she, like the Pandora of mythology, has all the world's delights and diseases for sale. However, a more poetic name for a barmaiden is *Hebe*, which the OED neatly defines as:

> 1. The goddess of youth and spring, represented as having been originally the cup-bearer of Olympus; hence applied *fig.* to:
> a. A waitress, a barmaid.

The male equivalent of a Hebe (pronounced *HE-be*) would be a *Ganymede*, which has a similar sort of definition:

> 1. A cup-bearer, a youth who serves out liquor; humorously, a pot-boy.

But they might balk at:

2. A catamite.

So it's best to leave mythology out of it and stick to something matey like *birler* or *bombard man*. Only if they fail to serve you within thirty seconds should you start hurling abuse at them. If it comes to that, *under-skinker* is a good Shakespearean word, but is unequal to the cruel contempt contained in the term *lickspiggot*.

Ordering

Once you have the *tapster*'s attention it is time to actually order your drinks. First, check to see whether there's a female present who wants brandy. If there is, you can say that she's a *bingo-mort*, and provided that the barman is fluent in the thieves' dialect of the eighteenth century, where *bingo* was brandy and a *mort* was a woman, then you'll be served straight away. Such fluency will also allow you to insist on a *soldier's bottle* (a large one) rather than a *bawdy house bottle* (a very small one), because even three hundred years ago they were trying to rip people off in such bars.

Gin may be referred to as *strip me naked*, but this should be done with caution as the tapster may take you at your word, so you might be better off asking for a glass of *royal poverty*. The same caution should be applied when referring to whisky as *spunkie*, or to strong beer as *nappy ale* (on the basis that it makes you want to take a nap).

It may be simplest to ask for *stagger-juice* all round and see what happens. After all, all that is really required is a memory-dulling *nepenthe*, a drink to make you forget. Or you may simply quote the Bible to the barman, the 31st chapter of the Book of Proverbs to be precise:

> Give strong drink unto him that is ready to perish, and wine unto those that be of heavy hearts. Let him drink, and forget his poverty, and remember his misery no more.

Fuddling

Ah, the sweet *guggle* of drink poured forth! The OED insists that drink guggles from a bottle, but it's a matter of onomatopoeic choice really. And ah, the happiness of the corner of the bar (or *snuggery*) to which you retire with your hard-won potations. Snuggery – despite its obvious rhymes of *thuggery*, *skulduggery* and *humbuggery* – is one of the pleasantest words in the English language.

Every pub used to have a snuggery of some sort or another, and they had supernatural qualities. A nineteenth-century Scottish writer observed that:

> The Snuggery, sir, has a power o' contraction an' expansion, that never belonged afore to any room in this sublunary world. Let the pairty be three or thretty, it accommodates its dimensions to the gatherin'.

Within the snuggery not only are the rules of sublunar space relaxed, but all human endeavours, all that mankind has ever fought, strived and died for is suddenly achieved without the slightest effort. Elsewhere on this petty orb, people are fighting and demonstrating and revolting and campaigning to achieve an equality that is somehow assumed in the snuggery over a few pints. Lord and commoner, billionaire and beggar, senior vice president in charge of sales and junior intern in charge of tea; all sit in parity around the beer mats. Cares, sorrows and injustices are abandoned somewhere near the till and all are equally jolly (except the nicotinians who have to go outside these days).

Of course, the table will probably require *pooning*. It usually does. To poon is:

> To prop up the piece of furniture with a wedge (a poon) under
> the leg (from 1856). Originally, to poon seems to have meant to
> be unsteady, and you propped up the leg that pooned.

That definition is taken from a dictionary of school slang peculiar to the Collegium Sancta Maria Wincorum or, in the common tongue, St Mary's College of Winchester. It seems astonishing that an action so bloody universal should have a name only in one boarding school in the nether regions of Hampshire, but that's how language works. Your dinner table probably needed to be pooned as well, but it was less necessary when the glasses were less full. Not that they will be full for long.

The results of fuddling

Once you are properly *vinomadefied* all sorts of intriguing things start to happen. Vinomadefied, by the way, does not mean 'made mad by wine', but merely dampened by it. It's the sister word of *madefied* meaning moistened, and on the other side of the family is a relative of *vinolent*, which has nothing to do with violence and merely means:

Addicted to drinking wine, tending to drunkenness.

It's a word that the Wife of Bath used in her grand and gaudy prologue:

For all so siker [surely] as cold engendereth hail,
A lickerous mouth must han [have] a lickerous tail.
In women vinolent is no defence –
This knowen lechers by experience.

Which may be rewritten for these more modern, more enlightened, post-feminist times as:

From lecherous women there is no defence
Especially when you're feeling vinolent.

But to return to the subject: vinomadefied is just a finer, more Latinate way of saying *beer-sodden* or *ale-washed*.

Once the vino has begun to madefy you, you may find that your hand becomes rather *wankle*, or unsteady. In fact, it may not even be your hand that's unsteady, just everything around it; after all, Thomas of Erceldonne noticed right back in the fifteenth century that 'Þe worlde is wondur wankill'.

The result of wankle hands is that whatever you're fuddling tends to divide itself neatly between your mouth, where it should be, and your nice clean top, where it shouldn't. The resulting spots were called *the tears of the tankard* by eighteenth-century drinkers, and in the messier officer's messes of the Second World War they were called *canteen medals*, on the basis that they tend to end up just where the silverware would on parade day.

There are, though, worse stains than the tankard's tears that can befall a fuddler through no fault of their own. Sailors used to refer to the

ADMIRAL OF THE NARROW SEAS. One who, from drunkenness, vomits into the lap of the person sitting opposite him.

This is pretty bad, and can ruin the whole atmosphere of the snuggery. However, it gets worse. Or at least it does if you take your shoes off while you're drinking. I assume that sailors used to drink barefoot – if not I can find no reasonable explanation for the following definition, which seems downright ungentlemanly:

VICE ADMIRAL OF THE NARROW SEAS. A drunken man that pisses under the table into his companions' shoes.

I mean, damn it all. That's hardly what you want to greet a probing toe at the end of the evening. Also, I don't quite see how one could manage to be a Vice Admiral of the Narrow Seas unless one had first picked up the shoe, or had quite fantastic aim beneath the table. There is no equivalent phrase for ladies, nor is there likely to be (even though there is, in the OED, an *admiraless*, meaning either a female admiral or the wife of a male one).

Arriving at the island

> ISLAND. He drank out of the bottle till he saw the island; the island is the rising bottom of a wine bottle, which appears like an island in the centre, before the bottle is quite empty.

Napoleon was not more sorry to spy St Helena, or Dreyfuss to sight Devil's Island, than the keen drinker is to see that dreaded lump appear out of the wine-dark sea. At this point it must be decided by those around the table whether this is an ordinary drink or one to be consumed *supernaculum*. *Super* is Latin for on, and *nagel* is German for fingernail, and like this odd combination, drinking supernaculum is a rather odd custom described in 1592 thus:

> Drinking super nagulum, a device of drinking new come out of France: which is, after a man hath turned up the bottom of his cup, to drop it on his nail and make a pearl with that is left which, if it slide & he cannot make stand on, by reason there's too much, he must drink again for his penance.

Supernaculum can either be an adverb, as above, or a noun to describe a drink so fine that not a drop is to be wasted. So a couple of hundred years later a dictionary simply defines it as:

Supernaculum, good liquor, of which there is not even a drop left sufficient to wet one's nail.

And a hundred years later it had become a toast or drinking cry. The novelist/Prime Minister Benjamin Disraeli has a description of a drinking contest in his first novel *Vivian Grey* (1827):

> The cup was now handed across the table to the Baron Asmanshausen. His Lordship performed his task with ease; but as he withdrew the horn from his mouth, all present, except Vivian, gave a loud cry of 'Supernaculum!' The Baron smiled with great contempt, as he tossed, with a careless hand, the great horn upside downwards, and was unable to shed upon his nail even the one excusable pearl.

The Baron was drinking a bottle of the finest Johannisberger, which is definitely a supernaculum drink. If you have been sipping at something less, then you should perhaps not get it down to the last drop. Instead, leave it to be mixed up in a bucket to be consumed by the poor of the parish. These mixed up *heel-taps* are known as *alms drinks* and go to people living in alms houses, although they're mentioned in Shakespeare as a quickfire way of getting somebody horribly, horribly plastered. Either way, whether you have pursued the Baron's path or the Christian one, you should now see a *marine officer* standing on the table.

> MARINE OFFICER. An empty bottle: marine officers being held useless by the seamen.

Well, that was the reasoning given in a dictionary of 1811. But come 1860 another slang dictionary has a different explanation.

> MARINE, or MARINE RECRUIT, an empty bottle. This expression having once been used in the presence of an officer of marines, he was at first inclined to take it as an insult, until some one adroitly appeased his wrath by remarking that no offence could be meant, as all that it could possibly imply was, 'one who had done his duty, and was ready to do it again.'

Ready to do it again? Splendid. But first, how drunk are you?

The stately progress of the drinker

The standard modern measurement of inebriation is the *Ose* system. This has been considerably developed over the years, but the common medical consensus currently has *jocose, verbose, morose, bellicose, lachrymose, comatose, adios*.

This is a workable but incomplete system, as it fails to take in *otiose* (meaning impractical) which comes just after jocose. Nor does it have *grandiose* preceding bellicose. And how they managed to miss out *globose* (amorphous or formless) before comatose is beyond me.

Back in the sixteenth century, medicine was a much less developed science. Still, in 1592 a chap called Thomas Nashe produced a good diagnostic system of the eight stages of drunkenness.

> Nor have we one or two kinds of drunkards only, but eight kinds.

The first is ape drunke; and he leapes, and singes, and hollowes, and danceth for the heavens;

The second is lion drunke; and he flings the pots about the house, calls his hostesse whore, breakes the glasse windowes with his dagger, and is apt to quarrell with anie man that speaks to him;

The third is swine drunke; heavie, lumpish, and sleepie, and cries for a little more drinke, and a fewe more cloathes;

The fourth is sheepe drunk; wise in his conceipt, when he cannot bring foorth a right word;

The fifth is mawdlen drunke; when a fellowe will weepe for kindnes in the midst of ale, and kisse you, saying, 'By God, captaine, I love thee. Goe thy wayes; thou dost not thinke so often of me as I doo thee; I would (if it pleased God) I could not love thee as well as I doo;' and then he puts his finger in his eye, and cryes;

The sixt is Martin[1] drunke; when a man is drunke, and drinkes himselfe sober ere he stirre;

The seventh is goate drunke; when, in his drunkennes, he hath no minde but on lecherie;

The eighth is fox drunke – when he is craftie drunke, as manie of the Dutchmen bee, that will never bargaine but when they are drunke.

---

[1] The *Martin* here may be a Pine Marten, or it may be an unidentified kind of monkey, or it may be an obscure reference to the Martin Marprelate controversy in which Nashe was involved and which is much too complicated to explain here.

All these species, and more, I have seen practised in one company at one sitting; when I have been permitted to remain
sober amongst them, only to note their several humours.

Animals have a strange knack of wandering into descriptions
of drunkenness, which is odd when you think about it, as they
rarely get served in pubs. And owls: the *Chambers Slang Dictionary*
has a whole entry on the different sorts of owl that you can be
as drunk as, without ever explaining how a 'fresh-boiled owl'
could be drunk at all, or why anybody would have boiled it.

The Aztecs (when not sacrificing humans) had an even
more wonderfully whimsical system of animal-based drunkenness. They used rabbits. Four hundred rabbits – the *Centzon
Totochtin*.

When the Aztecs fermented the sap of the maguey plant (or
Agave americana) they got a milky-looking drink called *pulque*,
which got them nice and tiddly. Therefore, in Aztec mythology, when Mayahuel, the goddess of the maguey plant, married
Patecatl, the god of fermentation, she gave birth to four hundred divine rabbits, which she fed from her four hundred divine
breasts.

These four hundred heavenly rabbits would meet for regular pulque-swilling parties, and were pretty much permanently
pissed. A couple of their names are recorded – Ometochtli (or
'Rabbit No. 2') and Macuiltochtli (or 'Rabbit No. 5') – and,
frankly, the rest can be guessed.

The point of all this is that the Aztecs measured drunkenness in rabbits. Fifteen rabbits was, apparently, ideal. But if you
were four hundred rabbits then you were completely gone. A
lovely little coda to this story is that though the conquistadors

stamped out the native religion, they never managed to quite stamp on the boozy bunnies. That's why there is, to this day, a Mexican phrase: 'As drunk as four hundred rabbits.'

There are uncountable terms for being drunk. Benjamin Franklin (when not taking the air baths described in Chapter 2 or writing interesting essays like *Fart Proudly*) observed that most vices have pleasant names. So misers can claim that they are being thrifty, spendthrifts that they are generous, lechers that they are passionate. But 'Drunkenness is a very unfortunate vice; in this respect it bears no kind of similitude to any sort of virtue, from which it might possibly borrow a name; and is therefore reduced to the wretched necessity of being expressed by round about phrases [...] Though every one may possibly recollect a dozen at least of these expressions, used on such occasions, yet I think no one who has not much frequented taverns could imagine the number of them to be so great as it really is.' So for the sake of the drunkards of posterity he made a list of over two hundred synonyms for sozzled.[2] It contains some beer-sodden gems. Back then a drinker could be *jambled*, *nimtopsical, super nonsensical, wise or otherwise* or *as drunk as a wheelbarrow.* He could delicately be said to have *smelt an onion*, or he could move up the social scale and have *made too free with Sir John Strawberry* and announce that *Sir Richard has taken off his considering cap.* Unfortunately there are no explanations included in Franklin's dictionary and we'll never know who Sir Richard might originally have been. However, for one of his phrases – *as drunk as David's sow* – there is a complete explication in Captain Grose's *Dictionary of the Vulgar Tongue*:

---

[2] The list in its entirety may be found in an Appendix at the back of the book.

As drunk as David's sow; a common saying, which took its rise from the following circumstance: One David Lloyd, a Welchman, who kept an alehouse at Hereford, had a living sow with six legs, which was greatly resorted to by the curious; he had also a wife much addicted to drunkenness, for which he used sometimes to give her due correction. One day David's wife having taken a cup too much, and being fearful of the consequences, turned out the sow, and lay down to sleep herself sober in the stye. A company coming in to see the sow, David ushered them into the stye, exclaiming, there is a sow for you! did any of you ever see such another? all the while supposing the sow had really been there; to which some of the company, seeing the state the woman was in, replied, it was the drunkenest sow they had ever beheld; whence the woman was ever after called David's sow.

But though David's wife may have appeared bedraggled to the company, I'm sure the company looked lovely to her, as she would have been wearing *beer-goggles*. Sober people always appear much prettier to drunkards than drunkards appear to the sober – and this is one of the chief advantages of inebriation: the elimination of ugliness. The psychological term for this is *kalopsia*: a wonderful form of madness whereby everything becomes beautiful.

It is enough to fill your head with *lovethoughts*, for as Shakespeare rightly observed, alcohol 'provokes the desire'. So perhaps now is the time to do something about it.

Chapter 17

10 p.m. – Wooing

On the prowl – observing your target – the chat-up – dancing – kissing – making rash proposals of marriage – fanfreluching – rejection

Now that you are thoroughly tanked up, it's probably time to attempt to mate, as it's well known that true love is merely a peculiarly painful sort of drunkenness. And anyway, it's *dragging time*, helpfully defined in the *Dictionary of Obsolete and Provincial English* as 'The evening of a fair day when the lads pull the wenches about'.

The dictionaries, though, are usually unkind to lovers. They tend to have all sorts of rude words like *lecher* or *slattern* that seem designed to make somebody ashamed of their natural obscene urges.

A much more pleasant term is *fleshling*, which the OED defines, rather coyly, as 'a fleshly minded person'. Fleshling sounds a little like *duckling* and a little like *gosling* and altogether makes you seem as innocent as a newborn baby. It's certainly a lot nicer than this definition in a late seventeenth-century dictionary of slang:

Mutton-Monger, a Lover of Women; also a Sheep-stealer.

However, if you flick a few pages back through that same dictionary you'll find a much more civilised term:

> *Give Nature a Fillip*, to Debauch a little now and then with Women, or Wine.

A *fillip*, incidentally, is the little movement you get if you brace the tip of a finger against your thumb and then release it. As that's a good way of tossing a coin to somebody, fillip came to refer to any little gift or treat.

A few pages onwards you find the true rustic joy of:

> *Green-Gown*, a throwing of young Lasses on the Grass, and Kissing them.

Ah, the beauties of a good dictionary! But before such herbaceous hedonism you will first have to find yourself a lass or lad, not to mention a comfortable lawn.

On the prowl

So you must set out into the great fleshy unknown to find yourself somebody to call your own, or at least to call when you're lonely. You must wander about on the pull. There are all sorts of delightful terms for this. In the seventeenth century you would have been:

> *Proling*, Hunting or Searching about in quest of a Wench, or any Game.

In the eighteenth century:

> **Caterwauling** Going out in the night in search of intrigues, like a cat in the gutters.

And in the nineteenth:

> OUT ON THE PICKAROON. Picarone is *Spanish* for a thief, but this phrase does not necessarily mean anything dishonest but ready for anything in the way of excitement to turn up; also to be in search of anything profitable.

And in Scotland you would have *sprunted*, or you would if you could find a convenient haystack:

> To SPRUNT, v, n, To run among the stacks after the girls at night

However, I contend that the best possible term for pootling around on the lookout for a lover is *Ogo-Pogoing*. This will require some explanation.

If you ask the average person what an Ogo-Pogo is, they will tell you to get stuffed. If, however, you ask somebody from British Columbia, they will tell you that the Ogo-Pogo is a sort of monster that lives in the Okanagan Lake and occasionally poses for extremely grainy photographs. It is, in short, the Canadian answer to the Loch Ness Monster. However, even they are unlikely to know that the real name of this unreal beast was Naitaka, and that Ogo-Pogo is a nickname taken from a British music-hall song that was a big hit in the 1920s.

It's a catchy tune, and it seems that people still remembered it in 1939, when pilots in the Royal Air Force would be sent out to fly around Britain on the off-chance that they would spot an enemy aircraft. The RAF pilots called this Ogo-Pogoing, presumably because while winging around scanning the skies they would sing to themselves the refrain from the song: 'I'm looking for the Ogo-Pogo/The funny little Ogo-Pogo.'

So Ogo-Pogo started out as a nonsense song, became the name of a mythical Canadian beast, and was taken up by the RAF meaning to fly around on the off-chance of meeting somebody. It would be a catastrophe if a word with such a rich history were to decline into disuse. And how better to describe the hopeless search for that mythical beast called Love? You even have, thanks to the RAF, the possibilities of sudden destruction or timeless glory built in. As tempting as the idea of proling, caterwauling, pickarooning or even sprunting may be, Ogo-Pogoing is without a doubt the finest word for wandering around with vague hopes of love.

Observing the prey

It is never easy to find a suitable target while Ogo-Pogoing. Many a female who sees the *Oxford English Dictionary*'s definition of *spanandry* – 'Lack or extreme scarcity of males in a population' – is liable to let out an all too familiar sigh. When you want a man, every party and every nightclub is dispiritingly spanandrous. In fact, one's *dioestrus* (a short period of sexual inactivity for females) can suddenly seem to stretch out into eternity.

But then it begins, very quietly, with a little *propassion*. A propassion is the first stirring of a proper passion, or indeed merely the feeling that there's a passion somewhere on its way, and that suffering is not far off. Our word passion, meaning love, as we saw in Chapter 1, derives from the Latin for suffering, on the simple basis that the two are one and the same; so the Passion of the Christ (his suffering upon the cross) is the same as our petty romantic passions, etymologically speaking.

For the moment you may merely *smicker*; it's a good way to start. To smicker is 'to look amorously or wantonly at or after a person', usually after, of course, although a glossary of medieval Scottish poetry (there are such things) says that to *smikker* is to 'smile in a seducing manner'. Either way, if you smicker enough you may well develop an acute *smickering*, or amorous inclination, towards someone. Smickering was a favourite word of John Dryden, who came up with the lovely line:

Must you be smickering after wenches while I am in calamity?

You can even smicker in very precise ways. For example, you may be particularly drawn to a pair of dark eyes, or a shapely nose, or an intriguing ankle. Those who study sexual attraction for a living (legally) call this *agastopia*, an immensely useful word that is defined in the *Descriptive Dictionary and Atlas of Sexology* thus:

Agastopia. A rarely used term for admiration of any particular part of the body.

Why it should be rarely used is a mystery, as agastopia was known even to the sexologists and sculptors of the ancient world. It is from the bottom-fond Greeks that we get the modern English term *callipygian*, meaning beautiful-buttocked.

There was a whole cult in ancient Syracuse devoted to Aphrodite Kallipygos, or Venus of the Beautiful Bottom, or at least there may have been. The only description we have of it comes from an ancient Greek chap called Alciphron who spent his time composing imaginary letters.

It is certain that the Greeks would commission all sorts of sculptures of callipygian Venus in which the main purpose was to make her as lovely-bottomed as possible. Lucian of Samosata records seeing one such statue carved by the greatest sculptor of antiquity: Praxiteles. This statue, apparently, was rather too good. So sexy was Aphrodite's posterior that a young man was discovered in the temple committing enthusiastic blasphemy with the marble goddess. He was rather embarrassed by this, as I suppose you would be, and cast himself into the sea. But though he died, the term callipygian lived on, and it can of course be applied to both sexes, mortal and immortal, marble and flesh.

But to move on from such *natiform* (or buttock-shaped) delights, one's agastopia might instead be directed at the *bathy-colpian*. Bathycolpian means 'deep-bosomed' and is an absurdly oblique and beautiful way of saying that a lady has voluptu-ous and luxuriant breasts. The advantages of describing a lady in such an incomprehensible manner will be evident to anyone who has ever been slapped or released on strict parole.

With all these different body parts to glance at, it is no wonder that you move your eyes from side to side using the *amatorial* muscles. One eighteenth-century dictionary is quite unnecessarily precise about it:

> AMATORII *Musculi* [among Anatomists] Muscles of the Eyes, which give them a Cast sideways, and assist that particular look called Ogling.

And there we have the problem. You are fast becoming an *ogler*, a *snilcher*, a *haker*. And if you thought hake was only a kind of fish:

> HAKE: To hanker after, to gape after, to sneak or loiter.

You must up your game if you do not wish to be thought merely a *gazehound* and amorous gongoozler. If you have decided upon your intended, it is high time that you did something about it. If you are a lady, you may give a coy *arrision* (which is the act of smiling at somebody) or practise your *minauderie* (coquettish manner). If you are a man, and you have picked out your *rum-strum* (a highwayman's term for a handsome wench) it may be time to *pavonize*, or act like a peacock showing off your magnificent tail in order to cow all the potential peahens with your magnificent masculinity.

But there's no use in just pavonizing; one is in danger of being a mere *dangler* ('To dangle – To follow a woman around without asking the question'). You must decide if this is a grand passion or a mere *velleity*, which the OED sternly defines as 'The fact or quality of merely willing, wishing, or desiring, without any effort or advance towards action or realization'.

Of course there may be reasons for your inaction. Perhaps the object of your affections is a *figurant*. This is, I confess, a technical balletic term for somebody who dances only in a group and never by themselves, but its usefulness in the discotheque should be self-evident. It is extraordinarily hard to sidle up to a figurant who has enclosed themselves within a protective fortification of bouncing shoulders and turned backs, but it must be attempted. Faint heart never won fair rum-strum.

You may even be covered in what the Old English liked to call *need-sweat*, which is the perspiration caused by acute anxiety. But what is such sweat compared with *anuptaphobia*, the morbid terror of remaining single? Though anuptaphobia is only a psychological term, she really should be a goddess, a cruel and terrible deity who directs all of humanity's most embarrassing actions. For who can disobey when Anuptaphobia commands? It is time to approach the object of your mute affections. And if Anuptaphobia tells you to *flichter* to him or her, then you must flichter.

And in case you were wondering:

FLICHTER v. To run with outspread arms, like a tame goose half-flying; applied to children, when running to those to whom they are much attached. [Dumfries dialect] Hence:

FLICHTER-FAIN adj. So fond of an object as to run to it in the manner above described.

The simplest methods are often the most effective.

The chat-up

Each species has its own particular mating call. A badger, for example, *shrikes* to his would-be beloved. A fox *clickets*. A goat *rattles*. A deer *croons*. A sow *breems* for her pig. A cow *eassins* for her bull. And an otter *whineth*. You should do none of these and if you hear a shrike, make your excuses and leave, as you are dealing with a badger in disguise.

Luckily for all of us, the correct way to initiate conversation has already been discovered and set down in writing by Christopher Marlowe:

> Come live with me and be my love
> And we will all those pleasures prove
> That hills and valleys, dale and field,
> And all the craggy mountains yield.

If that doesn't work, or if your intended expresses a distaste for craggy mountains, you could go for the 1950s standard: 'Suppose we get together and split a herring.' Unfortunately, everybody in the 1950s was too hep to record why it was a herring that needed splitting. A more explicable term was recorded by Cab Calloway: 'Wouldst like to con a glimmer with me this early black?', which he helpfully explains as 'the proper way to ask a young lady to go to the movies'. It should be noted here, that if the object of your affections replies 'Kill me', they are not requesting to be euthanatised and you should not actually murder them. *Kill me* is merely the Cab Calloway way of saying 'Show me a good time' and is the best response you could have hoped for. Jive was rather confusing in this way. *Murder* is defined in the *Hepsters Dictionary* as 'Something excellent or terrific', which is all very well provided that both parties are familiar with the idiolect, but it might lead to confusion and a rather feeble-sounding excuse in court.

Or one could go down the simpler route of throwing out a compliment or two. If you do so, you must try to be a little more gentlemanly than Dr Johnson was in his dictionary. In a rare moment of misogyny he wrote:

Bellibone n. A woman excelling in both beauty and goodness.
A word now out of use.

According to the OED the word was last used in 1586, which makes one wonder what occurred in 1587 that made ladies one or the other and rendered *bellibone* redundant.

Alternatively, you could call a lady a *wonder wench* (an old Yorkshire term for a sweetheart) or, if you're feeling ready to defend yourself, *cowfyne*, which even in a dictionary of Scottish terms is defined as 'a ludicrous term of endearment'. In fact, the only proper riposte that a lady can give to being called cowfyne is to reply that the chap is *snoutfair*, which means handsome, although the OED notes that it is usually used 'with some disparaging suggestion'.

What, though, if your initial blandishments and entreaties are met not with a flirtatious exchange of archaic endearments, but with indifference, incredulity, contemptuous laughter or sudden flight? Fear not. This may merely be a case of *accismus*.

Accismus is a rhetorical term meaning pretended lack of interest in that which you keenly desire.

Foolish Accismus hath a qualitie
To deny offer'd things in modestie:

Accismus was once considered the most necessary virtue of the female. For example, there's a rather peculiar polemic against girls' schools from the Victorian period that asserts:

A woman requires no figure of eloquence – herself excepted – so often as that of *accismus* ... On this account, mothers, fathers, men, and even youths, are their best companions; on the contrary, girls connected with other girls of a similar age, as in schools, provoke one another to an exchange of foibles, rather than of excellences, to a love of dress, admiration, and gossip, even to the forgetting of *accismus*.

But of course all of this raises the question of when accismus (male or female) is really accismus, and when (dare I broach the possibility?) it is true uninterest. This is a question that has puzzled young lovers through the ages, but which was long ago solved by the Church of England through the system of Nolo Episcopari.

Appointing a bishop is a tricky business. To be a bishop you have to possess the Christian virtue of humility; however, if you actually are humble you'll probably think that you're not worthy of being a bishop and turn the job down. Even if you secretly think that you'd make a splendid bishop and would look marvellous in a mitre, you can't just come out and say it. It would look bad. So you had to practise a little bit of accismus by announcing in front of the assembled company of churchmen that you'd really rather not become a bishop, or, in Latin, 'Nolo episcopari'.

When you had solemnly announced this, rather than saying 'Oh well, that's that, I suppose', the church council would ask you a second time, and for a second time you would humbly reply 'Nolo episcopari'. On the third go, you would say, 'Oh all right then, go on' or 'Volo episcopari' or somesuch line of assent. You would thus have displayed your humility and got the job.

However, it is dreadfully important to keep count, as if you said 'Nolo episcopari' a third time it would be assumed that you really meant it and your chances of promotion would be for ever scuppered. It's rather like the Rule of the Bellman described by Lewis Carroll in *The Hunting of the Snark*: 'What I tell you three times is true.'

Hope as you might, three cases of accismus are definitive and after that you deserve a slap.

This is often the stage of courtship where a woman wishes she were equipped with a *parabore*, or defence against bores. It is uncertain what a parabore would look like, although in the first (and only) usage recorded in the OED it is described as:

> ... a Bore-net, a para-bore, to protect me, like our musquito-curtains

So a parabore could perhaps be attached to a wide-brimmed hat. You could have some sort of rip-cord device, which when pulled would drop a thick veil around the whole head in the manner of a beekeeper. Thus, with a flick of the wrist, the beleaguered belle could make herself vanish from view and give a stern and certain message to her suitor. If parabores could be manufactured for a reasonable cost I imagine that they would become quite popular, though dispiriting to the poor chap who sees a whole group of girls reach for their rip-cords at his timorous approach.

If this unhappy fate does befall you, you can keep some semblance of honour by turning again to the dictionary of Hepster slang and crying, 'You're a V-8, baby, a V-8', where a *V-8* is, for some reason, 'A chick that spurns company'. However, it may be best not to get into an exchange of insults, as (from behind her thick veil) she could throw some hurtful barbs of her own. A few suggestions might be:

Twiddle-Poop An effeminate looking man
Smell-smock A licentious man

Or, most terrible of all, this from Dr Johnson's dictionary:

Amatorcultist. n.s. [amatorculus, Lat.] A little, insignificant lover; a pretender to affection.

There is no coming back from being called an amatorcultist; all you can do is dwindle away and disappear in a shower of tears.

But let us assume some little success at this early amatory stage. Where now? It's a fifty-fifty chance that your main aim is to be *thelyphthoric*, a word that comes from the Greek *thely* meaning 'woman' and *phthoric* meaning 'corrupting', thus the OED's simple definition: 'that corrupts or ruins women'.

Thelyphthoric began its life in English as the title of a smashing 1780 treatise:

THELYPHTHORA; OR, A TREATISE ON FEMALE RUIN, IN
ITS CAUSES, EFFECTS, CONSEQUENCES, PREVENTION,
AND REMEDY; CONSIDERED ON THE BASIS OF THE
DIVINE LAW: Under the following HEADS, viz. MARRIAGE,
WHOREDOM, FORNICATION, ADULTERY, POLYGAMY,
and DIVORCE; With many other Incidental Matters.

It's a promising title, and it gets better with the first sentence:
'The Author doth not scruple to call this TREATISE, one of
the most important and interesting Publications, that have
appeared since the Days of the *Protestant Reformation*.'

But as you read further (and who wouldn't?) it turns out that
far from being a useful instruction manual, the author is dead
against female ruin and all the accompanying pleasantness for
both parties. In fact, he has a high moral purpose of preventing
female ruin through the outlawing of divorce and the reintro-
duction of polygamy.

Thelyphthoric didn't keep its high moral tone for long and
instead toboganned off into the linguistic lowlands. Frankly, a
word like that is never going to remain in the purest of hands,
especially as most of the world's population either want to be
thelyphthoric or be introduced to somebody who is.

The dance-floor

The most common way of attempting thelyphthora is to dance,
jig, *shake a hough*, or *tripudiate*. The thelyphthoric qualities of
such rhythmic movements are amply recorded in the dictionaries. For example, from the eighteenth century:

Balum-Rancum A hop or dance, where the women are all prostitutes. N.B. The company dance in their birthday suits.

Or from the other perspective:

Gymnopaedic *Ancient Greek Hist.* The distinctive epithet of the dances or other exercises performed by naked boys at public festivals.

Or for both sexes:

Among the tramping fraternity a *buff-ball* is a dancing party, characterised by the indecency of those who attend it, the *costume de rigueur* being that of our first parents.

The most favourite entertainment at this place is known as '*buff-ball*,' in which both sexes – innocent of clothing – madly join, stimulated with raw whisky and the music of a fiddle and a tin-whistle.

But how to suggest such a thing in a manner both alluring and learned? In the 1960 film *Beat Girl*, Oliver Reed approaches a stylish young she-cat sitting in a bar and says: 'Say, baby, you feel terpsichorical? Let's go downstairs and fly.' Terpsichore is one of the nine ancient muses, and specifically the muse who inspires dancing. So Mr Reed's enquiry, in the context of the film, means: 'Do you feel inspired by the muse of dance? Let us go to the basement and do just that.' And, in the context of the film, it works. How or why Terpsichore got so famous in the mid-twentieth century is a bit of a mystery, but the OED even records the shortened verb *to terp.*

But what if you are not inspired by the moving muse? If you have not paid her sufficient sacrifices she may curse you with a flip of her immortal foot and leave you *baltering* upon the dance-floor. *Balter* is an old verb meaning to dance clumsily, although one dictionary defines it strictly as 'to tread in a clownish manner, as an ox does the grass'.

Make me immortal with a kiss

The Yaghan people of Tierra Del Fuego at the southernest tip of South America were one of the few tribes ever discovered who didn't wear clothes. This is not because Tierra Del Fuego is a warm and balmy place. It is not. Even in summer the temperature rarely rises above nine degrees centigrade. Yet naked they were, even when Charles Darwin visited them on the *Beagle* and, rather impolitely, called them 'miserable, degraded savages'. It would appear that the Yaghans simply hadn't invented clothing, but they did have an ingenious method for keeping warm, which was to smear themselves head to toe in grease and cuddle each other. This ingenious and energy-efficient practice must be kept in mind when considering their insanely useful word *mamihlapinatapai*.

Mamihlapinatapai is usually defined as 'Two people looking at each other each hoping the other will do what both desire but neither is willing to do'. Mamihlapinatapai is therefore generally reckoned to be one of the most useful words on earth. As two people stand at a doorway each gesturing 'After you', that is mamihlapinatapai. As two people sitting in a dull waiting room both hope that the other will start a conversation, that is mamihlapinatapai. And when two people look into each other's eyes, with that sudden realisation that lips can be used for something other than talking, but both too afraid to draw the other to them, that is Mamihlapinatapai Rex.

However, mamihlapinatapai is a rather controversial word. Experts on the Yaghan language (a group of which I cannot claim membership), while conceding that the word is theoretically possible, tend to pooh-pooh the idea that it ever actually existed. It could exist, just as in English the word *antifondlingness* could exist, but that doesn't mean it does. Mamihlapinatapai is, according to them, a whimsical invention of some unknown linguist.

This case looks, at first blush, rather convincing. How could a tribe that hadn't even invented clothes come up with a word so complex? However, I would contend that the two points are in fact connected, because if you spend half your time naked, cuddling and covered in grease, mamihlapinatapai is going to be a pretty common feeling. In fact it would probably be the dominant emotion of your nude, greasy existence.

So let us assume that the dancing is over, that your eyes have met, and that mamihlapinatapai has come upon you. What to do about it?

The simplest answer I can offer is to ask, 'Care for a biscot?', because *biscot* means 'to caress amorously' but the other person may not know that, and everybody likes a biscuit.

Less deceptive would be to ask the other party whether they are *osculable*. Osculable means 'kissable' but is a much more beautiful word. According to the OED, poor osculable has been used only once, in 1893, to describe the Pope. So the word is nearly virginal and should be taken out and shown to the world.

The Latin for to kiss was *osculare*, and the obscure English words thence derived are wonderful. There's an *osculatrix* (a lady who kisses), an *oscularity* (a kiss), and an *osculary* (anything that can and should be kissed, although this was usually a religious relic).

So, an alternative line could be: 'You are an osculary, and this is my religious duty', or somesuch.

And now it is time for the moment not of truth, but of kissing (the two are entirely separate notions). The eyes close. The lips of the lovers meet. *Cataglottism* is usually attempted by one or both parties, for the definition of which we should turn to Blount's *Glossographia* of 1656:

> *Cataglottism*, a kissing with the tongue.

This word, though rare, has survived for centuries. As the great biologist Henry Havelock Ellis[1] observed in 1905:

> The tonic effect of cutaneous excitation throws light on the psychology of the caress ... The kiss is not only an expression of feeling; it is a means of provoking it. Cataglottism is by no means confined to pigeons.

And a good thing too. But one thing leads to another and the tongue is often merely the thin end of the wedge. The moral dangers of kissing were perhaps most eloquently described by Sir Thomas Urquhart in his *Jewel* of 1652.

---

[1] Translating Charles Féré.

Thus for a while their eloquence was mute, and all they spoke
was but with the eye and hand, yet so persuasively, by vertue
of the intermutual unlimitedness of their visotactil sensation,
that each part and portion of the persons of either was obvious
to the sight and touch of the persons of both; the visuriency of
either, by ushering the tacturiency of both, made the attrecta-
tion of both consequent to the inspection of either.

Where *visuriency* means 'the desire to see' and *tacturiency* means
'the desire to fondle'. It is unfair, though, to judge somebody too
harshly on their desire to fondle. The OED records a word at
once splendid and tragic:

Fondlesome adj. Addicted to fondling.

It beats heroin. But it should be remembered that recidivist
fondlers often need treatment much more than they need punishment. If you object, you should never have given them a
fleshment in the first place.

Once upon a time you trained animals for the hunt by *flesh-
ing* them. If they did what they were supposed to do, you gave
them a little morsel of meat to encourage them; if they did not
do what they were meant to do, they were denied their fleshment. Exactly the same principle and the same word may be
applied to the actions now under consideration. After all, the
OED merely defines fleshment as 'the excitement resulting from
a first success'. A fleshment may therefore have the unfortunate
result of making people go too far too fast. In the current circumstances this could mean one of two things.

Proposing marriage

Mariturient means 'eager to marry' and is derived from the same sort of desiderative verb that gave us *visuriency* and *tacturiency* in the previous section. Maturiency is a relatively common and benign condition that leads to the most blessed state of matrimony and mutual comfort. But in extreme cases it can manifest itself as *gamomania* ('a form of insanity characterised by strange and extravagant proposals for marriage') and it is with the gamomaniacs that we are now concerned.

Every man is occasionally and honourably seized with the desire to make a woman what was called in the seventeenth century his *comfortable importance*, in the eighteenth century his *lawful blanket* and in these fallen and unimaginative days his *wife*. But gamomania goes beyond this.

The first signs may be detectable if he starts mumbling something about your being *fangast*. Fangast is an obsolete Norfolk dialect term meaning 'fit to marry' whose origins are chronically befogged. Few people know the word any more, and for that reason it could be terribly useful. Suppose that your insignificant other were to discover that you had drawn up a table of all your female acquaintances and next to each name had written 'marriage material' or 'not marriage material'. She'd flip her proverbial lid. But 'fangast' and 'not fangast' – unless she's a time-traveller from ancient Norfolk you're in the clear.

If just one other friend knows the word then the two of you can discuss whether somebody is fangast in front of their face with no danger of discovery: 'Have you met my new girlfriend? She's so pretty, and not at all fangast.'

'What?'

'Nothing, darling, nothing.'

But that's not how the gamomaniac thinks. To him (or her) all are fangast. To all will he bring his *subarrhations* (or gifts for a prospective wife). But you have to remember that though gamo, he's still a maniac and must be refused, however osculable. But of course he isn't necessarily a gamomaniac; he may have a title even less honourable, helpfully defined by Dr Johnson:

Fribbler One who professes rapture for a woman, but fears her consent.

Fanfreluching

The other possible result of fondlesome cataglottism is *fanfreluching*, which is another way of saying *swiving, meddling, melling, mollocking, wapping, flesh-company, quaffing, carnal confederacy, jelly-roll, jazz, jig-a-jig, jockumcloying, hot cockles, subagitation, interunion, the Venus exercise, the last favour, old hat, pom-pom, poop-noddy, Moll Peatley, Sir Berkeley*, or in a word: *sex*.

But here we reach something of a crux. First, this is a serious reference work and I am loath to add anything that may subject it to suggestions of levity. Second, there are as many carnal words as there are carnal actions, and one could get horribly bogged down in explaining exactly what is meant by *changing at Baker Street* – added to which my publishers have insisted that they will not stretch to illustrations. But thirdly and most importantly, this is a reference work that must maintain its relevance and usefulness. So the question that must be asked is whether you, dear reader, are going to pull tonight. And as you, dear reader, are the sort of person who reads books on obscure words, I fear that the answer is No.

It could be worse – you could be the sort of person who writes books on obscure words.

So let us sadly and sorrowfully assume that your *supersaliency* is met with an *imparlibidinous* response (that is, your attempting to initiate coitus by leaping upon the beloved is rebuffed by somebody who finds you less desirable than you find them). The course of true love never did leap smooth. There is a reason that you have never heard the word *equinecessary*, and that is that we so rarely are.

Silence and tears

It is important at this point to scrabble for whatever motes of dignity the situation affords. You could pretend, as you ruefully put your socks back on, that it was a mere *passiuncle* or insignificant passion. It may not be true, but none of the best things are. And as your beloved hurries off to obtain a restraining order, you can console yourself that you did at least have a *Pisgah sight*.

When Moses had led the Children of Israel through the wilderness he asked God to allow him to cross the Jordan into the Promised Land. But God would not let him set foot there, only have a glimpse.

And Moses went up from the plains of Moab unto the mountain of Nebo, to the top of Pisgah, that is over against Jericho.

And the LORD shewed him all the land of Gilead, unto Dan,
And all Naphtali, and the land of Ephraim, and Manasseh, and
all the land of Judah, unto the utmost sea, And the south, and
the plain of the valley of Jericho, the city of palm trees, unto
Zoar. And the LORD said unto him, This is the land which I
sware unto Abraham, unto Isaac, and unto Jacob, saying, I will
give it unto thy seed: I have caused thee to see it with thine eyes,
but thou shalt not go over thither.

So Moses the servant of the LORD died there in the land of
Moab, according to the word of the LORD. And he buried him
in a valley in the land of Moab, over against Bethpeor: but no
man knoweth of his sepulchre unto this day.

And from that sad passage English gained the term 'a Pisgah
sight', for something glimpsed but never obtained and never
obtainable. By a rather extraordinary feat of self-reference, the
OED's entry for Pisgah sight mentions its own first editor, Sir
James Murray, who 'led to within a Pisgah sight of completion a
larger and more scientifically organized work of linguistic reference than Dr Johnson could have produced', but died before he
could see his life's labours in print.

All you are left with is a case of *nympholepsy*, which is a longing for the unobtainable that afflicts any shepherd who happens
to come across a wood nymph in the course of his work. Such
shepherds are never happy again. They pine away. They neglect
their sheep and search the woods for the nymph whom they will
never find.

So turn for home. It's late anyway, and you have to get up
tomorrow I suppose. We generally do. Button yourself up,
pretend it never happened and set off, still perhaps humming

to yourself that miserable song in which all human sadness is contained:

I'm looking for the Ogo-Pogo
The funny little Ogo-Pogo
His mother was an earwig, his father was a whale
I'm going to put a little bit of salt on his tail,
I want to find the Ogo-Pogo.

Chapter 18

11 p.m. – Stumbling Home

*Setting off – getting lost – falling over
– attempts to sleep outdoors*

ﾠﾠﾠﾠﾠﾠﾠﾠﾠﾠﾠﾠﾠﾠﾠﾠﾠﾠﾠﾠﾠﾠ∽

The nymphs are departed, last orders have been called, and it is time to go home. Even Cab Calloway, a committed seeker of nocturnal amusements, went home in the end. His *Hepsters Dictionary* has a couple of helpful entries for things to say at *late bright* or the end of the evening:

> **Final** (v.): to leave, to go home. Ex., 'I finaled to my pad' (went to bed); 'We copped a final' (went home).

And:

> **Trilly** (v.): to leave, to depart. Ex., 'Well, I guess I'll trilly.'

But how will you get home? You could share a taxi. The OED insists that a shared taxi is called a *dolmus*, from the Turkish for 'filled'. But where are your *ale-knights* of the Round Table now, your boon companions in the night's struggle? Gone and bloody departed, that's where. Camelot is derelict, and you'll probably have to go home on foot.

If you are extremely lucky, a *white sergeant* may appear:

> A man fetched from the tavern or ale-house by his wife, is said
> to be arrested by the white sergeant.

But given your behaviour in the last chapter, I think that's
unlikely.

Heading home

In the *Canterbury Tales*, Chaucer explains the whole human
condition and search for happiness in terms of a drunk person trying to walk home. The general theme of his musing is
that though we all seek after happiness, we don't always know
where it is, and end up wandering hither and thither pursuing
the things we thought we wanted.

> We faren [fare] as he that drunk is as a mouse.
> A drunk man woot [knows] well he hath an house,
> But he noot [doesn't know] which the right way is thither
> And to a drunk man the way is slidder [slippery].
> And certes in this world so faren we;
> We seeken fast after felicity
> But we goon wrong full often, trewely.

If the way is particularly *slidder*, perhaps you can persuade
somebody to go *agatewards* with you. This charming old piece
of politeness is now confined to dictionaries of obsolete English:

Agate-Wards, adv. To go *agatewards* with any one, to accompany him part of his way home, which was formerly the last office of hospitality towards a guest, frequently necessary even now for guidance and protection in some parts of the country. In Lincolnshire it is pronounced *agatehouse*, and in the North generally *agaterds*.

Gate here is an old term for the public highway. So if you walked somebody agatewards you would accompany them along the dark, narrow, unfrequented lanes where robbers lurked, and then part with them at the wide open highway, where highwaymen lurked. Highwaymen were an altogether better class of thief. There were even

ROYAL SCAMPS. Highwaymen who never rob any but rich persons, and that without ill treating them.

There was also a *royal footpad*, who was just like a royal scamp except that he didn't have a horse. It is unfortunate that modern muggers seem to be universally republican.

Once you could hire a *moon-curser*, a boy who would walk beside you carrying a torch and lighting your way. Obviously, they were in permanent economic competition with moonlight, hence the name. They were not as honourable as royal scamps:

MOONCURSER. A link-boy: link-boys are said to curse the moon, because it renders their assistance unnecessary; these gentry frequently, under colour of lighting passengers over kennels, or through dark passages, assist in robbing them.

So perhaps it is best to be *solivagant*, to wander alone towards your far-off felicity. *Vagari* was Latin for 'wander', and solivagant is only one of the wonderful *vagant* words in the English language. If you wander outside – or *extra* – the bounds of your budget you are being *extravagant*. Indeed, originally extravagant had no financial connotations at all and simply meant 'wandering around too much'. So when Othello was described as 'an extravagant and wheeling stranger/Of here and everywhere', it just meant that he hadn't settled down. You can also be *mundivagant* (wandering the world), *multivagant* (wandering hither and thither), *montivagant* (wandering the mountains), *nemorivagant* ('wandering in the woods and groves'), *nubivagant* (wandering the clouds), and *omnivagant* (wandering absolutely everywhere).

These words are much more useful than they might appear. Aircraft are all nubivagant, gorillas are all nemorivagant, and a holiday in Snowdonia could be described as a montivagant weekend. In fact, one could be simultaneously montivagant, nubivagant, nemorivagant and extravagant simply by taking an expensive holiday in the Lake District.

The word that we need now, however, is *noctivagant*: wandering around at night. You must stumble like a *gyrovague* (or wandering monk), up blind alleys, *twitchels*, and *diverticulums*. You may well find yourself in a trance, but only because a *trance* is an old Scots term for a passage between two buildings. You will wander, *vagulate* and *wharve*; and it's as likely as not that you will end up a *night-foundered vicambulist*, or 'street-walker who has got lost in the darkness'.

At this point, you may wish to ponder the high-flown

concept of *nullibiety*, or state of being nowhere. It's usually used in theology, but can happily be transferred to trying to find your way home after a couple of drinks too many. It's also got a useful sister-word, *nullibiquitous*, which is the exact opposite of ubiquitous and means 'existing nowhere'. Thus you can search your house for your nullibiquitous car keys or whatnot.

Alternatively, you could look around you at the dark and unfamiliar streets and conclude that you had been *pixilated*, a splendid word and the cause of an awful lot of amusing typos in newspapers, if only you can spot them. Pixilated is completely different to *pixelated*. The latter, with an E, is something that happens to people's faces when they appear on television. But pixilated, with an I, means 'led astray by pixies'. It's astonishing, if you read the newspapers carefully, how many criminals have had their faces led astray by the Little Folk.

Pixies are a pest, and the cause of much wild wandering, or *skimbleskamble oberration* as Dr Johnson would have put it, leaving you *dog-weary* and *upon the wheady mile.*

The wheady mile is a very useful concept, defined in Nathan Bailey's *Universal Etymological Dictionary* of 1721 as 'A Mile beyond Expectation, a tedious one. *Shropshire*'. It's that last bit of a journey that goes on much longer than you had planned. Another dictionary calls it 'A mile of an extraordinary length'. This doesn't make much sense if you take it literally, as miles are, ordinarily, a mile long. But in your current state – drunk, weary and heartbroken – it is an utterly comprehensible idea and I wouldn't blame you if you sank to your knees in night-founded despair.

Devotional habits

When Diocletian entered Alexandria in 298 AD he was in a foul temper. The city had risen up in revolt against him and it had taken several months of siege before they finally gave in and opened the gates to the emperor, who was by now furious. He immediately ordered his legionaries to start killing the citizens and not to stop until his horse was up to its knees in the blood of the Alexandrians. The population of Alexandria was a little under a million at the time. The average human contains about a gallon of blood. This means that the resources available to the Roman soldiers would have been enough for – to use the standard Journalistic Unit of Measurement – an Olympic swimming pool and a half. Diocletian's plan was therefore thoroughly practicable.

Diocletian's horse had other ideas, though, for just as the soldiers were sharpening their swords and getting ready for the fun, the horse went down on its knees and refused to get up. Diocletian took this as an omen from the gods and immediately called off the massacre, thus saving the town. The Alexandrians erected a statue of the horse.[1]

The Victorians had a term for horses that fell to their knees all the time: they were said to have acquired *devotional habits*, on the basis that it looked as though they were kneeling down to pray. It's rather pleasant to imagine that a horse can't go twenty yards without kneeling to thank its creator. Pleasant for humans at least, not so for the horse, who is probably just old and tired

---

[1] It should be noted that many spoilsport historians think this story is much too good to be true.

and ready for the knacker's yard. Nor will anyone blame you if you acquire devotional habits of your own on your pixilated way.

Falling flat on your face

To Seel a Ship is said to *Seel*, when she tumbles suddenly and violent, sometimes to one side, and sometimes to another, when a Wave passes from under her Sides faster than she can drive away with it.

Universal Etymological Dictionary, 1721

Towards midnight a person is said to *seel* when they tumble suddenly and violent, sometimes to one side, and sometimes to another, when the pavement passes under their feet faster than they can stumble away with it, too exhausted and too well-refreshed to continue with this wheady mile.

Mischievous Reality notices you seeling and takes the opportunity to turn upside down and back to front. You totter, and before you have a chance even to cry out 'I *labascate!*', which means 'I begin to fall', you're actually falling in a terrible Newtonian *degringolade* onto your face.

Now is the time of *humicubation*: the act of lying on the ground, especially as a form of repentance. As a seventeenth-century bishop sternly observed:

Fasting and Sackcloth, and Ashes, and Tears, and Humi-cubations, used to be companions of Repentance. Joy may be a Consequent of it, not a Part of it.

Another useful word here may be *spartle*, to wave the limbs around vainly. Spartling is a common companion of evening humicubations, especially when the midnight creatures come curiously closer.

The moon-cursers and the *bug hunters* gather around. You catch a glimpse of the approaching *vespilone*, 'he that carries forth dead bodies in the night to be buried, as they use in time of plague and great sickness', with his *uncuses*, his *corpse-hooks*, his *eternity box* and his *danna-drag* on which the waste of the city is carried out. The Black Ox licks your cheek. The *barguest*, the ghost of broken walls, is watching with Old Split-Foot. The *hircocervus* blows a *mort*. The *donestres* call for you! The *whang-doodle* wails in the Yggdrasil! The skinless *écorchés* cavort! And Aboaddon, the Angel of the Bottomless Pit, beats time while the four hundred drunken rabbits dance an obscene can-can around you.

Now may be the time to indulge in a spot of *xenodocheion-ology*, which is the study of hotels and places to stay the night. There is the possibility of a *sheep bed*, i.e. the grass. But that won't keep away the *sooterkins* (strange, dark creatures said to grow inside Dutch women). Also, there is the question of warmth. If you are lucky enough to live in California all you will need to do is cover yourself with a newspaper, or *California blanket*. Those in chillier climes could knock on a few doors to see if anybody is feeling *xenodochial* – a slightly shorter relative of xenodocheionology that means 'given to putting strangers up for the night'.

Somebody who goes from house to house, even at this time of night, is *circumforaneous*, whether they're an encyclopedia salesman, a burglar or simply have something important to tell you about salvation.

But what is this? Is this *your mascaron*? Is this your own front door?

Chapter 19

Midnight – Nostos

*Making too much noise upon returning
– attempting to work – undressing
– arguing with spouse – falling asleep*

❦

The *Oxford English Dictionary* insists that *beauty-sleep* is 'the sleep secured before midnight'. So if you're still up, it's too late. Mind you, if you've gone to bed anywhere near a dairy farm, you may be sitting up in bed looking rather startled and consulting this humble, yet precise, reference work to find out what on earth that noise is. Luckily, I can refer you to *The Vocabulary of East Anglia; An Attempt to Record the Vulgar Tongue of the Twin Sister Counties, Norfolk and Suffolk as It Existed In the Last Years of the Eighteenth Century, and Still Exists* (1830). It's a saucy little page-turner of a dictionary filled with fantastical diseases of the turnip and explanations of why an *arseling pole* and a *bed faggot* aren't what you might have suspected.[1] On the subject of midnight it has this entry:

---

[1] Well, a bed-faggot sort of is. It's 'a contemptuous name for a bed-fellow'; but an arseling pole is utterly innocent and is to do with baking.

BULL'S-NOON, s. midnight. The inhabitants of dairy counties
can feelingly vouch for the propriety of this term. Their repose
is often broken in the dead of night by the loud bellowing of
the lord of the herd, who, rising vigorous from his evening
rumination, rushes forth on his adventures, as if it were broad
noon-day, and *blores* with increased rage and disappointment
when he comes to a fence which he cannot break through.

So if you have just woken up, don't worry. It's merely the lord
of the herd back from his evening rumination. If, on the other
hand, you *are* the lord of the herd, much the worse for wear
after your evening rumination, then you should try to make a
little less noise coming home.

The nightingale floor

If you wish to assassinate the Lord of Nijo Castle in Kyoto – and
who doesn't occasionally have strange whims? – several difficulties will immediately present themselves to you. There are
two rings of fortified wall, two rings of moats, and there hasn't
actually been a lord there since 1939. However, even once you've
surmounted these problems, you're going to have to deal with
the *nightingale floor*.

The Tokugawa Shogunate were not the sort of chaps who
took chances. So even if you made it to the sleeping quarters,
all the floorboards were specially designed to squeak when you
walked on them, meaning that you couldn't surprise anybody
in their bed. In fact, the squeakings were specifically designed to
be rather melodious and sound like nightingales. There was an

intricate system of nails and brackets beneath each corridor, and even though the results were rather approximate, it was possible to imagine that there was an aviary of indignant birds beneath your feet. It's a clever and ancient form of the burglar alarm, and though the original Japanese *uguisu-bari* has never made it into English, *nightingale floor* has an entry all to itself in the OED. The other peculiar thing is that though the Japanese make them deliberately, in the West we have been accidentally making nightingale floors for ages. Rare and extremely new is the house where the floorboards don't sing like a violated canary, or where the door doesn't *screak* on its hinges – a splendidly jarring word that sounds like a combination of *scream* and *shriek*.

You may plan to be as *surrepent* (or creeping stealthily underneath) as a *creep-mouse*, but you will probably sound more like a randy, post-ruminatory bull. The best you can do is, once beyond the nightingales, take Dr Johnson's advice and:

SOSS … To fall at once into a chair.

Lamp-life

Before actually tottering *bedwards*, you may wish to get a few things done. After all, you may be *clinophobic* and have a morbid fear of going to bed. You could, as the expression has it, get next week's drinking done early, although considering what happened a couple of chapters ago I cannot recommend this. Or you could take this opportunity to get some work done.

Winston Churchill was the grand old master of working at odd hours of the day. His brain seemed to rise with the bull, and there are numerous stories of how he won the Second World War at times of day when most of us are tucked up and dreaming. He used to hold cabinet meetings at just around this time, which were known to the poor people who had to attend as Churchill's *midnight follies*. Then he would pace around the cabinet war rooms during the small hours phoning people up and giving orders that were often complete nonsense and rightly ignored. Alan Brooke, Churchill's Chief of Staff, later recalled that 'Winston had ten ideas every day, only one of which was good, and he didn't know which one it was'.[2]

Those who feel philogrobolized all morning, so-so in the afternoon, and decent in the evening, but who are only truly awake after midnight are called *lychnobites*. Lychnobite comes from the Greek *lychno-bios* and means, approximately, 'lamp-life' (that's the same *bio* that you get in *biology*, 'the study of life'). The word was invented by Seneca, but found its way into the English language in the early eighteenth century.

If you are a hard-working lychnobite, like Churchill, or if you are a lazy lychnobite who simply failed to get anything done in the day, like me, now is the time to *lucubrate*. Lucubrate means to work by lamp-light, and is quite the most civilised form of working there is. There is nobody around to tell you how to do things, or how fast to do things, or that you can't do things with your feet up and a little whisky. This is especially true if you have a good strong lock on your *lucubatory*.

A lucubatory is 'a place of midnight study', a room that you work in when all the world is sleeping around you. They are

---

[2] Churchill's chief military assistant, Hastings Ismay, estimated that the numbers were in fact twenty ideas a day with five good.

very hard to find and rarely mentioned in estate agents' particulars. Some people like to add extensions to their houses – a games room, a gym, a private cinema – but if I ever have the money I shall add a lucubatory. I feel sure that it would increase my productivity no end, even though I would, of course, never go in there until I had heard the chimes at midnight. For the day, I would content myself with a *phrontistery*, which is 'a place for thinking'. There the eager phrontist can muse and ponder, ponder and muse to their heart's content, in a way that is utterly impossible in a utility room. Descartes, incidentally, had a phrontistery. He claimed to do all his best thinking sitting inside a stove. Not while it was lit, of course, that would be uncomfortable. But perhaps that would be the ideal lucubatory: a stove by day, and at night, when the embers have been raked out, a place of meditation and sooty solitude.

Dr Johnson didn't work late at night, and referred to lucubraters as *candle-wasters*, which is cruel. But perhaps he was right, and it is indeed time to *couch a hog's head*, *hit the hay*, and *head up the weary wooden hill to Bedfordshire*.

Disrobing

Apodysophilia is 'a feverish desire to undress'. It is usually a term of criminal psychology applied to people who do it in inappropriate places and get into trouble. The only appropriate places for an attack of apodysophilia are the *apodyterium*, or undressing room, of a Roman bathhouse, and your own bedroom.

Here you may play the *ecdysiast* at will – ecdysiast being a very learned term for a strip-tease artist invented by the

American satirist H.L. Mencken. He had received a letter from a lady called Georgia Southern, a distinguished stripper of the 1940s, who didn't like being called a stripper. She observed in her letter that:

> Strip-teasing is a formal and rhythmic disrobing of the body in public. In recent years there has been a great deal of uninformed criticism levelled against my profession. Most of it is without foundation and arises because of the unfortunate word strip-teasing, which creates the wrong connotations in the mind of the public. I feel sure that if you could coin a new and more palatable word to describe this art, the objections to it would vanish and I and my colleagues would have easier going.

H.L. Mencken, being a perfect gentleman, set himself to the task and eventually replied thus:

> I need not tell you that I sympathize with you in your affliction, and wish that I could help you. Unfortunately, no really persuasive new name suggests itself. It might be a good idea to relate strip-teasing in some way or other to the associated zoological phenomenon of molting. Thus the word moltician comes to mind, but it must be rejected because of its likeness to mortician. A resort to the scientific name for molting, which is ecdysis, produces both ecdysist and ecdysiast.

And ecdysiast it was. The term was instantly put to use by her publicist, got itself into the OED and even gave birth to the word *ecdysiasm* or 'the activity and occupation of strip teasing'.

You are nearly ready to leap into bed. First you must take your shoes off (a detail often omitted by ecdysiasts), which is technically noted as *discalcing*.

Finally, it is vital to check for *snudges*.

> Snudge, c. one that lurks under a bed, to watch an opportunity to Rob the House. (1699)

So down on your knees and have a good peek. There should be nothing down there except …

> BEGGAR'S VELVET, s. the lightest particles of down shaken from a feather-bed, and left by a sluttish housemaid to collect under the bed till it covers the floor for want of due sweeping, and she gets a scolding from her dame.

So it's time to get into bed – and, speaking of scolding, there is a risk that that is what you are now to receive.

Domestic dragons

As noted in the Preambulation, I have never been quite sure in this book whether you are married or not. I observed a couple of chapters ago that I feared the worst, but just to interpose a little ease, let our frail thoughts dally with false surmise and assume that you are possessed of a top-of-the-line, state-of-the-art spouse. In which case, I don't see why you haven't got to bed until this extraordinary late hour. And nor does your spouse.

The relevant word here is *dragonism*. Dragons, quite aside from their wings and halitosis, have the extraordinary quality of never going to sleep. Instead, they are eternally watchful, guarding their treasure and fair maidens. Thus dragonism is the practice of staying awake for ever, ready to attack. Prepare for a lecture.

> **Curtain Lecture** A woman who scolds her husband when in bed, is said to read him a curtain lecture.

The idea here is that you sleep in a four-poster bed and it's only once the curtains are drawn around you that your spouse, be they male or female, starts confessing your faults. The curtains stop the sound travelling too far, and also protect you from observation if you are *gymnologising*, or 'having an argument in the nude', as the ancient Greeks often did.

The ancient Greeks were masters of argument and spent a lot of time classifying methods of making yourself look good and your opponent look bad. They called this rhetoric. There are precisely a million and one rhetorical forms, but two of them are surprisingly common, almost universal, in a good domestic set-to.

Paralipsis is the practice of mentioning that you're not mentioning something, and saying what you're not saying. That may sound like a strange and preposterous paradox, but consider the following:

> I'm not going to bring up how you were late, late by half an hour. And I'm not going to mention how you disgraced yourself

at Percy's funeral, and I'm not even going to say a thing about your obsession with ferrets. All I'm saying is …

Do you see how it's done? You make a big show of saying what you're not saying. You list all the topics that you will not bring up. Now you know what paralipsis is – I am sure that you have used it yourself and had it used on you. It is the single most common rhetorical trope deployed in family rows. Any clause that begins with the words 'Not to mention' is paralipsis. Needless to say, it's a very clever technique because it allows you to score point after point without even allowing for a reply.

Epitrope is the granting of ironic permission, usually while listing all of the concomitant disadvantages. Consider the following:

Go right ahead. Don't mind me. Really, don't. Stay out late. Ruin your liver. It doesn't bother me that you're heading for an early grave and I'm going to be left bankrupt and alone with seventeen children and a wooden leg. Why should that bother me? You just do what you want to do.

Familiar? The only advantage of epitrope is that it usually means you're somewhere near the end of the curtain lecture. If you're not, you may become *fugacious* or ready to run away from home.

If you're lucky, your curtain lecture may be *subderiserous*, or gently mocking. And if you are truly blessed, you may receive *levament*, which Dr Johnson defined as 'The comfort that one hath of his wife'.

Lying down to sleep

Night-spel, was a Prayer against the Night-mar. (1674)

Finally, your *Scotch warming pan* has ceased to scold you (mind you, it might all start up again if you call them a Scotch warming pan). It is time to put out the lights and *dowse the glims*, as a highwayman would have said. Highwaymen could never say anything in ordinary English, and they would bid you good night by saying *bene darkmans*, pronounced *BEN-ay*, and deriving from the Latin for blessed. So if there is somebody with you, that is how to wish them good night.

Wrap yourself up in the *panes* and *counterpanes*. A dictionary of eighteenth-century dialect words defines *healing* as 'covering with the bed-cloaths', and it can often feel like that. Heal yourself among the lily-white sheets, say a night-spell to protect you from nightmares and, if you like, hold a quick *couchée* where all your courtiers come and pay homage to you as you lie in bed at night.

When the last courtier has departed and you are left silent in your *dreamery* (a place that favours dreams), your *consopiation* (or 'act of laying to sleep') may start. The Sandman, Morpheus, Billy Winks and all the other gods of sleep will approach; and soon a Norfolk farmer of the eighteenth century will appear and tell you that you *dream drumbles*, which is only his way of saying that you are half asleep.

Then, as you are half-dreaming, there is a little twitch known as a *myoclonic jerk*, which sounds like a spicy Jamaican sauce but is only your body shifting with your dreams. And then you are asleep, and nothing is moving but that strange 'nocturnal spirit' found only in Dr Johnson's dictionary, the Ponk.

Epilogue

Well that's it, I suppose. It's over. The ploughman homeward drops into the western bay and all that. I am feeling *finifugal*, and I have to say goodbye to my dictionaries.

It's nearly closing time at the British Library anyway. Seven minutes left, by my watch. There are only two of us left in Rare Books and Music, and I think the other fellow may be dead: at least he hasn't moved in the last twenty minutes. And when they close, I'll have to hand in all my dictionaries and they'll go back to the vaults and sleep again.

Every dictionary contains a world. I open a book of thieves' slang from Queen Anne's reign and they have a hundred words for swords, for wenches, and for being hanged. They did not die, they *danced on nothing*. Then I peek into any one of my rural Victorian dictionaries, compiled by a lonely clergyman, with words for coppices, thickets, lanes, diseases of horses and innumerable terms for kinds of eel. They gave names to the things of their lives, and their lives are collected in these dictionaries – every detail and joke and belief. I have their worlds piled up on my desk.

And the highwaymen are all hanged, the farmers are gone under their earth, and the RAF pilots who called the North Sea the *Juice*, the Atlantic the *Pond*, and the English Channel the *Drink* are lying at the bottom of all three.

All these worlds are departed, dead and dancing on nothing. They will not come back, but they are here in these books that I must hand in to the lady at the desk. It doesn't do to spend too

long with dictionaries, or I'll end up like Lot's beloved: salsicolumnified, gazing on my lost Gomorrahs.

That's it. The librarians are dowsing the glims, and even the
dead chap's getting up to leave. I shall return my dictionaries.
Bene darkmans, sleeping reader, bene darkmans.

Appendix

Paralipomenon
– The Drinker's Dictionary

Here is that list of Benjamin Franklin's terms for drunkenness in full:

The Drinker's Dictionary

He's addled, in his airs, affected, casting up his accounts, biggy, bewitched, black and black, bowzed, boozy, been at Barbadoes, been watering the brook, drunk as a wheelbarrow, bothered, burdocked, bosky, busky, buzzy, has sold a march in the brewer, has a head full of bees, has been in the bibing plot, has drunk more than he has bled, is bungy, has been playing beggar-my-neighbour, drunk as a beggar, sees the beams, has kissed black Betty, has had a thump over the head with Samson's jaw-bone, has been at war with his brains, is bridgy, has been catching the cat, is cogniaid, capable, cramped, cherubimical, cherry merry, wamble croft, cracked, half way to Concord, canonized, has taken a chirping glass, got corns in his head, got a cup too much, coguay, cupsy, has heated his copper, is in crocus, catched, cuts capers, has been in the cellar, been in the sun, is in his cups, above the clouds, is non compos, cocked, curved, cut, chippered, chickenny, has loaded his cart, been too free with the creature. Sir Richard has taken off his considering cap, he's chopfallen, candid, disguised, got a dish, has killed a dog, has taken his drops. 'Tis a dark day with him. He's a dead man, has dipped his bill, sees double, is disfigured, has seen the devil, is prince Eugene, has entered, buttered both eyes, is cock-eyed, has got the pole evil, has got a brass eye, has made an example, has ate a toad and a half for breakfast, is in his element, is fishy, foxed, fuddled, soon fuddled, frozen, will have frogs for supper, is well in front, is getting forward in the world, owes no man money, fears no man, is crump fooled, has been to France, is flushed, has frozen his mouth, is fettered, has been to a funeral, has his flag out, is fuzzled, has spoken with his friend, been at an Indian feast, is glad, grabable, great-headed, glazed, generous, has boozed the gage, is as dizzy as a goose, has been before George, got the gout, got a kick in the guts, been at Geneva, is globular, has got the glanders, is on the go, a gone man, has been to see Robin Goodfellow, is half and half, half seas over, hardy, top heavy, has got by the head, makes head way, is hiddey, has got on his little hat, is hammerish, loose in the hilt, knows not the way home, is haunted by evil spirits, has taken Hippocrates' grand Elixir, is intoxicated, jolly, jagged, jambled, jocular, juicy, going to Jericho, an indirect man, going to Jamaica, going to Jerusalem, is a king, clips the King's English, has seen the French king. The King is his cousin, has got kibed heels, has got knapt, his kettle's hot. He'll soon keel upward, he's in his liquor, lordly, light, lappy, limber, lopsided, makes indentures with his legs, is well to live, sees two moons, is merry, middling, muddled, moon-eyed, maudlin, mountainous, muddy, mellow, has seen a flock of moons, has raised his monuments, has eaten cacao nuts, is nimtopsical, has got the night mare, has been nonsuited, is super nonsensical, in a state of nature, nonplussed, oiled, has ate opium, has smelt an onion, is an oxy-crocum, is overset, overcome, out of sorts, on the paymaster's books, drank his last halfpenny, is as good conditioned as a puppy, is pigeon eyed, pungy, priddy, pushing on, has salt in his headban, has been among the Philistines, is in prosperity, is friends with Philip, contending with Pharaoh, has painted his nose, wasted his punch, learned politeness, eat the pudding-bag, eat too much pumpkin, is full of piety, is rocky, raddled, rich, religious, ragged, raised, has lost his rudder, has been too far with Sir Richard, is like a rat in trouble, is stitched, seafaring, in the suds, strong, as drunk as David's sow, swamped, his skin is full, steady, stiff, burnt his shoulder, has got out his top-gallant sails, seen the dog-star, is stiff as a ringbolt. The shoe pinches him. He's staggerish. It is star light with him. He carries too much sail, will soon out studding sails, is stewed, stubbed, soaked, soft, has made too free with Sir John Strawberry, right before the wind, all sails out, has pawned his senses, plays parrot, has made shift of his shirt, shines like a blanket, has been paying for a sign, is toped, tongue-tied, tanned, tipsicum grave, double tongued, tospey turvey, tipsy, thawed, trammulled, transported, has swallowed a tavern token, makes Virginia fame, has got the Indian vapours, is pot valiant, in love with varany, wise, has a wet soul, has been to the salt water, in search of eye water, is in the way to be weaned, out of the way, water soaked, wise or otherwise, can walk the line. The wind is west with him. He carries the wagon.

Dictionaries and Idioticons

(An *idioticon* is a dictionary of a particular dialect
or area of language)

Abedecarium Anglico-Latinum, Richard Huloet (1552)

Worlde of Wordes, John Florio (1598)

*A Table Alphabeticall, conteyning the true writing and
understanding of hard usual English wordes, borrowed from
the Hebrew, Greeke, Latine, or French. &c.*, Robert Cawdrey
(1604)

*A New Dictionary of the Terms Ancient and Modern of the
Canting Crew*, B.E. Gent. (1699)

*Glossographia Anglicana nova: or, a dictionary, interpreting such
hard words of whatever language, as are at present used in
the English tongue, with their etymologies, definitions, &c.*,
Thomas Blount (1656)

An Universal Etymological Dictionary, Nathan Bailey (1721)

Dictionary of the English Language, Samuel Johnson (1755)

Sports and Pastimes of the People of England, Joseph Strutt
(1801), enlarged by Charles Cox (1903)

An Etymological Dictionary of the Scottish Language, Reverend
John Jamieson (1808)

A Classical Dictionary of the Vulgar Tongue, Francis Grose etc. (1811). Grose died in 1791 but his dictionary continued to be expanded (and occasionally contracted) for a couple of decades after his death. I have used whatever edition I found most amusing.

The Vocabulary of East Anglia; An Attempt to Record the Vulgar Tongue of the Twin Sister Counties, Norfolk and Suffolk as It Existed In the Last Years of the Eighteenth Century, and Still Exists, Reverend Robert Forby (1830)

Westmoreland and Cumberland dialects: Dialogues, poems, songs, and ballads, John Russell Smith (1839)

A Pentaglot Dictionary of the Terms Employed in Anatomy, Physiology, Pathology, Practical Medicine, Surgery, Obstetrics, Medical Jurisprudence, Materia Medica, Pharmacy, Medical Zoology, Botany and Chemistry, Shirley Palmer (1845)

Dictionary of Obsolete and Provincial English, Thomas Wright (1857)

A Dictionary of Modern, Slang, Cant, and Vulgar Words Used at the Present Day in the Streets of London, John Camden Hotten (1860)

The Dialect of Leeds and its Neighbourhood Illustrated by Conversations and Tales of Common Life etc., C. Clough Robinson (1862)

A Dictionary of the Terms Used in Medicine and the Collateral Sciences, Richard D. Hoblyn (1865)

A glossary of words used in the wapentakes of Manley and Corringham, Lincolnshire, Edward Peacock (1877)

Shropshire word-book, a glossary of archaic and provincial words, &c., used in the county, Georgina Jackson (1879)

Slang and its Analogues, John Stephen Farmer (1893)

English Dialect Dictionary, Joseph Wright (1898–1905)

A Scots Dialect Dictionary, Alexander Warrack (1911)

Western Canadian dictionary and phrase-book: things a newcomer wants to know, John Sandilands (1912)

Cab Calloway's Hepsters Dictionary: Language of Jive, Cabell Calloway (1938–44)

Psychiatric Dictionary with Encyclopaedic Treatment of Modern Terms, Leland Earl Hinsie (1940)

Service Slang, J.L. Hunt and A.G. Pringle, Faber (1943)

Dictionary of Guided Missiles and Space Flight, Grayson Merrill (1959)

A Descriptive Dictionary and Atlas of Sexology, ed. Robert T. Francoeur, Greenwood (1991). N.B. This book does actually contain maps, although the term 'atlas' may be overstating it a bit.

Straight from the Fridge, Dad: A Dictionary of Hipster Slang (3rd edition), No Exit Press (2004)

Fubar: Soldier Slang of World War II, Gordon L. Rottman, Osprey (2007)

Chambers Slang Dictionary, Jonathon Green (2008)

The Oxford English Dictionary, OUP (2012)

*

However, a few words were not in any of these dictionaries:

Dysania is in use as a technical medical term (see, for example, *Myalgic Encephalomyelitis: A Baffling Syndrome with a Tragic Aftermath*, Ramsay, 1989) and also makes a show in a medical word-finder of 1958 called the *Reversicon*. But I've never found it in what I'd call a dictionary.

Groke is, or was, a Scottish dialect word mentioned in *History of the European Languages or, Researches into the Affinities of the Teutonic, Greek, Celtic, Sclavonic and Indian Nations* (1823) by Alexander Murray, who was Professor of Oriental Languages at the University of Edinburgh; he applied it exclusively to dogs.

Nooningscaup appears in *Clavis Calendaria* by John Henry Brady (1812), who mentions it as a contemporary term in Yorkshire.

The citation of *gongoozler* is from the 'Glossary of Canal Terms' skulking at the back of *Bradshaw's Canals and Navigable Rivers of England and Wales* by Henry Rodolph de Salis (1918).

The keys to the indoor tank park and *a meeting without coffee* come from my vast network of spies within the British defence establishment.

I was introduced to the term *gabos* by a Special Adviser to Her Majesty's Government who said it was commonly used round their way. I've since found various references to it on the Internet and one in a documentary that pins it down as a Miami criminal term. To my knowledge it has never made it into any print dictionary and has no currency outside of the Miami Mega Max Jail facility and the Palace of Westminster.

The tasseographical terms were culled from *Tea-Cup Reading and the Art of Fortune Telling by Tea-Leaves* by 'A Highland Seer', The Musson Book Co., Toronto (1920).

Shturmovshchina is a Russian term that has never made it into an English dictionary. However, it was much too delightful a word to exclude.

The definition of *cinqasept* is from *The Oxford Essential Dictionary of Foreign Terms in English*, ed. Jennifer Speake, Berkley Books (1999). I'm particularly fond of the idea that an afternoon visit to one's mistress could qualify as *Essential*.

Several of the terms in the shopping section do not appear in dictionaries. They were instead gleaned from people who work in the British retail trade.

The term 'drunk as four hundred rabbits' is mentioned in *México* by William Weber Johnson (1966). The Centzon Totochtin, from which the phrase must derive, are a standard part of Aztec mythology.

The definition of *smikker* comes from *A Chronicle of Scottish Poetry; From the Thirteenth Century to the Union of the Crowns: to which is added a Glossary*, J. Sibbald (1802).

There is also one word (quite aside from salsicolumnified) that I made up off the top of my head. But unless you check every word in this book against all the dictionaries listed above, you'll never find it. If you *do* check all the words in this book against all those dictionaries, I have nothing for you but my pity, and my curse.

Index

Chapter 17: 10 p.m.

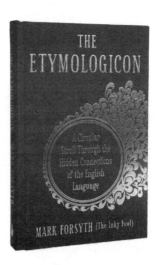

also available:

The Etymologicon

A Circular Stroll Through the Hidden Connections of the English Language

The *Sunday Times* Number One Bestseller

'I'm hooked on Forsyth's book … Crikey, but this is addictive'
—Matthew Parris, *The Times*

What is the actual connection between *disgruntled* and *gruntled*? What links church organs to organised crime, California to the Caliphate, or brackets to codpieces?

As heard on BBC Radio 4, *The Etymologicon* – which springs from Mark Forsyth's Inky Fool blog – is an occasionally ribald, frequently witty and unerringly erudite guided tour of the secret labyrinth that lurks beneath the English language. It takes in monks and monkeys, film buffs and buffaloes, and explains precisely what the Rolling Stones have to do with gardening.

ISBN 978-184831-307-1

£12.99

The Etymologicon

– the unabridged audiobook read by
Simon Shepherd – is published
by AudioGO (9781445847429)
and available now from
audiogo.co.uk